SPICY TASTY VEGAN CUISINE

An Informative Health Guide for the Melaninated (People of Color)

ALL RECIPES ARE VEGAN, GLUTEN-FREE & NON-SOY!

MAMA NAASIRA AGEELA & DR. GREGORY JOE BLEDSOE

SPICY TASTY VEGAN CUISINE

"EAT AND HEAL AT THE SAME TIME"

MAMA Naasira Ageela &
Dr. Gregory Joe Bledsoe, J.D.

Source Of Light Publishing
P.O. Box 27504 • Oakland, CA 94602
www.spicytastyvegan.com
spicytastyvegan@gmail.com
Phone: 510–473–6579

ISBN 13:978-1515181002

Book Design by black ink + paper
Photography by Jamil Wallace & Naasira Ageela
Edited by Mary Anne McNease
Editor Assistants: Mardeen Cassell, Drexel Lyles, Linda Odumade
Subtitle Quote from Thelma Carrington

Notice: The information contained in this book is for educational purposes only; it should not be used for diagnosis or to guide treatment without the opinion of a health professional. Any reader who is concerned about his/her health should contact their Health Care Practitioner.

Ordering Information: Quantity sales. Special discounts are available on quantity purchases by corporations, associations, and others. For details, contact the "Special Sales Department" at the address above.

Special thanks to the Most High (our Ancestors, Mother/Father God, Divine Spirit) and all the others who, without their love, inspiration, information and guidance this book would not be. Below are listed some of the individuals and businesses we would like to recognize for their support. This list is far from complete.

Ruthie Mae Fletcher (Mom)
Mary Anne McNease
Chamaine Woffard
Caroline & Richard Cannon
Rev. Diana McDaniels
David de la Vega
Kimone Gooden
Olric Carter
Howard & Claudette Morrison
Josefa Perez
Rainbow Grocery – San Francisco
William Taylor, Esq.
Dr. Delbert Blair
Dr. Veronica Hunnicutt
Rev. Eloise Oliver
Dr. Christopher Kox
Harold Manley
Barbara & Truman Hildreth
Jamil Wallace
Atiba Wallace
Dulani Wallace
Thelma Carrington
Henry Crater
Marilynne Davis
Alton Byrd
Michele McKenzie

JacQueene Hedquist
Brotha Ra
Diana Lynch
Nubia Sutton
Leonard Franklin
Barbara Bridgewater
Pio Winston
Bonnie Strong
Kristin Graetz
Carol Jean Jones
Fevn Cintron
Far–I Shields
Elaine Shelly
Veronica Butler
Anna Marie Coleman
Dr. Gail Meyers
Ms. Tessie Bledsoe
Virna Tarvarez
Roselind Hildreth
Areca Smit
James Sandoval
Rebecca Clemons
Rose Joyner
Herma Jean Gardere
Monique Levi
Debra Jones-Davis
Miliani Wallace
Gracie Taylor

Contents

Naasira Ageela's Introduction 5
Transitioning to Healthy Foods 7
Testimonials 9
Forgiveness 29
Most Men Are Slow 33
Naasira's Approach 37
My Journey 47
My Soy Story 57
Cooking Oil Alternatives 65
Gregory Joe Bledsoe's Introduction 95
Barefootin' 119
Coffee 123
Organic Foods 133
GMO Foods 141
Fruit 145
Vegetables 151
The Dirty Dozen and Clean 15 161
Herbs And Spices 165
Healthy Grains 201
Diseases And Bad Nutrition 207
Uterine Fibroids 215
Prostate 233
Melanin and What Melanin Does 237
Vitamins 259
Antiperspirant and Deodorant 263
Water 267
Microwave Ovens 291

Food for Thought 295
Cookware – from the worst to the best 303
Polystyrene (Commonly known as Styrofoam) Containers 319
Plastics and Recycle Codes 323
Basic Kitchen Safety Tips 329
Recipes 333
Spicy African Stew 335
Almond Arugula Pesto 339
Almond Coconut Date Rolls 340
Almond Banana Smoothie 341
Almond Milk 342
Baked Butternut Squash 343
Baked French Fries 344
Banana Fruit Cookies 345
Banana Fruit Loaf 347
Blueberry Almond Butter Smoothie 349
Wild Rice 350
Citrus Drink 351
Cocoa Mousse 352
Collard Green Wraps 353
Wrap Sauce: 355
Vegan Real Cornbread 356
Daikon Kale Stir–Fry 357
Earthy Root Detox Tea 358
Egg Substitute 358
Fruit Grain Cereal 359
Simple African Fufu 360
Shallot Popcorn 361
Tasty Guacamole 362
Natural Hair Conditioner 363
Hemp/Basil Dressing 364
Hemp Milk 365

Kale Chips 366
Simple Kale Stir–Fry 367
Lasagna with Basil Cashew Cheese 368
Tasty Millet 372
NaaCereal 373
Quinoa, Black and Red Rice Mix 375
Real Banana Pancakes 377
Pineapple Rind Drink 379
Pizza 380
Plant Protein Filling 382
Spicy Vegan Plantain 384
Tasty Polenta 385
Portobello Mushrooms 386
Tasty Potato Salad 387
Pulp Burger/Juice 389
Raw Ice Cream 390
Raw Salad 391
Vegan Real Waffles 392
Roasted Eggplant Vegetable Casserole 394
Salad Dressing 396
Steel Cut Oats 397
Baked Sweet Potatoes/Yams 398
Quinoa Tabouli 399
Mixed Spiced Tossed Salad 400
Variety Fruit Salad 401
General Index 402

PART 1

CHAPTER 1

Naasira Ageela's Introduction

IT IS AMAZING WHEN you can live long enough to learn there are many realities to life. I am happy today to have learned there is a more natural and sustainable diet to nurture the body. I learned to care for my health by getting sick and then reading and asking questions to help myself get better. If you know and believe natural remedies will help you feel better, instinctually you will explore other options.

If I had not contracted Hepatitis B from sticking myself with a needle, while working as a phlebotomist at the UCSF Medical Center at the tender age of nineteen, I would not be living the healthy, vibrant, invigorating, creative life I enjoy today. That needle stick turned out to be a divine blessing.

When I became ill, I had no idea that the food we ate was supposed to nourish our bodies.

My doctor warned me that if I wanted to live, I would have to change my diet. The candy and fast food had to go. I began researching healthy foods and so embarked on my journey from illness to wellness. I discovered the healing properties of fruits and vegetables, grains, herbs and spices. Where I lived was brimming with restaurants, health food stores and fruit stands, and I learned new and different ways to make healthy meals without meat.

What started out as a misfortune, became my great fortune. I have been blessed in many ways by the benefits of eating a healthy diet and have become part of a wonderful community along the way. Twelve years ago, I became a vegan and was honored to share my vegan cooking experience with Gregory Joe Bledsoe and others through our cooking classes.

What we endeavor to do in this book is share our knowledge and passion for life, learning and abundant health. It's not just knowing enough to get by, not just making do, not settling for less, but expanding, growing, sharing, supporting each other and re–creating our community. I accepted my calling to prepare spicy, tasty food to remain healthy and to support the folks who are interested in being healthy as well.

We have learned over a period of sixty years that the words we use are powerful. It is so important to watch what we say. Words can enslave, words can empower and everything in between. Think of your words as electromagnetic boomerangs that you throw and that come right back to you. Another way of putting it is – put good stuff in, get good stuff out. Like cooking, like life. I know I am so thankful for the many gifts I have been blessed with and grateful to be able to share with others who are open to receive them. Hopefully, the ideas and information in this book will help you in your journey, wherever it takes you. Be healthy, be well, my friends!

CHAPTER 2
Transitioning to Healthy Foods

ONCE YOU DECIDE TO make a transition to healthy foods, the first thing to do is to list all of the foods and drinks you are currently consuming that are unhealthy for you. Then, next to each unhealthy food or drink, write in the name of a healthy alternative. At your own pace, substitute out the unhealthy foods and drinks by replacing them with more healthy alternatives.

An example would be to "substitute out" drinking cow's milk by replacing it with almond or hemp milk. The almond and hemp milk is certainly healthier for most. You can also make the hemp and almond milk yourself. Another example would be to replace vegetable oils with extra virgin olive oil or raw coconut oil (especially for high heat cooking). Continue to "substitute out" until your list of unhealthy foods has been completely replaced with healthy alternatives.

Remember, it took a lifetime for you to get where you are today. But the time it will take for you to transition to optimum health can be relatively short. Your motivation will be the way you look and feel. As you eat better, you think and can do better. Just as one must take a step to begin a mile journey, you can begin your journey to eating healthy foods by switching, one at a time, unhealthy choices for healthy ones.

Also, it is important to keep in mind that as you change your diet and lifestyle your body will begin to detoxify. This means, your body will start to eliminate toxins. Generally, this is done through your bowels cleaning out and becoming more regular.

CHAPTER 3
Testimonials

When you eat something Naasira and Gregory Joe have made, you can actually taste their spirit. They are akin to modern day explorers on a treasure hunt for optimal health and wellness.

–Areca Smit, Oakland, CA

It is with great pleasure that I applaud Gregory and Naasira on the exceptional work they have done in showing Americans how to prepare and enjoy vegan cuisine. Their food is healthy and delicious! What a blessing this couple is to all of us!

–Dr. Veronica Hunnicutt, San Francisco, CA

For meat eaters, they will not be dissatisfied. The seasonings are wonderful. I have experiences with many vegetarian restaurants and much vegetarian cuisine and I can say without a doubt that Greg and Naasira's recipes are wonderful.

–Mali Vincent Williams, Oakland, CA

If you thought meat WAS good, try this alternative. You will be hooked for life.

–Hajjah Roslyn Abdullah, Oakland,CA

A culinary magician, Naasira's cooking is simply magical. As a born soul food meat eater I appreciate texture, seasoning, variety and ultimately a filling meal. I have found all of the above in Naasira's vegan dishes. Among the many dishes she creates, her stews, salads and cornbread stand out as the best dishes I have ever eaten. They burst with flavor engulfing all of the senses in a melody of Caribbean, African, Asian, and Eastern taste, all carefully balanced by deliciousness.

Her dishes are hearty and they have the power to lure, cure and win over even the most skeptical eaters. Eating her dishes made me realize that even I could become a vegan and eat fulfilling foods that are both satisfying and healthy. One taste is all it takes to realize a glimpse of heaven is attainable by tasting Naasira's dishes.

–Dr. Shaute Tosten, Temecula, CA

Every time I taste or experience Naasira's food I get an electric charge going through my body. I have never tasted food that lifts my vibration that high. I would recommend this book to anyone and everyone who is sick and tired of being sick and tired.

–Nubia I, Oakland, CA

Delicious! The food is a life changing experience. It's new and fresh. It is the total opposite of a hard brick in the stomach feeling after eating a double cheeseburger that is hard to digest.

–Ms. Tessie Bledsoe, Las Vegas, N.V.

A new definition of what eating is ... a combination of herbs and spices on veggies that speak a new language of pure goodness to your inner being. This is vegan fuel that lights you up like an old fashioned pinball machine. It is a twist and shout of flavor to a vegan vegetarian cuisine. The taste is truly a hallelujah moment.

–Dr. A.B.Bruce, D.C., Stockton, CA

Sistah Naasira and Brotha Greg's food is very nutritious, delicious and satisfying. It's prepared in a clean environment with love, wisdom, and "overstanding". On the benefits of their foods: It cleans the colon. Thus, helping to prevent colon cancer. The food has the natural vitamins the body needs to maintain good health and longevity. Try it. You will love it. It's good for you and refreshing too.

–Raslam Atiba, Oakland, CA

Naasira's food is nourishment for the soul. More than just a meal, it satisfies desires you didn't even know you had! Every time I eat her food it realigns my body, mind and spirit in new ways and I gain energy and reach new levels of clarity. To call her a chef is an understatement. She is a healer using food as medicinal alchemy. She truly embodies the spirit of how to eat to live.

–Zakiya Harris, Visionary, Catalyst, Cultivator, Oakland, CA

This is good and nutritious food without the salt, sugar and grease. When you finish eating you feel like you've been nourished. This book is back to the essentials of healthy eating. This is medicinal food with love.

–Leon Williams, Berkeley, CA

I really enjoyed the African Stew dish. It has a variety of vegetables and spices. This particular dish has given me more energy to help deal with my asthma. Thank you and congratulations on this book.

–Shelby Hammonds, Daly City, CA

When she put the plate in front of me I said "What a plate." It was tasty. She used a lot of herbs and spices. It was healing. It was a meal where you just wanted to savor the flavor.

After eating I felt the food healing me or giving a positive healing effect. I did not feel bloated or stuffed. I felt great. I also really enjoyed the collard green wraps.

–Khatia Washington, Columbia, MD

My girlfriend and I have known Greg and Naasira as a couple for ten years. Years ago, we started stir–frying our vegetables the way Greg and Naasira showed the two of us. We have become healthier (I have lost twenty pounds and still, to this date, continue to lose weight). As the result of the more healthy way of cooking and eating a vegetable–based diet, our lives have certainly been enriched.

The two of us are grateful for Greg and Naasira, vegans, and advocates for a vegetable based diet. Their passion for a healthier way of living has touched the lives of so many people. May they continue to be blessed as they continue to be a blessing to so many people through their healthy cooking.

–Stephen Nunley and Katrytae McCraw, Fremont, CA

My testimony is on the pulp sandwich: Now some people would think, how in the world could a sandwich made of pulp be inviting? Let the truth be told, this sandwich was outstanding!

It is very flavorful and filling (I got full, and I can eat!). This sandwich contains the pulp of all the healthy foods like carrots, celery, beets, pineapple, and so on. It was topped off with mustard, catsup and avocado.

It was also like bringing your health and five senses back to life while eating. You could enjoy this sandwich and get a raw detox at the same time. This was a seriously healthy MAN'S sandwich.

Bro. Karl Grant, El Sobrante, CA

Naasira and Greg are on a mission to improve the health of their community one meal at a time. These recipes are not only good for you, they're also good to you.

–Michele, CA

Naasira and Gregory's delectable creations have nourished and comforted me for years. They consistently remind me of the importance of taking the time to prepare wholesome, tasty meals. It is such a gift that they are sharing their recipes, which I feel are relatively easy to prepare and offer healthy and hearty vegan options. Naasira and Gregory also have an immense understanding of the many facets that contribute to good health. I consider them to be wonderful resources and examples of healthy living in general.

–Jamillah Sabry, Oakland, CA

Delicious, wholesome, and absolutely filling epitomizes this vegan cuisine. The soups and stews delight your palate with a rich and robust mixture of spices, topped off with a homemade spread on pita bread creates a dish fit for a king, queen, or family. Contrary to your mother's twist on it, their homemade pizza is amazing and a must for gatherings both, small or large. Trust me, your guests will thank you for it!

My favorite, however, is the fruitbread. With four different flours and every fruit you can imagine, you won't be able to take a bite without devouring a wealth of

–Nubia I, Oakland, CA

Delicious! The food is a life changing experience. It's new and fresh. It is the total opposite of a hard brick in the stomach feeling after eating a double cheeseburger that is hard to digest.

–Ms. Tessie Bledsoe, Las Vegas, N.V.

A new definition of what eating is ... a combination of herbs and spices on veggies that speak a new language of pure goodness to your inner being. This is vegan fuel that lights you up like an old fashioned pinball machine. It is a twist and shout of flavor to a vegan vegetarian cuisine. The taste is truly a hallelujah moment.

–Dr. A.B.Bruce, D.C., Stockton, CA

Sistah Naasira and Brotha Greg's food is very nutritious, delicious and satisfying. It's prepared in a clean environment with love, wisdom, and "overstanding". On the benefits of their foods: It cleans the colon. Thus, helping to prevent colon cancer. The food has the natural vitamins the body needs to maintain good health and longevity. Try it. You will love it. It's good for you and refreshing too.

–Raslam Atiba, Oakland, CA

Naasira's food is nourishment for the soul. More than just a meal, it satisfies desires you didn't even know you had! Every time I eat her food it realigns my body, mind and spirit in new ways and I gain energy and reach new levels of clarity. To call her a chef is an understatement. She is a healer using food as medicinal alchemy. She truly embodies the spirit of how to eat to live.

–Zakiya Harris, Visionary, Catalyst, Cultivator, Oakland, CA

This is good and nutritious food without the salt, sugar and grease. When you finish eating you feel like you've been nourished. This book is back to the essentials of healthy eating. This is medicinal food with love.

–Leon Williams, Berkeley, CA

I really enjoyed the African Stew dish. It has a variety of vegetables and spices. This particular dish has given me more energy to help deal with my asthma. Thank you and congratulations on this book.

–Shelby Hammonds, Daly City, CA

When she put the plate in front of me I said "What a plate." It was tasty. She used a lot of herbs and spices. It was healing. It was a meal where you just wanted to savor the flavor.

After eating I felt the food healing me or giving a positive healing effect. I did not feel bloated or stuffed. I felt great. I also really enjoyed the collard green wraps.

–Khatia Washington, Columbia, MD

My girlfriend and I have known Greg and Naasira as a couple for ten years. Years ago, we started stir–frying our vegetables the way Greg and Naasira showed the two of us. We have become healthier (I have lost twenty pounds and still, to this date, continue to lose weight). As the result of the more healthy way of cooking and eating a vegetable–based diet, our lives have certainly been enriched.

The two of us are grateful for Greg and Naasira, vegans, and advocates for a vegetable based diet. Their passion for a healthier way of living has touched the lives of so many people. May they continue to be blessed as they continue to be a blessing to so many people through their healthy cooking.

–Stephen Nunley and Katrytae McCraw, Fremont, CA

My testimony is on the pulp sandwich: Now some people would think, how in the world could a sandwich made of pulp be inviting? Let the truth be told, this sandwich was outstanding!

It is very flavorful and filling (I got full, and I can eat!). This sandwich contains the pulp of all the healthy foods like carrots, celery, beets, pineapple, and so on. It was topped off with mustard, catsup and avocado.

It was also like bringing your health and five senses back to life while eating. You could enjoy this sandwich and get a raw detox at the same time. This was a seriously healthy MAN'S sandwich.

Bro. Karl Grant, El Sobrante, CA

Naasira and Greg are on a mission to improve the health of their community one meal at a time. These recipes are not only good for you, they're also good to you.

–Michele, CA

Naasira and Gregory's delectable creations have nourished and comforted me for years. They consistently remind me of the importance of taking the time to prepare wholesome, tasty meals. It is such a gift that they are sharing their recipes, which I feel are relatively easy to prepare and offer healthy and hearty vegan options. Naasira and Gregory also have an immense understanding of the many facets that contribute to good health. I consider them to be wonderful resources and examples of healthy living in general.

–Jamillah Sabry, Oakland, CA

Delicious, wholesome, and absolutely filling epitomizes this vegan cuisine. The soups and stews delight your palate with a rich and robust mixture of spices, topped off with a homemade spread on pita bread creates a dish fit for a king, queen, or family. Contrary to your mother's twist on it, their homemade pizza is amazing and a must for gatherings both, small or large. Trust me, your guests will thank you for it!

My favorite, however, is the fruitbread. With four different flours and every fruit you can imagine, you won't be able to take a bite without devouring a wealth of

–Nubia I, Oakland, CA

Delicious! The food is a life changing experience. It's new and fresh. It is the total opposite of a hard brick in the stomach feeling after eating a double cheeseburger that is hard to digest.

–Ms. Tessie Bledsoe, Las Vegas, N.V.

A new definition of what eating is ... a combination of herbs and spices on veggies that speak a new language of pure goodness to your inner being. This is vegan fuel that lights you up like an old fashioned pinball machine. It is a twist and shout of flavor to a vegan vegetarian cuisine. The taste is truly a hallelujah moment.

–Dr. A.B.Bruce, D.C., Stockton, CA

Sistah Naasira and Brotha Greg's food is very nutritious, delicious and satisfying. It's prepared in a clean environment with love, wisdom, and "overstanding". On the benefits of their foods: It cleans the colon. Thus, helping to prevent colon cancer. The food has the natural vitamins the body needs to maintain good health and longevity. Try it. You will love it. It's good for you and refreshing too.

–Raslam Atiba, Oakland, CA

Naasira's food is nourishment for the soul. More than just a meal, it satisfies desires you didn't even know you had! Every time I eat her food it realigns my body, mind and spirit in new ways and I gain energy and reach new levels of clarity. To call her a chef is an understatement. She is a healer using food as medicinal alchemy. She truly embodies the spirit of how to eat to live.

–Zakiya Harris, Visionary, Catalyst, Cultivator, Oakland, CA

This is good and nutritious food without the salt, sugar and grease. When you finish eating you feel like you've been nourished. This book is back to the essentials of healthy eating. This is medicinal food with love.

–Leon Williams, Berkeley, CA

I really enjoyed the African Stew dish. It has a variety of vegetables and spices. This particular dish has given me more energy to help deal with my asthma. Thank you and congratulations on this book.

–Shelby Hammonds, Daly City, CA

When she put the plate in front of me I said "What a plate." It was tasty. She used a lot of herbs and spices. It was healing. It was a meal where you just wanted to savor the flavor.

After eating I felt the food healing me or giving a positive healing effect. I did not feel bloated or stuffed. I felt great. I also really enjoyed the collard green wraps.

–Khatia Washington, Columbia, MD

My girlfriend and I have known Greg and Naasira as a couple for ten years. Years ago, we started stir–frying our vegetables the way Greg and Naasira showed the two of us. We have become healthier (I have lost twenty pounds and still, to this date, continue to lose weight). As the result of the more healthy way of cooking and eating a vegetable–based diet, our lives have certainly been enriched.

The two of us are grateful for Greg and Naasira, vegans, and advocates for a vegetable based diet. Their passion for a healthier way of living has touched the lives of so many people. May they continue to be blessed as they continue to be a blessing to so many people through their healthy cooking.

–Stephen Nunley and Katrytae McCraw, Fremont, CA

My testimony is on the pulp sandwich: Now some people would think, how in the world could a sandwich made of pulp be inviting? Let the truth be told, this sandwich was outstanding!

It is very flavorful and filling (I got full, and I can eat!). This sandwich contains the pulp of all the healthy foods like carrots, celery, beets, pineapple, and so on. It was topped off with mustard, catsup and avocado.

It was also like bringing your health and five senses back to life while eating. You could enjoy this sandwich and get a raw detox at the same time. This was a seriously healthy MAN'S sandwich.

Bro. Karl Grant, El Sobrante, CA

Naasira and Greg are on a mission to improve the health of their community one meal at a time. These recipes are not only good for you, they're also good to you.

–Michele, CA

Naasira and Gregory's delectable creations have nourished and comforted me for years. They consistently remind me of the importance of taking the time to prepare wholesome, tasty meals. It is such a gift that they are sharing their recipes, which I feel are relatively easy to prepare and offer healthy and hearty vegan options. Naasira and Gregory also have an immense understanding of the many facets that contribute to good health. I consider them to be wonderful resources and examples of healthy living in general.

–Jamillah Sabry, Oakland, CA

Delicious, wholesome, and absolutely filling epitomizes this vegan cuisine. The soups and stews delight your palate with a rich and robust mixture of spices, topped off with a homemade spread on pita bread creates a dish fit for a king, queen, or family. Contrary to your mother's twist on it, their homemade pizza is amazing and a must for gatherings both, small or large. Trust me, your guests will thank you for it!

My favorite, however, is the fruitbread. With four different flours and every fruit you can imagine, you won't be able to take a bite without devouring a wealth of

fruit. Although sweet, this organic desert is going to be one of the best vegan goodies you'll ever have! All the recipes within this cookbook are life giving, healing, and have assisted me on my journey of healthy eating and living. So begin yours today!

–Vanessa Dilworth, Oakland, CA

The Vegan Love Doctors Naasira and Gregory Joe are the ones I refer to when my body is in need of some medicinal cleansing and healing with food. One of my favorites is their pulp sandwich and beet juice. I believe that we must have a relationship with the food we choose to put in our bodies. Their food makes this relationship a loving, spiritual and healthy connection. Vegan love forever.

–Margo Harper, San Pablo, CA

The food that Naasira has cooked for me is super fantastic. It's the type of food that gives one a long life expectancy. I call it my healing food and the way that it is prepared is simply amazing. You have every root and herb and vegetable known to man and the way it's prepared and the mixture of it is outstanding. I call Naasira my vegan queen. It's amazing how she knows how to prepare the right types of food for any type of ailment that one may be experiencing in their bodies.

Once you have a mindset to eat properly and eat what God has put on this earth for us to digest and to eliminate in the proper way, we find ourselves having more energy and your thinking capacity is very clear. So, I must say you can't lose with the stuff my vegan queen does use.

–Deborah Benefield, Oakland, CA

Proper eating, Dr. Joe says, is one of the secrets of life. I agree and the vegan vegetarian cuisine is very good and truely "soul" food. The waffles were excellent! They were a lot better than mine. They are a part of a fabulous vegan cuisine by people who are very conscious about their diet. And thanks to Dr. Joe I am now getting back into the waffle game in a more healthy way.

–Leonard Franklin. Oakland, CA

One of my favorites is Naasira's Guacamole. It is "the bomb", "to die for". The vegan popcorn with garlic, cumin, and the many spices is wonderful. When I want to eat something sweet, this is the thing to eat. It is so much better for you. It keeps me from eating anything that is sweet that I should not eat and it is very delicious. This is cooking that will embrace you when you have the mind–set for living a healthy, longer and productive life. You will feel great too!

–Diana Lynch, Oakland, CA

I have dined on their delicious vegan meals and it has really made a believer out of me that vegetables and spices can be combined in such a way that it can tantalize your palate and make you want more and more. I have eaten pulp sandwiches that were just fabulous made from the remnants they utilize of what was not cooked up into their delectable dishes. They are also so delicious and delightful to the palate as well.

–Marilyn Richburg–Reynolds, Oakland, CA

I think it is a wonderful thing that we have decided that the way we used to eat is really not healthy and that we have people such as Naasira and Greg that take the expressed time not only to cook the right foods and be healthy, but to teach everyone else how to do it. I think that it's extremely important that we do this and they walk as superior examples that we are what we eat and we should eat well so we can look well.

–Rhonda Crane, Oakland, CA

I love the taste and the flavors. It is good and it makes you feel good. I wish I could eat like this all the time.

Teresa Daigle, San Pablo, CA

The fruitbread is delicious and amazing. I never expected vegan food to be so filling, satisfying and yummy.

–Stephanie DeVito, Oakland, CA

Because I was privileged to have access to Naasira's health sustaining foods, my vitality and overall sense of wellbeing has increased. The foods and recipes along with their good water and exercise have helped to stabilize my health.

–Harold Manley, Age 82, Claremont, CA

I had the awesome pleasure of not only dining on some of Gregory and Naasira's delectable cuisine, but watching them prepare it as well. It was total Love in action. Their food is thoroughly satisfying not only for the body, but the soul and mind as well. I know if we took all of Gregory and Naasira's healing advice and ate the way they suggest, the world would be in a much healthier place. I thank God for these two angels. Peace and Blessings.

–Rebecca Clemons, Oakland, CA

For a couple of years Naasira served up a variety of recipes, which she was developing and testing, to the delight of many who worked at the City College of San Francisco Libraries. I was the beneficiary of great and wonderful, natural whole foods, both raw and cooked, which surprised the palate by many subtle flavors from start to finish, and satisfied the body's needs no less than the soul. A meal from Naasira's cuisine was never short of color, texture, flavor, love and good will. I treasure the memory and crave the cooking.

–Dr.Christopher Kox Interim Dean, Library City College of San Francisco

I have had Naasira's vegan breakfast meals. They are nourishing, filling and delicious. Sometimes when you are trying to eat healthy some of the foods may not taste good. But this is not the case with Naasira's food. It is very tasty. I would eat a half bowl of the breakfast cereal and eat the other half the following day. Everything that should be in a good healthy breakfast meal was in it. There are raisins, fruits, oats, and vegetables. The fiber has helped improve my digestive system and the meals gave me more energy. After eating the breakfast, I would feel good all over. Naasira's breakfast food really put me on the road to healthy eating.

–Phyliss McFee, Oakland, CA

Naasira's food is a miracle. I once had a stomachache for about a week. I ate some of the vegetable stew, cornbread, salad and collard green wraps. Suddenly, my stomachache was gone. When I was sick with the flu I drank some of her citrus drink. It gave me energy and I felt so much better. I could drink it every day. Her smoothies are also amazing. Her food is natural, medicinal and tasty. I can feel the energy flowing through my body as I eat it.

–Marissa Tampoya, Oakland, CA

I love them. Their food is food of knowledge, learning, healing and love.

–Herma Jean Gardere, Richmond, CA

I used to work with Dr. Bledsoe at a junior high school in Oakland, California. I had the opportunity to inquire about why he had so much energy, was always so slim, very active and very alert all the time. He was one of the teachers that never got sick. If he took off it was because he was planning something else. But he was never sick, which raised my curiosity about his diet.

I had the pleasure of tasting the breakfast made of quinoa, different types of rice, vegetables and fruits with superfoods. I had never tasted it before. But it was delicious. I really enjoyed the breakfast. I felt a sense of wellbeing without being full. It was very tasty, especially for me, not being accustomed to quinoa.

I told my sister about it and she was so curious that she started to order the quinoa breakfast. She also had that sense of wellbeing and wanted to continue ordering that special recipe which was very tasty. I continued eating the breakfast and always felt so energized knowing I was eating clean organic food.

I highly recommend this new cookbook and any of the recipes. They are 100% organic and most of all are healthy and very good for you.

–Yolanda Carrillo, Daly City, CA

I have known Gregory for the past five years. And I have enjoyed his recipes and his advice in the field of healing. This has helped me physically to overcome illnesses. Gregory also strengthens my knowledge of self–healing through natural foods.

–Kareem Zuniga, born in Guatemala, Central America, currently residing in Oakland, CA

Naasira and Dr. Bledsoe may not fully realize how significantly they made a difference in my life. They helped me change the way I eat. It really does take a village! Thanks. –Greg McNamara, Placerville, CA

I want to express my appreciation for the wonderful things Naasira and Gregory have done and the beautiful menu they have created. I didn't know very much about vegan or vegetarian food. But thanks to them a whole new world has been opened. They have prepared meals showing how delicious this food could actually taste. The food is prepared in such a way that it is attractive, smells good, and it is good for you. That is a delightful combination. Thanks again for showing us a better way of eating. –Anna Coleman, Long Beach, CA

I first experienced Naasira's excellent food a year ago. Leftovers left too soon. When I found out they were coming back to the DMV. I had to set up a chance to allow good vegetarian friends to experience this wonderful banquet of love, taste and color. Every one at Eden Valley was overjoyed. We all ate ourselves blissful. I look forward for the ability to take Naasira's recipes and attempt to create a feast 1/3 as delicious as hers because I know 100% is impossible.

–Drexel Lyles, Washington, D.C.

I really appreciate the vegan food. The wholesomeness has helped heal me in my sicker days and helped give me vitality. I recommend all of these recipes to each and every one to help you become more whole and also have a tasty time doing it.

–Alton, CA

I am privileged to have met Naasira and Dr. Joe (Gregory Joe). I met Naasira while working at the Rosenberg Library at City College San Francisco. She introduced me to some of her smoothies and vegan food. The smoothies gave me such a boost of energy it was like I was running around cleaning up the building. The stress of my job seemed to go away. I had so much energy I started each day walking a mile around the college track. I no longer had the cravings to eat the chips and junk food that I had eaten before.

Being a carnivore, I had no idea food without meat could taste so good. I have eaten everything they have fixed for me. It is so hearty and filling. After eating it I feel like I am on cloud nine. I now make my own smoothies two to three times a week. It helps keep my energy up and tastes great too. My experience with Naasira and Dr. Joe's smoothies and food has changed my life for the better. I am no longer anemic nor a borderline diabetic.

–Doretha Evans, San Leandro, CA

With the help of Naasira's food I have changed my diet. By changing my diet to vegan I can truly admit that this is the best way to go. I feel great. I look great. This is the best I have felt in over 10 years. Change your diet and you will live a lot longer.

–Sharon Yasin, San Francisco, CA

As a friend and supporter I have gained from your superb efforts, knowledge and sacrifices in bringing forth your outstanding wisdom and life saving recipes. Your work has resulted in me improving my eating habits and becoming self–educated about what to eat and how to eat to live. My whole hearted thanks are due to the both of you who are truly One. Congratulations! Its time the world knows real truth and real Love.

–JacQueene Hedquist, Las Vegas, NV

The cornbread is excellent. My son loves it. He is always asking me when I am going to make more. I am so glad that Naasira and Greg are caring and sharing this wonderful way of eating. The food is good to you and better for you.

Thelma Carrington, Age 83, Okemah, OK

Naasira is very passionate about the vegan lifestyle and healthy eating. She is very knowledgeable about what ingredients are necessary for an authentic vegan dish. Furthermore, Naasira understands what foods are required for healing and nourishment for the body. I will definitely continue to use her recipes on my voyage to a healthy lifestyle.

–Lakysha Cummings, Oakland, CA

I can always speak about Sister Naasira's vegan cuisine with sheer delight because it is both delicious and life saving. One day Naasira entered the classroom with an aroma that had entered before her. The fresh healing smell let me know this was the way to go. It was appetizing, flavorful and magnificent to the body, mind and soul.

Under the presence of her food you quickly are made aware just from the smell alone it has healing qualities to both the spirit and the body. This makes her food nurturing love in action.

My favorite foods are her wonderful sandwiches. The pulp and humus sandwiches are simply amazing. And...Oh my God!, the stir–fry. It is a variety of spices combined with moist vegetables bursting with flavor. Each and every bite is an experience you will not forget.

Naasira's fine preparation of food has taught me that if I change the way I eat, I will change the way I heal.

–Linda D. Lovett, San Bernardino, CA

Dr. Bledsoe and his wife Naasira have provided incredible inspiration for my eating habits and me. When I first met Dr. B, at the middle school where I currently work, I was a full–blown meat–eating carnivore. I was sluggish and would routinely get tired and fatigued throughout the day, which is a huge problem when you work with teenagers. I would see how Dr. B was so energetic and enthusiastic throughout the day and decided to talk with him about how he maintains his high energy. He told me about his vegan diet and healthy eating habits. He then began to bring me a smoothie every morning.

Not only did I find myself feeling better and having more energy, but also they tasted delicious! After this experience I began to do some research into the factory farm system in this country. I read a book called Eating Animals by Jonathan Safran Foer and The Omnivore's Dilemma by Michael Pollan. Both of these books along with my conversations with Dr. B convinced me to change my eating habits and become a vegetarian.

This was the best decision of my life. It was over three years ago and I have not looked back. I've never felt better! I have energy throughout the day, I feel more clear-headed and my immune system has vastly improved. In fact, I cannot remember the last time I was sick and I am around "germ factories" all day! I am forever grateful to Dr. B and Naasira for providing a wonderful model of healthy living and showing me that a vegetarian/vegan diet can be not only very satisfying but extremely tasty as well.

–Nicholas Miller, Oakland, CA

I really love the salads Naasira makes. Eating her salads changed my way of eating. They are wonderful. I loved them so much I had to ask her to make me some every week. I never had any type of salads like those before. I love the colorful variety of vegetables. The salads are very natural with good nutrients you can feel going through your body. The fruitbread is the BOMB too. You cannot find food like this on the open market. I am waiting for Naasira and Dr. Joe to open a restaurant so I can daily eat her delicious healthy food.

–Lawrence Reese, San Francisco, CA

Naasira and Dr. Joe have recipes that support your immune system, which promotes a hearty healthy thyroid. This is one of the major concerns of many African American women. Armed with love, a cozy kitchen and a genuine traditional African concern for authentic foods, they are on a single mission to promote healthy eating lifestyles.

They teach cooking and eating the way we need to know. Both Naasira and Dr. Joe compliment each other in their joint effort to promote healthy eating. Naasira's gourmet style embraces Dr. Joe's support and inspiration.

They are true representatives in letting "food be their medicine, and their medicine be their food". They both illuminate great health. Whether raw or freshly cooked vegan dishes, they are both joined at the apron in demonstrating a healthy and better alternative to the way most of us have eaten. They are a sweet couple deserving a "Best Seller". Love, peace and blessings,

–Aminah Huang, Oakland, CA

Naasira's food is easy to eat. It is very tasty, nutritious, good for you and your digestive system. It is a great colon cleanser. I mean, it really helps to clean you out. I also enjoy her smoothies that seem to be made with love and magic.

–Donna White and Ferondus Ellis, Richmond and Emeryville, CA

2014 is the year of vegan cooking. This cookbook is a must to have because these recipes are extraordinary. I ate Naasira's food for seven days. My digestive system was much better. My bowel movements improved. My skin looked better and my eye stopped twitching. Eating Naasira's food was detoxing me as I dined on her delicious, nutritional cuisine.

–Rahima DuBose, Atlanta, GA

I was born and raised in San Francisco. Somehow, I ended up in Point Hope, Alaska. Like most, I eat some good food. But most of it is really not good for me at all. Not too long ago I came down from Alaska. My sister hooked me up with some of her mean, lean, vegan cuisine. In the short time I was there I could tell the difference. Her food really lifted me up. I could feel it go through my entire body. I could tell that this is the way I should be eating. My wife also likes the food. Naasira's cooking has inspired me to change my diet.

–Richard Cannon, Point Hope, AK

I came home real tired one day. I started eating some of Naasira's stew. I enjoyed the taste. It warmed my body and made me feel better. I do like the stew!

–Cynthia Taylor, Treasure Island, CA

Last year, I pulled a muscle in my stomach. The doctors didn't seem to know what was going on. But I did know that I was sick. I had been in the house for 17 days. I had lost 40 pounds. I could not eat, nor hold anything down. I was "toe up". Then my wife appeared like an angel with Naasira's food. It was one of the best stews I have ever eaten. It was prepared well. The salad was good and healthy. It was the only food I was able to keep down at the time. I ate it for 3–4 days.

After eating Naasira's food I felt so much better. I am now off the medication and a lot of unhealthy stuff. Whatever it is that she puts in her stews does the trick. I would recommend her recipes for anybody.

–Ken Taylor, Treasure Island, CA

I love Naasira's food. It doesn't just push you out and make you feel fat and all like that. I especially enjoyed the breakfast Gregory made. It was delicious.

–Ruthie May Fletcher, Age 85, Las Vegas, NV

Nutritional is a word that is used by many chefs and cooks all over the world. I believe most of them only speak about these values from the point of the foods they prepare. But Naasira and Gregory's food hold the nutritional value and taste that allow our bodies to do all the talking.

I am a survivor of Type 2 Diabetes. I had struggled with many years of pains and inconsistency with my sugar levels. Let's put it this way, I love food! For years I would consume any dish that was put in front of me, even if it wasn't good for my body. I was raised on Naasira's food and because of this my body was never subjected to any major illnesses during my youth and adolescence.

As a young man from twenty to twenty eight years, my ignorance to the blissful consumption of the unnecessary would steer me to those burger and fries, "we all love so much". I felt prescribed medicine would have done more damage to me only because I was on the border of being a Type 1 Diabetic. I was afraid that if I took the medicine, I would have been much more careless about the foods I consumed and my illness would eventually accelerate.

Pain would strike constantly in my legs, feet, and joints. I would even have problems with my vision. Then I came home, I tasted Naasira and Gregory's food for the first time. I say it was my first time only because my eyes were finally opened and I could see clearly. The freshness of their organic salad's, soups, and smoothies give me all the nutritional value my body needed.

Thank you very much Naasira and Gregory for opening my eyes.

–Atiba Wallace, Anchorage, AK

Naasira and Dr. Joe make food for the Spirit. I have known them for going on two years and see them nearly every week at the farmer's market. I can attest to the fact that they are people who practice what they preach. That is, positivity, health, knowledge and love. Having tried a number of their always delicious and nutritious creations and knowing the love and care they put into all aspects of their lives, I have found myself highly anticipating the release of this book. It will be a welcomed and necessary addition to any kitchen.

–James Sandoval, Oakland, CA

I am truly a food connoisseur. I love to eat. I have eaten all kinds of food. I've eaten Indian, Greek, Italian, Japanese, Russian, Kosher and so many more. My favorite food is Naasira's for the following reasons. It is healthy and healing. It is filled with the best of herbs that Naasira has studied, thought about and figured out what they all are good for. In other words, which herbs were healing for the body, mind, and soul. I don't want you to take my word for it. Please, try it yourself.

My brother was in the hospital for over a month. I went to see him every day, two to three times. The only thing I could think of was getting him to eat Naasira's food when he got out of the hospital. Even if I would have to tie him up and put it down his throat, I was willing to do that. But as it turned out, he was willing to try it.

Thank God, within a week he was recovering well. I would say about 70% of the recovery was Naasira's food. The rest was lots of sleep and personal love and care from his daughter and me. So, I can say thank you Naasira and Greg for your support and always being there delivering the food and every delivery was different.

You will never find it being cooked the exact same way. It is always different and it gets better and better. It changes with the four seasons. I could go on and on (smile). But this is her book, not mine. I have been eating Naasira's food for about twenty–two years or more. It is the best thing that can happen to a human being. Thank you Naasira and Greg.

–Bonnie Strong, San Francisco, CA

My sister had recommended Naasira's cooking to me in an effort to get me healthier. I did not try her food until after my hospitalization. When in the hospital I ate food on the hospital menu, which included meat. After my hospital stay I discovered the benefits of Naasira's food with its many herbs and spices. Before eating Naasira's African stews and stir–fries, the medication I was taking seemed to drag me down. I seemed to have little or no energy. But Naasira's food made me feel better. I no longer had the desire to eat meat. I portion out the stew and eat it with my other food. It is a great pick–me–up. It has helped to boost my immune system and build up my body. I now feel so much better. In fact, I feel like a new person.

–Henry Crater, San Francisco, CA

I had cancer and was undergoing chemotherapy a few years ago. I did not go through what a lot of people went through. I mean, the throwing up. I did not go through any of that because of Naasira's food, citrus drink and tea. It kept my body cleansed. I had no poison backing up in my system.

The citrus drink is incredible! Whenever I would start to get a cold, congestion, or a sniffle I would drink it. The problem was gone. The cereal is good. The stew, with all those vegetables and spices is delicious. It includes turmeric, which is good for any inflammation in my body. My cancer in now gone and I appreciate Naasira for being there for me. –Maxine Dempsey, Oakland, CA

I would like to thank you and Joe for what you did to help my mother. I know what you did had an impact on my mother's recovery. I could feel the energy in the food and your citrus drink you gave her. When I saw my mother drinking the citrus drink, I had a cold and I wanted to give it a try. When I drank the citrus drink it heated my chest. Suddenly, everything came right out. The cold was gone. What you do is lovingly amazing.

–Bryant Dempsey, Stockton, CA

I'm no Foodee, but I thoroughly enjoyed the dish you guys prepared for me at lunchtime that day. You put it in a "to go" container allowing me to stay on schedule. That was love in true form. Thank you. Thank you very much. Your new creations with vegetables, oils, herbs and spices are so delicious, even sexy, that the taste stayed with me thoughout my day.

I know you two will continue this grand nutritional effort. We are what we eat and your creations will make us all better people. I miss our retirement planning sessions. You guys have arrived and are blessed. May God continue to bless you two.

–Tillman Pugh, MBA, CFP, Oakland, CA

After eating what Naasira and Gregory prepared I felt like Wow! Could this actually taste this good without meat? Keep in mind, I'm a true Inupiat, Eskimo from the Arctic of Alaska. In order to survive in this harsh environment we need protein (all our traditional food). But once I tasted the food I thought I could actually get use to this stuff and enjoy it at the same time, knowing all the nutritional benefits of the food. The salad was very delicious! When I see Naasira and Greg preparing the food I also see the energy and love that they put into it.

Had I not known them, with the energy they have, I honestly would have thought they were in their early forties. When actually, they are in their early sixties. That's living proof as to how healthy this food truly is. With that said, I highly recommend for everyone to check this food out.

–Caroline Cannon, Point Hope, Alaska

I had the opportunity of having Greg and Naasira visit me during the summer. They introduced me to their wonderful way of cooking. I watched both of them as they prepared their meals. I was fascinated as they took the time to intricately cut up each vegetable and herb.

I always tried to eat right. But watching them made me feel a little closer to healthy eating and living. I enjoyed the meals that included kale, greens, broccoli and cauliflower. Everything was fresh.

I also introduced this way of cooking to my grandchildren, ages 4 and 8. To my surprise they really enjoyed the vegetarian dishes. I now prepare vegan food most Sundays for them. At 63, I am very impressed with what I have learned from Greg and Naasira as I try this new way of eating. Thank you, Greg and Naasira.

–Kazzandra Greene, New York City

On the food preference continuum that extends from the carnivore on the right to vegan on the left, you two were always considered by me to be to the left of my fish and chicken diet. And, since getting joy out of eating is such a personal thing, I immediately felt a bit of trepidation upon receiving your invitation to sample your Food of Life. The trepidation came out of my respect for your culinary attainments and not wanting to make negative comments about your choice of foods.

[Background – I am not a gourmet. Therefore, whenever I dare to comment on some food I have been given, in all likelihood, I will be expressing to the inquisitor why my

brain is processing – that my preferences in eating were either: not disturbed by this menu or that my preferences in eating were, in fact disturbed. The verbal expressions of those brain processes usually gets further reduced down to the words "I like it" or "I have problems with this." Rarely–to–never would I give any qualitative assessment of the food: I might get kicked out of the host's house]

So, when you gave me your Food of Life dishes, I felt a bit of trepidation. Very timidly, I opened the lids of your "to–go" containers, and immediately recognized the rice and the striking fresh salad. And surprise, surprise, once heated, the flavors of the main dish poured out and drove me to devour everything over the course of two days – except the avocado sandwich.

The salad was quite alive and included greens (as opposed to just lettuce), which greens proved to be a pleasant surprise. The dressing you provided was a revelation. The latent sweetness of the main dish (possibly from the tomatoes or their sauce) balanced the spicy rice quite nicely. The breakfast mix was used as ice cream scoop–sized balls along side my everyday breakfast fruit.

Thank you for opening my palate. Thank you for the deft touch of giving me "to–go" containers that allowed me to sneak a taste away from your public viewing. The superiority of the food gave me everything I would have had at a formal sit down dinner – except you watching me eat (again, the trepidation). Thanks again.

–William Taylor, Esq., Oakland, CA

I would like to sing my praises for the most delicious and remarkably nutritious fruitbread ever made. It is moist and sweet without the sugar or butter. This taste along with the nutritional qualities would never happen in regularly baked commercial goods. Vegan cooking and baking are pleasant surprises to the healthy side of culinary art. Thanks.

–Marguerite Versher, Oakland, CA

As a vegetarian for over 25 years and event planner for nearly 20 Collard Greens Cultural Festivals and Cook–Offs between California and Georgia, I believe I am well qualified to judge any collard green dish raw or cooked. The Collard Green Wrap – Um, Umm, Ummm. Absolutely delicious! It is a dish for any time of the day... breakfast, lunch, dinner or as a snack. Naasira and Greg are true food scientist. They know exactly what herbs and spices bring out the flavor of any vegetable. Eating their colorful and delicious meals prepares you for a healthy journey of peace, love and longevity.

"The Collard Green Queen"

–Dr. Mama Nobantu Ankoanda

The food was invigorating! The raw ingredients left me feeling energized and uplifted. It was like a pick–me–up food. The taste was delightfully wonderful, with a natural savory sweet taste. I felt the energy of the soul in the food. In all honestly, it was the best raw sandwich I have ever experienced.

I love you both. –Khadijah Grant, El Sobrante, CA

Naasira's Vegan dishes were always a hit when my student organization held events. The fresh salad and vegan pasta was delicious. I loved the sauce for the pasta, and so did everyone at the events. That is why it would be eaten very quickly. The food was truly appreciated by people of all cultures. It was a delight to serve food that not only satisfied your taste buds, but that was also good for those you are serving. After seeing how much people loved the vegan food from Naasira, I made sure to have some at every event.

–Jesse James, Sacramento, CA

I have known Naasira to be an excellent cook for all of the past forty years we have been friends. She always loved cooking, sharing her talents and family recipes, while taking excellent care of her children and overcoming personal health challenges. When she became a vegetarian and later a vegan, her passion increased and blossomed into an avenue for change in the community and the world, one person and one plate at a time. Her food is delicious, beautiful and healthy. What more can you ask food to be? Her partnership with Gregory has only added to her inventive spirit and her search for the truth. Their collaborative efforts are a gift to all who seek an enlightened awareness along with a healthy and happy tummy.

–Mardeen Cassell, Antioch, CA

I remember a time being very ill and Naasira's wonderful, wholesome food totally nourished me back to health very quickly. Naasira cooks soul food the way it should be. It is healthful as well as tasteful. I can only imagine how much healthier the black community and everyone else for that matter would be if they could cook food the way Naasira prepares it with her loving hands. The community would no longer battle health problems like obesity, high blood pressure, high cholesterol, etc. This is healing food and everyone would be blessed immensely to have the opportunity to taste Naasira's amazing cooking!

–Samantha Mathews, Istanbul, Turkey

No one else has done what MAMA Naasira and Dr. Joe have done to help improve my health. Since meeting them, I have had nothing but success with my health. I really appreciate the quality of their food. They used the highest quality ingredients of organic, unrefined unprocessed foods.

They uniquely prepare the food in a way that tastes like special gourmet meals, which is something not easy to do when preparing vegan food. When you eat their food you are eating close to the way God intended for us to eat. I feel they are closest to the creator in that sense.

I will continue to deal with them for my health. And I would also recommend to anybody and everybody that they should definitely buy their book and listen to what they have to say. It will make the quality of your life so much better.

–Anthony Edwards, San Leandro CA

One Friday afternoon I experienced a literal smorgasbord of vegetarian delight. It was delicious! I had a lovely veggie pulp sandwich with fresh veggie juices in a variety of combinations. There were lentils and Dr. Joe's cornbread, steel cut oats with sliced apples and pears with a little banana, goji berries, raisins, pea protein and psyllium husk. I have to admit, I pigged out.

The food they serve is spiritual, a ritual. It is an offering. It is sacred, like the vessel it enters. I certainly want to live a long healthy life. MAMA Naasira and Dr. Joe are scientists in this field. I am certainly consulting them (smile).

Thanks so much for the food.

Peace and Blessings,

–Wanda Sabir, San Francisco Bay Area

CHAPTER 4
Forgiveness

TOTAL HEALING TAKES PLACE when there is no judgment, which includes resentment, envy, or jealousy. Since our thoughts affect the very cells of our bodies, it is best to maintain loving, not destructive thoughts. Loving thoughts promote healing. One sure way to heal is to forgive. Since this is not always easy to do, I have set forth steps that lead to forgiveness. Forgiveness allows healing to take place at our cellular level.

It also creates a tremendous release of thoughts that no longer serve our highest good. This will permit a greater opportunity to replace those thoughts that no longer serve us with thoughts of love, joy, gratefulness, and blessings for others. Keep in mind that whatever you focus your attention on or put your mind on most, you will create more of the same in your life.

Forgiveness Challenge

This is a three (3) step challenge.

Step one (1) Write down all the things you did or did not do this life that you could have done differently.

Forgive yourself for all of those things. At the time you acted or chose not to act, you were doing the best you could based on your level of awareness, comprehension, and your desire or willingness to do better. In other words, you could not do better if you did not know better and you can't make change unless you have the desire and will to do so.

Step two (2) Write down the names of all the people and what you think they did that may have caused you hurt, harm, or suffering this life.

Forgive them. They were also doing the best that they could at that time of their actions or inactions with their level of awareness, comprehension, and desire or willingness to do better.

Often, we find that we may have been mistaken in thinking someone wronged us. For example: We may later discover that someone other than the person we originally thought actually ate our apple or cookie. Another example would be to think a brother, sister, or friend wore our shirt or blouse losing a button or soiling it, only to later discover that someone else did it.

Step three (3) Forgive yourself again. You played a part in everything that has happened to you this life. It could be karma you are paying off from other life times or karma you are paying off for things that you have set in motion this life.

You can attract what you fear or attract more love and happiness into your life. Whatever you focus on the most becomes a reality in your life. Focus on forgiving yourself and others each day.

This challenge is designed to bring out thoughts, experiences and feelings that you may have suppressed. Uncovering these suppressed ideas and thoughts will allow you to forgive yourself and the person(s) involved. Forgiveness is the key to releasing you from the past pain. It also allows you to release and let go and to release your judgment of others for the wrong they may have caused you.

Keep in mind that everyone is you on some level. Truly, we are all one.

Forgiveness: The Greatest Healer of All by Gerald Jampolsky, M.D. Published 1999 by Atria Books/Beyond Words Publishing Inc.

Radical Forgiveness by Colin Tipping, Revised Edition Published 2010 by Sounds True Inc.

Forgive for Good by Dr. Fred Luskin, Published 2003 by HarperCollins Publishers Inc.

Let It Go: Forgive So You Can Be Forgiven by T.D. Jakes, Published 2012 by Atria Books

CHAPTER 5
Most Men Are Slow

A MESSAGE FROM GREGORY JOE TO MEN

WHEN A MAN COMES into this life, I believe it is karmic. Being born as a man is the cost we pay for what we did or did not do in a past or past lives. That is why the average man that comes here seems to be so much slower than most women. Most men are so slow that they are not aware or have any idea that they are slow. What do I mean by slow? It's an attitude I characterize as unaware, unconscious, and disconnected from an appreciation of the value of other perspectives.

Some men are so slow that they think they are fast. It takes about 50 years before the average man begins to mature.

By the time they start to mature at about 50, most men have accumulated many physical and social challenges. These challenges have usually come about because they were too slow to listen or comprehend what someone (often a woman) tried to tell them to do or not to do differently. Some men are so slow, they arrogantly feel or believe that a woman can't tell them anything.

To add to that challenge, when they come into this life, men are told one of the biggest stories, along with Santa Claus, the Easter Egg Bunny laying chocolate eggs, and God being a white man, that they have to work through all their lives. That story is that man is superior to woman. While it is true that most men might be able to carry a heavy object or even run with it for a short distance, that is about where a man's superiority ends.

Females possess a more efficient and powerful immune system than males. This provides women greater immunity against infections and a faster recovery time than men. There are more women 100 years and older than there are men. That explains why there are more widows than there are widowers.

A woman's body weight is about 25% fat compared to a man's 14%. Perhaps that is why women are better insulated against the cold and can endure cold weather on a general basis better than men. Fewer women have hardening of the arteries than men. More men have incidences of stomach ulcers, baldness and gout than women. Women can adjust their blood pressure quicker than men.

At high altitudes like the Andes Mountains, where there is 18% less oxygen, women survive better than men. Women also can carry heavier loads at these high altitudes than men because women's oxygen capacity is larger. Women have a higher pain threshold and can bear pain much more, without complaining, than men. If a man had to endure menstrual cramps or the pain of childbirth, there would be considerably fewer people on this planet.

Women have a larger thyroid gland than men. A girl at the age of 7 has a brain capacity that a boy does not get until he is past puberty, usually about age 14, because of high levels of thyroid rich hormones. That is one of the reasons why the female is mentally superior to males during childhood. The female brain, relative to overall body weight, is ¼ heavier than a male brain. The female brain has a finer texture and has a more complex organization than that of a male.

Women's brains have more nerve cells in their frontal lobes than men. These frontal lobe nerves regulate higher brain functions such as language, judgments, and planning future actions. This may shed some light on why many men will not ask for directions when lost or will not admit when they are wrong. It also points to the fact that females learn to speak foreign languages more quickly and accurately than males and is why most women can out talk men and are better able to successfully plan for future events than men.

Men have more heart attacks and strokes caused by brain hemorrhage than women. Suicide rates at all ages are higher for males. Women in general are better at multi–tasking and more intuitive than men. Women miscarry or are less likely to carry to full term more male babies than female babies. Baby boys are much more likely to die in the first year than baby girls.

In light of these facts, I believe men should see women in a different light. Give thanks that women take time and put up with us. It is not easy dealing with someone who is slower than you. In fact, men should continuously thank females in their life for being patient and loving them.

A man should strive to be the best that he can be. No lying, stealing, cheating, littering, or acts of unkindness. If they do this, men have a better chance of being appreciated by righteous women. Also, they will have a better opportunity to understand, know, and become aware of the beauty and power of women. But if they don't try to do right this life, they might come back in another life as an even slower man...or worse.

Man, Women, And Child Dr. Delbert Blair 2012 http://bit.ly/1dVhtEM

The Natural Superiority of Women by Ashley Montagu, fifth Edition, 1999

"Women Have More Frontal Lobe Neurons Than Men" http://bit.ly/1H437PU

Mail Online: "Baby boys are a quarter more likely to die in their first year of life" http://dailym.ai/1L7MEdj

Why it's not "Rain Woman" http://econ.st/1Ip9Xde

CHAPTER 6
Naasira's Approach

A SUSTAINABLE PLAN FOR FOOD PREPARATION

OPTIMUM HEALTH IS A desire for many of us and we know that proper nutrition, healthy lifestyles, and a good diet are essential to this quest. There are many approaches to healthy eating, just as there are many former vegans and vegetarians. Some have abandoned the vegan or vegetarian diet because they no longer wished to cook or prepare food. A lack of a sustainable approach to weekly vegan or vegetarian cooking has been the main reason. We invite you to try Naasira's approach, as she has used it to create optimum health for herself and others and is now sharing it with you. This will require setting aside time to prepare and cook for the week. This will turn out to be one of the best times in your life.

To start off, we need to stock our kitchen. Below is a working list of the fruits, vegetables, spices, herbs, breads, flours, spreads and nut butters, seasonings, oils, sweeteners, plant–based milks such as almond or hemp milk, beans, grains, super–foods, and snacks we will use.

I would not suggest getting everything at once. Obtain the items required for each recipe you are working on. I would suggest listing all the recommended items for your kitchen. Pick up a few non–perishable items such as rice, beans, nuts, or grains on the list each time you go to the market, farmer, or store.

Fruits and vegetables are best eaten fresh. Only purchase the fruits and vegetables you will eat during the week. This keeps the fruits and vegetable fresh. They contain more minerals, vitamins, and healthy fruit fiber. Always remember, fresh is best.

Your stocked kitchen will provide you flexibility, options, and creativity. You can also think of your kitchen as your health science laboratory. Here, you will assemble herbs, spices, fruits, grains, and vegetables to give your body food to aid in its optimal repair and healing. Make sure you put your food in safe containers. This will protect your food against spoilage and not expose your food to unhealthy substances.

Stock Your Kitchen

Organic, non–genetically modified organisms (GMO), non–pesticide sprayed foods are best. But if they are not available, use Grocery/Health Food Stores/Online.

- **Beans**
- Adzuki beans
- Black beans
- Black–eyed peas
- Chickpeas (garbanzo beans)
- Lentils (French, green, red, black)
- Navy beans
- Red Kidney beans
- Split peas
- Any other type of bean you like
- **Breads/Flour/Pasta**
- Spouted–grain bread(raisin, cinnamon, or sesame)
- Whole–grain pita bread
- Barley Flour
- Brown Rice Flour
- Buckwheat Flour
- Quinoa Flour
- Rye Flour
- **Condiments**
- Black sesame seeds

- Catsup
- Mustard
- Pickles
- **Dried Fruit**
- Apricots
- Figs
- Goji Berries
- Medjool dates
- Mulberries
- Prunes
- Raisins

- **Herbs And Spices**
- Allspice (whole, powder)
- Basil
- Bay leaf
- Black Pepper
- Cardamon (seed, powder)
- Cayenne
- Cinnamon powder
- Cinnamon sticks
- Chipotle
- Cloves (whole, powder)
- Coriander (seed, powder)
- Cumin (seed, powder)
- Curry
- Dill (seed, powder)
- Fennel (seed, powder)
- Fenugreek (seed, powder)
- Herbes de Provence
- Italian
- Mineral salt
- Nutmeg (whole, powder)
- Nutritional yeast
- Marjoram

- Oregano
- Paprika
- Rosemary
- Sage
- Sea salt
- Sumac
- Thyme
- Turmeric
- Vegan bouillon cubes
- **Fresh fruit** (seasonal purchases are best)
- Apples
- Avocados
- Bananas
- Blueberries
- Cherries
- Cucumbers
- Figs
- Grapes
- Kiwi
- Mangoes
- Oranges
- Papayas
- Peaches
- Pears
- Persimmons
- Plantain
- Strawberries
- Tomatoes (including cherry)
- Watermelon
- Or any other fruit you like.
- **Fresh Herbs**
- Basil
- Dill
- Fennel

- Ginger
- Rosemary
- Thyme
- **Fresh Vegetables** (seasonal purchases are best)
- Arugula
- Asparagus
- Basil
- Beets
- Beet Greens
- Bell Peppers (green/red/yellow)
- Bitter Melon
- Broccoli
- Cabbage (red, Napa, green)
- Cauliflower
- Carrots
- Celery
- Cilantro
- Collard Greens
- Dandelion Greens
- Dill
- Eggplant
- Fennel
- Ginger
- Kale
- Leeks
- Mushrooms
- Mustard Greens
- Peas
- Parsley
- Peppers (hot)
- Rosemary
- Shallots
- Scallions
- Spinach

- String Beans
- Swiss Chard
- Thyme
- Turnip Greens
- Sweet potatoes
- Yams
- **Frozen Fruit** (freeze it in season)
- Bananas
- Blackberries
- Blueberries
- Cherries
- Raspberries
- Strawberries
- **Grains**
- Barley (hulled)
- Couscous
- Millet
- Polenta
- Quinoa
- Black, Wild, Red, Jasmine or Brown Basmati Rice
- Rolled Oats
- Steel Cut Oats
- **Liquid Seasoning**
- Bragg Liquid Aminos
- Shoyu
- **Nuts/Seeds**
- Almonds
- Cardamom seeds
- Caraway seeds
- Cashews
- Chia seeds
- Coriander seeds
- Flax seeds
- Hemp seeds

- Pine nuts
- Pistachios
- Pumpkin seeds
- Sesame seeds
- Sunflower seeds
- Walnuts
- **Oils**
- Extra Virgin olive oil
- Virgin Coconut oil
- Flaxseed oil
- Omega Twin
- **Plant–Based Milks**
- Almond milk
- Coconut milk
- Hemp Non–Dairy Beverage
- Hemp milk
- **Spreads and Butters**
- Almond butter, raw
- Cashew butter, raw
- Miso (made from fermented soybeans and salt) red or white
- Organic Raw Black Sesame Tahini
- Tahini butter
- **Snacks**
- Non–dairy, non–soy yogurt
- Popcorn
- Plantain
- **Sweeteners**
- Black Strap Molasses
- Maple Syrup
- Coconut Nectar
- **Superfood**s
- Maca
- Protein power

- Psyllium husk
- Moringa
- Pea Protein

The goal of this method is to ensure you have fresh, healthy food readily available so you will not resort to unhealthy food choices. A well stocked kitchen will serve you well in your new, healthy eating lifestyle. When preparing food for the week, keep in mind the goal. The items you purchase or select will be for cornbread, stir–fry (sauté), salad, smoothies, juices, and African vegetable stew. The collard green wraps, spaghetti sauce, tacos, Sloppy Joes, pizzas, lasagna, and other dishes are spin–offs of the African vegetable stew.

Farmers' Markets

Most of your fresh fruit, nuts, olive oil, and vegetables may be purchased at the Farmers' Market. Here are some helpful tips.

The farmers can give you lots of information about the items you purchase, like the health benefits, the different varieties and ways to prepare the produce.

If you are a regular customer, most farmers will charge you less. Once farmers get to know you, they generally will look out for you. This can be in the form of saving goods for you, letting you know when certain foods are in season, or bringing goods for you.

There is generally a discount on the goods sold near closing time. That is because the farmers would rather sell the goods at a lower price or give them away to avoid having to pack them up to take back to the farm or warehouse only to be packed up and sold another day. Also, the goods might be too ripe to sell another day.

There are a few disadvantages of coming to the Farmers' Market near closing. The best looking fruits and vegetables are usually sold early in the day, so by the time you arrive, what's left may have been picked over and not look so pretty. But once it is washed, chopped, and cut up for salads, stews, roasted vegetables or stir–fry, the initial look of the produce will not matter.

Grocery/Health Food Stores/Online

The items that cannot be obtained from the Farmers' Market usually can be found at the grocery or health food store. Many large groceries have a health food or organic food section. Most health food stores will have some of the items listed above. Many of these items may also be purchased online.

Now, some of you may hesitate when you discover organic or non–pesticide sprayed, non–GMO fruits and vegetables cost more than conventional fruits and vegetables. But I invite you to compare the price of the average medical bills you receive for treatment because of the damage caused by pesticides and waxes from conventionally grown fruits and vegetables to the price paid for organic or non–pesticide sprayed , non–GMO fruits and vegetables. Your body will appreciate the healthy choice.

The Food Industries are motivated by profit. If there is a demand and a profit can be made selling organic or non–pesticide sprayed, non–GMO food, the food industries will find a way to make it available to the consumers. As more people voice their demand for organic, non–pesticide sprayed, non–GMO foods, the food industries will comply. This will create more competition between competing food companies. This results in prices in stores being lowered as more companies rise to meet the consumer's demands.

There are growing numbers of people who desire a healthier way of eating. This includes, the "hipsters" and "baby–boomers" that have considerable economic influence. Talk to your local store managers. Tell them that you want them to obtain organic or non–pesticide sprayed, non–GMO fruits and vegetables.

CHAPTER 7
My Journey

GREGORY JOE BLEDSOE

MY JOURNEY IN PURSUIT of abundant life began in a family of six brothers and four sisters. My parents were from the South. My grandmother (my mother's mother) earned a living washing clothes and cooking for affluent White people in the areas where she lived. With such meager earnings, she was barely able to help raise my mother and uncle. My grandmother passed that cooking on to my mother that was later to be called "Soul Food".

My Mother's Kitchen

I started off eating the "Soul Food" diet inherited from my parents: chicken smothered with brown gravy, corn on the cob with melted butter and salt and greens cooked until they wore a dirty brownish–green color, having the green of life boiled out of them. Candied yams and soft white yeast rolls would generally round out a typical Sunday meal.

My mother's kitchen experienced her sweet potato pies, smothered pork chops, red beans with neck bones and white rice, cinnamon rolls with white sugary icing, hot water cornbread, gumbo, liver with onions, meatloaf, catfish, fried chicken, turkey, mashed potatoes, salmon croquettes, potato salad, chicken and dumplings, beef and chicken stew, black–eyed peas with okra, chitterlings, stuffed bell peppers, and boiled cabbage with salt pork.

My father, a former Marine, had one dish for which he was known. Creamed tuna or "Shit on a Shingle", as it was called in the military. It was made with all purpose white flour, milk, shortening, salt, pepper, and canned tuna. The sauce was served over toasted white bread. Whenever my mother was having a baby or out of town, creamed tuna would make its appearance.

Sugar Jones

There was also the barbeque. The sauce was made of sugar, mustard, liquid smoke, garlic powder, hot sauce, tomato paste and catsup. This barbeque sauce generously covered the links, ribs, hot dogs and hamburgers, and was poured into the beans. I could not leave out the Kool–aid, Coke, Diet Pepsi, luncheon meats, buttered pound and upside–down cakes.

At that time, I did not know that refined flour and sugar are substances that were never meant to be in the body. My Aunt Peal was very dear to me. At the age of six, I remember living with her in Bakersfield, California. Each morning she would serve us hot buttered white rice, with evaporated condensed milk, and sugar. It is safe to say that she was most likely addicted to the sugar. At that time she was diagnosed with high blood pressure and diabetes. It was not long after that she went blind and died.

Hot Dogs And Buns

I once knew a person who boiled and ate a whole package of hot dogs. I remember doing that twice in my life. Both times I was about 16 years old, very athletic, and ignorant of nutritional facts. I did not know that a plain single hot dog or frankfurter has about 717 milligrams of sodium. One with catsup and/or mustard has about 900 milligrams of sodium.

Luckily, I survived eating the ten hot dogs twice. I did not continue this unhealthy practice. The person I knew, at age 49, was diabetic, on dialysis, and not so lucky. He suffered a heart attack and died.

I had no knowledge at that time that mixing carbohydrates and proteins could cause gas, heartburn, indigestion, headaches, joint pain, inability to lose weight, fatigue, acne, and more. No one told me that carbohydrates and proteins should not be combined unless they are in eighteen percent (18%) proportion to each other.

The Infamous Pig

As a teenager, I was influenced by the Honorable Elijah Mohammad's book, "How to Eat to Live". In this book, he states the advantages of adults eating one meal a day and fasting. Fasting allows the body's organs to take a deserved break. This results in more efficiency in the work of rested organs.

My family was no stranger to eating pork. The pig (swine) was eaten from his snout to his tail. We ate pork fried, baked, or boiled. I remember one of my aunts preparing a dish made from the pus coming out of the pig's forelegs. This was called "pork blood". It was served with mashed potatoes.

I recall my cousins and I purchasing a large bag of pork rinds at the local neighborhood store. Pork rinds are the tough skin layer of pigs that remains after the meat has been removed. It is rehydrated in water with added flavoring and a generous slathering of salt before it is sliced and deep–fried in very hot pork fat, twice. This causes water to expand as steam and is what causes them to bubble. The rinds are removed from the fat, flavored, and air–dried.

We ate the rinds with hot sauce and drank soda. At times we purchased pickled pig feet that came from a large jar of water, vinegar, and salt solution. The pig feet were eaten with crackers. "Pig tails" were put in stews and beans to add flavor. The process of preparing chitterlings, the intestines of the pig, left an awful smell in the house. But we ate them. We ate the pig from the "rooter to the tooter".(See also page 108 "Eating Pork")

Steps Toward Veganism

At fourteen, I began hanging out at my best friend's house a lot. His family were Seventh Day Adventists. Many Seventh Day Adventists are vegetarians. This family ate no red meat or pork. His mother cooked chicken and many dishes served with cheese. She was a good cook. It was quite a departure from the "Soul Food".

What she did in the kitchen was fascinating to me. I now knew life without red meat or pork was possible. I gave up eating beef and pork. Her cooking made it easy. I recalled the many maladies that came about as the result of family members eating pork and red meat. It strengthened my resolve to keep away from red meat and pork (swine). However, her frame of 5' feet tall and over 220 pounds lead me to believe that there had to be an even better way of eating.

Meat

During College, I read more about the advantages of life with no meat. I learned about the abuse animals are made to endure so they can be eaten. The hormones and antibiotics given to the animals that are to be consumed in our bodies are alarming. In 2010, the Bolivian President, Evo Morales, stated that "When we talk about chickens, it's pumped full of female hormones, and so when men eat chicken, they sway from being men". When women eat chicken pumped full of female hormones and antibiotics it seems to contribute to uterine fibroids and promote fibroid growth.

Dr. Roba

According to Dr. Anteneh Roba, "Africans ate no meat over 5000 years ago and were able to communicate with the animals". This was enough for me. I became a vegetarian. Having given up red meat and pork before, it was now time to say goodbye to chicken and seafood. I ate more fruit, vegetables, and grains. The last to go was the dairy (cheese and milk products).

I taught in the Oakland Public Schools for thirty years. I rarely got a cold. If I did get a cold, it didn't last long. I am perceived as being younger than my true chronological age. I still do many things people far younger than me have stopped doing, either because their knees hurt, or because they have shortage of breath, backs out, or because they have other physical challenges. I feel so blessed to have learned at an early age that your health is your wealth.

Family Reunion

At our family reunion in Arkansas, soul food was served. The families met in the school auditorium set for the grand meal. Mashed potatoes, packaged salad mix, macaroni and cheese, turkey, ham, fried chicken, green beans, store bought pound, white, and lemon cakes, and sodas were served. Many of the family members were not in the best of shape. Waist lines were scarce. Some were walking to the side. I pointed out to my wife that we should do better. It made no sense for our people to continue to kill themselves with their knives and forks.

The next night, at the family banquet, one of the elder clan spoke. He said that he wanted to report that three family members were sick. One is still hospitalized. Fortunately, this experience was enough to prove the point. The committee putting on the reunion next year will have vegetarian and vegan food. We will assist this effort.

Needless to say, my family was riddled with heart attacks, gout, diabetes, strokes, obesity, nervous breakdowns, cancer, and short life. So, as not to follow the pack, I changed my way of eating and most importantly, my way of thinking. This has led to a welcomed lifestyle.

Meeting Naasira

I met Naasira in 1999. She was working at a branch library in Oakland, California. I had gone there to replace some of my music. Patrons enjoy my music so much they will check it out and not return it. Naasira saw my music, said she would support me, and purchased a cassette tape. We spoke briefly. She told me she was married. I was married too at the time. I looked forward to talking to her again.

Three years later, I saw her in a health food store in Berkeley, California. She told me that she was no longer married and was living with a housemate. When Naasira described her roommate, I knew her and where she lived. I too, was no longer married. I invited Naasira to lunch at the Organic Café. She was intriguing. I enjoyed her so much I asked her to join me for a concert at Stern Groove in San Francisco.

She brought the food she had prepared the day before. She had put it away when I invited her to lunch. Now, it was displayed. Her food was amazing. The food had smells, flavors, colors, and incredible taste. She got my attention and that of another friend who had joined us.

The following morning I was in San Francisco on a radio interview. It was about two a.m. I called Naasira to find her preparing food. I told her I would come by after the interview if she were still up. After the interview, I called her. Naasira said she was up cooking for the week. When I arrived I was introduced to a new way of cooking. Soon herbs, spices, vegetables, and legumes were marinating in a delicious stew. There were stir–fries, cornbread, yams, plantain, and salad.

Soon we were cooking together. I witnessed many people loving Naasira's food. Her phone was constantly ringing. Friends, relatives, co–workers, and colleagues were asking for her food. Many claimed that the herbs and spices in the food helped them to feel better. I know of two who claim that after a regular diet of Naasira's food they were no longer considered diabetic. Some said the food is tasty. Most said it is a combination of healthy eating and great taste.

There was no way Naasira could keep up with the demand of the many people who wanted her food. We thought of different ways to help them. She reasoned that some did not learn how to cook and others did not know how to manage their cooking time. I suggested a cooking class demonstrating her style of cooking using healing herbs and spices and her method for cooking for the week.

We held several cooking classes with great success. But with me teaching full time, and Naasira's heavy workload at City College San

Francisco Library, we could not continue. So we both retired and put together this cookbook to assist those on their way to an abundantly healthy life.

DAY 1: Shopping and Chopping

Purchase fruits and vegetables. Below is an example of a week's purchase for two people.

4–6 tomatoes
1 bunch cilantro
2 medium sized potatoes (blue, purple, red, Yukon)
2 bunches kale (curly, purple, dinosaur)
1 medium sized broccoli
1 bunch chard (Swiss, rainbow, rhubard)
1 cabbage (Napa, green, red)
1 bunch parsley
1 bell pepper
4 carrots
1 Jalapeno pepper
3-4 bunches shallots
1-2 bunches scallions
1 medium sized ginger root
2–3 zucchini (yellow, green)
1 bunch beets with greens (2–4 beets)

Chop vegetables, scallions, shallots, ginger and tomatoes small enough for salad.

A. Wash all fruits and vegetables thoroughly.
B. Put chopped items into separate covered containers.
C. Place all covered containers in the refrigerator for the next day.

DAY 2: Making and Baking

You are going to make a large salad, baked yams or sweet potatoes, cornbread and an African vegetable stew. The salad, stew, yams or sweet potatoes, and cornbread will last 5 days.

To make the salad you will need a large bowl with a lid or top.

A. Take all containers, except for the potatoes and tomatoes, out of the refrigerator and place on the table or on a large surface.

B. Take the tops off the containers.

C. Place small amounts of each vegetable in the large salad bowl until filled.

Cover or place lid on top of the salad bowl and refrigerate.

The salad can last 5 days when refrigerated. Top with tomatoes before each serving. Putting tomatoes in salad during refrigeration or before serving time can make the salad too watery.

Cook African vegetable stew using the rest of the vegetables and tomatoes. See our recipes for African vegetable stew, baked yams, stir–frys and many more.

Eat your serving for the day. It will taste great. But remember, this is a weekly approach to cooking. Don't eat too much the first day. You may portion your food for the next 4 days with the use of food containers.

DAYS 3, 4, & 5: Eating and Enjoying

Warm up your daily portions of food. Use desired spices to perk up your daily servings. Food loses flavor over time. A dash of Bragg Liquid Aminos and a few spices and herbs will bring out the flavor in your food.

Supplemental Dishes: If you find that your daily portions are eaten faster than planned or you would like to add more food to cover the 5 days, there are many dishes you may add including rice, polenta, quinoa, millet, pasta, fufu or plantain. We have many recipes for you to sample.

DAY 6: Creating and Constructing

Sauté, bake, or stir–fry any leftovers. Prepare any of the supplemental dishes mentioned above. Any stew left over can be used in preparing collard green wraps, Sloppy Joes, pizza, spaghetti sauce, and lasagna. See our recipes for these dishes. Be creative in your new kitchen.

DAY 7: Resting and Fasting

This is your free day. You have a variety of choices. You can choose to fast. Fasting as an art has been practiced for thousands of years. It has been used for rejuvenation, clarity, cleansing, strengthening, and curing illness. This gives your digestive system a rest.

This system is very busy, hard working, and requires high amounts of energy. Just as we take vacations to rejuvenate from stress, our digestive system needs a vacation. Once rested, our digestive system works more efficiently. Without the job of digesting food, the body's enzyme system is allowed to work more quickly and efficiently in detoxifying and breaking down toxins in the body.

You could pick other recipes in this book to cook or prepare. You can choose other activities: take a long walk or bike ride, swim, dance, nap, go see a good movie, or go to the park. You could read a good book in a good location, go out to eat, go to the beach, desert or mountain.

Making Naasira's Approach Work for you

This is one example of how you can cook for the week. You might choose to fast, juice for the week, or go raw. You might want more vegetables, grains, sautés, stir–frys, baked or roasted food. You can gear your selections toward what your body requires at the time. The same approach to weekly cooking or preparing foods can be used when preparing different foods.

This is a sure way of having what your body requires for optimum health. This weekly preparation method helps ensure that you will always have the best optimal health. You will avoid turning to food you know will not serve your best interest.

CHAPTER 8
My Soy Story

MY STORY OF USING soy is probably familiar to some. In 1992, the soy industry started an incredible soy marketing campaign. Many consumers had started to change their lifestyles and eat in a healthier way. I was a vegetarian at that time. My meals consisted mostly of fresh fruits, vegetables, and a few recipes.

The soy industry started promoting soy as "heart" health. The industry ads claimed that soy could alleviate symptoms associated with menopause, reduce the risk of certain cancers, and lower levels of the "bad" cholesterol. They used studies that showed that Asians, particularly in Japan and China, had a lower incidence of breast and prostate cancer than people in the United States. The industry also pointed out that Asians eat soy and live longer than Americans. That got my attention.

Soon soy proteins and oils appeared in markets and grocery stores. My food was fried or baked using corn, canola, and vegetable oil or had these oils poured over it. Soy burgers, tofu, tempeh, miso, soy sauce, soy cheese, soy sausage, soy ice cream, and soy wieners (hot dogs) were part of my new found diet. I delightfully tasted the many textures of soy. Tofu was a welcomed addition since it seemed to take on the flavor of the herbs and spices added to it. Soy was embraced as a great tasty substitute for meat and dairy products.

The soy industry profited too. From 1992 – 2008, the soy industry's profits rose from $300 million to $4 billion dollars annually. It was an amazing marketing scheme. They manipulated the facts about the soybean to make a profit. They used the method of telling a lie and repeating it again and again through massive advertising. Soon the victims (consumers) would start to believe it.

I soon noticed that all was not perfect in my soy paradise. I experienced excess gas and my skin would start to burn and itch soon after eating soy products. I would drink more water to try and clean out my system. I even started to exercise more, thinking my body was in need of more physical conditioning. It was only after researching the truth about soy, I was able to stop eating it and free myself from the gas, burning, and itching.

Brother Karl Grant had a more interesting story. In 2000, after hearing many advertisements proclaiming soy beverages as a healthier alternative to milk, Brother Karl made the switch from cow's milk to soy. He brought soy beverages home to share with his family. He earnestly drank soy beverages. After 6 months, Brother Karl looked in the mirror at his chest and saw that he had developed female breasts. He said they looked like a size "C" cup.

Like myself, Brother Karl began to search for answers. It was not long before he was able to make the connection to soy and his newly grown breasts. He told God that if he would help him to get off soy, he would never touch it again. True to his word, Brother Karl gave up the soy. Soon afterwards his female breasts disappeared and his regular chest came back.

At this point, I think it may be clear that consuming soy causes the body serious problems. Many of the problems occur because soy prevents the body from absorbing the nutrients the body requires and provides excess estrogen. In addition, most soy is GMO. But if you would like more details of the problems soy gives your body, continue to read the information below.

People began to speak out against the marketing ploy by the food industry. Many were aware that the food industry seemed to be more influenced by financial gain than concern for the health of the American people. Those that tried to warn of the dangers of soy were met with stiff opposition. The Food industry spent millions of dollars in marketing and misleading ads. Those opposing the food industry had quite a battle.

The industry's financial influence placed pressure on any station that dared to "air" the truth. The money that could possibly be lost by any station giving "air" to the truth about soy kept a lot of information from getting out to the public. Coupled with the steady flow of misinformation, and our desire to have the perfect substitute for the "meaty" taste many had grown accustomed to, it was very hard for the truth to be widespread.

The ugly truth is that the soybean is toxic. Originally, in China and Japan, fermented soy was considered the poor farmer's or peasant's "meat". They ate this when they had little access to meat. When the Asians discovered how to ferment the soybean, they began to incorporate soy foods into their diet. This traditional fermentation process deactivates or reduces the effects of many contaminates in soy. The properly fermented soy foods included tempeh, miso, natto, shoyu, and soy (tamari) sauce.

These foods are a source of vitamin K2, which help prevent osteoporosis (brittle bones), dementia, and cardiovascular disease. Asians did not eat large portions of this soy. They used soy foods as condiments, not an entree. Their diet included about nine grams of soy products a day. That is less than 2 teaspoons. Also, the typical Asian will also consume soy with nutrient–dense and mineral–rich foods such as fish broth, naturally high in iodine and other minerals which support the thyroid.

By contrast, in the United States, we ate unfermented processed soy. We ate most of it in the form of soy beverage, tofu, textured vegetable protein (TVP), and soy infant formula. We also eat it in large amounts. An example would be that processed soy food snacks or shakes contain over 20 grams (1/2 cup) of non–fermented processed soy protein in one serving.

There are many reasons unfermented processed soy is considered toxic. Here are a few. Most modern soy foods are not fermented to neutralize toxins in soybeans, and are processed in a way that increases levels of carcinogens. Since the introduction of genetically engineered foods in 1996, about 90–95 percent of all soybeans grown in the United States are produced from genetically modified seed. These seeds are produced from organisms that have specific changes introduced into their DNA using methods of genetic engineering.

Nearly 100 percent of fast foods and 60 percent of all processed foods contain soy. People can develop sensitivities to a food that has antigens or bacteria not originally in the DNA chain, as in the case of genetically modified (GM) foods. Since the introduction of genetically engineered foods in 1996, we have had an upsurge in low birth weight babies, infertility, and other problems in the U.S. Lab animals fed genetically modified organisms (GMO) have shown immune dysfunction, cellular, and metabolism changes including allergies, sterility, birth defects, and offspring death rates up to five times higher than normal.

Except nuts and oilseeds, the soybean is higher in phytoestrogens than any other food source. Soy phytoestrogens are potent antithyroid agents that can cause hypothyroidism (goiters) and can cause thyroid cancer. They can disrupt endocrine function and may cause infertility and breast cancer. That is because they are plant–based estrogens that basically act like or mimics estrogen in our bodies. This can cause excess estrogen in the body leading to uterine fibroids, prostate, and breast cancer.

Unfermented soy contains antinutrients that will leave your body mineral–deficient and anemic if eaten in large quantity. Antinutrients, such as trypsin inhibitors in soy, have been shown to interfere with enzymes needed for protein digestion. This may cause pancreatic disorders. In test animals, soy containing these inhibitors caused stunted growth. The naturally occurring phytates in soy block the uptake of essential minerals. This would include calcium, magnesium, copper, iron and zinc.

Another example of the body not getting the required nutrients because soy blocks the uptake of nutrients came from a man who had switched from regular milk to soy milk because he believed the misinformation given about soy being a more healthy alternative than cow's milk. He told me that after some time, his daughter's baby teeth were coming in with cavities. After doing research on soy, he discovered that soy prevented his daughter's body from absorbing the calcium needed to keep her teeth healthy.

Soy foods contain high levels of aluminum. Acid washing in aluminum tanks, designed to remove some of the antinutrients, leeches aluminum into the final product. This is toxic to the nervous system and the kidneys. Aluminum can have adverse effects on the brain causing symptoms such as antisocial behavior, learning disabilities, Alzheimer's disease and dementia.

Glutamate (MSG), a potent neurotoxin and aspartate (a component of aspartame), which causes brain–cell death, is formed in the processing of soy food. Even more glutamate (MSG) is added to some soy products to mask soy's unpleasant taste. Soy has also been linked to erectile dysfunction. Two natural drugs found in soy, genistein and daidzein, mimic estrogen so well that they have been known to cause breast enlargement, decreased libido, and low sperm count.

Soybeans also contain haemagglutinin. This is a clot–promoting substance that causes red blood cells to clump together. This clumping of red blood cells makes them unable to properly absorb and distribute oxygen to your tissues. Soy also has one of the highest percentages of contamination by pesticides of any of our foods.

In infants, the highest risk is for those who are fed soy formula. In her book, The Whole Soy Story, Dr. Kaayla T. Daniel states, "The estrogens in soy will affect the hormonal development of these children, and it will certainly affect their growing brains, reproductive systems, and thyroids." Soy formula contains large amounts of manganese, which have been linked to attention deficit disorder and neurotoxicity in infants. Even the Israeli health ministry recently issued an advisory stating that infants should avoid soy formula altogether.

In animal studies, the second and third generations of those animals fed GMO were found to be sterile and infertile with high infant mortality rates. Sadly, it is possible that the GM food eaten today will result in the sterility or infertility of your yet to be born child or grandchild. The FDA relies on GMO–producing companies to conduct their own safety research. Ironically, the United Kingdom Monsanto restaurant does not serve GMO at the company's workers' request.

If you insist on eating soy, it's better to eat organic non–GMO soy products. But all soy products include naturally occurring antinutrients, toxins and plant estrogens. Except for the different kinds of fermented soy products, given the fact that nearly all soy grown in the United States is genetically modified (GM), and the known challenges presented to our bodies by unfermented soy, it would seem prudent to avoid most soy products at this time. As of the time of this writing we would consider fermented organic Miso, Tamari Sauce, Tempeh, Liquid Bragg Aminos and Shoyu safe to consume.

"Genetically Modified Food Research On Why You should Avoid Soy" http://bit.ly/1dVhtVe

"The Dark Side Of Soy" http://bit.ly/1Nbo2fU

"Dangers Of Soy" http://bit.ly/1CisFRI

"Phytoestrogens" http://bit.ly/1ewwYEf

"Soy Dangers Summarized" http://bit.ly/1BC6DPm

"The Health Dangers Of Soy" http://huff.to/1d71OkU

"Could Your Diet Be Causing Uterine Fibroids?"
http://bit.ly/1GbuAJG

"Why Are Factory Farmed Animals Given Antibiotics And Hormones Such As rBGH?" http://abt.cm/1MTIowg

"Evo Morales Says Eating Chicken Makes You Gay"
http://bit.ly/1CiV8Hk

Dr. Roba: *"Soul Food–For–Thought"* February 12, 2010

The International Fund For Africa
http://www.iFundAfica.org

PART 2

CHAPTER 9

Cooking Oil Alternatives

BEFORE THE EARLY 1900S, most cultures consumed fats like coconut oil, palm oil, butter, tallow and ghee. Heart disease was a rare occurrence then. But the rate of heart disease began to rise in the 1950s, when a governmental campaign was launched to convince people to eat vegetable oils and margarine. In the early 1980s, polyunsaturated oils became popular after the American Soybean Association (ASA) launched a series of attacks against tropical oils produced outside the U.S.

The marketing attacks of the ASA were aimed at turning consumers away from tropical oils such as coconut and palm. The food industry was looking to make more money by eliminating the competition. They marketed their genetically engineered polyunsaturated oil as "heart healthy oils," and a good alternative to those "artery clogging saturated fats." These polyunsaturated oils could be cheaply manufactured, and many consumers were influenced by the mass advertising campaign to purchase these oils. The food industry was set to cash in on the anti–coconut and palm oil panic it had created.

With the panic created by the ASA about saturated fats, fast food restaurants quickly jumped on the bandwagon and switched to polyunsaturated vegetable oils. Processed food companies stopped using coconut oil. They replaced it with soybean and canola oils. Margarine (advertised as healthier than butter) was substituted for real butter. Soybean oil and canola oil replaced olive oil and coconut oil in many American diets. Even today, many containers of "olive oil" are nothing more than soybean or canola oil with a bit of real olive oil in it.

History

Dr. Bruce Fife tells the history of this tropical oil war in his two books, "The Coconut Oil Miracle" and "The Palm Oil Miracle". According to Dr. Fife, until the late 1980s tropical oils were common ingredients in many foods because they did not go rancid (spoiled) as do polyunsaturated oils. Foods made with tropical oils remain fresh longer.

In 2001, at the time of one of Dr. Fife's writings, nearly 80% of vegetable oil came from soybeans, of which 75% was partially hydrogenated (containing up to 50% trans fatty acids). In 1982, a restaurant meal contained 2.4 grams of trans fatty acids. In 2001, the same meal contained 19.2 grams.

According to Dr. Fife, the oil war began in the mid 1980s. It was launched by the American Soy Association (ASA) to increase the sales of soybean by getting rid of competition from imported tropical oils, such as palm and coconut. It appeared to be well planned. The media started warning the public about the newly discovered health threat – coconut oil. It was proclaimed that coconut oil was a saturated fat that would cause heart disease.

In response to the media warning, the movie theaters began popping popcorn in soy oil. Food makers switched to soybean oil and partially hydrogenated soybean oil (margarine) instead of the tropical oils they had used for years. Restaurants also stopped using tropical oils in favor of soybean and other vegetable oils.

In 1986, the ASA sent a "Fat Fighter Kit" to soybean farmers to scare people away from using tropical oils. The Kit encouraged them to write government officials and food companies and to protest the use of highly saturated tropical oils. The wives and families of some 400,000 were encouraged to lobby praising the health benefits of soy oil. Misguided health groups such as the Center For Science In

The Public Interest (CSPI) joined the lobby, issuing news releases referring to tropical oils as "artery–clogging fats."

In October 1988, Nebraska millionaire, Phil Sokolof, a heart attack survivor and founder of the National Heart Savers Association, began running ads accusing food companies of "poisoning America" by using saturated tropical oils. One ad showed a coconut "bomb" with a lighted wick and cautioned consumers about the health threat of tropical oils.

The Truth Is Suppressed

Despite testimonies of well–respected medical professionals and researchers, the media paid little attention. Major newspapers, radio, and television networks picked up the anti–saturated fat ads and developed alarming news stories. One article was titled "The Oil From Hell."

Those who knew the truth were ignored and criticized by the brainwashed media. The fictional message won out over scientific fact. Even popular doctors like Andrew Weil said in his newsletter "saturated fats, all saturated fats, promote heart disease and, therefore, should be avoided."

By the early 1990s, the tropical oil market was only a fraction of what it used to be. The oil exporters from Malaysia prepared a public relations campaign against what it called "vicious scare tactics." The tropical oil industry, with few allies, did not have the financial means to retaliate. It could not match the combined efforts of the ASA, CSPI and others.

Gradually, coconut oil began to re–emerge in the early 2000s after Dr. Fife began writing the scientific truth about coconut oil. His first book, Saturated Fat May Save Your Life appeared in 1998. To date, Dr Fife has written six books on coconut oil and other books on coconut flour and coconut water. His books are all easy to read. Even to the obviously uninformed reader, it is very easy to conclude that coconut oil is indeed the healthiest oil you can eat.

Steps To Truth

In the late 1990s, Dr. Fife was told by one of his colleagues that the stories about saturated fats were not true. Dr. Fife began his research. He learned several things. He learned that coconut oil is an incredible food with many health benefits. He learned that it does not promote heart disease, but fights against it. He also learned that saturated fat is not the villain it was made out to be and that polyunsaturated fat and hydrogenated vegetable oil are actually the real troublemakers.

In 2000, Dr. Fife published another book titled "The Healing Miracles of Coconut Oil." This was the first book published devoted entirely to the health benefits of coconut oil. Before it was published, Dr Fife gave a copy of the manuscript to Jon Kabara, PHD for his review. Dr. Kabara was an emeritus professor of chemistry and pharmacology at Michigan State University. He was one of the most outstanding researchers on fats and oils. He had studied the health benefits of coconut oil for nearly 50 years.

He told Dr. Fife his book was factual and accurate. But he advised him not to publish it because it would be a waste of his time. He told him that no one would buy his book because they would not believe it. He also told Dr. Fife that he would open himself up to a multitude of criticism. Dr. Kabara stated that he had tried for decades to tell people of the benefits of coconut oil but was only criticized. He said that he only wanted to spare him the pain.

The Truth Emerges

Dr. Fife went ahead and published the book. At first it met a lot of resistance. The media ignored the book so he could get no reviews or publicity. People did not believe coconut oil was good for them. The sales of the book started off slowly. Dr. Fife got one person to read it. Soon word of mouth spread the book.

In 2001, more companies began selling coconut oil, many over the internet. The Price–Pottenger Nutrition Foundation and the newly formed Weston A. Price Foundation spoke positively of coconut oil in their newsletters. More Health food stores began stocking coconut oil in their stores.

By 2003, the sales of Dr. Fife's first book were increasing. He published a second book titled, "Eat Fat, Look Thin. In this book Dr. Fife discussed briefly the weight loss aspects of coconut oil. After submitting the book to the editors of Women's World Magazine, they published an article on coconut oil that had an enormous impact. The magazine had a readership of several million. That single article created an instant demand for coconut oil throughout the country.

All coconut oil suppliers and distributors sold out in a matter of weeks. Overseas, coconut oil producers were backlogged for months with orders. Those who had never sold coconut oil before began to stock it in their stores.

Dr. Fife's books created renewed interest and demand for coconut products. With the rising demand for coconuts, factories went back into full production, farmers started harvesting, and trucking of coconut came back into full swing. Thanks to Dr. Fife and others that spoke the truth coconut oil has now been selling well.

Make good choices

Our aim is to encourage you to educate yourself and make the best choices you can based on reliable information. Healthy cooking oil alternatives exist. We want to avoid being led astray by faulty media reports, particularly those based on corporate profit incentives. We recommend reading Dr. Fife's books and other references listed below if you would like to learn more.

"Mamma Natural: Counterfeit Olive Oil" http://bit.ly/1RiskFy

"Coconut Oil vs Soybean Oil" By Lita Lee, Ph.D.

http://bit.ly/1TCKfee

Dr. Bruce Fife, *The Healing Miracles of Coconut Oil* Published 2003, copyright 1999, 2000,2002,2004, Piccadilly Books Ltd.

Bruce Fife ND *The Coconut Oil Miracle* Published 2003, Piccadilly Books Ltd. previously published as "The Healing Miracles of Coconut Oil"

Bruce Fife ND *Eat Fat, Look Thin : A Safe and Natural Way to Lose Weight Permanently* published 2002, Piccadilly Books Ltd. copyright 2002, 2005

Dr. Bruce Fife The Palm Oil Miracle published 2007 copyright 2007 Piccadilly Books Ltd.

Brian Fife ND Saturated Fat May Save Your Life published 1999 Piccadilly Books Ltd.

Polyunsaturated Oil

Polyunsaturated oils are oils like soybean, canola, sunflower, safflower and corn oil. They are called "industrialized oil" because they are clear and odorless. This is mainly because they have been heavily refined, bleached, and deodorized with chemicals after a high–heat processing. Vegetable oils are manufactured, usually from genetically engineered soybeans, corn, and rapeseed (canola). The majority of these industrial oils have been heavily sprayed with Round–up (glyphosate) or atrazine, a highly toxic herbicide (plant killer), and other toxic pesticides.

Take canola oil, for example. It is created after making a hybrid version of the rapeseed. Rapeseed oil contains high amounts of toxic erucic acid. This is poisonous to the body. Canola oil is an altered version, called Low Erucic Acid Rapeseed (LEAR). It is commonly genetically modified and treated with high levels of pesticides. It was given its name in the 1980s as part of a marketing effort. After all, how many people would buy oil called "rape "? Not many.

Canola (modified rapeseed oil) is removed from the seed by high temperature mechanical pressing and a petroleum solvent to extract the oil. Since traces of the solvent usually remain in the oil, acid is used to remove nasty solids (wax) that occur during the first processing. It is then further refined, degummed, and bleached treated with more chemicals to improve color and separate the different parts of the oil. Each step requires exposure to high temperatures and chemicals.

The large amounts of omega 3 fatty acids in canola oil become rancid (spoiled) and foul smelling during these high heat processes. It therefore, has to undergo another chemically refining process to be deodorized to be edible. This deodorization process eliminates a large portion of the omega–3 fatty acids by turning them into trans (changed or transformed) fats.

Hydrogenation

If the vegetable oil is to be made into margarine or vegetable–based shortening it undergoes an additional process called hydrogenation. Hydrogenation is the chemical process by which hydrogen gas is pumped into vegetable oil at very high pressure. This process turns the oil into a product that will remain solid at room temperature. It does this by turning oils containing unsaturated fats, the kind often used for deep–frying, into those containing saturated fats, into a partially solid form like margarine.

This process creates a substance that is made up of stiffened fat molecules that keep from separating or spoiling as quickly as unsaturated oils. Hydrogenation raises the melting point above room temperature. It also makes the liquid oil become solid in a process called hardening. The solid product is used as a margarine or spread. Examples of the properties of hydrogenated oils can be found in the hardness of stick margarine or the flakiness of pastry.

Fats can be fully or partially hydrogenated using the hydrogenation process. Fully hydrogenated oil would be as thick as animal lard. This oil is firmer and turned from a liquid to a solid during hydrogenation. Hydrogenating vegetable oils is generally less expensive than using saturated animal fats. Food items that are fully hydrogenated have no dangerous trans fat and a comparatively long shelf life. But most food manufacturers do not let the hydrogenation process go that far.

Fully hydrogenating the oils makes them too hard and solid to easily spread. To keep the margarine or shortening slightly soft, the oils used to make margarine and shortening are partially hydrogenated. Partially hydrogenated oils, such as those found in commercial peanut butter (not fresh–ground) prevent separation and produce hardened, but not solid, fats. Partially hydrogenated oil can withstand repeated heating and increase flavor stability.

Partial hydrogenation has been utilized by the food industry as a means of cost–effectively producing fats that remain solid at room temperature but then melt upon either consumption or baking. This achieves 'mouth feel'. An example would be the pleasurable "melt in the mouth" experienced with chocolate. Partially hydrogenated oils also have the added benefit of being more resistant to becoming rancid (spoiled). This means a much longer shelf life.

Trans Fats

Large amounts of omega 3 fatty acids in vegetable oils become rancid (spoiled) and unpleasant smelling during the high heat processes of hydrogenation. It therefore, has to undergo another chemically refining process to deodorize the oil so that it is consumable. This process removes a large portion of the omega–3 fatty acids by turning them into trans (changed or transformed) fats or trans fatty acids. Simply put, trans fats are a negative byproduct of the process of hydrogenation.

Merely cooking with polyunsaturated oils at modern heat can damage the structure of the oils. The oils will oxidize very quickly. These oxidized oils become trans fats. That is why trans fats or trans fatty acids tend to show up in high–fat dishes that are not that good for your body. They can be found in a long list of foods including vegetable shortening, margarine, fried foods, cookies, crackers, cake mixes, biscuit, pancake and cornbread mixes, frostings, cereals, granola bars, chips, salad dressing, candies, and many other processed foods.

Trans fats were developed during the time Americans were told that saturated fat was bad for you. The food industry waged a campaign against the "artery–clogging animal fats" found in meats, butter, and cream, while promoting vegetable oils as a "heart healthy" replacement. This massive misinformation campaign was designed to keep Americans away from saturated oils such as coconut and palm kernel.

Shelf Life

The food manufacturers soon realized that trans fats lasted longer than butter without going rancid. This increased "shelf stability" of food products made with trans fats and meant more potential profit to the food manufacturers. Many companies use trans fats because they are cheap and easy to make. Today, trans fats are in over 40 percent of all food products on the grocery shelves.

The majority of trans fats consumed come from foods that are manufactured. Humans have long been exposed to natural trans fats coming from animal food sources. These sources, however, historically, have not seemed to pose a threat to our health. Trans fats occur naturally in some animal source foods including beef, lamb, pork, butter, and milk. The amount of trans fats in these animal sources is in small quantities compared to those that come from partially hydrogenated oils.

Dangers

Oils that are fully hydrogenated don't contain any of the dangerous artery–inflaming trans fat found in partially hydrogenated oils. Only partially hydrogenated oils contain trans fats. An example would be margarine. Made from vegetable oil, it undergoes considerable processing, and the more solid it is, the more trans fats it contains. In the stick form, margarine typically contains more trans fat than margarine in a tub.

Even though fully hydrogenated oils do not contain trans fats, they do still contain fat. Use them sparingly to maintain a healthy weight.

In addition, some hydrogenated oils may cause other health risks. If hydrogenated oils are exposed to heat or light, which routinely occurs during processing, they oxidize and turn rancid (spoiled). These oils are so fragile that they can begin to oxidize even at room temperature and in low–light conditions. This process creates free radicals. Free radicals have been implicated in everything from aging to cancer and should be absolutely avoided.

The damage that some artificially manufactured trans fats cause is due to the fact that they can inhibit the body's production of enzymes. They can also interfere with the production of important molecules that are essential for cell function. Adding the hydrogen atoms to the oil changes the fat. With this artificial change in the fat, the fat (lipase) enzymes in your body cannot break it down effectively.

Your body requires fats for rebuilding cells and hormone production. But it has to use the building blocks we give it. When we give our body a high concentration of polyunsaturated fats instead of the ratios it needs of saturated fats, it has no choice but to use these polyunsaturated fats in our cells for cell repair and creation.

The problem is that polyunsaturated fats are very unstable and oxidize easily in the body. Often, they have already oxidized before consumption during processing or by light or heat exposure while sitting on the grocery store shelf. These oxidized fats are known to cause inflammation and mutation in cells. In the arterial cells, these mutations can cause inflammation that can clog arteries. When these fats are incorporated into our skin cells, their mutation can cause skin cancer. This accounts for many people often getting the most dangerous forms of skin cancer in places where they are never exposed to the sun.

Trans fats contribute to clogged arteries, heart attacks, and strokes. They can increase LDL (bad) cholesterol levels in the blood and decrease HDL (good) cholesterol levels. In general, it is best to avoid hydrogenated oils, especially since most of the vegetable sources of oil are genetically modified herbicide resistant crops that can cause harm to your body. Free radicals are a serious concern since they are created during the processing, on the grocery shelves as the oil is exposed to heat and light, and often when the oil is exposed to low light conditions.

Caution: When looking at the ingredient list on food packages, keep in mind that another name for trans fats is "partially hydrogenated oils." That is because the mere process of making partially hydrogenated oil creates trans fats. So, if you read a food package that simply lists "partially hydrogenated oil", think trans (changed) fats.

Food manufacturers are allowed by the FDA to list 0 percent of trans fat on a food package if there is less than 5 percent of trans fats per serving. The food manufacturers use a trick allowed by the FDA. They reduce the size of the servings in order to have less than 5 percent trans fats in a serving. So, if you see servings that are ridiculously small (two cookies or 5 chips per serving), the food probably contains more trans fat than the food manufacturers want you to know.

Also, if you read a package that lists "hydrogenated oil," without expressly stating whether it is partially or fully hydrogenated, it may not be trans–fat free. Sometimes the terms "partially hydrogenated" and " hydrogenated" are used interchangeably. If the package clearly states that it contains fully hydrogenated oil, then it is free of trans fatty acids. If the package does not clearly state whether it is partially or fully hydrogenated, it is better to side with caution and assume the food contains trans fat.

"Trans Fats" http://bit.ly/1K2q3Or

"Trans Fat Foods To Avoid" The 5 Worst Offenders

http://bit.ly/1dViIDW

"Why You Should NEVER Eat Vegetable Oil or Margarine!"

http://bit.ly/1J9pDqV
"Fats Of Life" http://bit.ly/1IpFZpE
"Do All Foods Listing Hydrogenated Oils Contain Trans Fats?" http://abt.cm/1Gbv2HD
"What Are Hydrogenated Oils?" http://bit.ly/1H4zpKz
"What Foods Contain Hydrogenated Oils?" http://bit.ly/1LkYYrF
"List of Fully Hydrogenated Oils" http://bit.ly/1J9pRhH

Rancidity/Free Radicals

Polyunsaturated oils go rancid very easily, particularly when heated and exposed to oxygen. After the oxidation that takes place in the industrial processing, the oils are already somewhat rancid. If this processing does not turn the oils rancid, sitting the containers of oil on the store shelf exposed to light, heat, or moisture certainly can. So this oil is usually rancid before it is purchased. Most people will not be aware that the oils are rancid. That is because you can't detect it from smell or taste. Any unpleasant smells or odors are disguised by deodorizers and bleach used in the processing.

Avoiding processed foods can do a lot to protect you from rancid polyunsaturated oils. Eating rancid oils will not kill you or make you immediately ill. It may produce damaging chemicals and substances that can harm you over time. Chemicals such as aldehydes and peroxides can damage your body's cells and contribute to atherosclerosis. Free radicals produced by rancid oil can damage DNA in your cells and cause damage to arteries. They can also act as carcinogens. That means substances that can cause cancer.

How Free Radicals Work

Rancid oil is oxidized oil. It is a form of spoilage in the fat or oil portion of food that gives off an unpleasant odor and flavor. Rancid oil forms free radicals in the body. Free radicals are organic molecules responsible for aging and tissue damage.

They are known to cause cellular damage and have been associated with diabetes, Alzheimer's disease, cancer, heart disease, autoimmune diseases, and premature aging. Free radicals are normally produced in the body as a by–product of utilizing oxygen to produce energy. When we metabolize, or break down food, our bodies break down the food we eat into usable energy. As a side effect from this, oxygen creates the formation of free radicals.

Oxidation in the body is unavoidable. So long as we breathe oxygen there will be oxidation in our body and thus the creation of free radicals. Another source of free radicals is the immune system. Your immune system will create free radicals in order to fight off bacteria and harmful disease.

Free radicals are simple oxygen molecules with an electron missing. These molecules do not have an even number of electrons. This makes them unstable. So they are always roaming freely and seeking out other chemical structures (tissue) in our bodies from which they can steal an electron in an effort to become 'whole' again.

The problem is that when these unpaired electrons "steal" an electron from another chemical structure (tissue), that chemical structure (tissue) is left seriously damaged. The electron "stolen" is usually from a chemical structure (tissue) close to the molecule with the unpaired electron. This "stealing" creates another molecule with a missing electron and damage to its chemical structure (tissue). This often results in a cascading effect, with many molecules stealing electrons from other chemical structures (tissue) in an effort to stabilize themselves. Out in the world, this may be a normal process. But in the body, it can result in unwanted body damage. The uncontrolled action by free radicals in this cascading effect can wreak havoc in the body.

Free radicals in small and controlled quantities are necessary and indeed helpful in everyday metabolism and normal reactions in the body. Problems start when the production of these free radicals are increased and out of control. A combination of consuming oxidized oil, animal source food, your body's metabolizing (breaking down) food, and your immune system creating them can certainly cause an excess. This excess of free radicals will accelerate your aging and can do damage to your cells, organs and body as a whole.

Neutralizing Free Radicals

How do antioxidants 'neutralize' free radicals"?

In simple terms, eating a diet rich in antioxidant–containing foods, such as fruits, vegetables and whole grains neutralizes free radicals. That is because the antioxidants contained in these foods voluntarily give one of their electrons to a free radical molecule. Antioxidants can do this without damaging themselves. Melanocytes (melanin producing cells) also freely give electrons to free radicals without damaging themselves. It is the way nature keeps the oxidation process in check. Oxidation is an essential tool in nature. If oxidation did not occur, nothing would ever degrade or decompose.

Omega 3s and Omega 6s

Another major concern with vegetable oils such as corn, canola, soybean, cottonseed, safflower, or sunflower is that they contain a large amount of omega–6 fatty acids. Our bodies require both omega–3s and omega–6s in our diets for general health. They are called "essential" fatty acids because our bodies cannot make them. We must obtain them from food.

Omega–3s come primarily from fatty fish such as tuna, salmon, and mackerel. They are found in green vegetables like Brussels sprouts, kale, spinach, and salad greens. They are also in flax, hemp, pumpkin seed, beans, walnuts, and some vegetable oils. Omega–6s mostly comes from plant oils such as corn oil, soybean oil, and sunflower oil, as well as from nuts and seeds.

In general, hormones derived from the two essential fatty acids have opposite effects. Hormones from omega–6 fatty acids tend to increase inflammation, which is an important part of the immune response. They also increase blood clotting, and building cell membranes in the brain. Hormones from omega–3 fatty acids decrease those functions. Cell membranes with abundant omega 3 fatty acids are associated with lowered rates of heart disease, diabetes, depression, and violence.

To maintain optimum health humans must consume omega–3 and omega–6 fatty acids in roughly equal amounts. Problems occur when there is not a balance between the two families of hormone fatty acids. Anthropological research suggests that our hunter–gatherer ancestors consumed omega–3 and omega–6 fatty acids in a ratio of roughly 1:1. It also indicates that both modern and ancient hunter–gatherers did not have the modern inflammatory diseases, like heart disease, diabetes, and cancer.

Omega Balance

Today, some health educators advocate the range of 1:1 – 4:1, omega–6 to omega–3. Most Americans eat a ratio closer to 20:1, which creates a host of problems in the body. Simply put, this means that the more omega–3 fat you eat, the less omega–6 will be available to the tissues to produce inflammation. Omega–6 is considered pro–inflammatory, while omega–3 is considered neutral. A diet with lots of omega–6 and not much omega–3 will increase inflammation. A diet with lots of omega–3 and not much omega–6 will reduce inflammation.

There are many sources of omega–6 fatty acids in modern diets. Meats, oily salad dressings, and cooking oils are common sources of omega–6 fatty acids that many people consume in large servings too frequently. As vegetable oil consumption rose, the ratio of omega–6 to omega–3 fats in the American diet increased. Refined vegetable oils, such as soy oil, are used in most of the snack foods, crackers, sweets, cookies, as well as in fast food.

Today, on average, people consume, about 70 lbs of vegetable oils a year. Soybean oil is the number 1 source of omega 6s in the American diet. Soybean oil is in 100 percent of all fast foods and 60 percent of processed foods in America. 20 percent of the calories in the American diet are estimated to come from soybean oil. This is over the recommended amount of omega 6s humans should consume. The American Heart Association recommends that only 5% to 10% of food calories come from omega–6 fatty acids.

The key to maintaining healthy levels of essential fatty acids is to maintain a good ratio between the sources of foods rich in omega–3 and omega–6 fats and avoid the foods that disrupt their absorption. Eating products with refined flour, white sugar, fried foods, and foods made with trans–fats (partially hydrogenated oils) can interfere with the absorption of essential fatty acids. Avoid or limit foods made from highly processed grains. This will help fight inflammation and reduce risk of the diseases of modern civilization such as obesity, asthma, depression, heart disease, cancer, arthritis, and even a tendency toward violence.

"Why You Should Never Eat Vegetable Oil Or Margarine" http://bit.ly/1J9pDqV

"Omega–6 fatty acids | University of Maryland Medical Center" http://bit.ly/1CiVYUr

"Balancing Omega–3 and Omega–6?" http://bit.ly/1K2qhFd

"If We Are What We Eat, Americans Are Corn And Soy" http://cnn.it/1LkZdTz

"Omega–3 and Omega–6: The Essential Fatty Acids to Include in Your Diet" http://bit.ly/1BC7Czo

"How Too Much Omega–6 And Not Enough Omega–3 Is Making Us Sick" http://bit.ly/1GXR4BB

"What Oil Should You Be Cooking With, And Which Should You Avoid?" http://bit.ly/1IUtl4I

Storage

Vegetable oil stored at room temperature will continue to oxidize. That is because oil exposed to air, light, or moisture will continue to oxidize. An example would be the oils setting in a cupboard or on a kitchen counter. It oxidizes even further every time the cap is opened and closed. So, if you must continue using vegetable oil, remember, it is prone to oxidation.

If you must use polyunsaturated vegetable oil, buy only vegetable oil that is cold pressed, unrefined and organic. Buy it fresh, as you need it. Keep it stored in dark (opaque) bottles and away from heat. Get only small amounts that you know you'll finish using in a few weeks or less. These oils are best suited for sprinkling lightly over salads and not for cooking, since even medium heat can damage them.

"Effects Of Eating Rancid Oil"

http://bit.ly/1BC7I9U

"What Are The Dangers of Rancid Oil" http://bit.ly/1TCLc6k

GOOD OILS

Coconut Oil

Over 1/3 of the world's population depends on coconut for food. Populations around the world have thrived for many generations eating large amounts of coconut. The populations that eat a lot of coconuts are among the healthiest people on the planet. An example of such a population is the Tokelauans, which live in the South Pacific. They eat over 60% of their calories from coconuts. They are the biggest consumers of saturated fat in the world. These people are in excellent health with no evidence of heart disease. Another example of a population that eats a lot of coconut and remains in excellent health is the Kitavans, inhabitants of Kitava, one of the Trobriand Islands of Papua New Guinea.

Coconut oil is one of the few foods that can be classified as a "superfood." It is one of the healthiest oils that can be used in cooking. This oil contains primarily saturated fats, but does not contain cholesterol. In fact, coconut oil is one of the richest sources of saturated fat known to man. Almost 92% of the fatty acids in it are saturated. That is why coconut oil fats are stable when exposed to light and heat.

It is one of the few oils that do not turn rancid when heated at high temperatures. This makes it ideal for using as your all–purpose cooking oil. This includes frying, and stir–frys, where it gives it a tropical flavor. In baking, coconut oil can be substituted 1–for–1 in most baking recipes that call for butter or oil. I've used it for smoothies, banana bread, waffles, pancakes, muffins, and corn bread.

I would suggest using organic coconut oil whenever possible. Organic means that the coconuts are from places that don't use chemicals. Generally, coconuts grown without the use of synthetic pesticides are more nutritious. Eating organic will reduce the amount of carcinogens (cancer causing agents) in your blood. Thus, you will decrease your chances of illnesses significantly.

Types of Coconut Oil

"Raw", "unrefined" and "refined" are terms that have to do with how much heat is used to process the coconut oil.

Raw virgin coconut oil is cold pressed from only fresh coconuts. The coconut oil is usually pressed at temperatures below 113 degrees Fahrenheit (45° Celcius). This ensures all nutrients and antioxidants are not lost. This differs from the other virgin coconut oils produced by either of the expeller (screw) or centrifuge (spinning) methods. Both of which raise the temperature during production. The raw coconut oil is best suited for raw diets.

"Extra virgin" and "Virgin" are about the same, there are no industry standards to gauge this. Since coconut oil comes from other countries where these terms may not mean the same, the meanings may mean different things depending on the country it comes from. Both terms have to do with how many times the coconut meat (or coconut "meal") was pressed to get the oil out. A one time press is usually called "extra virgin", "virgin or "first pressed". In some countries "extra virgin" means the least amount of pressure (and therefore less heat) that is used. "Virgin" means there is more heat used, more friction, but results in higher yields of oil.

Unrefined coconut oil is typically labeled as "pure" or "virgin" or "extra virgin" coconut oil. The coconut oil is extracted from fresh coconut meat rather than dried. The fresh coconut meat is processed either by wet milling or quick drying. Quick drying is the most common method used. Here, the coconut meat is quickly dried and the oil is mechanically expressed. In wet milling, the coconut milk is expressed from the fresh meat and then boiled and fermented, or separated from the meat using enzymes or centrifuge (spinning). Unrefined oil does not require bleaching or additives. It isn't exposed to high heat levels and retains the distinct flavor and odor of coconut.

Refined coconut oil is bleached, and deodorized. The oil is obtained from dried coconut meat known as copra. Oil obtained from copra has to be purified with bleach because contaminants arise during the drying process. High heat is used to deodorize the oil to remove its odor and flavor. Sodium hydroxide is often added to give a longer shelf life. Some brands use chemical solvents to extract oil from the meat. They may partially hydrogenate the oil. This means it will contain trans–fats.

Why Coconut Oil?

Generally, oils that benefit our bodies are from places where our DNA originates. Highly melaninated people are best served with coconut oil. Coconut trees are grown in tropical areas and places that get very warm or hot. These are the places of your ancestors. Oils that originate from there are best suited for your body.

Easily Absorbed and Digested

Coconut oil is easily digested, absorbed by the body and improves vitamin and mineral absorption. It requires less energy and fewer enzymes to break it down for digestion. Unlike other oils, it does not need pancreatic fat–digesting enzymes for digestion. Enzymes in the saliva and gastric juices break it down. Then, it is absorbed directly from the intestines and sent straight to the liver.

In the liver, it is, for the most part, burned as fuel and used directly for energy. It seldom ends up as body fat or as cholesterol in arteries. Since no bile or pancreatic enzymes are needed for coconut digestion, this makes coconut oil a healthy food for those with diabetes or those who have gallbladder problems.

Boost Metabolism

Coconut oil can help boost metabolism. This is the rate at which your body burns calories. Since the fats in coconut oil travels directly to the liver, it is converted into energy and not stored as fat. Because the oil is easily absorbed by the energy–producing organelles of the cells, metabolism increases. This gives the body a boost of energy. This burst of energy results in a stimulating effect on the entire body.

In addition to increasing your energy level, there are other important benefits from boosting your metabolism. The immune system will function better. This helps to protect you from illness and speeds the rate of healing. Cells function at a higher rate of efficiency. Injuries heal quicker, old and diseased cells are replaced faster, and young new cells are generated at an increased rate, replacing worn–out ones.

Many health problems such as heart disease, obesity, and osteoporosis (weak bones) are more common in those people who have slow metabolism. Any health condition is made worse if the metabolic rate is slower than normal. This is because cells cannot heal and repair themselves as quickly. Increasing the metabolic rate provides an increased degree of protection from both infectious and degenerative illnesses.

Weight Loss

When you add coconut oil into your diet, you'll feel more full and eat fewer calories. The saturated fat in coconut oil triggers a natural satiation (fullness) response and keeps your blood sugar steady. It can reduce your hunger and make you eat less without even trying. Coconuts oil increases your metabolic rate. The metabolic rate is the rate at which your body burns calories. This increase causes you to burn more energy (fat). Since coconut oil can increase fat burning and reduce appetite, it makes sense that it can also help you lose weight.

Other Benefits

Energy and Performance

Coconut oil is easily and quickly absorbed into the digestive system and converted into an important source of quick energy to your body. This is a function usually served in the diet by simple carbohydrates. Many athletes are now using coconut oil to boost performance and control weight. So, for a quick energy boost, you could simply eat a spoonful of coconut oil, or add it to your food.

Immunity Booster

Coconut oil contains the most lauric acid of any substance on earth. About 50 percent of the fat in coconut oil is lauric acid, which is rarely found in nature. Lauric acid is found in abundance in breast milk. Your body converts lauric acid into monolaurin, which has amazing antibacterial, antiviral, antiparasitic, and antimicrobial properties. Both lauric acid and monolaurin can destroy harmful pathogens like bacteria, viruses and fungi.

The monolaurin's antifungal properties have been shown to help fight yeast infections and reduce candida and yeast in the body. It helps improve the immune system and fights everything from the common cold to serious lipid–coated viruses such as herpes, measles, influenza and HIV. Lauric acid can help lower blood pressure and cholesterol. It helps keep arteries flexible and prevent atherosclerosis and does not increase LDL (bad) cholesterol.

Vitamin E

Coconut oil has vitamin E. It gives skin–nourishing properties. Vitamin E is essential for healthy skin growth. It repairs weathered skin, protects against cracking, and keeps skin smooth. Additionally, it prevents aging and the wrinkling of skin, due to its good antioxidant properties.

Good Fat

Most people think that fat is bad. In fact, fat is critical for optimal health. It is a basic component of nutrition along with carbohydrates, proteins, vitamins, minerals, and water. Fat is necessary for normal body functions. It protects all vital organs, promotes cell growth, supplies energy, and assists anti–inflammatory fat soluble vitamins like A, D, E, and K in their function. Also, importantly for women, fat regulates hormones.

Coconut oil provides your body with high–quality saturated fat that is vital for health. It also helps improve absorption of fat–soluble vitamins. It can increase bone strength by allowing better absorption of vitamin D, calcium, and other minerals. Taking a spoonful of coconut oil along with your vitamins may help boost their effectiveness.

No Insulin Spike

Coconut oil does not produce an insulin spike in your bloodstream. It acts on your body like a carbohydrate, without any of the negative insulin–related effects associated with long–term high carbohydrate consumption. Diabetics and those with pre–diabetes conditions can benefit from this fast–acting energy source. In fact, coconut oil added to the diets of diabetics and pre–diabetics has actually been shown to help stabilize weight gain, which can dramatically decrease the likelihood of getting adult onset type–2 diabetes.

Reduce Heart Risk

Coconut oil improves important risk factors like LDL (bad) and HDL (good) cholesterol, which may translate to a reduced risk of heart disease.

Other uses

Coconut oil has been shown to boost brain function in Alzheimer's patients and reduce seizures. It can boost thyroid function. The oil can be used as homemade deodorant, body lotion, toothpaste, facial moisturizer, eye makeup remover, and hair conditioner. It can also be used for lice treatment, maintaining healthy and youthful looking skin, cardiovascular health, blood sugar regulation, and to soothe sunburns.

How To Get A Good Deal On Coconut Oil

In general, the cost of coconut oil available in most stores can get quite pricey. One way to save money on purchasing coconut oil is to buy it in bulk. We would suggest buying anywhere from a gallon to 3 gallons at a time. Coconut oil is so stable it can keep for at least 6 months or more. Buying in large amounts saves money and it is worth it in the long run.

But before you commit to purchasing a large order, we would suggest that you buy a small amount of the brand or variety you might be interested in. This would ensure that you actually like the taste and smell before you purchase a large order. We would also suggest teaming with like-minded friends to place an order with you. This will allow you to obtain a large amount of oil at a cheaper price and reduce shipping costs.

"The Many Benefits of Coconut Oil http://bit.ly/1J9quIa

"Coconut Oil and Medium-Chain Triglycerides"
http://bit.ly/1Bu73qz

"Coconut Oil: This Cooking Oil Is a Powerful Virus-Destroyer and Antibiotic"
http://bit.ly/1IVuVmX

"The Truth About Coconut Oil"
http://wb.md/1Jaqbgd
"Why Coconut Oil Is The Best Vegetable Oil"
http://bit.ly/1d7SUnx
"The Benefits Of Using Coconut Oil"
http://dailym.ai/1L7MEdj
"Top 10 Evidence–Based Health Benefits of Coconut Oil"
http://bit.ly/1H5vGMN
"A Little Story About Coconut Oil And Its Healthy Benefits"
http://exm.nr/1d7SYn9
"Fats to Avoid: The Polyunsaturated Oil Epidemic"
http://bit.ly/1BCWCBu
"How To Choose A Good Coconut Oil" http://bit.ly/1Ftj4I3

Olive Oil

For thousands of years the people of the Mediterranean have enjoyed the benefits of olive oil in their diets. It is well known for its health benefits and for its wide range of flavors and savory uses. Olive oil has a distinct flavor and can be used in dishes where you can taste it. Sprinkling in soup, over steamed vegetables, or dipping with bread, for example. It is an excellent choice when you're using it cold to make salad dressing or sautéing vegetables over low to medium heat.

If you're cooking over high heat, don't use olive oil. Olive oil has a lower smoke point than some of the other oils. That means, the point at which oil will begin to smoke. For olive oil, this is between 365° and 420° Fahrenheit (185° and 215° Celsius). When you heat olive oil to its smoke point, its antioxidant properties start to degrade. The oil begins to oxidize, producing free radical molecules and other potentially health–harming compounds.

Olive oil is an excellent choice when you're making salad dressing or sautéing vegetables over medium heat. I would suggest setting the oil temperature at 360–365° Fahrenheit (182 – 185° Celsius) with a maximum of 380° Fahrenheit (193°Celsius). After frying, you can filter the cooled oil through a coffee filter and use 2–3 more times for frying only. Since it has a distinct flavor, it should be used in dishes where you want to taste it. An example would be to pour it over bread, steamed vegetables or soup.

Extra virgin and virgin olive oils are best when added after cooking or used for dipping with bread, in marinades or on salads. They have a stronger flavor than the more refined olive oils. The refined grades of olive oil have higher smoke points and are more suitable for frying and roasting. They may also be used for dishes that benefit from a lighter flavored oil. Remember, the refined olive oils are for high temperature cooking. Extra virgin is for the maximum of antioxidants.

Types of Olive Oil

Some grades of olive oil depend on an "acidity rating". As olive oil degrades or breaks down, fatty acids are released from the oil. This results in olive oil having an unpleasant flavor. It also causes the oil's acidity level to rise. The more degraded the oil is, the greater it's acidity level. Oleic acid is commonly formed when olive oil is damaged. The acidity level of olive oil is measured by the percentage of oleic acid it contains.

Extra virgin olive oil: This is the best olive oil you can get. It is rich in antioxidants. This oil is derived from the first pressing of the olives. It is not from olive pulp that has previously had oil extracted. The oil is extracted by mechanical means only, without the use of heat or chemicals. This is called "cold–pressing". It also has an acidity rating of 0.8% or less.

Virgin olive oil: This oil is also produced by mechanical means from a first pressing. It has a slightly higher acidity rating of between .9% – 2%. Virgin olive oil does not undergo chemical refinement. Like extra virgin oil, it is a good source of antioxidants.

Fino olive oil: (meaning fine in Italian) is a blend of extra virgin and virgin olive oils.

Olive oil or "Pure" olive oil: This grade of olive oil is made from oil that has been refined by heat or chemical means. It has an acidity rating of no more than 1.5%. The refinement process uses chemicals and deodorants to remove any odor. It is then mixed with a small amount (less than 5%) of virgin olive oil to return some of the flavor. The refining process removes many of the antioxidants and health–giving nutrients contained in extra virgin and virgin olive oils.

Light and Extra light olive oil: This oil is a blend of refined olive oils that are usually derived from the lowest quality olive oils available through chemical refining processes. It may contain some virgin oil (1%–2%). The "lightness" in these oils refers to the color, fragrance and flavor.

Due to the refining process, it is lighter in color and has little or no flavor. This is because of the chemicals and deodorants used in the refinement. The lighter quality is achieved by an extremely fine filtration and refining process. The refinement does not lower the amount of calories in the oil. This increased refinement creates a great reduction in the health benefits by decreasing the amount of antioxidants.

This oil is a good choice for baking and other purposes where the heavy olive oil flavor is not important. This refinement process also gives the oil a higher smoking point. When the oil hits its smoke point it starts to degrade and oxidize. This produces free radicals, the very things we are trying to reduce by eating olive oil. This makes this oil a prime candidate for high–heat cooking such as frying or sautéing.

Why Choose a California Olive Oil Over a European One?

The California Olive Oil Council's (COOC) evaluation criteria are stricter than those of the International Olive Oil Council (IOOC). The COOC calls for a 0.5% oleic acid (monounsaturated fat) content to the IOOC's 0.8%. Keep in mind, the lower the fatty acid content, the lower the chance of rancidity.

Some Spanish and Italian "extra virgin" oils that have widespread distribution in U.S. supermarkets are considered clearly subpar to "extra virgin" oils meeting COOC's evaluation standard. This would indicate a flaw in the certification process. A recent investigation found that many large Italian producers were purchasing oils from other Mediterranean countries and falsely labeling the oil as their own. According to a 2007 article in The New Yorker about the investigation, only 40% of Italian olive oil sold as "extra virgin" actually meets the requirements.

Lastly, there is the issue of cultural preference. One example is where olives were left to mold in a bag on a Tunisian estate because they said their consumers actually prefer a musty olive oil taste. You can probably find some U.S. oils that are also bad. So, the best suggestion would be to do your own research and find a few labels you can trust. Stick with those labels until your palate can tell the difference when trying new oils.

Health Benefits

Olive oil is rich in vitamins A, B–1, B–2, C, D, E, and K, as well as iron. It contains antioxidant substances that help prevent artery clogging, damage to blood vessels and cells, and chronic disease by attacking free radicals. This may also result in playing a role in slowing down the aging process of cells and tissue. Olive oil also contains monounsaturated fatty acids that control LDL (the bad cholesterol) levels while raising HDL (the good cholesterol) levels.

Freshness and Storage

To get the best of great taste and positive health benefits, choose your olive oil carefully. The fresher the oil, the greater will be its antioxidant (health) properties and the less it will have degraded. This means, the more the oil breaks down or deteriorates chemically. Olive oil has a shelf life between one and two years. So, be sure to check the use–by date. Don't hoard it. Buy an amount that you'll use up quickly. Once opened, store it in the refrigerator and use it within a month.

When choosing olive oil, go for varieties that are sold in dark green glass bottles, in tins or in packaging that shields it from light. This is because light contributes to the degradation of olive oil. Store it in a dark, cool place or wrap the bottle in aluminum foil to shield it from further sunlight. Avoid plastic. Protect it from heat and oxygen, the other two enemies of good oil, which speed spoilage. Even the best of oil can rapidly go rancid when left sitting under a half–bottle of air, in heat or brightly lit conditions. When that happens, all those healthful properties you paid for are lost.

How To Get A Good Deal On Olive Oil

In general, the cost of olive oil available in most stores can get quite pricey. One way to save money on purchasing olive oil is to buy it in bulk. This may be online or at the mill. I would suggest buying anywhere from a gallon to 3 gallons at a time. Olive oil can keep for one to two years. Check the use–by date. Buying in large amounts saves money and it is worth it in the long run.

Buy as close to the mill as possible. Visit it during the harvest to see how olives are picked, crushed, stirred, and spun into olive oil. If a mill is out of reach, find a store where you can taste olive oils in a range of varieties. Seek out freshness, choosing oils that smell and taste lively and vibrant. It is also helpful where the staff can answer a few basic questions about how, where and by whom the oils were made before you buy them.

But before you commit to purchasing a large order, I would suggest that you buy a small amount of the brand or variety you might be interested in. This would ensure that you actually like the taste and smell before you purchase a large order. We would also suggest teaming with like–minded friends to place an order with you. This will allow you to obtain a large amount of oil at a cheaper price and reduce shipping costs.

"How to Buy Great Olive Oil" http://bit.ly/1I5OIl3

"Designations and definitions of olive oils"
http://bit.ly/1IqK8tB

"Why You Shouldn't Always Cook With Olive Oil"
http://bit.ly/1L9URxx

"How to Choose Olive Oil" http://bit.ly/1FtjOg1

"Extra Virgin Olive Oil"
http://bit.ly/1Rjr85O

"The Secrets to Buying Olive Oil" http://thebea.st/1K2TKi9

"In Search Of The Best Extra–Virgin Olive Oil By Elaine Corn"
http://bit.ly/1FtjSwy

"Choosing An Olive Oil" http://bit.ly/1LlIQWL

CHAPTER 10
Gregory Joe Bledsoe's Introduction

ALL READING THIS BOOK are part of a greater, grander plan than most can only imagine. This book is one result of our collective thinking. Our collective consciousness has demonstrated ways to maintain the body on the path to optimum health. This book is one of the ways. There was a need for preparing and cooking vegan and vegetarian food. There are many ex–vegetarians and ex–vegans because of this. The book provides an easy to follow approach for weekly cooking.

This book introduces foods, herbs, and spices that provide the body better assimilation, circulation, and elimination. It is a guide for those just starting on their path to optimum health. It speaks to those knowing that their present way of eating, cooking, or preparing foods no longer serves them. It introduces a healthy and sustainable way of cooking and preparing food that can adapt to our varied schedules.

Information is provided on herbs, spices, fruits and vegetables used in the recipes that assists your body's growth, repair, and maintenance. Based on the information provided, one can tailor the amount of healing herbs and spices according to their particular health challenge(s). If you are not experienced in the kitchen, this book is for you. If you know your way around the kitchen, heavenly experiences await you sooner.

We consider revealing misinformation on nutrition to be part of the quest for optimum health. It is essential to uncover the many myths and deceptive practices that abound concerning the foods commonly accepted as healthy that make up the daily food intake of so many and that have led to much illness and loss of the enjoyment of life.

White Foods (Refined Sugars & Flour)

Today, the food industry comprises 17 percent of our economy. Millions are spent on misinformation campaigns to convince consumers and health care professionals of the safety of refined or processed foods that are called "White Foods". They are called "White Foods" because the vitamins and minerals that are essentially the darker substances are removed during the refinement process. This results in the starch or "White Foods" being left.

These processed or refined foods are essentially, "bad carbs" (carbohydrates), like white rice, pasta, bread, cereals, table sugar, high fructose corn syrup, and baked goods made with white flour. The "good carbs" are good sources of dietary fiber that include beans and legumes, fruits, vegetables, whole grains, whole grain cereals, and whole grain breads.

White Flour

White flour has an even worse effect on the body than sugar. It is nutritionally dead and slowly kills you. If you were to try to live on white bread alone for 60 days, you would die of malnutrition. As a result of the refinement and bleaching process, nearly 100 vitamins are removed from the whole wheat kernel. This includes B–vitamins (niacin, thiamine, and riboflavin).

In addition to the missing vitamins, white flour lacks the two important healthy fibers –bran and germ– necessary for digestion.

This leads to a product that is so nutritionally depleted that manufacturers are required by law to replace certain vitamins.

That is why the word "enriched" is seen on the food labels. The bran, germ, and vitamins are replaced with synthetic, small quantities of calcium, iron, B and D vitamins.

The refined or processed foods ("White" foods such as table salt, milk, sugar, white breads, and white flour) cause nutrient deficiencies that promote chronic disease and illness. They upset the body chemistry resulting in degenerative diseases and obesity.

White Sugar

Sugar is Addictive

Sugar is addictive. When we eat sugar, dopamine is released in the brain. Dopamine is a neurotransmitter that helps control the brain's reward and pleasure center. When dopamine is released it gives us a feeling of pleasure. This is how drugs of abuse such as cocaine function.

Our brain is hardwired to seek out activities that release dopamine. The ingestion of sugar is an activity that is desirable because it releases an enormous amount of dopamine. In certain people with a predisposition to addiction, this causes a reward–seeking behavior that is typical of an addiction to abusive drugs.

A 2012 study by Dr. Robert Lustig of the University Of California, San Francisco revealed that sugar is just as addictive to the human brain as cocaine, setting off the same dopamine triggers and forcing us to crave more and more of it.

Lustig, Robert H., MD. *Sugar: The Bitter Truth.* UCSF Mini Medical School for the Public. University of California– San Francisco, San Francisco, CA. 30 July 2009 Speech.

High Fructose Corn Syrup

High fructose corn syrup (HFCS) is much worse than white sugar. This food product is also known as corn sugar, corn syrup, fructose syrup, fructose, glucose/fructose, or high–fructose maize syrup. It is a corn–based sweetener made from corn stalk. Most of the corn used to make HFCS is genetically modified. It is used in candy, beverages, including soft drinks, fruit juices, salad dressings, and many food products. On average, Americans consume about 60 pounds of HFCS per year.

HFCS is used by food producers because it is cheaper, dissolves more easily in liquids than table sugar, and gives these food products a longer shelf life. The government farm bill subsidizes (pays part of the price for producing or pays producers not to grow) a certain few large agribusinesses and large farm owners that grow corn, not vegetables. This means that our tax dollars are paying them a higher price for their corn or paying them for not growing corn.

This form of sugar is extracted from corn stalks through a chemical process. Table sugar (sucrose) consists of a chemical structure of two sugars molecules tightly bound together, fructose and glucose, in an equal ratio. HFCS has a sweeter taste because fructose is sweeter than glucose. There is more fructose than glucose in HFCS.

HFCS and cane sugar are not biochemically identical. They are not processed the same way. In cane sugar, sucrose is slowly absorbed into the bloodstream. It takes the enzymes in our digestive track longer to break down the sucrose into glucose and fructose than HFCS.

In HFCS, the two sugar molecules, fructose and glucose, have no chemical bound or boundary. Without the boundary, no digestion is required so they are rapidly absorbed into the bloodstream. Fructose is much more readily metabolized (broken down) into fat in the liver than glucose. Most fats are formed in your liver. When sugar enters your liver, it decides to store it for later energy use, burn it, or turn it into fat. High levels of cholesterol block the flow of blood to and from the heart. This weakens the heart muscles and the circulation of oxygen throughout the body. This also leads to deposits of fat on the liver.

This is the major cause of liver damage in this country. This condition is called nonalcoholic "fatty liver" disease (NAFLD). It affects about 70 million people today. NAFLD in turn leads to hepatic insulin resistance, type II diabetes, and a host of other obesity–related conditions.

High doses of free fructose have punched holes in the intestinal lining. That is because free fructose requires more energy to be absorbed by the gut. This depletes the energy fuel source required to maintain the integrity of the intestinal wall or lining. When this lining is compromised because of the depletion of the body's energy source, food and bacteria "leak" across the intestinal membrane. An immune reaction and body wide inflammation are triggered when toxic gut bacteria and partially digested food proteins enter your bloodstream. This inflammation is the root of obesity, heart disease, diabetes, accelerated aging, dementia and cancer because of the affect on the immune system.

When glucose is rapidly absorbed into the bloodstream, this triggers spikes in insulin. Insulin is a hormone produced by the pancreas to regulate carbohydrates and fat metabolism in the body. The continued spikes in insulin lead to leptin being inhibited. Leptin is a protein hormone that acts on receptors in the hypothalamus of the brain where it controls appetite. When leptin is limited, appetite control is hindered since this interferes with the body's hormones signaling the brain that one is full (satiated). This leads to increased food intake, weight gain, diabetes, heart disease, cancer, dementia, and more.

Obesity and irregular fluctuations of insulin lead to diabetes in many people. This is because of the continual damage to the pancreas caused by these irregular spikes of insulin production. This overworking of the pancreas causes the pancreas to stop producing insulin, or insufficient amounts of insulin are produced to regulate carbohydrates and fat metabolism.

High fructose corn syrup (HFCS) and foods rich in sugars and sweeteners like HFCS, rot the teeth by decaying the enamel coating. Like other refined sugars, HFCS contain no vitamins or nutrients.

The vitamins and nutrients needed to digest the carbohydrates must be drawn from your body's bone and tissues. This depletes your body of its valuable nutrients.

Even though foods that contain high levels of HFCS provide lots of calories, those calories have no nutritional value. Foods containing high amounts of HFCS are a source of body fatigue because they cause your body to release great amounts of hormone and endorphins. Too much of this refined sugar will cause your body to crave more. This results in mood swings when trying to cut back because the desires and craving only increases.

Lastly, HFCS often contains possible contaminants including mercury that are not regulated by the FDA. Mercury in the body acts as a neurotoxin, interfering with the brain and nervous system. Even in low dosages, mercury may affect a child's development by shortening attention span, delaying walking and talking, and causing learning disabilities. In adults, mercury poisoning can cause loss in memory and vision. It can cause tremors, and numbness in fingers and toes. It can also adversely affect regulation and fertility, and may possibly be the reason for some heart attacks. I am saddened to witness any teenager consume a 20 ounce HFCS sweetened soda, sports drink, or tea. These drinks contain 17 teaspoons of sugar. This happens much too often. The average teenager consumes two of these HFCS beverages each day.

Carbohydrates

Our bodies require carbohydrates for energy, especially the brain and the nervous system. The percentage of dietary energy our bodies require from carbohydrates varies. The percentage ranges from 45–65% (the Institute of Medicine) to 55–75% (the Food and Agriculture and World Health organizations). This energy is mostly used for normal body functions such as heartbeat, digestion, body movement, and breathing. Sadly, most eat only about half of the recommended amounts from the best sources.

The most common and abundant forms of carbohydrates are sugars, fibers, and starches. They are found in bread, milk, beans, potatoes, popcorn, cookies, spaghetti, corn, sodas, and sweet potato pie. The best sources of carbohydrates are found in fruit, vegetables, beans, and whole grains. Our digestive system handles all carbohydrates in much the same way. It breaks down (or tries to break down) the carbohydrates into single sugar molecules. Single sugar molecules are small enough to cross into the bloodstream. An enzyme called amylase helps to break down carbohydrates into glucose (blood sugar) that is used as energy for the body. This energy is necessary for the production of body tissues and insulation.

Carbohydrates are classified according to their chemical structures and how quickly sugar is digested and absorbed. There are simple and complex carbohydrates. Simple carbohydrates are simple sugars with a chemical structure of one or two sugars linked together. They have very little nutritional value, like the HFCS. These are refined sugars that are quickly digested. An example is how fast sugar–based candy melts in your mouth.

Simple carbohydrates that consist of one sugar are called galactose (found in mother's milk), fructose (found in fruit), dextrose (found in corn) or glucose (blood sugar). The simple carbohydrates with two chemically linked sugars are lactose (found in animal milk), maltose (found in certain vegetables and beer), and sucrose (table sugar). Examples of foods containing simple carbohydrates include products with white flour, milk, honey, chocolate, candy, soda, jam, yogurt, fruit, molasses, fruit juice, table sugar, and packaged cereals.

Complex carbohydrates consist of a chemical structure that is made up of three or more sugars linked together. Examples of foods that contain complex carbohydrates include beans, spinach, broccoli, lentils, yams, zucchini, skimmed milk, whole grains and cereals. These sugars are mostly rich in fiber, vitamins, and minerals. Complex carbohydrates act as the body's fuel and contribute significantly to energy production. They absorb certain minerals and are important in the formation of fatty acids.

Due to their complexity (three or more linked sugars), complex carbohydrates take longer to digest than simple carbohydrates. They don't raise the blood sugar level as quickly as simple carbohydrates. The fiber helps temper blood sugars by slowing the rate of absorption of sugar into your bloodstream. This results in you feeling full longer (satiated) and less likely to over eat later.

Refining Or Processing

What happens when food in its natural state is processed or refined?

Foods are refined or processed to prolong the time they can be on the store shelves to be sold. The longer the time a food can last on the store shelf, without spoiling, the greater the opportunity to sell the product. This is called "shelf life". Since goods are now processed to last longer on the store shelves, this speaks to a profit motive.

The refinement process transforms a complex carbohydrate into a simple carbohydrate by removing the original vitamins and minerals contained in the fiber. Fiber comes from plant foods. There is no fiber in animal products such as fish, eggs, milk, and poultry. Fiber is the indigestible part of plant foods. This includes vegetables, fruits, nuts, whole grains, and legumes (a class of vegetables that includes lentils, peas, and beans). Most of the fiber consumed passes through the intestines and is not digested. It assists in keeping your bowels regular.

Lets take a kernel of wheat for example. A kernel of wheat consists of three parts, the Bran, Germ, and Endosperm.

The Bran is the tough fibrous outer hard shell of the grain. It is the part of the grain that provides most of the B vitamins, important antioxidants, minerals, and fiber. The benefits of B vitamins are awesome. They ease stress, aid memory, mood, relieve PMS, and reduce heart attacks. Even migraines can benefit from the B's in the right amount. Some B vitamins help with the production and repair of DNA. Some assist cells to burn glucose and fat for energy. Others help create neurotransmitters (substances involved in the transmission of nerve cells) like serotonin.

Serotonin is a hormone located in four areas of the brain. In the pineal gland its major effects include improving mood and giving you that satiated or "satisfied" feeling from food. In the lining of the digestive track it regulates intestinal movement. In the central nervous system it regulates appetite, sleep, muscle contraction, mood, memory, and learning. In the blood platelets, it regulates constriction of blood vessels and blood clotting.

Bran contains many healthy oils and minerals. They are necessary for building strong teeth and bones, converting eaten food into energy, and controlling body fluids in and outside cells. Minerals are found in vegetables, fruits, (especially dried fruit), nuts, cereals (including cereal products such as bread), meat, milk, and dairy foods.

Your body needs larger amounts of some minerals like calcium and iron to grow and stay healthy and small amounts of what is called trace elements each day. Trace elements are essential nutrients that your body needs to perform necessary functions, grow, develop, and repair itself, but in much lesser amounts than vitamins and minerals. Examples of trace elements are iodine, chromium, copper, selenium, and zinc.

The Germ is the next layer. This is the embryo that will transfer into a plant. It is packed with nutrients including fatty acids and vitamin E. Fatty acids promote healthy cell transference. Fatty acids create healthy skin with a membrane that keeps water and nutrients in, and allows waste to pass out. This helps dissolve fatty deposits that block pores and cause acne. They repair skin damaged by pimples and blemishes.

Fatty acids reduce the appearance of cellulite, acne, sagging and aging skin. They fight cancers, help oxygen circulation throughout the body, work with red blood cells, and help prevent arthritis. A lack of these fatty acids could lead to problems. There could be problems with memory, vision, irregular heartbeat, blood clots and a decrease in the functioning of your immune system.

Vitamin E is a fat soluble antioxidant. This means it can be dissolved in fat and it removes free radicals. Free radicals are unstable compounds that damage the cell structure. Vitamin E reduces cholesterol, thins the blood, prevents blood platelets (blood cells that help stop bleeding) from clumping, reduces the risk of sunstroke, coronary artery disorder, and heart disease. Vitamin E also helps alleviate fatigue, nourish cells and strengthen capillary walls.

The **Endosperm** is the soft part in the center of the grain. It contains the starch. The starch is the part left after the refining process. The most nutritious parts of the grain, the bran and germ, containing concentrated amounts of fiber, vitamins, minerals, and antioxidants are removed. What is left, the endosperm, is composed mostly of starchy carbohydrates low in nutrients.

There you have it. Whole grains are rich in fiber providing long lasting energy that will keep you fueled for hours. Refined grains are quickly digested into simple sugars and absorbed into your bloodstream. This can cause blood sugar levels to spike and then quickly crash. These rapid swings in blood sugar often drain your energy resulting in feeling moody and fatigued.

Digesting Refined Foods

When foods such as sugar or flour are refined and processed, the body suffers when digesting them. That is because the body's digestive system requires the same minerals and vitamins contained in the fruit, vegetable, or plant to digest it. When cane sugar, for example, is ground and stripped of its outer layer where the fiber is located, the minerals and vitamins are removed.

The minerals required to digest sugar are calcium, manganese, phosphorous, magnesium, cobalt, copper, zinc, and chromium. Sugar cane in its natural state is rich in these minerals. It also contains vitamins C, B1, B2, B6, iron, niacin, and pantothenic acid. These vitamins and minerals work with the natural sugar cane's enzymes and fiber to nourish the body. The fibers of the natural sugar cane help to slow down the absorption of the sugars. This prevents the sharp rise in blood sugar that is associated with refined sugar.

When the body is given refined sugar, it knows what is required to digest the sugar. The refined sugar is devoid of the minerals and the corresponding enzymes needed to digest the sugar. The body tries to adapt by pulling stored nutrients from its own bones and tissues.

For example, calcium is needed to digest refined sugar. There is no calcium left in refined or processed sugar. Calcium is pulled from your bones and tissue where it is stored to digest the refined sugar. The depletion of calcium from your bones and tissues on a regular or daily basis weakens the bones, potentially leading to osteoporosis, and other degenerative diseases.

In addition to refined food robbing the body of stored nutrients, refined carbs are less satisfying (less feeling of being full) than "good carbs". The body absorbs processed grains and simple sugars relatively quickly. The increased blood sugar triggers a release of insulin, and in about an hour or two after eating, the hunger returns.

"Harvard School of Public Health"

http://bit.ly/1RjsVaa

http://bit.ly/1NddFeh

"The Dangers of High Fructose Corn Syrup" http://bit.ly/1LlJBiv

"10 Side Effects of High–Fructose Corn Syrup" http://bit.ly/1FtlnK

"5 Reasons High Fructose Corn Syrup will Kill You" – Dr. Mark Hyman http://bit.ly/1Rjt3Xb

"What's So Bad About Flour and Sugar"
http://bit.ly/1SyQApy

"9 Reasons to Avoid Sugar As If Your Life Depended On It"
http://bit.ly/1SyQMVC

Aspartame (NutraSweet/Equal, Canderel)

The history of Aspartame being approved by the FDA is like a tangled web of bribery that makes your average politician look like a saint. In 1970, Aspartame's approval was initially rejected by the Federal Drug Administration (FDA). But G. D. Searle, the developer of Aspartame, presented to the FDA 100 studies that showed it was harmless. These were studies G.D. Searle had funded. They knew if Aspartame was approved they would make millions.

But each time an independent study was done it was found to be dangerous for human consumption. For the first time in history the FDA began criminal investigation into Searle for misrepresenting the results of experiments. What the investigation revealed was startling. Tumors were cut out of mice and they were labeled as having no tumors. Some animals were not autopsied for months resulting in rotting that ruined data. Obvious tumors were also labeled as normal swelling.

When the FDA ruled that Aspartame would not receive final approval what followed was a series of dirty political tricks. In January 1977, while the grand jury probe was underway, G.D. Searle arranged to hire the U.S. Attorney, Samuel K. Skinner who was leading the investigation. Then Searle hired Donald Rumsfeld, a former member of Congress and Secretary of Defense in the Ford Administration, as the new CEO. Rumsfeld appointed several political buddies to top management positions. He vowed to get Aspartame approved.

In December 1977, Skinner's withdrawal and resignation as U.S. Attorney stalled the Searle grand jury investigation so long that the statue of limitations on the Aspartame charges ran out. The investigation by the grand jury was dropped. Skinner then left the U.S. Attorney's office and took a job with Searle's law firm.

After Ronald Reagan's inauguration in1981, Rumsfeld became part of Reagan's transition team that was in charge of choosing a new FDA commissioner. Rumsfeld appointed Arthur Hayes Hull, Jr. as the new commissioner. One of Hull's first official acts as FDA commissioner was to appoint a five–person panel to review Aspartame.

Three of the five voted not to approve Aspartame citing the animal tumors as a big concern. Hull appointed a sixth member to tie the vote. Then Hayes, a man who knew nothing of food additives appointed himself, as commissioner to vote also. He then casted the deciding vote in favor of approval. Shortly after this Hayes resigned as commissioner of FDA and was hired by Searle at a position paying 100's of 1000s dollars a year.

Aspartame is a popular low–calorie sweetener. It does not occur naturally but is a manufactured substance. You can find it in diet soda, tabletop sweeteners, chewing gum, yogurts, cooking sauces, crisps, drink powders, sugar–free products, flavored water and cereals. Although it is present in diet foods, it is not calorie–free. Aspartame contains 4 calories per gram. It is about two hundred times sweeter than sugar. Only a very small amount of Aspartame is required to create a sweet–tasting product with few or no calories.

Aspartame is highly addictive. The phenylalanine and methanol in Aspartame increases the dopamine levels in the brain and causes a certain high feeling. This creates an addiction that is only made worse by the release of methyl alcohol or methanol, which is classified as a narcotic. So, it was only natural that humans would begin to consume foods containing Aspartame at a high rate. This can lead to obesity.

Fifty percent of Aspartame is Phenylalanine. On February 17, 2004, Dr. Richard Wurtman of MIT told Congress that Phenylalanine is a neurotoxin (substance toxic to nerves) that goes directly in the brain because it contains no other amino acids that keep it from getting into the brain. It lowers the seizure threshold. That is, it raises the chances of having seizures. It also depletes serotonin. Lowered serotonin triggers manic depression (bipolar), mood swings, anxiety, paranoia, hallucinations, insomnia and panic attacks.

Aspartame also contains aspartic acid and methanol, a neurological poison that can't be made non–poisonous. Methanol is used as paint thinner. It breaks down into formaldehyde and formic acid in the body. Formaldehyde is a known carcinogen. It causes retinal damage, birth defects and interferes with DNA replication.

Free methanol is one of the most toxic products put out in the population. It is created from Aspartame when it is heated to above 86° Fahrenheit (30° Celsius). When free methanol is ingested into the body the absorption of methanol is sped up considerably. Since it has been put in food products brain cancer numbers have soared. Every primate developed grand mal seizures (unconsciousness, convulsions, muscle rigidity) when it was used on them.

This is one of the worst products ever approved by the FDA. It leads to headaches, brain tumors, seizures, optic nerve degeneration and cancers.

How Aspartame Became Legal – The Timeline By Rich Murray rmforall@att.net http://bit.ly/1Ndexjc

"Watch The Video" http://bit.ly/1QILU2U

"Nothing Natural About Natural" http://bit.ly/1CjRnBp

"The top 10 worst sources of aspartame – Natural News" http://bit.ly/1GcQgoD

"Congressional Record, Dr. Richard Wurtman, Aspartame"

http://bit.ly/1H5yf1t

"Aspartame...The Bad News" http://bit.ly/1K2UNi4

Stevia

Stevia and many of the calorie-free sweeteners are highly processed. Some of the chemicals used in the processing are known carcinogens (substances that cause cancer). The processing begins with GMO corn. "Natural flavors" is another ingredient added to powdered and liquid stevia products. This is likely due to the fact that once the stevia leaf is processed it can develop a metallic taste. However, the food industry allows synthetic and dangerous chemicals to be defined as natural. Many of these chemicals in "Natural Flavor" can lead to addiction.

Coconut Sugar

Coconut sugar is a better sugar alternative than Stevia. It is low glycemic (making it more diabetic friendly) and one of the most natural unprocessed forms of sugar available. Coconut sugar is naturally high in amino acids. It has 10,000 times more potassium, 20 times more iron and magnesium than conventional sugar.

Agave Nectar (or syrup)

Sugar is addictive. Most Agave nectar (or syrup) is a highly concentrated sugar. It is 1½ times sweeter than table sugar. Because Agave has a low-glycemic index (it has minimal impact on blood glucose levels) and doesn't spike your blood sugar like regular sugar does, it was thought to be a good alternative for diabetics. However, most Agave doesn't contain a lot of glucose. It contains more fructose than any other common sweetener, including high-fructose corn syrup (HFCS). Regular table sugar is about 50% fructose, HFCS is about 55% fructose, and most Agave is about 70–90% fructose.

Commercially processed Agave is not raw nor "natural and organic", despite being labeled as such. This can be blamed on the lax regulation and enforcement of raw food labeling by the FDA. In order to change the pineapple-like bulb of the agave plant into sweet syrup, most Agave goes through an extensive process of chemical refining, using heat, which changes the enzymatic structure of the syrup. This converts it into a man–made chemical fructose. Most companies remove the natural enzymes to prevent agave syrup from fermenting and turning into tequila. This process makes many Agave brands sold in health food stores and supermarkets, neither raw, organic nor natural.

Once consumed, refined fructose is processed through the liver and converted into triglyceride, which is essentially stored as body fat. This can contribute to the fatty arterial plaques responsible for cardiovascular disease. As it gets metabolized (broken–down), uric acid and free radicals form, which can trigger damage to cells and inflammation. Excess amounts of this fat have been linked to everything from Type II diabetes to heart disease. High fructose consumption can make your body resistant to leptin. This is a hormone that tells your body when you're full. As such, a common result is a larger appetite that can lead to weight gain. Other challenges linked to a diet high in fructose include depletion of the body's minerals, hardening of the arteries, obesity, cancer growth, memory loss, irritation of the liver and a tendency toward insulin resistance, a predecessor to diabetes.

Recommendations: Limit all forms of sugar. If you must use sugar, consider using dates, persimmons, coconut nectar and maple syrup.

"Why I NEVER Use Agave" http://bit.ly/1fo9mS9

"This Sweetener Is Far Worse Than High Fructose Corn Syrup" http://huff.to/1Ndf1px

"Agave: Why We Were Wrong" http://dailym.ai/1L7MEdj

"What's Your Take on Agave Nectar?" http://bit.ly/1d7W36B

Artificial Food Coloring

Adding artificial colors to foods can make them look a lot more appealing. This is a tactic the food industry has been capitalizing on for decades. But many children react to the red, blue and other dyes contained in junk food. In the U.S., more than 15 million tons of artificial food color is used in food manufacturing each year. The Center for Science in the Public Interest (CSPI) points out that food dyes should be banned from use in consumable goods because they have no nutritional value.

According to CSPI executive director Michael F. Jacobson, "These synthetic chemicals do absolutely nothing to improve the nutritional quality or safety of foods, but trigger behavior problems in children and, possibly, cancer in anybody". The children's reaction to the dyes that are usually accompanied with refined sugar, has helped to get many of them diagnosed with Attention Deficit Hyperactivity Disorder (ADHD).

Gluten

Gluten is responsible for the elasticity of dough. It helps the dough rise and keep its shape and often gives a chewy texture. Gluten is added to many things in the food processing industry and is one of the fake meat options for vegetarians. It is used in hair products, cosmetics and skin preparations.

It is estimated that up to 15% of the U.S. population is gluten intolerant (gluten sensitive). This was not always the case. The wheat of today is not the same wheat our forebears ground into their daily bread. It has changed considerably in the past 50 years under the influence of agricultural scientists. The original wheat was about 5% gluten. Now, the Canadian variety is 55% gluten. Today, whole wheat bread increases blood sugar as much as or more than table sugar.

Pure strains of wheat have been crossbred and hybridized with non–wheat grasses to introduce altogether new genes, using techniques like irradiation of wheat seeds and embryos with chemicals, gamma rays, and high–dose X–rays to induce mutations. This was done to make the wheat plant resistant to environmental conditions, such as drought or pathogens, fungi or bacterium and to increase yield per acre. Intense crossbreeding created significant changes in the size of the wheat and structural change in the amino acids in wheat's gluten proteins. No human safety or animal testing was conducted on the new genetic strains that were created.

Small changes in wheat protein structure can point out the difference between a devastating immune response to wheat protein versus no immune response at all. Wheat has undergone a drastic transformation to yield something nearly unrecognizable when compared to the original wheat. These changes may account for wheat sensitivity in many and for the 400 percent increase in celiac disease over the past 40 years. For these reasons we would recommend avoiding gluten whenever possible.

"CSPI Says Food Dyes Pose Rainbow of Risks" http://bit.ly/1I5TTlo

"Is Gluten Bad for You?" http://bit.ly/1LlK8kK.

"10 Signs You Are Gluten Intolerant" http://bit.ly/1JautUX

Wheat Belly by William Davis, M.D. Publisher: Rodale Books; 1 edition (August 30, 2011)

Table Salt: Do not eat table salt. Table salt is created by taking natural salt or crude oil flake leftovers and heating it at 1200° Fahrenheit (648° Celsius). This heat kills the essential minerals and beneficial trace elements that naturally occur in salt. Bleach gives the white appearance, and anti–caking agents are added during the refinement process. Anti–caking agents such as Ferrocyanide, talc and aluminium derivatives, a potential cause of Alzheimer's disease, are added to increase shelf life and allow an easier pour. But the chemicals added to keep salt from absorbing moisture on the shelf interfere with the body's ability to regulate hydration in your body.

The Federal Drug Administration (FDA) has a special provision to allow talc, a known carcinogen, in table salt. Although it is prohibited in all other foods, due to toxicity issues, under current regulations, table salt can be up to 2% talc. Your body retains water for its protection. But your cells must release water to help neutralize, dilute, and break down the table salt. This water loss dehydrates and weakens your cells. This can even cause them to die prematurely.

The natural forms of iodine are lost when salt is refined. Without this iodine, the thyroid is severely harmed, leading to metabolism and growth issues. Because of this, the salt industry began to add synthetic forms of iodine to their products. But it's in such small amount; it's insufficient to provide the iodine needs of the body.

Table salt has been exposed to many toxic chemicals, which can include sulfuric acid or chlorine during its refinement process. Iodized salts, at super markets or on the table of restaurants, have synthetic chemicals added to them. These chemicals may include fluoride, sodium bicarbonate, iodide and potassium iodide. Common table salts add white sugar and toxic MSG (mono–sodium–glutamate).

Considered toxic to the body, it is also highly addictive. The body craves more of this fake sodium the more it becomes use to it. It is responsible, in large part, to the onset of many diseases including thyroid and metabolic dysfunction. It causes high blood pressure and excess fluid in your body tissue, which can contribute to rheumatism, gout, arthritis, kidney and gall bladder stones and cellulite.

"The Truth About Table Salt and The Chemical Industry" http://bit.ly/1Ftm2vU

"The Health Dangers of Table Salt" http://bit.ly/1MVeFTC

"The Benefits of Himalayan Salt" http://bit.ly/1JauI29/

"Real Salt, Celtic Salt and Himalayan Salt" http://bit.ly/1TDUoZB

"Types of Salt: Himalayan vs Kosher vs Regular vs Sea Salt" http://bit.ly/1K2VcRE

Mixing Carbohydrates And Proteins

No more than 18% carbohydrates should be combined with proteins or no more than 18% proteins should be combined with carbohydrates. Vegetables, herbs, and salad ingredients are considered neutral foods. Together with spouted legumes and seeds they may be combined with either food group.

The percentage is based on the work of the pancreas. When a carbohydrate is put in the mouth, this triggers the pancreas to produce an enzyme called amylase to digest the carbohydrates. Protease is an enzyme produced by the pancreas that digests protein. The pancreas can only produce up to 18% of protease or amylase when it has to produce more than one of the two enzymes.

When the combining ratio is unbalanced one gets digested completely while the other is not. This results in fermentation, putrification and poor digestion. Yeast and harmful bacteria grows in the digestive tract because none of the enzymes can do their job properly.

Vegetable protein–rich foods are whole grains such as quinoa, whole grain bread, brown rice, and barley. Beans, lentils, and legumes are an excellent source of protein. Nuts, seeds and nut butters are protein sources. All food made from meat (animal protein), poultry, seafood, eggs, processed soy products are considered protein.

The protein food that you eat requires a certain level of acid in order to be properly digested and expelled. Protein bonds are broken up by hydrochloric acid in the stomach. An enzyme called pepsin breaks the protein strands into smaller fragments. Protein digestion continues into the large and small intestine.

The digestion of carbohydrates or starches, such as potatoes or rice requires an alkaline balance to be properly digested and expelled. The process begins in the mouth with the release of enzymes called ptyalin from the salivary glands located inside the jaw, under the cheek, and under the tongue. The starches are broken down in part before they reach the stomach. As the process continues into the stomach, an acid is produced to assist in the digestion. The process continues into the large and small intestine.

When the proper percentages of combining are not adhered to, many problems persist. First, the digestive environment is unable to get acid enough or alkaline enough to properly digest either food group. When this happens neither are absorbed well and necessary nutrients are lost. It takes longer for the digestion to complete. Fermentation and toxicity occurs.

Carbohydrates are digested faster than proteins. If both carbohydrates and proteins are combined without the proper percentage, the protein is digested first. The carbohydrates are shelved waiting their turn to be digested. Unfortunately, the next meal may arrive too soon. Once again, the protein is digested first which could result in the carbohydrates being stored as fat.

Eating Pork

China is the largest producer of pigs, one of the most consumed meats in the world. Pigs carry many viruses and parasites in their body and meat. According to The Center for Disease Control and Prevention (CDC), each year more than 100 viruses come to the United States from China through pigs. This includes H1N1, better known as 'the swine flu." This is another virus that has made the leap from the pig to humans.

The pig (swine) is a foul animal that is a scavenger, often eating anything they can find. This includes insects, leftover scraps, bugs, their own feces, and carcasses of sick animals, including their own young. The pig is so poisonous (99.9 per cent) you can hardly kill him with other poisons, including lye.

The bite of a snake will not poison the pig. The pig can eat snakes with no ill affects. It has no sweat glands to rid its body of toxins. This leaves many toxins in the pig's body. When you eat pork meat, you too are consuming all these toxins that weren't eliminated from the pig. The pig is so filthy and poisonous nature has prepared him a sewer line, which you may find at the openings on his forelegs that oozes pus.

The pig contains a parasitic worm called trichina (commonly known as pork worm). Trichina can be found in the stomach and intestinal walls of its eaters. There, it breeds and works its way into the muscles of the body. The parasites then work themselves into the spinal cord and travel to the brain. This causes the victims to suffer with fever, rheumatism, back, stomach, and headaches.

Eating pork (swine) destroys or alters the appearance of its eaters. Trichina even changes the color of the eyes of some swine eaters to a dull brown or dull red. The pork eaters tend to be slow thinking, slow moving and have the tendency to be easily irritated. It can take up to seven years for these parasitic worms to depart your body.

To kill off any worms, the CDC recommends freezing and thoroughly cooking pork before eating it. We don't know how you would feel, but we would not feel comfortable eating anything that has to be first frozen and then thoroughly cooked to kill off its worms.

"Why You Should Avoid Pork" http://bit.ly/1GZCRUQ

Elijah Muhammad. How to Eat to Live Vol. 1 (1967) Reprinted 1997 How To Eat To Live Book One Published by Secretarius MEMPS Ministries 5025 N Central Ave #415 Phoenix, AZ 85012

"H1N1 Flu" http://1.usa.gov/1dW1x5e

"6 Horrifying Things About Pork Everyone Should Know" http://bit.ly/1MVfbB3

"PORK!! The consequences of eating it!!" http://bit.ly/1QINQbG

"Food Combining: The Little–Understood Secret to Optimal Health & Weight Revealed" http://bit.ly/1GZD2j4

"How To Combine Foods For Optimal Health" http://bit.ly/1GZD2j4

Stevia "7 Things You Didn't Know About Stevia" http://huff.to/1GyInMN

"Why I Quit Stevia" http://bit.ly/1GqBZUr/

"Is Stevia Safe?" http://bit.ly/1GZDEFp

"4 Health Side Effects of Stevia" http://bit.ly/1SyTLxp

Coconut Sugar "What Are the Benefits of Coconut Sugar?" http://bit.ly/1I5Xkbk

"Coconut Sugar – Healthy Sugar Alternative or a Big, Fat Lie?" http://bit.ly/1IqP6q7

"Dr. Oz Recommends Coconut Sugar" http://bit.ly/1CjSXmT

CHAPTER 11
Barefootin'

HAVE YOU EVER NOTICED the difference you feel when you take off your shoes and walk, stroll, or sleep on the ground with the skin of your body touching the earth? This has been called "grounding" or "earthing". It stems from the idea that in our modern daily city life we have little or no direct contact with the earth. Without this contact, we lose out on the health benefits of our bodies exchanging negatively charged electrons with the surface of the earth.

We can stop the inflammatory processes in our bodies by walking barefoot on the earth. This may be one of the most important overlooked factors in maintaining one's health. This has been called the ultimate antioxidant and anti–inflammatory. It has been considered the cheapest, easiest way of helping to create optimum health. The physical disconnect with the earth creates abnormal physiology and contributes to inflammation, fatigue, stress, and poor sleep. Recent research explains why this happens.

For most of our evolutionary history, we humans sat, stood, walked, and slept with the skin of our bodies touching the earth. This contact serves as a conduit for transferring earth's gentle negatively charged electrons underfoot into the body. Electrons from the earth have antioxidant effects that can protect your body from inflammation, which is said to be the root of most disease.

Traditionally, shoes or moccasins were made of leather. Leather is made of the hides of animals and is electrically conducive. This is because it includes a layer of dermal connective tissue mostly made of collagen, which has been shown to be a semiconductor. Leather actually conducts electrons and therefore maintains a conductive contact between the earth and your feet.

It is only recently that substances such as wood, rugs, plastics and asphalt have separated us from contact with the earth. Modern day plastics and rubber are electrical insulators. Many are walking around insulated from the earth because they are wearing shoes and soles made of rubber or plastic. Both of these insulators block the beneficial flow of electrons from the earth to your body. We also no longer sleep on the ground as we did in the past.

Our bodies contain free radicals. They are positively charged. These chemicals come in many shapes, sizes, and configurations. They are capable of damaging cells and genetic material. The body generates free radicals as byproducts of turning food into energy. Others are in the air you breathe and the food you eat. Some free radicals are generated by sunlight's action on the skin and eyes. Some come from immune responses to injury or exposure to pollutants or toxins.

Free radicals all share a voracious appetite for electrons. They steal electrons from any nearby body substances. This electron theft can radically alter the structure or function of the substance. The damage can change the instructions coded in a strand of DNA. It can alter a cell's membrane, changing the flow of what enters and leaves the cell. It can also make a molecule of circulating low–density lipoprotein (LDL, often called bad cholesterol) more likely to get trapped in an artery wall.

When you are injured or cut, your body has evolved a means to kill bacteria. Reactive oxygen species (ROS) are delivered to the site of injury by white blood cells. ROS are very effective at this task. But ROS are also very reactive biochemically and can damage nearby healthy tissues. ROS are usually positively charged molecules that need to be neutralized immediately to prevent them from damaging nearby healthy tissues.

You soak up millions of negatively charged electrons by putting your feet on the ground. These negatively charged electrons intercept and neutralize free radicals and ROS. This starts to detoxify the body. Within 2 seconds from the time your skin touches the earth, there will be a change in skin conduction. This will improve heart rate variability because it makes the blood thinner and shifts the nervous system to a point where it has more tranquility.

So instead of the blood being thick and sluggish like catsup, it flows more like red wine. The most common cause of a heart attack or stroke is caused by sluggish blood. It is also a major factor in degenerative diseases, cancer, tumors and diabetes. The immune system functions optimally when your body has an adequate supply of electrons. Studies have shown that "grounding" or "earthing" decreases the effect of potentially disruptive electromagnetic fields given off by all the electronic devices that surround us.

The entire skin is conductive to the mobile electrons that flow from the earth to your body. But there is one particularly important area on the bottom of the foot. To an acupuncturist, this area is known as "Kidney 1". It provides the best connection between the feet and the earth. It is located on the sole of the foot, approximately 1/3 the distance between the base of the 2nd toe and the heel, between the 2nd and 3rd metatarsal bones.

A meridian is an "energy highway" in the human body. Qi (chee) energy flows through this energy highway to all parts of the body. "Kidney 1" is the point where the kidney meridian ends. It ultimately connects to all of the other meridians and delivers earth's antioxidant electrons to every part of the body. As antioxidant electrons from the earth enter the body through the bottoms of the feet, they neutralize the free radicals widely thought to be responsible for premature aging and chronic diseases.

Recommendations

Spend as much time as you can barefoot on the earth.

If you are injured, connect your body to the earth as soon as possible.

When engaging in a sport that involves a risk of injury, spend 15 minutes with your feet in contact with the earth before you begin. This builds up the number of electrons in your connective tissues.

When it is not possible to be outside to put your feet on the earth, a number of devices that conductively connect you to the earth may be used. These include grounded floor mats, grounded sleep systems, conductive patches, ankle and wristbands. These devices can be connected with a wire to a ground rod inserted into the earth or to a ground port that has been properly tested by an electrician.

"Dr. Mercola: Why Does Walking Barefoot On The Earth Make Your Feel Better" http://bit.ly/1CjT2H7

Energy Medicine Technologies: Ozone Healing, Microcrystals, Frequency Therapy, and the Future of Health Edited by Finley Eversole, PH.D. ã 2013 by Finley Eversole Inner Traditions One Park Street Rochester, Vermont 05767 http://bit.ly/1h3Yc5P

Earthing: The Most Important Health Discovery Ever? by Clinton Ober, Stephen T. Sinatra, Martin Zucker: Publisher: Basic Health Publications; 1st edition 2010

Dr. Weils: "There Anything to "Earthing?"

http://bit.ly/1Ftnaj8

CHAPTER 12
Coffee

COFFEE IS AMERICA'S FAVORITE drug. Over 150 million Americans start most days with a caffeine shot. Studies have shown that it can improve alertness and long term it may reduce the risk of developing kidney stones, Parkinson's disease, gallstones, and liver cirrhosis for heavy drinkers. Good–quality ground coffee is a source of antioxidants that can make you feel good and may help with weight loss. Purchase fresh, high–quality and ideally organic coffee. Regular coffee is one of the most pesticide intensive crops in the world.

Coffee Contains Caffeine. Caffeine is the same drug you probably ingested in your beloved colas and chocolate bars since early childhood. It affects your body just like any drug. You may start off taking it slowly. But as your body develops a tolerance to it, you will need more and more to feel the same effects. Eventually, your body will reach a point where it may seem it can't be without it. You will start to experience withdrawal symptoms when you attempt to stop.

Most become addicted to the caffeine in coffee thinking they don't drink nearly enough to become addicted. It may take less to become addicted than most would think. Research conducted by the department of psychiatry and behavioral sciences at Johns Hopkins University School of Medicine demonstrated that low to moderate caffeine intake (as little as one 14–ounce mug per day) can quickly produce withdrawal symptoms.

One caffeinated drink, whether tea, soft drink, or coffee, will put your body on the caffeine rollercoaster. Once consumed, caffeine begins its effects by initiating uncontrolled neuron firing in your brain, according to Stephen Cherniske in his book, Caffeine Blues. This excess neuron activity triggers your pituitary gland to secrete a hormone that prompts your adrenal glands to produce stress hormones called adrenalin.

Adrenalin is what gives winning athletes that burst of energy and the ability to rescue people by lifting cars or other heavy objects. This is also the source of our "fight–or–flight" response. This normally occurs when you perceive an external threat or danger. Your muscles will tense. Your blood sugar elevates for the extra energy in case it is needed. Your pulse and respiration rates speed up. Your general state of alertness is increased as you ready to fight or run.

You may be just sitting at your desk or in your chair drinking a cup of coffee, but your body is put in the mode to fight or run. With this "caffeinism" or adrenal high you may feel a charge of alertness. When it wears off within the next hour or so, you will probably feel tired, irritable and hungry.

At these times of "low energy", many people simply drink another cup of coffee, or eat a sugary snack to "perk up" and stay alert. Both caffeine and sugar give only temporary feelings of increased energy. This feeling soon dissipates. This cycle of low energy followed by ingesting caffeine and food continues all day for some people.

Like sugar, coffee constantly stimulates the production of adrenalin. Sipping on coffee, caffeinated soda or tea, the entire day puts excessive wear and tear on the adrenal glands. After prolonged "caffeinism" or adrenal high your body enters into a state of adrenal exhaustion. Caffeine consumption has simply pushed the adrenal glands so much that they are burned out.

The body's constant state of alert and the ups and downs in energy your body endures throughout the day drains your energy. This drain produces more irritability, anxiety, sleep disturbance, mood swings and depression. This makes you more and more fatigued over time. Over the years, if you drink coffee, as with any addiction, it will take ingesting more and more to get the same result.

Other Health Challenges Associated With Coffee

Many people drink coffee first thing in the morning. Drinking coffee on an empty stomach stimulates hydrochloric acid (HCI) production. Your body is designed to produce enough HCI to digest meals. If your body has to make HCI more often in response to regular cups of coffee, there can be a problem.

It may have difficulty producing enough HCI to deal with a large meal. This can lead to problems with protein digestion associated in a variety of health problems, from gas and bloating to Irritable bowel syndrome (IBS), diverticulitis and even colon cancer.

Acid reflux and heartburn problems can be caused by coffee. Studies show caffeine in coffee relaxes the lower esophageal sphincter. This small muscle should remain tightly closed once you've eaten. This prevents the contents of your stomach from coming back into the esophagus and burning its delicate lining with hydrochloric acid. When caffeine relaxes this muscle acid reflux and heartburn may occur. Coke and other high caffeine "energy drinks" can also contribute to these conditions, but coffee is particularly problematic for this.

Excessive coffee consumption may have some very negative effects on our digestive system. Many of the compounds in coffee like caffeine and the various acids found in coffee beans can irritate your stomach and the lining of your small intestine.

Coffee elevates cortisol levels. Cortisol is a stress hormone that causes you to age more quickly. It also makes you store body fat. In the longer term it has been associated with an increased risk of high cholesterol, heart disease and osteoporosis.

Coffee affects iron absorption in your stomach and particularly your kidneys ability to retain zinc, calcium, magnesium and other important minerals. Magnesium absorption is particularly worrying as it is necessary to maintain bowel regularity.

Coffee has been shown to be one of the major sources of Acrylamide in American diets. Acrylamide is a potentially carcinogenic (cancer–causing) substance. It forms when coffee beans are roasted at high temperatures. The darker the coffee roast, the higher the levels of this dangerous chemical are likely to be.

After reading this far, perhaps you have a feeling that there could be some value in cutting down a bit or even replacing coffee altogether. If you are experiencing any of the problems above, or just feel coffee has you too on edge consider these recommendations.

Recommendations

You are considered a caffeine junkie if you consume more than 3 cups of coffee a day and can't get through the day without your caffeine fix. If you are low–level coffee drinker (one cup every second or third day), you may be able to replace coffee 'cold turkey' with peppermint tea, teeccino or another coffee alternative you enjoy.

To avoid being addicted, do not drink coffee daily. If you chose to drink coffee, do it semi–regularly. This will avoid you getting withdrawal headaches when you don't drink it.

To start breaking the addiction, you need a week minimum of freedom from caffeine in all its forms. Get any coffee out of the house as soon as possible to avoid temptation. This includes caffeinated colas, "energy drinks" and coffee flavored foods. Go slowly with your reduction to zero caffeine.

Drink plenty of water to flush out toxins and prevent brain fog and caffeine withdrawal headaches. If you use caffeinated green tea as your coffee replacement initially, reduce your use after a day or two and replace it with ginger or peppermint tea for at least a week. Alternatively, you may use a decaffeinated green tea.

Reduce caffeine withdrawal problems by switching to ginger tea, teeccino and caffeine-free herbal teas, and coffee alternatives. Each morning take one of the red ginseng tinctures. Eat plenty of organic fruit. This will energize and provide you body with antioxidants.

"How to Give Up Coffee in 10 Simple Steps"

http://bit.ly/1MVgHTS

Caffeine Blues By Stephen Cherniske MS Publisher: Warner Books December 1, 1998

"Seven Negative Effects of Coffee"

http://bit.ly/1FtnezD

"10 things Never To Eat" by Dr. Ted Broer Aug 8, 2013 – Uploaded by Allen Wright http://bit.ly/1GZDVrN

"The Hidden Dangers Of Caffeine: How Coffee Causes Exhaustion, Fatigue And Addiction"

http://bit.ly/1IqPmW8

Milk

Breast Milk

The best milk you can get is mother's milk. Breast milk has a higher fat content than whole cow's milk. This is needed for the baby's brain growth. The nutrients of human breast milk are significantly more bioavailable (absorbed by body) than those of cow's milk because it is species specific. That means, designed only for humans. There are also many components of mother's milk that are not present in cow's milk.

Cow's Milk

Contains high amounts of calcium (around 300 mg per cup). But many scientific studies have shown many detrimental health effects directly linked to milk consumption. The most surprising link is that not only do we barely absorb the calcium in cow's milk (especially if pasteurized), but also it actually increases calcium loss from the bones. That is why the countries with the highest rates of osteoporosis (brittle bones) are the ones where people drink the most milk and have the most calcium in their diets.

Like all animal protein, milk acidifies the body pH. This triggers a biological correction. Your body seeks to neutralize the acid to restore a healthy body pH balance. Calcium is an excellent acid neutralizer and the biggest storage of calcium in the body is in the bones. Calcium that our bones need to stay strong is pulled out of the bones to neutralize the acidifying effect of milk. It leaves the body via the urine, resulting in an actual calcium deficit.

Cow's milk contains on average three times the amount of protein than human milk. This creates disturbances in the process your body uses to get or make energy from the food you eat that have detrimental bone health consequences. Today, many milking cows are given antibiotics. Some cows are also given steroids and artificial growth hormones made by Monsanto called recombinant bovine growth hormone (rBGH).

This man–made or synthetic hormone keeps the mother cow lactating for a long time to artificially increase milk production. rBGH also increases blood levels of the insulin–growth factor 1 (IGF–1) in those who drink it. Higher levels of IGF–1 are linked to several cancers. It's been used since the FDA approved it in 1993 but it's not permitted in the European Union, Canada and 27 other countries.

Milk also causes inflammation and constant production of immune cells can cause permanent damage, which can lead to cancer, Alzheimer's, arthritis, heart disease and more. For those concerned with a convenient source of calcium, protein, fats, vitamin D, etc., there are many people in many parts of the world who still manage to get all the calcium, protein, fats, vitamin D, etc. that they need and do not drink milk. Calcium may be derived from many nondairy sources and Vitamin D can be supplied by sunlight exposure and food sources.

The inhumane treatment of cows is another reason to give up milk. All milk at the grocery store is not from happy cows. The mother cow and baby calf are separated at birth. Their cries for each other can be heard from far away. Some conventional dairy "farmers" have cows by the thousands confined to filthy, crowded stalls and feedlots that are brutalized to maintain high milk production. Cows must be routinely impregnated, usually once a year, causing greater stress, and greater likelihood of illness and premature death.

Some cows will suffer mastitis, become cripple, unable to walk and will be left for dead. Mastitis is the inflammation of the mammary gland and udder tissue and is a major and most common endemic disease of dairy cattle in the United States. Most of the cows are sick, so their milk contains pus, blood, drugs, and other dangerous pathogens, which is why it must be pasteurized to be safe for human consumption. When dairy cows can no longer produce milk, they are sent to auction to be slaughtered, many are sick, weak, and in an emaciated condition.

Soy Milk

This milk is a complete protein that has about the same amount of protein as cow's milk. It can replace animal protein and other sources of dietary fiber, minerals and vitamins. It contains little digestible calcium because calcium is bound to the bean's pulp, which is indigestible by humans.

In her book, The Whole Soy Story, Dr. Kaayla T. Daniel states, "The estrogens in soy will affect the hormonal development of these children, and it will certainly affect their growing brains, reproductive systems, and thyroids." Soy formula contains large amounts of manganese, which have been linked to attention deficit disorder and neurotoxicity in infants. Even the Israeli health ministry recently issued an advisory stating that infants should avoid soy formula altogether.

Soy blocks the uptake of nutrients by the body and interferes with the assimilation of essential minerals. Soy plant estrogens are potent antithyroid agents that can cause hypothyroidism (goiters) and can cause thyroid cancer. They can disrupt endocrine function and may cause infertility and breast cancer. That is because they are plant–based estrogens that basically act like or mimics estrogen in our bodies. This can cause excess estrogen in the body leading to uterine fibroids, prostate, and breast cancer.

Hemp Milk

Hemp milk is made from the seeds of the same plant used to make marijuana. However the seeds don't contain any THC, the psychoactive component in marijuana. So, you will not get high. They are one of nature's most perfect foods, plus they taste great! Hemp seeds are a nutritionally complete food. They contain all 20 amino acids. Hemp seeds are noted for their high concentrations of omega fatty acids, which is great for your memory by helping your brain's neurons to communicate properly.

Omega 3"s in the seeds can help to reduce inflammation, lower your risk for cancer, arthritis, heart disease, improve brain function and be helpful for people with atherosclerosis (hardening of the arteries). The gamma–linolenic acid in these seeds can help reduce nerve pain in your digestive system. This cleans the walls of your colon. Other nutrients include magnesium, phytosterols, ascorbic acid, potassium, beta–carotene, calcium, iron, fiber, phosphorus, riboflavin, thiamin and niacin.

Grinding the seeds, blending them with water and straining out the solid residue, makes hemp milk. Sweeteners, such as coconut nectar and maple syrup can be added. Additionally, spices such as cinnamon, cloves, nutmeg, vanilla extract, and cardamom may be used. Those who suffer from soya and nut allergies will face no problem if they take hemp milk. Hemp Milk will help you to feel energetic. It is full of vitamins, especially A, B, D. It is an excellent source of protein, making it a perfect food for vegetarians, whose diet often lacks in these.

Hemp milk is low in saturated fats, cholesterol and lactose free with a creamy and nutty taste. It improves the immune system, maintains the hair, skin and nails in good condition. Hemp milk is known to sharpen the mental abilities. It is ideal for those who suffer from a heart disease or those who are trying to lose weight. If you purchased Hemp milk you should still avoid any product that uses carrageenan as a thickening agent. *See Hemp Milk recipe page 345.

Almond Milk

Almond milk is one of the most nutritional milk substitutes available today. Almond milk is lactose, gluten, casein and cholesterol free. It is low in calories, at only 40 calories per eight ounce serving. It is low in fat, containing only three grams of fat per eight ounce serving. The milk is a rich source of vitamin E, which is needed to maintain the cells of the body in proper shape. It contains minerals, such as, magnesium, manganese, selenium, phosphorous, potassium, iron, fiber, zinc and calcium, which help in keeping the bones and teeth healthy, improving the immune system and preventing cell or tissue damage.

Almond milk contains high levels of antioxidants, so it can help prevent many types of cancer and slow the signs of aging. The potassium in almonds helps keep blood pressure normal. Since almond milk is free of both saturated fat and cholesterol, it makes it a healthier choice for reducing the risk of heart disease and for those with heart problems. The only thing that cow's milk has more of than almond milk is protein. Cow's milk has eight grams of protein per serving while almond milk has only one gram per serving. Make sure you're getting enough protein from the rest of your diet or consider adding half a scoop of protein powder to almond milk smoothies.

Those with tree nut allergies should avoid almond milk. Almonds are considered Goitrogenic. This means, along with broccoli, flax, cabbage, kale and soy it contains chemicals in it that are considered harmful to the thyroid if consumed in large amounts by those with low functioning thyroids. Commercially available almond milk is often enriched with vitamins A and D, as well as calcium, to make it seem more like regular milk. Sweeteners are added while making almond milk and its sugar content can be much higher than the regular milk. Avoid almond milk with carrageenan, an additive used as a stabilizer and thickener.

Almond milk is alkalizing (as almonds are), yet almond milk can energize a person like the regular cow's milk. You can make almond milk. It is easy to do. This avoids unwanted additives and sweeteners. *See Almond Milk recipe.

Samuel S. Epstein, M.D. What's In Your Milk? Published by Trafford Publishing 2006

"Debunking The Milk Myth: Why Milk Is Bad For You And Your Bones"

http://bit.ly/1SyUaA3

"Nutrition for Breastfeeding Toddlers"

http://bit.ly/1K2FGH2

"What's A Healthier Choice Than Cow's Milk: Rice, Soy or Almond?" http://bit.ly/1Lq8vL1

"The Healthier Choice: Almond Milk vs. Milk"

http://bit.ly/1LlLImB

"Here are 8 Reasons to Eat Hemp Seeds from Healthy Body Now"

http://bit.ly/1MVgT5q

"What about Humanely Raised Milk and Dairy Products?"

http://bit.ly/1QIPU3r

"Almond Milk Vs. Hemp Milk"

http://bit.ly/1TDWpU7

CHAPTER 13
Organic Foods

INDUSTRY ANALYSTS ESTIMATE THAT U.S. organic food sales exceeded $35 billion in 2012 (over 4 percent of total at–home food sales of 760 billion). It is predicted to generate about 42 billion U.S. dollars in 2014. Organic non–food products such as lawn care, household products, flowers, pet food, and fiber are currently almost $2.8 billion of the total organic market. Organic non–food sales have jumped nearly eight–fold since 2002.

National Organic Program (NOP)

The United States Agricultural Department's (USDA) Agricultural Marketing Service implemented a National Organic Program (NOP) in 2002. This program supports organic processors and farmers and provides consumer assurance. USDA uniformed the varying standards among dozens of State and private certification organizations that had emerged by the late 1990s. It also continues to update rules on organic processing and production.

NOP makes certification mandatory for operations with organic sales over $5,000. It has accredited 56 U.S. State and private certification programs, and over 40 foreign programs. Certifying agents review applications from farmers and processors for certification eligibility. Qualified inspectors conduct annual onsite inspections of organic operations.

Products certified as manufactured or produced in compliance with NOP can be identified with the "USDA ORGANIC" seal. This seal conveys the following product information: (1) No synthetically compounded fertilizers and pesticides were used in production except in rare approved instances. (2) There was no application of synthetically formulated fertilizers or pesticides used on the land used in organic production within the last three years. (3) Raw manure was applied to the soil and not applied directly to growing plants, followed by a soil–fallow (plowed but left unseeded) period of 90 or 120 days, depending on whether the manure was composted with defined temperature limits for specific periods of time prior to application or the product grows in contact with the soil. (4) No sewage sludge was used as fertilizer. (5) Irradiation was not used to preserve or sterilize the product. (6) No genetically modified organism (GMO) products or plant varieties were used. (7) Both livestock and poultry had access to out–door space and no growth hormones or antibiotics were used. (8) Processed foods with the USDA ORGANIC seal have 95–100 per cent organic ingredients.

Organic Material Review Institute

The Organic Material Review Institute (OMRI) was founded in 1997 as a non–profit organization. It provides an independent review of products intended for use in certified organic production to organic certifiers, manufactures, growers, and suppliers. OMRI reviews products against the NOP standards. Accepted products are "OMRI Listed" (a registered trademark). All acceptable products appear on the OMRI Products List.

Price–Look–Up Codes (PLU).

Another way to find out if your food is organic is the Price–look–up codes (PLU). These are small stick–on labels in grocery stores on many pieces of produce. These numerical codes give valuable information to checkout clerks. They often list the produce cultivar name and the country of origin. Additionally, if the PLU has 4 numerical digits, the produce was grown conventionally. If the PLU has 5 digits and the first is a 9 followed by 4 other digits, the produce was grown organically. If the first digit is an 8 followed by 4 other numbers, the produce is genetically modified, a GMO.

Children Are More At Risk

Relative to body weight, children take in more toxic chemicals than adults. Their developing organ systems are especially sensitive, more vulnerable and less able to detoxify such chemicals. They are three to four times more prone to allergies than adults. Infants below two years of age are at greatest risk and have the highest incidence of reactions. Michael Meacher, the former minister of the environment for the UK, said, "Any baby food containing GM products could lead to a dramatic rise in allergies."

Milk and dairy products from cows treated with the genetically engineered bovine growth hormone (rbGH) contain an increased amount of the hormone IGF–1. This is one of the highest risk factors associated with prostate and breast cancer. Children generally eat a high percentage of corn in their diets, making GM corn particularly problematic for them.

Breast fed infants can be exposed by way of the mother's diet. Fetuses may possibly be exposed in the womb. Because children's bodies develop at a fast pace, they are more likely to show the effects and be influenced by genetically modified (GM) foods. The EPA's "Guidelines for Carcinogen Risk Assessment" suggest that in the first 2 years of life, children receive 50 per cent of their lifetime cancer risks.

"Higher Risks for Children" http://bit.ly/1TDWt6e

"Statistics and facts on the organic food industry in the U.S." http://bit.ly/1H5AIJc

"Organic Sales In 2013 Grew Nearly 12 Percent" http://bit.ly/1IqPGnH

"Organic Certification" http://1.usa.gov/1I5Ytzz

Energy Medicine Technologies: Ozone Healing, Microcrystals, and the Future of Health Edited & Copyrighted by Finley Eversole, PH.D 2013 Inner Traditions One Park Street Rochester, Vermont 05767 http://bit.ly/1BD1Mxo

Natural versus Organic

All organic foods are natural. All natural foods are not organic. NOP defines the way organic foods are produced and raised. Items labeled "natural" should be suspect. Manufacturers can claim "natural" on their nutritional products if at least 10 percent of the product comes from natural food sources. Some small producers applying organic techniques in their operations vend their goods as "all–natural" at farmer's markets.

Pesticide Data Program (PDP)

The USDA's Pesticide Data Program (PDP) is a national pesticide residue database program. Through the cooperation with State agriculture departments and other Federal agencies, PDP manages the collection, data entry, analysis, and reporting of pesticide residues on agricultural products in the U.S. food supply. There is an emphasis on those products highly consumed by infants and children. The data produced by PDP are reported in an annual summary, which can be used to determine pesticide residue on any U.S. products in the food supply.

Less Pesticides

Organic foods have less pesticide residue than non–organic foods. But all organic production is not pesticide free. A low level of pesticides is expected in organic food since a few pesticides are approved for the use on organic foods. These pesticide used are less toxic, applied at a lower rate, and have shorter residual periods (normally measured in hours) than pesticides used on conventional food.

More Nutritionally Dense

Organic produce is more nutritionally dense, having higher levels of nutrients than conventional produce. This is partly because organics promotes the practice of eating a diet consisting of food harvested within a hundred mile radius. This reduced distance in food being transported produces fresher food. It uses less fossil fuel and creates strong local food systems that support environmental sustainability. The possibility of contamination is also reduced when there is no highly concentrated national food system.

Poultry, Eggs, Beef and Pork

There are organic guidelines for the production of poultry, eggs, beef products and pork. There must be humane treatment of the animals and settings where the animals have access to outdoor space and have room to exercise. The health of these animals is maintained by a diet that does not rely on antibiotics for survival. Organic feed must be used.

The industrialization of meat production has introduced large confined animal feeding operations (CAOs). They provide low cost meat in vast quantities. The efforts to efficiently operate these CAOs are not without the concerns for the healthfulness of the food products generated and the environmental costs.

Antibiotics

Cattle and corn are transported many miles to a CAO for the final "finishing". During this period while the animals are waiting to be slaughtered they are fed a predominant diet of corn. It is believed that corn tenderizes and flavors the meat with fat deposits between the muscle fibers. Cows are designed by nature to eat only grasses. They can't survive a concentrated corn or grain diet without the aid of low–level antibiotics. Over 80 percent of all antibiotics used in the United States are used in food animals.

Since the 1950s, it has become routine practice to add low–levels of antibiotics to the water or feed of even healthy cattle, poultry, and swine. This was to promote faster growth and prevent infections that tend to occur when animals are housed in unsanitary, crowded, stressful conditions. Giving animals continuous low–levels of antibiotics creates a major health concern. The concern is the rise of drug–resistant bacteria that pose a growing public health risk.

That is because bacteria such as E. coli exposed to continuous low–levels of antibiotics can become resistant to the antibiotics and may contaminate meat products through contact with fecal matter during the "finishing" process. Bacteria can share the traits that make them drug–resistant with other kinds of bacteria. This makes the drugs doctors rely on to treat illnesses like strep throat, childhood ear infections and pneumonia less effective. It can lead to widespread drug–resistance and the creation of bacterial super–bugs.

There are a few new antibiotics to replace those that prove no longer effective. But many of them are expensive and have greater side effects associated with them. "Antibiotic resistance" has been reported as a growing health concern by the American Public Health Association (APHA), American Medical Association (AMA) and the National Institute of Health (NIH). A decrease in resistance has been reported in European countries where antibiotics have been banned in animal production.

"Science and Laboratories" http://1.usa.gov/1LlM2lc

"What You Need to Know About Antibiotics Abuse on Farms" http://on.nrdc.org/1I5YHa7

Hormones

Organic production of animal products does not allow the use of growth hormones. Milk from dairy cows on organic farms, particularly pasture–based operations, often contains 30 percent higher levels of conjugated linoleic acids (CLAs) than conventional milk. CLA is best known for its anti–cancer properties, reducing the risk for cardiovascular disease, weight management and helping fight inflammation.

Factory farms in the U.S. use hormones to promote milk production in dairy cows and promote growth in beef cattle. This is done with the approval of the United States Dairy Association (USDA) and Federal Drug Administration. It is estimated that two thirds of all U.S. cattle raised for slaughter are given growth hormones. The Europeans banned the use of growth hormones for beef in 1988.

The European Commission Committee reported in 1999 that residue in meat from animals injected with hormones could affect the hormonal balance in humans. This could cause reproductive issues, and breast, colon, or prostate cancer. The European Commission does not allow the importation of any beef treated with hormones, meaning no U.S. beef is accepted.

About 22 percent of all dairy cows and 54 percent of large herds in the U.S. use recombinant bovine growth hormone (rBGH) to get 8–17 percent increase in milk production. Bacterial bladder infections in cows increase by 25 percent when rBGH is used. This necessitates the use of antibiotics to treat the infections. Another hormone called insulin–like growth factor–1, linked to breast and colon cancer in humans, is in high levels in the milk of cows given rBGH.

Regulations do not allow the use of hormones in poultry and pigs. But antibiotics are used routinely. Tight confinement of chickens and pigs encourage the use of low levels of antibiotics to promote faster growth, insure health and prevent infections that tend to occur when animals are housed in crowded unsanitary, stressful conditions. This continuous use of antibiotics can impact not only the consumers of eggs and meat, but the animal caretakers as well.

The benefits of using organic foods are noticeable and far reaching for anyone concerned with their own health and the health of our planet.

"Health Benefits of Organic Milk" http://bit.ly/1FtnLS2

"Factory Farming and Human Health" http://bit.ly/1dW3bnk

"Why Are Factory Farm Animals Give Antibiotics and Hormones Such As rBGH?" http://abt.cm/1MTIowg

"rBGH or rBST" http://bit.ly/1MVhuUR

CHAPTER 14
GMO Foods

Genetically modified organisms (GMOs) have been linked to premature aging, immune problems, infertility, faulty insulin regulation, and changes in major organs and the gastrointestinal system. Genetically modified (GM) foods were made possible by technology developed in the 1970s. Genes from one species are forced into the DNA of another. Genes produce proteins, which in turn can generate traits or characteristics.

The promised traits associated with GMOs by biotechnology companies were that their engineered crops yield more, require less pesticide use, have no impact on the environment and are safe to eat. Sadly, the research shows none of the promises have come true. The only two traits found to exist in nearly all commercialized GM plants are pesticide production and herbicide tolerance.

Herbicide–resistant canola, soy, cotton and corn plants comprise about 80% of all GM plants. They are engineered with bacterial genes that allow them to survive otherwise deadly doses of herbicides. This may give farmers more flexibility in weeding, but it also gives the GM seed company lots of profits. Farmers who buy GM seeds must sign a contract to buy only that seed producer's brand of herbicide.

The corn and cotton varieties, which account for about 20% of all GM plants, produce a pesticide in every cell. This is accomplished due to a gene from a soil bacterium called Bacillus thuringienesis (Bt). Bt produces a natural insect killing poison called Bt–toxin. Disease resistant zucchini and crook–neck squash make up under 1% of GMO plants.

The Food and Drug Administration (FDA) has regulatory jurisdiction over food and food additives. The FDA labeled GM foods as "generally recognized as safe" (GRAS). This status allows a product to be commercialized without the need for additional testing. Under U.S. law, to be considered GRAS the substance must be the subject of a substantial amount of peer–reviewed published studies or the equivalent. Additionally, there must be an overwhelming consensus among the scientific community that the product is safe. GM foods had neither requirement.

The government's desire to boost U.S. exports was evidenced by Vice President Dan Qualye on May 26, 1992 where he chaired the Council on Competiveness, which identified the GM crops as the crops to boost our exports. He announced reforms to simplify and speed up the process of GM products to market without being hampered by unnecessary regulations.

There was also the powerful influence of large agricultural corporations on the government. The passage of the non–regulation policy on GM foods would result in large profits for the providers of GM foods. They would save the time and cost associated with additional testing, peer–reviewed published studies, and an overwhelming consensus that the product is safe among the scientific community.

The agriculture biotech company with the greatest influence was Monsanto. Michael Taylor, a former outside attorney for Monsanto and the Food Biotechnology Council had a special position created for him at the FDA in 1991. He oversaw the development of the policy on non–regulation of GM foods. Soon after working with the FDA he became Monsanto's vice president and chief lobbyist. In 2010, he was appointed to another newly created post at the FDA, this time as Deputy Commissioner for Foods.

"The person who may be responsible for more food–related illness and death than anyone in history has just been made the US food safety czar," writes foremost healthy food consumer advocate Jeffrey Smith over at the Huffington Post.

In 1992, 3 days after Quayle's announcement, the FDA unveiled its policy on non–regulation with respect to genetically modified foods. It provided that foods developed through genetic modification are not inherently dangerous and, except in rare cases, should not require extraordinary premarket regulation and testing.

Under this non–regulation policy, GM foods are regulated as ordinary foods, and not food additives. There are no required labeling or safety evaluations of GMOs. A company can introduce GM foods to the market without telling the FDA. Also, the self–policing of GM foods by the producers, will ensure that GM crops are GRAS as long as their producers say they are.

The experts at FDA were extremely concerned. Internal memos made public from a lawsuit showed that the overwhelming consensus of the FDA scientists was that GM crops can have hard to detect, unpredictable side effects. Many experts believed this radical technology carried "serious health hazards". They called for careful, lengthy research that would include human trials before any genetically modified organisms (GMOs) could safely be released into the food supply. Their concerns were largely ignored in favor of the non–regulation of GM foods.

There are many reasons GM plants present dangers. GMOs are inherently unsafe because the process of engineering it of itself creates unpredictable alterations. The gene insertion process creates mutations around the insertion site and elsewhere. Because of the mutations harmless protein may be transferred into a deadly or dangerous version.

Studies demonstrate that GM diets show toxic reactions in the digestive tract. Examples of this include rats fed GM potatoes. They showed proliferated cell growth in both the stomach and the intestinal walls, less developed brain, liver, and testicles, partial atrophy (shriveled up) of the liver and damaged immune system. The other example, GM peas, produced an inflammatory response in mice, suggesting that the peas might trigger a deadly anaphylactic shock in allergic humans. These peas were destroyed before commercialization.

Both dangerous crops could have been easily approved for commercialization. They were only discovered because the researchers used advanced tests that were never applied to GM crops currently on the market. These unsafe crops would have passed the normal tests that companies typically used to get their products approved.

Mice fed potatoes engineered to produce the Bt–toxin developed damaged and abnormal cells. Cell proliferation can be a precursor to cancer.

A number of safety studies show that GM diets cause liver and organ damage, reproductive failures, infant mortality and higher death rates in rats, mice and rabbits. GM crops have been shown to trigger immune reactions and may cause allergies. Many farmers have reported livestock sterility and deaths when feeding them Bt. (Bacillus thuringienesis) corn

Recommendations

Do not eat GM foods and GM ingredients. Avoid them whenever possible.

"Who is Michael Taylor, Really? Monsanto, The FDA And A History Of Evil" http://bit.ly/1focSvS

"The Food And Drug Administration Policy On Genetically Modified Foods" http://bit.ly/1RjxO2Y

"Former Pro–GMO Researcher Tells It Like It Is"
http://bit.ly/1BD2dHK

Smith, Jeffrey M. Seeds Of Deception: Exposing Industry and Government Lies About The Safety Of The Genetically Engineered Foods You're Eating. Published by Yes Books 2003

CHAPTER 15
Fruit

THE NATURAL SUGARS AND invigorating quality of fruit make it a wonderful substitute for food containing chemical or refined sweeteners. Compared to animal products, fruits are generally higher in fiber and lower in calories and fat. Fruit contains health–enhancing minerals, vitamins, enzymes and fiber. They are also packed with potent protective plant compounds such as antioxidants.

Juice

Eating the whole fruit is healthier for you than drinking the juice. When eating the whole fruit, the natural sugars and fibers help to keep your blood sugar stable and make you feel full. Fruit juice that has no fiber and nutrients is basically just a concentrated source of sugar. It lacks the supportive nutrients to help it digest and metabolize (break down). Fruit juice elevates blood sugar quicker than whole fruit. The level of sugar obtained from fruit juice is higher than the level found in whole fruit.

Drinking fruit juices all day long between meals weakens the body. Notice infants who drink apple juice most of the day. They lose their appetite and become irritable and weak. Infants should not be given juice and put to sleep. The sugary juice on the infant teeth will begin the journey to tooth decay.

Listed below are some of the top rated healthy fruits and their benefits:

Blueberries – contain rich antioxidants, which breaks down fat and cholesterol and helps protect against cancer, heart disease, obesity and diabetes. They have a substantial amount of lutein, a potent antioxidant that helps prevent cataracts and macular degeneration. They also contain compounds that can protect against urinary tract infections.

Watermelon – Watermelon is actually a vegetable, belonging to the cucumber and squash family. It originated in Africa. At 92 percent water and 8 percent sugar, it is a perfect remedy for constipation, lowering blood pressure, and treating diabetes. Watermelon is used to treat urinary difficulties. It is packed with lycopene, a powerful antioxidant, which helps to reduce cancer risk. Eat watermelons with seeds.

Apples – Red Delicious, considered the healthiest apply variety, has the most health–promoting antioxidants. Gala and Granny Smith are the runners–up. Eat the skin for a high dose of fiber that helps lower cholesterol and keeps you regular. An apple is packed with antioxidants and supplies 15 percent of your daily fiber needs.

Grapefruit – Grapefruit is packed with vitamin C, the antioxidants that can substantially lower triglyceride (fat in the blood) levels and cholesterol. It is high in enzymes that burn fat. Grapefruit treats poor digestion, lung congestion and helps overcome alcohol intoxication. It is used to alleviate gas, pain, and swelling.

Kiwi – Ounce for ounce, kiwis contain more than twice the amount of vitamin C as oranges. One large fruit contains enough vitamin C to meet your daily requirements. Kiwis are an excellent source of fiber, potassium, and vitamin E, which is good for healthy skin and a healthy immune system. Kiwis may lower the risk of cataracts and could even protect DNA from damage.

Cantaloupe – Cantaloupes contain a good source of a potent antioxidant, vitamin C. This helps fight free radicals in your body spreading damage to your cells, causing diseases and signs of aging. Cantaloupe has concentrated amounts of beta–carotene, a powerful antioxidant that strengthens your immune system, which makes you less susceptible to flu and colds.

Half a cantaloupe gives you nearly a full day's supply of beta-carotene. The body converts beta-carotene into vitamin A, which is essential for the maintenance of healthy eyesight. A rich source of potassium, which normalizes the heartbeat and promotes the supply of oxygen to the brain, makes you feel more relaxed and focused.

Papaya – Half of a papaya gives you over 150 percent of your daily vitamin C. Papaya is also a great source of potassium, which normalizes the heartbeat, promotes the supply of oxygen to the brain and makes you feel more focused and relaxed. It is a good source of folate, which protects against birth defects. Papaya contains a substance that helps improve your digestion, papain. It is used for treating the pain of rheumatism. For a great facial mask treatment, simply rub the inside of the papaya skin on your face.

Pears – Once called the "gift of the gods" by Homer, pears are packed with nutrients, antioxidants and fiber, making them a delicious but healthful snack. One pear gives 11 percent of our daily requirement of vitamin C and 9.5 percent of copper. It is an excellent source of dietary fiber, which can lower levels of bad cholesterol and reduce the risk of stroke, colon and breast cancer.

Doctors generally consider pears to be a "safe" or hypoallergenic fruit because they are less likely than other fruits to produce an allergic response when eaten. For this reason, pears are often one of the first fruits given to infants. Because they are high in fiber the bloodstream slowly absorbs a pear's carbohydrates. This prevents a spike in blood sugar and helps to control blood glucose levels, making them a smart snack for those with diabetes. Pears are used for constipation, injuries to the skin, and loss of voice.

Strawberries – A handful each day provides antioxidants that help prevent heart disease, control type 2 diabetes and reduce inflammation. They are very rich in silicon and vitamin C, which is useful for all arterial and connective tissue repair. Strawberries are used for sore throat. They strengthen teeth and gums, improve appetite and relieve urinary difficulties.

Tomato – Often considered a vegetable, tomatoes are a citric fruit. They are high in vitamin A and Vitamin C. These important antioxidant vitamins work to defend DNA damage from free radicals. Thus, tomatoes may help prevent age related diseases such as diabetes and atherosclerosis. Tomatoes contain important nutrients that help reduce inflammation, heart disease and prevent cancer.

Studies have shown the more tomatoes people eat the lower their risks of certain cancers, especially, stomach, lung and prostate cancers. A substance responsible for tomatoes red color, lycopene, is thought to be the reason for this cancer protection. Cooked tomatoes contain even more lycopene than raw ones. Cooking breaks down the cell walls, helping to release the lycopene. Also, eating tomatoes with a little bit of fat, such as olive oil, helps the body to better absorb lycopene.

Tomatoes clean the liver, purify the blood and detoxify the body in general. They are used in cases of diminished appetite, indigestion and constipation. Tomatoes relieve high blood pressure, red eye and headache. Since they upset calcium metabolism (break down), they should not be used in cases of arthritis.

Bananas – They are relatively low in calories and almost fat free. Bananas are high in potassium yet low in sodium. Bananas help reduce blood pressure. This lowers your risk of high blood pressure and stroke. Bananas help to detoxify the body and lubricate the intestines and lungs. They also treat constipation and depression. Bananas contain protease inhibitors that can help eliminate bacteria that have been targeted as a primary cause of stomach ulcers.

Grape – Grapes make a great snack for children. They contain resveratrol, a powerful antioxidant that helps fight heart disease. While red wine is a source, you get almost as much resveratrol in a cup of dark–colored grapes as you do in a five–ounce glass of merlot. Grapes help to build and purify blood and improve cleansing functions of the glands. Grapes benefit the kidneys, liver, bones and are used to treat rheumatism and arthritis. They are also valuable for liver malfunctions such as hepatitis and jaundice

Orange – A single medium sized orange gives you almost a full day's vitamin C, plus potassium. The membrane around each wedge contains hesperidin, a potent bioflavonoid and antioxidant which may lower cholesterol. Oranges are a general tonic for weak digestion and poor appetite. They benefit gums and teeth and are valuable for inflammation. According to research, even the scent is calming. Tangerines make a good substitute for commercial oranges. They have many of the same properties but are sprayed less with chemicals.

Tracye Lynn McQuirter *By Any Greens Necessary* Published by Lawence Hill Books © 2010

Paul Pitchford Healing With Whole Foods Published by North Atlantic Books Berkeley, California © 2002

"Fruit Or Vegetable — Do You Know The Difference?"
http://mayocl.in/1FtoaUx

"The 8 Healthiest Fruits You Should Be Eating"
http://bit.ly/1FtoeDR

"How Does Fruit Juice Compare To Whole Fruit?"
http://bit.ly/1SyVmmX

"5 Health Benefits of Cantaloupe" http://bit.ly/1I5ZMyF

"5 Health Benefits of Pears"
http://bit.ly/1JayhWo

"5 Health Benefits of Tomatoes" http://bit.ly/1LlMqA5

CHAPTER 16
Vegetables

VEGETABLES, PARTICULARLY LEAFY GREENS, have numerous health benefits. Leafy vegetables are packed with fiber along with minerals, vitamins, and plant–based substances that may help protect you from heart disease, diabetes, and perhaps even cancer. According to the Center for Science in the Public Interest (CSPI), the minerals, vitamins, and phytochemicals in green leafy vegetables reduce colon cancer, improve memory, build strong bones and decrease the risk of stroke. Vegetables give you the most for your money of all foods. They have the fewest calories and the most nutrition.

Below is a list of the top healthy leafy vegetables and some of their benefits:

Kale – If a vegetable wore a cape, it would be kale. It is full of the most vision and bone–protecting vitamins of the greens on this list, lutein and K. It is an excellent source of chlorophyll, calcium, potassium and vitamins A and C. Vitamin A helps in the maintenance of good vision and strengthens your immune system. Vitamin C provides protection against free radical injury and flu–like viral infections.

Kale is also high in folate (water–soluble B vitamin). Folate, also called folic acid, has an important role in DNA synthesis. When it is given before, and during early pregnancy it may help prevent neural tube defects in newborn babies. It also helps to ease lung congestion and can be used to treat ulcers.

Spinach – Popeye's favorite vegetable is low in calories and high in nutrition. It has 20 calories per serving. Spinach is rich in iron, folate (water–soluble B vitamin), and vitamins A and C. It helps cleanse the blood of toxins that cause skin disease, prevent the risk of constipation and protect against heart disease. It is also a source of omega–3 oils.

Swiss Chard – A member of the beet family. It is a good source of vitamins A and C. Swiss Chard is high in the antioxidants that help to protect against mascular degeneration. Also, Swiss Chard's unique phytonutrients may offer special benefits for blood sugar control.

Cabbage – Low in calories and high in water content, cabbage is a good source of fiber. This makes it a good choice for those who are trying to prevent or manage type 2 diabetes, heart disease or weight lost. Purple cabbage is packed with antioxidants, one of the cheapest vegetables to buy, lasts a long time in your refrigerator crisper, and can easily be eaten cooked just as deliciously raw.

Cabbage is high in vitamin and mineral content. A single serving of raw purple cabbage contains about 20 percent of your daily recommended intake (DRI) for vitamin A and about 80 percent of your DRI for vitamin C (more than oranges). It also contains notable levels of folate, vitamin K, calcium, magnesium and potassium. Cabbage benefits the stomach and improves digestion. It is used to treat constipation, the common cold, whooping cough and frostbite. Cabbage helps rid the digestion system of worms.

Collards – If any vegetable should wear a cape, it should be the collard greens. The cholesterol–lowering ability of collard greens may be the greatest of all commonly eaten cruciferous vegetables such as cauliflower, cabbage, cress, bok choy and broccoli. Collards are high in vitamin K, which helps keep bones strong. They contain folate (water–soluble B vitamin), niacin, thiamine, phosphorus and potassium. The phytonutrients in collards helps protect against obesity, diabetes, heart disease, ovarian and breast cancers.

Consuming collars help to promote a healthy complexion, hair and increased energy.

Turnip greens – Low in calories yet rich in vision–protecting lutein. Turnip greens are also high in folate (water–soluble B vitamin), vitamins A, C and K and calcium. Calcium helps to support the health of your teeth, prevent bone softening, fractures, and osteoporosis. Turnips help to detoxify the body and build the blood. It is helpful for indigestion, hoarseness and diabetes.

Mustard greens – The cholesterol–lowering ability of steamed mustard greens is second only to steamed collard greens. The strongest of the bitter greens, these spicy greens are an excellent source of vitamins C and A, which helps in the maintenance of good vision and strengthens your immune system. It also contains an excellent source of several essential minerals such as calcium, iron, magnesium, potassium, and manganese.

Mustards contain an essential nutrient that is necessary for blood clotting, vitamin K, and antioxidants that help remove free radicals from your body, thus preventing cancer. Regular consumption of mustard greens in the diet is known to prevent arthritis, osteoporosis, iron deficiency anemia and believed to protect from cardiovascular diseases, asthma, colon and prostate cancers. It also helps to clear chest congestion and improves energy circulation.

Beet greens – Beet tops are a great source of iron and vitamins A, C, and K. These vitamins help to strengthen your immune system, improve vision, remove free radicals from your body and boost the strength in your bones.

Dandelion greens – Low in calories yet high in calcium. One cup of chopped dandelion greens has 10% of the recommended daily value of calcium. That is slightly more calcium than kale. These greens are rich in Iron and loaded with antioxidants. Dandelion greens are high in vitamins A and C. Vitamin C helps facilitate iron absorption. High in protein, these greens have more protein per serving than spinach.

The nutrients in dandelion greens may help reduce the risk of stroke, cancer, cataracts and age–related macular degeneration. Dandelion contains anti–inflammatory properties, which may help those with asthma and other inflammatory diseases. These greens are known to help detoxify and cleanse the liver.

Non–leafy Vegetables

The non–leafy vegetables listed below contain good sources of vitamins, minerals and antioxidants. Antioxidants are natural substances that may prevent or delay some types of cell damage. Eating a diet rich in vegetables and fruits as part of an overall healthy diet may also reduce the risk for heart disease, stroke and may even protect against certain types of cancers.

Choose your vegetables from a rainbow of colors. Vegetables are like fruit. They need not be cooked. They are already done. Eat them fresh (raw) as often as possible. Vegetables can be steamed, stir–fried, baked or sautéed. Adding the right herbs and spices can make your vegetable more healthy, tasty, and delicious.

Below is a list of the top non–leafy vegetables and some of their benefits:

Sweet potatoes – This is another vegetable that should ware a cape. It is high in folate. Folate, also called folic acid, has an important role in DNA synthesis. When it is given before, and during early pregnancy it may help prevent neural tube defects in newborn babies.

Sweet potatoes contain almost twice as much fiber as other types of potatoes. The high fiber content gives them a "slow burning" quality resulting in their caloric energy being used more slowly and efficiently than a low–fiber carbohydrate. This helps with weight management.

They contain a large amount of vitamin B6, which prevents hardening of the arteries and blood vessels. The high amounts of potassium plays an important role in lowering blood pressure by ridding the body of excess sodium and regulating fluid balance. Potassium helps regulate the natural rhythm of the heart, and maintains normal function of the central nervous system and brain.

Sweet potatoes contain Beta–carotene, which the body converts to Vitamin A, an important antioxidant. One medium sweet potato provides your body with the complete recommended daily allowance of vitamin A. Vitamin A is useful in the prevention of several different types of cancer. It helps to internally protect your skin from sun damage. It is also an excellent nutrient for eye health, useful for night blindness and helps prevent macular degeneration.

These potatoes contain Manganese, a trace mineral that has great health benefits. It helps support healthy blood sugar levels, which can help stabilize the appetite for hours as opposed to the temporary satisfaction that comes with most other carbohydrates. Sweet potatoes are also rich in vitamins C and E, potent antioxidant vitamins that play an important role in disease prevention and longevity.

Asparagus – Asparagus is packed with powerful antioxidants. It is ranked among the top vegetables and fruits for its ability to neutralize cell–damaging free radicals. According to preliminary research, this may help slow the aging process. This plant is low in calories, high in water content and a good amount of fiber. This makes it a good choice for those who are trying to prevent or manage type 2 diabetes, heart disease or weight lost.

It is a good source of folate. A half–cup serving provides nearly 60 percent of the recommended daily allowance. This is good news for pregnant women. Asparagus is a good source of fiber, vitamins A, C, E and K, as well as chromium, a trace mineral that is important to your body's insulin performance.

Asparagus contains a rich source of Glutathione (GSH), an important antioxidant that helps break down cancer causing substances (carcinogens) and other harmful compounds like free radicals. This is why eating asparagus may help prevent certain forms of cancer, such as colon, larynx bone, breast, and lung cancers.

Asparagus helps to cleanse the arteries of cholesterol and is used for hypertension and hardening of the arteries. It also contains high levels of an amino acid, which serves as a natural diuretic and helps rid the body of excess salts. This is beneficial for people who suffer from an accumulation of fluids in the body's tissues (edema) and those with high blood pressure or other heart–related diseases.

Broccoli – Broccoli shares the immune boosting, cancer fighting properties with other cruciferous vegetables such as Brussels sprouts, cauliflower and cabbage. Broccoli is packed with soluble fiber that draws cholesterol out of your body, maintains low blood sugar, prevents constipation, curbs overeating and aids in digestion. Broccoli contains high levels of calcium and vitamin K, which are important for bone health. Of all the cruciferous vegetables, broccoli has the most concentrated source of vitamin C.

Broccoli's anti–inflammatory properties may be able to prevent (or reverse) some of the blood vessel linings damage that can be caused by inflammation due to chronic blood sugar problems. A good source of potassium and folate, broccoli helps protect against prostate cancer. Used for nearsightedness and eye inflammation, it is low on calories. It is also a good source of potassium, and vitamin A, which benefits rough skin, helps vision and is required for the immune system and production of red blood cells.

Carrots – Low in calories and high in water content, carrots are a good amount of fiber. This makes it a good choice for those who are trying to prevent or manage type 2 diabetes, heart disease or weight loss. High in beta–carotene, they help improve your vision, especially night vision. The potassium in carrots helps preserve bone health and lower blood pressure.

Carrots contain an essential oil that destroys roundworms and pin worms. They protect against ear infections and improve liver function. Carrots treat indigestion and heartburn. In addition to helping maintain healthy hair and skin, the antioxidants in carrots may also help to prevent macular degeneration, arthritis, heart disease and cancer.

Eggplant – Actually a fruit, eggplant blends with other foods like a non–starchy vegetable. Eggplant is high in dietary fiber, which keeps the digestive system working properly, protects against colon cancer and keeps the stomach feeling full after a meal. Low in carbohydrates and calories, eggplants contains no fats, so they can easily be included in one's daily diet without the fear of weight gain.

Eggplant contains vitamin C, folate, B vitamins, and vitamin A, which improve the body's overall health and boost the immune system. It is high in chlorogenic acid, a strong antioxidant that helps to lower low density lipoprotein (LDL) ("bad" cholesterol) and fights the free radicals that cause cancer. Furthermore, experts believe that chlorogenic acid has antiviral properties, which can help prevent and treat diseases caused by viruses.

Eggplant contains properties, which protect and prevent cells from mutating into cancerous cells. Eggplant has a rich source of flavonoids (super–antioxidants found in many natural foods). The flavonoids help to renew arteries, reduces swelling and helps prevent strokes. The phytonutrients in eggplants help protect cell membranes from free radical damage.

Celery – Low in calories and high in water content, celery has a good amount of fiber. This makes it a good choice for those who are trying to prevent or manage type 2 diabetes, heart disease or weight lost. Celery hydrates your body and helps flush out toxins, keeping your skin and other organs healthy. It is very high in silicon, which helps renew bones, joints, arteries and all connective tissues.

Celery is a good source of quercetin, an anti–inflammatory antioxidant, which some research suggests may help prevent memory loss and arthritis. It contains potassium, which help preserves bone health and lower blood pressure. Celery benefits the stomach, treats high blood pressure, eye inflammation and acne. It is helpful in headaches caused by high blood pressure. Celery also contains luteolin, an antioxidant, which may help protect against brain inflammation that can lead to dementia.

Peppers –The richest source of vitamins A, C, and K are found in sweet red peppers, They contain high amounts of cancer–fighting lycopene, an antioxidant compound that gives tomatoes and certain other fruits and vegetables their bright red color. The capaicin contained in peppers that gives hot peppers their heat also protects against stomach ulcers, reduces LDL (bad) cholesterol and boost the immune system. Red peppers prevent malaria and cold conditions. Black peppers expels gas and are recommended for pain in bowels.

Watermelon – Watermelon is actually a vegetable, belonging to the cucumber and squash family. It originated in Africa. At 92 percent water and 8 percent sugar, it is a perfect remedy for constipation, lowering blood pressure, and treating diabetes. Watermelon is used to treat urinary difficulties. It is packed with lycopene, a powerful antioxidant, which helps to reduce cancer risk. Eat watermelons with seeds.

The juice of the watermelon is highly alkaline. Watermelon is the most alkaline of all the melons. Bacteria and viruses can't thrive nor live in a highly alkaline environment. By maintaining a highly alkaline environment in your body as opposed to an acidic one, viruses are avoided. Here are some human diseases caused by viruses: Burkitt's lymphoma, chicken pox, colds, Colorado tick fever, dengue, encephalitis, fever blisters, genital herpes, German Measles, mononucleosis, mumps, oral herpes, polio, rabies, shingles, smallpox, warts, and yellow fever.

Watermelon should contain seeds. If the melon is seedless (contains no seeds) it can't germinate. That means, you have no seed to grow another watermelon. Seedless watermelons are melons with altered DNA (Deoxyribonucleic acid). DNA is a molecule that encodes the genetic instructions used in the development and functioning of all known living organisms. Seedless watermelon or any other fruit without seed is just not natural. The reason a plant produces fruit is to house the seed.

A seedless watermelon is a genetically modified watermelon. This genetic modification is done chemically. To create a seedless watermelon, seed producers must treat natural watermelon seed with Colchicines, a chromosome altering chemical. Colchicines change the chromosomes number in the seeds from 2 to 4.

Once this is done, the seeds are pollinated with the natural 2 chromosome watermelon. The result is an un–natural, genetically modified watermelon with 3 chromosomes.

Does this sound natural to you?

Some consider genetic engineering to be only when there is cutting, splicing and the introduction of DNA material. But when chemicals are used which alter the DNA of watermelons the results are similar. Chemically altering genetic material is still a modification of the DNA.

Yams – There are about 200 varieties of yam. The flesh may be varying colors including ivory, yellow, purple or white. Yams contain vitamin B6, which has been shown to reduce the risk of heart attack and stroke. They are a good source of potassium, a mineral that helps to control blood pressure. Yams' complex carbohydrates and fiber slow the rate at which their sugars are released and absorbed into the bloodstream, providing help with blood sugar and weight control.

Tracye Lynn McQuirter *By Any Greens Necessary* Published by Lawence Hill Books © 2010

Paul Pitchford Healing With Whole Foods Published by North Atlantic Books Berkeley, California © 2002

"Leafy Greens — Ranked and Rated" http://wb.md/1Lq9ASR

"What are the health benefits of collard greens?" http://bit.ly/1I60bRG

"10 Reasons You Should Use Dandelion Greens In Your Green Smoothie" http://bit.ly/1TDXUSh/

"What's New and Beneficial About Mustard Greens" http://bit.ly/1K2X6Sr

"What Are the Health Benefits of Collard Greens, Turnips, Kale & Mustard Greens?" http://bit.ly/1CjUbhI

"What's New and Beneficial About Swiss Chard" http://bit.ly/1fodDVP

"3 Benefits of Beet Greens" http://bit.ly/1SyVVxd

"5 Huge Health Benefits Of Sweet Potatoes" http://bit.ly/1QIREtu

"5 Powerful Health Benefits Of Asparagus You Probably Didn't Probably Didn't Know" http://bit.ly/1TDY8IX

"Vegetables: How Food Affects Health" http://bit.ly/1I60ETX

"7 Health Benefits of Broccoli" http://bit.ly/1GyKfoL

"What Are the Health Benefits of Carrots?" http://bit.ly/1JayWGX

"Following Are Top 3 Health Benefits Of Eggplants" http://bit.ly/1d80vT0

Jeffery M. Smith *Seeds of Deception* Publisher: Yes! Books, 2003

Jeffery M. Smith *Genetic Roulette* Publisher: Yes! Books, 2007

Jeffrey M. Smith "Non GMO Shopping Guide" http://seedsofdeception.com

Seedless Watermelon Is GMO" http://bit.ly/1fodUbf

"Backgrounder on Genetic Modification of Crops and Animals" http://bit.ly/1MViS9W

"Seedless Watermelon and GMO Facts" http://bit.ly/1FtoZwz

CHAPTER 17

The Dirty Dozen and Clean 15

THE FOOD QUALITY PROTECTION Act of 1996 authorized the Environmental Working Group (EWG) to assess pesticides in light of their particular dangers to children and to ensure that pesticides posed a "reasonable certainty of no harm" to children or any other high–risk group. EWG analyzes pesticide residue testing data from the U.S. Department of Agriculture (USDA) and Food and Drug Administration (FDA). This law is credited with reducing the risks of pesticide residues on food. It forced American agribusiness to move away from some of the riskiest pesticides.

But all troublesome chemicals are not completely out of the food supply. A handful of foods still contain residues of many hazardous pesticides. EWG publishes its annual shopper's guide rating of conventional foods. It lists the produce with the most and least pesticide residues. This agency was designed to fill the void left by the U.S. Environmental Protection Agency (EPA), which has largely failed to tell Americans they have a right to know about the risks of pesticide exposure and ways they can reduce pesticides in their diets.

EWG has come up with rankings for these popular produce items listed below. All 51 foods are listed below from worst to best. The lower the numbers, the more pesticide residue the produce contains. The top 12 produce items contain the most pesticide residue. These are considered the "Dirty Dozen". Buy these organic whenever possible. The last 15 produce items, having less pesticide residue than the rest, are considered the "Clean 15". These are the least sprayed. There is no need to buy them organic.

(Dirty Dozen)

1. Apples
2. Strawberries
3. Grapes
4. Celery
5. Peaches
6. Spinach
7. Sweet bell peppers
8. Nectarines (imported)
9. Cucumbers
10. Cherry Tomatoes
11. Snap Peas (imported)
12. Potatoes
13. Hot Peppers
14. Blueberries (domestic)
15. Lettuce
16. Kale/Collard Greens
17. Plums
18. Cherries
19. Nectarines (Domestic)
20. Pears
21. Tangerines
22. Carrots
23. Blueberries (Imported)
24. Green Beans
25. Winter Squash
26. Summer Squash
27. Raspberries
28. Broccoli
29. Snap Peas (Domestic)
30. Green Onions
31. Oranges

32. Bananas
33. Tomatoes
34. Watermelon
35. Honeydew Melon
36. Mushrooms

(Clean 15)

37. Sweet Potatoes
38. Cauliflower
39. Cantaloupe
40. Grapefruit
41. Eggplant
42. Kiwi
43. Papayas
44. Mangoes
45. Asparagus
46. Onions
47. Sweet Peas (Frozen)
48. Cabbage
49. Pineapples
50. Sweet Corn
51. Avocados

EWG's 2014 Shopper's Guide to Pesticides in Produce http://www.ewg.org/foodnews/

CHAPTER 18

Herbs And Spices

HERBS AND SPICES HAVE more disease–fighting antioxidants than most fruits and vegetables.

Allspice (whole, powder): Allspice, also called pepper, Jamaica pepper, English pepper, pimenta, pimento, myrtle pepper or newspice. It is a cured, unripe berry from a tree native to the tropical evergreen rain forest of Central American region and Caribbean islands. Generally, it takes five years before the plant starts to bear fruits.

Ground allspice has a strong spicy taste. The aroma closely resembles a mixture of nutmeg, black pepper, cinnamon and cloves.

The spice contains a good amount of potassium, which helps control blood pressure and heart rate. It has a good amount of a copper, selenium, magnesium and iron, required for red blood cell production in the bone marrow.

The spice also contains very good amounts of vitamin A, vitamin B–6, riboflavin, niacin and vitamin C, a powerful natural antioxidant. Regular consumption of foods rich in vitamin C helps the body develop resistance against infectious diseases and harmful, pro–inflammatory free radicals. The active principles in allspice have been found to have anti–inflammatory, carminative, soothing, warming and anti–flatulent properties. Allspice improves digestion.

By Any Greens Necessary by Tracye Lynn McQuirter Publisher: Lawrence Hill Books 2010

"Allspice" http://www.rxlist.com/allspice/supplements.htm
"Pimento/allspice"
http://www.herbwisdom.com/herb–pimento.html

Basil: Basil is also called Albahaca, Basilic, Basilic Commun, Basilic Grand, Basilic Grand Vert, Basilic Romain, Basilic aux Sauces, Basilici Herba, Basilici Herba, Common Basil, Garden Basil, Krishna Tulsi, Munjariki, Ocimum basilicum, St. Josephwort, Surasa, Sweet Basil, Vanatulasi, Varvara, and Visva Tulsi.

It's highly aromatic leaves have a pleasant spicy odor that smells similar to and tastes somewhat like cloves or anise.

The herb was common in the eastern Mediterranean and later brought to England by the Crusaders. It may be used fresh or ground.

It contains a good amount of vitamins K, C, iron, omega–3 fatty acids and calcium, which helps bone health. Basil is complete with antioxidants and phytonutrients. Some of these phytonutrients in basil have been found to protect cell structures and chromosomes from radiation and oxygen–based damage.

The antibacterial nature of basil is linked to its essential oils. The essential oil in the leaves of basil has an anti–inflammatory effect. Basil can help improve blood flow and help stop cholesterol from oxidizing in the blood stream. Adding basil essential oil to your natural cleaning supplies, in a low concentration (1% or less) can add natural antibacterial (antimicrobial) properties.

Bay Leaf: Also called Apollo's Bay Leaf, Bay, Bay Laurel, Grecian Laurel, Indian Bay, Laurel, Nobel Laurel, Poet's Laurel, Roman Laurel, Royal Laurel, Sweet Bay, Sweet Laurel, Turkish Laurel and Wreath Laurel.

The bay tree is native to the Mediterranean region and Asia Minor. Bay Leaves are strongly aromatic with a woody flavor and a pleasant, subtle minty aroma. The fresh leaves are very mild. They do not develop their full flavor until several weeks after picking and drying.

The spice is a very good source of many vitamins that help in enzyme forming or building, nervous system function, and regulating body metabolism. Fresh leaves are a very rich source of vitamin C (ascorbic acid), one of the potent natural antioxidants that helps remove harmful, pro–inflammatory free radicals from the body. Ascorbic acid has wound healing, immune booster, and antiviral effects.

It is an excellent source of vitamin A, a natural antioxidant essential for healthy visual sight, maintaining mucus membranes and skin health. Bay leaf is a good source of minerals like copper, potassium, calcium, manganese and iron, essential for red blood cell production. It contains selenium, zinc, magnesium and potassium, which help control heart rate and blood pressure. Fresh leaves and herb parts are very good in folic acid. Folates aid in the prevention of birth defects.

This spice has components known to have been antiseptic, antioxidant, digestive, and thought to have anti–cancer properties. Eating natural foods rich in vitamin A helps prevent lung and oral cavity cancers and colic pain. Infusions of herb parts with water are reputed to soothe the stomach and relieve flatulence. It has diuretic, and appetite stimulant properties.

http://www.turkishbayleaf.com/laurel–leaves–other–names/

Black Pepper: Some of the other names for Black pepper include Piper nigrum, Peppercorn, Pepper, Piper nigrum, Pimenta, Pimienta, Extract, Pepper Plant, Kosho, Blanc Poivre, Extrait de Poivre, Grain de Poivre, Hu Jiao, Kali Mirchi, Krishna, Marich, Maricha, Pepe Pfeffer, and Pimienta Negra

Black Pepper is a flower–producing climbing shrub native to the forests of Malabar and Travancore in India, where it is found in abundance. It was later introduced to other tropical countries, such as the Philippines, the Malay Peninsula, Sumatra, and West Indies. Currently, Vietnam is the world's largest exporter of pepper.

Harvested for use as a seasoning, spice, or health supplement, when dried, the fruit is referred to as a peppercorn. The black powdery form is derived from grinding mature peppercorns until they reach a fine texture.

It has been used as a stomachic remedy for relief from nausea and "upset stomach". Studies have suggested that piperine in black pepper helps prevent heart disease, stroke and can significantly increase the body's absorption of beta–carotene, vitamin B and selenium. It causes the stomach to increase the flow of digestive juices. In addition, black pepper extract has been found to contain antioxidant properties and anti–carcinogenic effects.

Black Pepper was believed to cure conditions such as constipation, earache, diarrhea, gangrene, insect bites, heart disease, hernia, tooth decay, sore throats, liver problems, indigestion, insomnia, joint pain and lung disease. Black pepper is still widely used in standard Indian medicine as a natural treatment for colds, sore throats and chest congestion.

"Pepper" http://www.herbwisdom.com/herb–pepper.html

"Common Name: Black Pepper | Scientific Name: Piper Nigrum" http://bit.ly/1Ndnnxh/

Cardamom (seed, powder): A member of the ginger family, other common names include Brown cardamom, Bengal cardamom, Java cardamom, Kravan, and Siamese cardamom. It embraces a spicy, citrusy, herbal, slightly sweet and savory flavor.

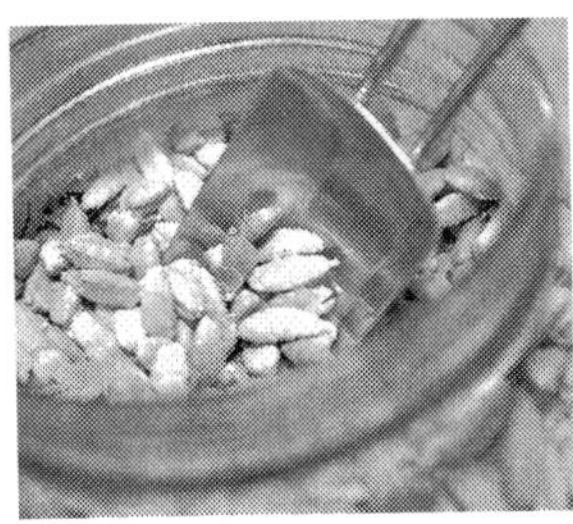

Found mainly in India and it is farmed in only a few places in the world, including Laos, Vietnam, Sri Lanka, China, Nepal, pockets of India, and Guatemala. Due to its therapeutic properties and rich aroma, it is considered one of the most valuable spices in the world. In Indian cooking, it is one of the primary ingredients of Garam Masala.

The seeds of the cardamom plant contain important minerals such as calcium, phosphorus and sulfur. They also contain volatile oil, which makes up about 5 percent of the seed's mass that has aromatic and medicinal properties. Studies confirm that cardamom oil acts as a pain reliever and helps relieve digestive problems induced by garlic and onion.

Cardamom has been used to relieve medical problems including bad breath, tooth, gum, and oral disorders, digestion, urinary problems, depression (when used as aromatherapy), and cancer prevention. In addition to these medicinal uses, cardamom contains a large amount of antioxidants, which protect the body against aging and stress.

"Cardamom"

http://www.herbwisdom.com/herb–cardamom.html

Cayenne: Also known as paprika, Vapsicum annuum,Bird pepper, Guinea spice, Cow–horn pepper, and Aleva. Originated in the Americas, spread across the world, it is used in both food and medicine. The peppers can be grown in a variety of locations, preferring moist, warm, nutrient–rich soil in a warm climate. They only need about 100 days to mature. Today, India is the world's largest consumer, producer, and exporter of chili peppers.

Cayenne is often used as a natural pain killer, fat burner, to improve circulation, increase metabolism, aid digestion and boost the immune system. It is used as a tonic for the kidneys, lungs, spleen, pancreas, and to treat shingles, and rheumatism and herpes. It contains anti–inflammatory properties to combat chills, to treat bunions, psoriasis, and prevent heart disease. Cayenne improves circulation and aids digestion by stimulating gastric juices. It stimulates the appetite, reduces inflammation and is a mild stimulant or tonic. This spice relieves gas, colds, and stops bleeding from ulcers.

Recently, cayenne has been used successfully to treat cluster headaches, a painful type of headache. Used externally, cayenne liniment may soothe the pain and stiffness of rheumatism and arthritis. It can be taken for cramps, stomach and bowel pains. Small amounts of the powder on fresh fruit may expel worms. Cayenne is also said to increase fertility and delay senility.

"Cayenne Pepper" http://en.wikipedia.org/wiki/Cayenne_pepper

"Chili Peppers" http://en.wikipedia.org/wiki/Chili_pepper

"Cayenne" http://www.herbwisdom.com/herb–cayenne.html

Cinnamon powder: Ground up cinnamon sticks.

Cinnamon sticks: There are two types of cinnamon, Cassia (Chinese), and Ceylon. The spice originated from Ceylon, an island southeast of India. Currently, the largest producer is Sri Lanka (formerly called Ceylon). Cassia is a more common kind that grows wild all over China and other parts of East Asia. It was used in ancient Egypt for embalming and added to food to prevent spoiling.

Also called "quills", cinnamon comes from the dried bark of a special genus of evergreen trees. Although there are hundreds of varieties of cinnamon, only 4 types are used for commercial purposes.

These are Ceylon, Cassia, Saigon and Korintje Cinnamon. Cassia, Saigon and Korintje are classified under the Cassia Cinnamon category because they are very similar to each other with only slight variations in taste, color, shape and Coumarin content.

All Cassia type Cinnamon contains high levels of Coumarin, a substance known to cause liver damage. Ceylon is the only soft and brittle cinnamon with very low Coumarin levels. It smells very mild and is slightly sweeter in taste. Cassia Cinnamon is used by about 70% of North America. Indonesia is the major supplier of Cassia Cinnamon. Ceylon is used mostly used in Europe and Mexico.

Cassia is much cheaper than Ceylon, which tends to be expensive because of the handcrafted process required to harvest it and roll it in many thin layers. Cassia Cinnamon is a hard bark that has a spicy, strong and sometimes bitter aroma. Ceylon Cinnamon sticks are soft, crumbly and rolled like a cigar with layers of soft brittle cinnamon bark. Cassia Cinnamon sticks tends to be hard, hollow and have only one rolled layer. Ceylon Cinnamon is lighter in color while Cassia Cinnamon tends to be darker in color.

Cinnamon may help soothe an upset stomach including gastrointestinal problems, diarrhea and morning sickness. One German study showed that Cinnamon "suppresses completely" the cause of most urinary–tract infections and the fungus responsible for vaginal yeast infections (Candida albicans). It can help clear up urinary–tract infections and allow diabetics to use less insulin by helping people with diabetes metabolize (break down) sugar better.

Cinnamon with each meal may help control blood sugar levels. It aids digestion by helping the body process food by breaking down fats during digestion. Cinnamon oil and cinnamon extract have anti–fungal, anti–bacterial, and anti–parasitic properties that kill many disease–causing fungi and viruses such as Candida albicans and thrush (oral yeast infection) and head lice. Cinnamon is considered a pain killer because it reduces inflammation. Cinnamon aids in lowering blood sugar, triglycerides, LDL, and total cholesterol in people with type 2 diabetes.

"Types Of Cinnamon" http://bit.ly/1K2XyzY

"Cinnamon" http://bit.ly/1Gec17D

Chipotle: A smoke–dried jalapeño pepper that originated in the area surrounding Mexico City. People who lived there before the Aztec may have invented it. It loses very little of its heat through the smoking process, and many enjoy its spicy slightly sweet and wood smoke taste. Drying chipotle peppers removes some of the heat content, which makes it easier to add to your foods. Chipotle is often used in Mexican cuisine.

Researchers have found that Capsaicin, the compound that gives chili peppers its powerful kick can help burn more calories immediately after a meal. Hot peppers help reduce cholesterol levels and help increase your body's ability to dissolve fibrin, a known substance that forms blood clots. It lowers free radical damage, which leads to atherosclerosis (hardening of the arteries).

The chemical compounds in chipotle can improve circulation, dilate blood vessels, and reduces the risk of heart disease. Weight control is made easier with improvements to circulation and metabolism. The capsaicin levels in chipotle peppers help to stop prostate cancer cells from spreading and can even help prostate cancer tumors to shrink in size. It also lowers your risk of diabetes.

It aids fat oxidization, which is the way your body uses up stored fats to produce energy, leading to increased weight loss. Since the development of type 2 diabetes goes hand in hand with obesity, this is another way this spice reduces the risk of type 2 diabetes.

"Chipotle Supports a Healthy Heart And Blood Sugar"
http://bit.ly/1GscoKXf

"What is a Chipotle Pepper?"
http://bit.ly/1LbxKCH

Cloves (whole, powder): Other names include clove oil and oil of cloves, engenol, clavo, clau, cravinho and clovas. A dried flower bud and stem from an aromatic evergreen tree, it grows in the tropics of South America and Asia. Cloves have quite a strong aroma and a burning flavor to the taste.

The oil extracted from the plant is used in herbal remedies and some dental practices. Cloves are well known for their medicinal properties regarding treating toothaches. Approved for use in dentistry as a topical anesthetic, it might also help as far as reducing heart disease and insulin deficiency as well.

Studies suggest that clove oil may fight bacteria, fungi, and even skin mites (scabies). Bacteria in the mouth can cause both bad breath and toothaches. Using a clove has antiseptic qualities, which nullifies the action of the bacteria. They may also have cholesterol–lowering abilities.

"Cloves" *http://bit.ly/1KxEjOl*

"Cloves"http://bit.ly/1ezHHh6

Coriander (seed, powder): Cilantro originated in the Mediterranean basin, and presently grows wild in SE Europe. It has been cultivated in India, Egypt, and China for thousands of years.

A member of the carrot family, cilantro or coriander has two common names, and two different identities and uses. The Spanish word for coriander leaves is cilantro. It is also sometimes called Mexican or Chinese parsley or Dhania. Coriander refers to the entire plant. Cilantro describes the first vegetative stage of the plant's life cycle. It is referred to as coriander after the plant flowers and develops seeds.

Coriander is the dried, round, tiny ball seed of the cilantro. They are used ground or whole as a flavoring or seasoning. The essential seed oil is used in various herbal remedies, dietary supplement and perfumery.

This powerful herb has many health benefits. It is rich in micronutrients and nutritional elements. It contains vitamins and minerals like calcium, magnesium, potassium, sodium and dietary fiber. Coriander seeds and leaves, aside from being used in cooking, have been used to reduce fever, strengthen the stomach and lower cholesterol levels.

In parts of Europe, cilantro has been referred to as an "anti–diabetic" plant because its seeds have hypoglycemic effects. In India, coriander is known for its anti–inflammatory proprieties. Coriander may also be used in treating headaches, stiffness and muscle pain. Individuals who suffer from diabetes can benefit from using it. It contains linalol, an essential oil that can help increase the appetite and detoxify the liver.

It's rich source of iron and phytonutrients help prevent nausea, protect the body against urinary tract infections, lower blood sugar levels and protect against damage from free radicals. Recent studies have shown that coriander can be successfully used in treating anxiety, depression and panic attacks.

Dry coriander has been effective in treating diarrhea. Boiled coriander seeds are beneficial for women suffering hormonal mood swings and heavy menstrual flow. Coriander contains antimicrobial substances that help prevent and cure small pox. It freshens breath, reduces the accumulation of heavy metals in the body, which aids in preventing Alzheimer's disease and loss of memory. It also helps cure sores and ulcers in the mouth.

Coriander juice is beneficial in treating hepatitis, dysentery, indigestion and colitis. Mixed with a pinch of turmeric powder, it serves as a potent remedy against pimples and blackheads.

"What Is The Special Nutritional Power Found In Fruits And Vegetables?"

http://bit.ly/1BuYSu6

"Cilantro vs. Coriander: What Is Cilantro – What Is Coriander"

http://bit.ly/1Lmzhqz

Cumin (seed, powder) Native to China, Mexico, India and the Mediterranean, it is also known as Kemun, Kamoun, Kamun, Green cumin, White cumin, Cummin, Cumin blanc, Kreuzkümmel, Weißer Kreuzkümmel, Römischer Kümmel, MutterkümmelJira, Jeera, Saphed, Duru, SuduruComino, Comino blanco, Jilakara, Duru, Suduru, Comino, Comino blanco, Jilakara, Jilakarra, Kimyon, Acem kimyonu, Kemnon, Jilakarra, Kimyon, Acem kimyonu, Kemnon and Jira, Today, cumin is cultivated and grown in many countries including China, Saudi Arabia, Malta, Sicily, India, Mexico and Iran.

Its use goes back over 5000 years. The ancient Egyptians used it in the mummification process and as a spice in foods. The small, flat seed provides a peppery flavor used in Mexican dishes, as well as in combination with curry in Middle Eastern and Indian food. A member of the parsley family, this seed has a warm aroma and distinct flavor. It is a major ingredient in curry and chili powder.

Cumin is high in iron and manganese, calcium, many vitamins and fiber. Cumin is said to prevent gas, clear jaundice, reduce muscle spasms, and stop diarrhea. It may also reduce seizures, strengthen bones and lower blood sugar. It aids digestion, relieves constipation and aids the body's ability to absorb nutrients because the enzymes in cumin help break down the food. The fiber in cumin helps get rid of the piles when consumed daily.

Cumin's anti–fungal properties will help to clean out the digestive tract. Cumin helps relieve colds, sore throats and fevers. It contains a great source of iron, which is key in keeping your immune system healthy, maintaining your metabolism and producing energy. Females going through their menstural cycle, who are pregnant or nursing need to consume more iron and cumin is a potent source.

It is a stimulant, antiseptic and a benefit for digestive disorders. The seeds themselves are rich in iron and are thought to help absorb nutrients into the system. It has been shown to boost the power of the liver's ability to detoxify the body. Recent studies have revealed that cumin seeds might also have anti–carcinogenic properties. Due to its antiseptic properties, Cumin is also said to help relieve symptoms of the common cold. Boil the seeds in a tea and then drink it a couple of times a day. If you have a sore throat, try adding some dry ginger to help soothe it.

Cumin can also be applied as a salve for boils by making a black cumin paste by grinding seeds with water and applying it to the affected area. Cumin is said to increase the heat in the body, which makes metabolism more efficient. It is also thought to be a potent kidney and liver herb and can help boost the immune system. Some believe black cumin seeds may even be able to help treat arthritis and asthma.

"Cumin in History" http://bit.ly/1Fu1zqXl

"Cumin" http://bit.ly/1Lrlo7k

Dill (seeds, powder) A member of the parsley family, dill weed is native to the eastern Mediterranean region and western Asia. It's other names include Dill Weed, Dillweed, Dill Herb, Dill Oil, Indian Dill, Dilly, American Dill, European Dill, Sowa Aneth, Aneth Odorant, Anethi Fructus, Anethi Herba, Anethum graveolens, Anethum sowa,

Eneldo, Faux Anis, Huile d'Aneth, Fenouil Bâtard, Fenouil Puant, Madhura, Peucedanum graveolens, Satahva, Shatpushpa and Sotapa.

Dill is native to southern Russia and the Mediterranean region. It grows in southern Europe and in Mediterranean climates. Currently the largest commercial producers are Pakistan and India. The United States and several other countries have commercial production areas.

The whole plant with the immature seeds is known as dill weed. Dill weed is a unique herbal plant because both its leaves as well as seeds are used as a seasoning. The leaves and seed are not used the same way. Dill Seeds have a pungent, caraway seed–celery like flavor. While dill has a similar but milder taste, it is typically used in salads, soups, potatoes, fish, and other dishes. Dill pickles are made with the mature seed heads.

Dill seeds, used as spice, are similar in appearance and taste to caraway seeds. They feature a flavor that is sweet, aromatic and citrus, but also slightly bitter. I would suggest buying whole dill seeds instead of its powder since often it contains other spicy powders. The seeds can be stored in a cool, dry place.

The benefits of dill weed include chemical compounds that are known to have been antioxidant, disease preventing, and health promoting properties. It also has been shown to control blood cholesterol levels. The essential oil, Eugenol, contained in the dill has been in therapeutic usage as a local anesthetic and anti–septic. Eugenol has also been found to reduce blood sugar levels in diabetics. It also has carminative, digestive, disinfectant, sedative, anti–spasmodic properties and helps breast milk secretion in nursing mothers.

Fresh dill herb is an excellent source of vitamin C, the antioxidant. Vitamin C helps the body develop resistance against infectious diseases and harmful, pro–inflammatory free radicals. It is a good source of minerals like manganese, calcium, copper, potassium, and iron. These minerals help to regulate growth and development, sperm generation, digestion, control heart rate and blood pressure. The sprigs of the dill weed are said to have anti–septic, digestive, and carminative properties.

Dill has been used for heartburn, insomnia, and stomach ailments. It contains compounds associated with attacking and limiting the growth of cancer cells within the body. Rich amounts of calcium help strengthen the bones and assist in reducing the time a cold lingers within the body. It also aids bad breath.

"Where Does Dill Weed Come From?"
http://bit.ly/1IWrDzM
"Dill Weed (Herb) Nutrition Facts"
http://bit.ly/1GA3oqm
"What Other Names Is Dill Known By?"
http://bit.ly/1Fu1DHb

Fennel (seed, powder) A flowering plant in the celery family and a native to southern Europe and the Mediterranean area, it is now widely cultivated in China, Italy, Hungary, Bulgaria, Romania, Greece, Turkey, Germany, France, Egypt, and India.

It is also known by other names including Fenkel, Fennel Oil, Fennel Essential Oil, Fennel Seed, Bitter Fennel, Common Fennel, Fenouil, Bari–Sanuf, Anethum Foeniculum, Anethum piperitum, Carosella, Fenouil Amer, Fenouil, Bulbeux, Fenouil Commun, Fenouil de Florence and Fenouil des Vignes.

Fennel has a mild anise–like flavor, more aromatic and sweeter to taste. It is a licorice flavored aromatic herb. It grows to be several feet tall and looks similar to a dill plant. The stalks are topped with feathery green leaves. Flowers grow near these leaves and produce fennel seeds. The seeds, leaves, stalk, and bulb are all edible.

This digestive herb is one of Germany's more important medicinal plant crops. Fennel is said to cure everything from hiccups to earaches, toothaches, and asthma. The seeds can be chewed to sweeten breath and help a toothache. A gargle with fennel can relieve hoarseness or a sore throat.

Fennel is often used for colic, lungs, irritable bowel, spleen, kidneys, liver, suppressing appetite, promoting menstruation, breast enlargement, improving digestive system, milk flow in nursing mothers and increasing urine flow. It is used to treat absence of a menstrual period (amenorrhea), chest discomfort due to poor blood flow through the blood vessels in the heart (angina), anxiety, heartburn, lower blood pressure, depression, water retention, respiratory congestion, coughs and has been used for high blood pressure and boosting sexual desire.

Excellent for obesity, fennel is a mild appetite suppressant that is also used for cancer patients after chemotherapy and radiation treatments to help rebuild the digestive system. It is a tested remedy for gas, acid stomach, gout, cramps and spasms. Ground fennel made into tea is believed to be good for snake, insect bites or food poisoning.

"Fennel"

http://wb.md/1TF4uIc

"History,Region of Fennel Origin"

http://bit.ly/1d8W7Dk

"Fennel (Foeniculum Vulgare)"

http://bit.ly/1IrW1zk

Fenugreek (seed, powder): A member of the legume, pea, or bean family, it is a native to southern Europe, the Mediterranean region, and Western Asia.

Today, the largest producer is India. Other major fenugreek-producing countries are France, Nepal, Pakistan, Afghanistan, Iran, Bangladesh, Argentina, Egypt, Spain, Morocco and Turkey. It is also known by other names including Methi, Menthulu, Venthyam, Abesh, Bird's Foot, Bockshornklee, Greek Hayseed and Goat's Horn.

Fenugreek's dried or fresh leaves are used as an herb, the seeds as a spice and the fresh leaves, sprouts, and greens as a vegetable. Uncooked fenugreek seeds have a bitter, unpleasant taste. The seeds should be lightly dry roasted before using to enhance the flavor and reduce the bitterness of the spice. The seeds can be sun dried, powdered and stored. Because the seeds are very hard and difficult to grind, a mortar and pestle work best.

Because it is both a seed and a legume, it is rich in vitamins, minerals and high in protein. Fenugreek seeds are an important source of diosgenin, which is widely used in the production of synthetic estrogen, steroids, oral contraceptives, sex hormones and veterinary medicine. The seed is used in Ethiopia in the treatment of diabetes. Topically, the seed may have some benefit for soothing skin that is irritated by eczema or other conditions. As a warm poultice, it has been applied to relieve gout pain and muscle aches.

Research shows that fenugreek lowered cholesterol levels as well as blood sugar levels. Its ability to balance hormone levels helps in treating menopause and PMS. Its antioxidants help prevent disease and slow aging. Fenugreek has been used against sore throats, wounds, bronchitis, ulcers, fevers, swollen glands, skin irritations, diabetes and in treating cancer. Fenugreek has been used to improve the milk flow of nursing mothers and to increase sexual desire.

Considered the finest herb for enhancing feminine beauty, fenugreek has a long history as a breast enlarger. It promotes the growth of new breast cells and increases the size and fullness of the breasts. An ancient Ayurvedic cure for dandruff, it also tones the hair, giving it a silky shine and feel. Fenugreek seed paste in powder form can be used as a face pack to help tone the skin and cure acne. It was known to cure constipation, is used to break up respiratory congestion and for weight gain. It also contains choline, an essential nutrient, which aids the thinking process.

"Fenugreek (Trigonella Foenum–graecum)" http://bit.ly/1BuYWtQ

"Menthi – Methi, Fenugreek Seeds (Indian Spice)"

http://bit.ly/1H6kL5j

"Fenugreek"

http://bit.ly/1TF4HLil

"Fenugreek" http://en.wikipedia.org/wiki/Fenugreek

Garlic: A member of the onion family, garlic is native to central Asia and is mentioned in ancient Egyptian, Indian, Greek, and Chinese writings. Today, China is the largest producer, followed by India, South Korea, Egypt, Russia and the United States. The other names for garlic include Garlic Oil, Garlic Clove, Aged Garlic Extract, Ajo, Arishtha, Ail, Lashuna, Vellaipundu, Lasan, Lasun, Lasuna, Allii Sativi Bulbus, Allium, Allium Sativum, Camphor of the Poor, Da Suan, Nectar of the Gods, Poor Man's Treacle, Rason, Rust Treacle and Stinking Rose.

Garlic contains a substance called Allicin, which has anti–bacterial properties equivalent to a "weak" penicillin. A natural antibiotic, it is useful in treating everything from tonsillitis to allergies. Studies suggest garlic destroys cancer cells, may disrupt the metabolism of tumor cells and that one or two cloves weekly provide cancer–protective benefits.

It helps reduce clotting, remove heavy metals and parasites, clean the arteries and retards the growth of viruses, yeasts (including Candida albicans), eliminates worms, unfavorable bacteria and expels coldness. It is used for snake bite, hay fever, asthma, pneumonia, tuberculosis, diarrhea, abscesses, hepatitis and warts. It also promotes the growth of healthy intestinal flora.

Garlic contains many sulfur compounds, which boost the immune system, lower blood pressure, detoxify the body, and improve circulation. It is also used to help prevent plaque buildup in the arteries that cause blockage and may lead to a stroke or heart attack. It is known to reduce coughs, colds, and bronchitis.

Garlic helps repel fleas from dogs and other pets when combined with their food. It relieves poison ivy, poison oak, sore throats and sinus headaches. It is used as a remedy for athlete's foot. Poultices made with chopped garlic have been used to draw out swelling from boils.

"Allium Sativum (Garlic)"

http://bit.ly/1LmzHod

"Garlic" http://www.rxlist.com/garlic/supplements.htm

"Garlic" http://www.herbwisdom.com/herb–garlic.html

Healing with Whole Foods by Paul Pitchford Publisher North Atlantic Books, Berkeley, California ©2002

Ginger: A member of the plant family including turmeric and cardamom, Ginger is native to India and China and it spread to the Spice Islands, other parts of Asia, West Africa and the Caribbean. The largest producer is India, followed by China, Nepal, Nigeria and Thailand.

The other names include, Black Ginger, African Ginger, Indian Ginger, Ginger Root, Jamaica Ginger, Race Ginger, Cochin Ginger, Ginger Essential Oil, Amomum Zingiber, Ardraka, Gan Jiang, Gingembre, Gingembre Africain, Gingembre Cochin, Gingembre Indien, Gingembre Jamaïquain, Gingembre Noir, Huile Essentielle de Gingembre, Imber, Jengibre, Jiang, Kankyo, Kanshokyo, Zinziber Officinalis Nagara, Racine de Gingembre, Rhizoma Zingiberi, Rhizoma Zingiberis, Rhizoma Zingiberis Recens, Shen Jiang, Sheng Jiang, Shoga, Shokyo, Shunthi, Srungavera, Sunth, Sunthi,

Vishvabheshaja, Zingiber Officinale, Zingiberis Rhizoma, Zingiberis Siccatum Rhizoma, Zinzeberis, and Zinziber Officinale.

The underground stem (rhizome) of the herb is used for cooking, tea and medicine. Ground ginger is more potent than fresh ginger. Fresh ginger can be substituted for ground ginger at a 6 to 1 ratio. The flavors of dried and fresh ginger are somewhat different. Ground ginger root is typically used as a flavoring for recipes such as, crackers, ginger beer, cookies, cakes, ginger ale and gingerbread.

Ginger root is well researched and known as a food preservative, remedy for motion sickness, indigestion and nausea. It is used for colic, irritable bowel, flu, cold, chills, loss of appetite, poor circulation, menstrual cramps, bloating, heartburn, flatulence, indigestion and gastrointestinal problems and stomach cramps. Ginger has been shown to work against skin, ovarian, colon and breast cancer. It has been used for headaches, coughs, toothaches, arthritis, fevers, bronchitis and brittle bones (osteoporosis). It has also been used to ease tendonitis, lower blood pressure and also hinder blood clotting.

A warming remedy, it is ideal for keeping the blood thin in higher doses and boosting the circulation. Ginger is a powerful anti–inflammatory herb that has been known to ease inflammation of the joints and muscle tissue. Due to its amazing qualities of circulation increasing, ginger is thought to improve the complexion. It has eased tendonitis, reduced nervousness, and helped sore throats. Studies demonstrate that ginger can lower cholesterol levels by reducing cholesterol absorption in the blood and liver, and actually suppresses cancer cells.

Ginger: http://www.rxlist.com/ginger/supplements.htm

Garlic: http://www.herbwisdom.com/herb–garlic.html

Herbes de Provence: This combination of herbs takes its name from the region of Provence, in the southeast tip of France. Created in the 1970's, Herbes de Provence is a seasoning blend that features many of the herbs that grow abundantly in southern France that are used in a lot of the cooking from that region. Meant to be an easy short cut for seasoning dishes, the mixtures, known as Provencal herbs, are typically made from dried herbs.

These dried mixtures sold in supermarkets will be slightly different from one to the next. But typically, the blend can include any of the following herbs: rosemary, lavender, basil, thyme, marjoram, bay leaf, chervil, sage, savory, fennel, oregano, dill, and tarragon. In some mixtures basil, fennel seeds, sage, citrus zest and mint may or may not be included. Which herbs get used and their exact ratio depends on the cook and the recipe. Like Curries, there is no set formula for blending Herbes de Provence.

"Herbes de Provence" http://www.herbes–de–provence.com

"From the Spice Cupboard: Herbes de Provence"
http://bit.ly/1Rl28KA

"Herbes de Provence" http://bit.ly/1H12vZh

Italian Seasoning: Like Curries and Herbs de Provence, there is no set recipe for what should or should not be included in the blend of spices. Most manufacturers start out with a basic blend of basil, rosemary, oregano, thyme, and marjoram that are popular in Italian cooking. But often they add different tastes to make their blends more distinctive. Sage, parsley, savory and garlic powder are popular additions. Coriander and cilantro might be added for color. Red pepper flakes can be included for the heat they give the food.

"What Is Italian Seasoning?" http://bit.ly/1ezIChy

Marjoram: A member in the mint family, it originated in Egypt and Arabia. Today, it grows wild in the Mediterranean region and is grown in gardens around the world. Often mistaken for oregano, although related plants, they are two different species. They taste similar. Oregano often has a stronger flavor. But both contain high amounts of antioxidants.

Marjoram is called by many names, including Wintersweet, Joy of the Mountains, Sweet Marjoram, Knotted Marjoram, Origanum Majorana, and Majorana Hortensis.

There are four forms of Marjoram: essential oil, fresh or dried leaves, or powder (ground up). It is used mostly as seasoning in cooked dishes but is also found in health care and beauty products. As an essential oil, fresh or dried leaves or powder, it has many health benefits. The essential oil is used in aromatherapy treatments, where it is said to be spicy, warming and have a soothing effect. Applied topically, it has been known to relieve toothaches, backache, sore muscles and sprains. Often recommended as a treatment for stress and insomnia, it is used as a tea to help relieve both nausea and gas.

Marjoram contains the compound Eugenol, which has antiseptic, antifungal, and antiviral properties. This can numb sensations, kill germs and relieve swelling. It is used to help with digestion, relieve diarrhea, constipation, cramps and increase menstrual flow. Taken internally, it is used to relieve a variety of problems caused by inflammation, including asthma, migraine, fever, muscle spasms, sinus headaches and body aches.

It has been known to benefit the cardiovascular and circulatory system by lowering the blood pressure, reducing the risk of hypertension, heart problems, preventing the build up of cholesterol, and reducing risk of hardened arteries. It also aids in improved blood circulation by dilating the arteries as necessary and increases control of sexual desire. Most experts recommend that medicinal amounts not be taken during pregnancy.

"Marjoram" http://bit.ly/1H6look

"What Is Marjoram?" http://bit.ly/1GA46DV

Mineral Salt: Mineral salts come from salt caves that formed about 250 million years ago as ocean salt settled in certain geologic areas around the earth. The salts come in different varieties. They include phosphate, calcium, chloride, sodium and potassium. Iodized salt, essential to the function of the body, is one of the most common mineral salts.

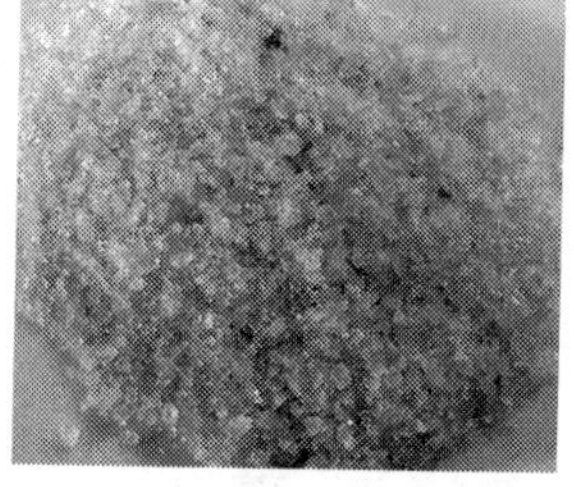

Himalayan Pink Salt is considered a good example of mineral salt. It contains the full spectrum of 84 minerals and trace elements that include calcium, potassium and magnesium. The pink color is due to the presence of iron oxide. Unrefined, unprocessed "raw" salt from a large salt mine in Pakistan is hand harvested, hand–crushed, hand–washed and sun dried. Free of any additives or anti–caking agents, it is known to be the purest, highest quality salt available.

The health benefits of using Himalayan Crystal Salt may include regulating and controlling water levels within the body for proper functioning, promoting circulation support, increased absorption of food elements within the intestinal tract and acidity balance in the cells and the brain. It improves blood sugar, healthy respiratory function and naturally promotes healthy sleep patterns.

It aids in reducing the common aging signs, supports vascular health and increases bone strength. It lowers incidences of sinus problems, promotes sinus health, reduces cramps and creates a healthy libido. It also promotes gall bladder and kidney health when compared to common chemically treated table salt. Himalayan Pink Salt is higher in potassium, magnesium and lower in sodium than sea salt.

Today, most of the commercial supply of Himalayan Pink Salt comes from the mountains of Pakistan

Sea Salt: Sea salt is obtained from the evaporation of seawater. It is typically not processed, or undergoes very little processing which allows it to retain trace levels of minerals like magnesium, calcium, potassium and other nutrients. If it is harvested from a polluted sea or lake it can also contain trace amounts of heavy metals. Sea salt is only 84% sodium chloride and is not exposed to harsh chemicals. Table salt is almost 98% sodium chloride.

Pure unrefined sea salt is not harmful in moderate amounts. Healthy sea salts make a body a hostile environment for pathogens, such as parasites and bacteria. Like Himalayan Crystal Salt, sea salt contains essential minerals and trace elements. It naturally contains selenium, which helps to expel toxic heavy metals from the body.

It contains chromium, which regulates blood sugar levels and boron, which helps prevent osteoporosis. Copper helps the body to form new arteries when the main arteries become clogged and sea salt is one of the few sources for safe copper ingestion. In most individuals, small amounts of sea salt will lower the blood pressure because it contains the trace minerals that aid with blood pressure regulation.

Nutmeg (whole, powder) Nutmeg is known by other names, such Pipo, Myristica fragrans, Mace, Magic, Muscdier, Muskatbaum, Myristica, Myristicae Aril, Noz moscada, Jaatipatree, Jatipatra, Jaiphal, Jatikosha, Nuez moscada, Nux moschata, Fleur de Muscade, Jatipatri, Jatiphal, Jatiphala, Javitri, Jatiphalam, Jayapatri, Macis, Muscade, Muscade et Macis, Muskatnuss, Myristica fragrans, Myristica officinalis, Myristicae Semen, Noix de Muscade, Noix de Nuez Moscada, Nuez Moscada y Macis, and Ron Dau Kou.

Nutmeg is used as a general name for many trees in the Myristica family. These trees grow mainly in Indonesia, mostly in the Banda

Islands. It is now cultivated in the West Indies. The nutmeg tree is the source of both nutmeg and **mace**. Nutmeg is the shelled dried seed of the tree. Mace is the dried covering of the shell of the seed. Other commercial products, including nutmeg butter, essential oils, and extracted oleoresins are produced from the trees.

Nutmeg has been known to relax the body, which helps reduce anxiety and makes falling asleep easier. It can be taken to stimulate the brain and fight lack of energy and stress. The Myristicin contained in nutmeg can be effective against Alzheimer's and other memory related conditions. It has been used as Chinese medicine for pain, inflammation and arthritis. Some practitioners use the essential oil on joints or other parts that are experiencing pain.

The medical industry has recognized the antibacterial ingredients in nutmeg to be effective against strep throat. The antibacterial properties may help relieve gum and mouth sores, inflammation and bad breath. The essential oil can be used on a sore tooth. It is used to increase the appetite and help relieve bloating by removing excess gas. Some believe nutmeg can help remove toxins from the liver and kidneys and can help remove kidney stones.

The essential oil can be applied to the skin or used with other oils or ingredients to help relieve skin conditions. Nutmeg with honey or Orange lentil powder can be used to create a scrub that may relieve blackheads and reduce marks from acne. Nutmeg butter can be used in place of cocoa butter. For a fresh taste and daily cleanse, add a little to your toothpaste.

"Nutmeg" http://www.herbwisdom.com/herb–nutmeg.html

"Nutmeg And Mace" http://bit.ly/1K3A6nM

Nutritional Yeast: Like mushrooms, it is a member of the fungi family. Its other names include Savoury yeast flakes, Brufax, Nooch, Yeshi. Vegetarian food yeast, Vegetarian Support Formula and Hippie dust. While gaining in popularity in the late 1900's, ancient Egyptians used it as early as 1550 BC.

Nutritional yeast is made from a single–celled organism, Saccharomyces Cerevisiae, which is grown on enriched purified cane and beet molasses. It is then harvested, washed and dried with heat to kill it. Since it contains no live enzymes, it is not like active dry yeast or baking yeast, which makes bread rise. It's not the same as Brewer's yeast, which is a product of the beer–making process that has a very bitter taste.

It has a distinct flavor often identified as cheesy, nutty and slightly sweet. It is popular as an ingredient in cheese substitutes and as a popcorn topping. This yellow shaded product is usually found packaged as either flakes or powder. If you're using the powder, you will need only about half as much as the flakes. It is packaged under many brand names in the natural food section. You can typically find it in the bulk bins at local natural food stores. If you can't find it locally, you can purchase it online.

It is naturally low in sodium and fat, free of sugar, soy, dairy, gluten, preservatives and animal products. It is often used as a condiment in the place of salt, cheese or butter for vegans and non–vegans. Adding a small amount enhances the flavors. Check the label carefully before buying to see if there are any whey or animal products.

Nutritional yeast contains B–vitamins, folic acid, selenium, zinc, as well as other vitamins. It is a complete protein (containing 18 amino acids) and some brands are fortified with vitamin B12. B vitamins help reduce stress, balance the systems of the body, and convert food to energy. They help minimize fatigue, depression, nervousness, irritability, insomnia, trembling, loss of appetite, PMS, and mood changes. B vitamins can also help improve memory, hair, skin, and nails.

"Nutritional Yeast Demystified" http://bit.ly/1fpE7pL

"What Is Nutritional Yeast?"
http://bit.ly/1BDXB4q
"Nutritional Yeast"
http://bit.ly/1JQkOOk
"What the Heck is Nutritional Yeast?"
http://bit.ly/1GA3UV8

Oregano: A member of the mint family, it is also known as Pizza herb, Marjoram, Wild marjoram, Mountain Mint, Wintersweet, Origanum vulgare, Oregano Oil, Oil of Oregano, Organy, Origan Européen, Origani Vulgaris Herba, Origano, Origanum, Origanum vulgare, European Oregano, Mediterranean Oregano,Thym des Bergers,Carvacrol, Dostenkraut, Huile d'Origan, Marjolaine Bâtarde, Marjolaine Sauvage, Marjolaine Vivace, Phytoprogestin, and Thé Sauvage.

Grown in Italy, it is native to the Mediterranean region including southwestern and western Eurasia. Warm, aromatic, and slightly bitter taste, oregano can vary in intensity. Quality oregano may almost numb the tongue. The herb is widely used in Egyptian, Spanish, Italian, Palestinian, Latin American, Turkish, Lebanese, Syrian, Greek, Philippine, Portuguese and Italian–American cuisine.

Used for centuries, the ancient Greeks used it for curing a variety of ailments from convulsions to heart failure. Hippocrates used oregano as a cure for respiratory, and stomach ailments, and as an antiseptic. In the traditional Austrian medicine oregano herb has been used internally as a tea or externally as an ointment for treating nervous system, respiratory tract and gastrointestinal tract disorders. Herbal doctors prescribed it as a general well being tonic in the 1800's as well as to promote menstruation.

A USDA study found that, gram for gram, the highest antioxidant activity belonged to the herbs of the oregano family. It reduces damage due to oxygen, such as that caused by free radicals. The antibacterial and antifungal properties of oregano have been demonstrated. Research has shown that it attacks microbes and inhibits the growth of infections, including yeast and Candida (Candida albicans).

Other studies show that oregano oil is effective against a large array of bacteria. Oregano aids indigestion, heartburn, and low stomach acidity by reducing gas in the stomach as well as soothing a churning stomach. Topically, it has been applied for treatment of microbial infections, such as athlete's foot.

Oregano: http://en.wikipedia.org/wiki/Oregano

Oregano: http://bit.ly/1d8WxJJ

Oregano:http://bit.ly/1fpE916

Paprika: Made from dried and ground chile peppers (capsicum annuum), it is a member of the nightshade family, which includes tomatoes and potatoes. It is native to tropical areas of the Western Hemisphere, including the West Indies, Central America, South America, and Mexico. Christopher Columbus is given credit for bringing the chile to Europe.

Other names for paprika include Sweet paprika, Sweet pepper, Bell pepper, Pod pepper, Pimentón, Pimiento dulce, Papurika, Paprika, Paprika de Hongrie, Édes paprika, Pimentón, Piros paprika, Fulful halou, Fulaifilah halwa, Cherven piper, Piperka, Piment annuel, Piment doux, Piment doux d'Espagne, Degi mirch , Deshi mirch, Desi mirch, Mithi mirch, Fűszerpaprika, Pimiento morrón, Kırmızı biber and Pul biber.

The largest producers of paprika are India, Peru, Spain and China. Different regions grow peppers with different heat. It can range from mild to hot. Flavors also vary from country to country. But most plants produce the sweet variety. The most well known producers of sweet paprika are the Szeged and Kalocsa regions of Hungary.

A spice that adds color, paprika is richer in vitamin C than the citrus fruits. Vitamin C provides protection against cardiovascular disease including stroke and heart attack. The abundant amount of vitamin C enables the body to absorb the iron in paprika, which is involved in the formation of red blood cells. The vitamin E contained in paprika is an antioxidant that prevents damage by free radicals and also reduces the risk of heart disease.

It is rich with minerals like magnesium, phosphorus, iron and potassium that help prevent anemia, improve heart health and purify your blood. Paprika contains an antibacterial protein that has been found to inhibit the growth of certain bacteria such as E.coli and Salmonella that are sometimes transferred through ingestion. It also aids in digestion by normalizing acid in the stomach and the vitamin A in paprika plays a crucial role in maintaining healthy eyesight.

Capsaicin helps lower blood pressure by relaxing the blood vessels and may lower the risk of cancer. Its anti–inflammatory properties are beneficial for people suffering from inflammatory and autoimmune diseases. It aids in relieving swelling caused by arthritis and other pains and aches in the body. It is rich in beta–carotene, which gets converted to vitamin A in the body. Vitamin A plays an important role in the maintenance of healthy skin by promoting a bright complexion and preventing the occurrence of wrinkles, freckles and age spots.

A rich source of vitamin B6, it helps in preventing hair loss and is involved in the production of melanin, the pigment that gives color to your hair. In fact, sweet paprika powder added to henna gives a reddish tint to hair while coloring it. However, to avoid an allergic reaction, it is best to do a patch test on the inside of your wrist before using it on your scalp. Its antibacterial properties make it effective for the treatment of skin problems caused by bacteria, including acne.

"What is Paprika?" http://bit.ly/1BuZcsM

"Paprika History" http://abt.cm/1H13cBV

"Paprika (Capsicum annuum L.)" http://bit.ly/1BDXGov

Rosemary: A member of the Mint family, which includes oregano, basil, thyme and sage, it is native to the Mediterranean. It is well suited to growing in the dry, high wind, sandy soil, high salt, rocky areas, especially along the coast. Rosemary can survive on just the spray of the seawater in the air. It is widely used in Europe for medicinal and cooking use. Today, the largest producers of Rosemary are Spain, France and Egypt.

The other names include Rosemarine, Garden rosemary, Incensier, Rosmarinus, Compass Plant, Compass Weed, Old Man, Polar Plant, Romero, Romarin, Romarin, Rusmari, Rusmary, Rosmarinus officinalis, Encensier, Herbe Aux Couronnes, Des Troubadours Rose de Marie, Rose Des Marins and Rosée De Mer.

It is highly aromatic, with the flavor hinting of both pine and lemon. It can be used to flavor dishes, added to dressings and as a medicinal herb. It is used as a natural antiviral and antibacterial. The leaves are often used to make tinctures that are applied to the skin to treat sprained ankles and muscle soreness. Studies have shown that it promotes memory and reasoning function by increasing blood flow to the brain.

Research has shown that the antioxidants in rosemary are highly effective in fighting damage caused by oxidative stress that occurs during many diseases. Other studies have also shown that it contains carnosic acid, which offers protection against harmful substances that have cancer causing potential (carcinogens). Used externally, it has been used to help prevent premature hair loss by increasing circulation and stimulating the hair follicles to renewed activity.

Use of the herb has been effective in fighting Candida or yeast infections. It contains an antioxidant that has demonstrated its ability to prevent damage to skin cells by UV–A radiation. It is used to help prevent damage to the blood vessels. This damage raises heart attack risks and gene mutations that could lead to Parkinson's, Alzheimer's and cancer. It is often used in hair care products and lotions for its anti–aging qualities. Rosemary is used in mouthwash and gargles.

"Rosemary" http://bit.ly/1I7R7eZ

"Rosmarinus Officinalis" http://bit.ly/1QKo8Aw

"Rosemary" http://bit.ly/1TF5hJd

Sage: A member of the Mint family, it is native to the Mediterranean. Today, the top producers are Turkey, USA, Ukraine and Spain. More than half of the world's supply is still wild–collected. Its leaves and stems are used fresh or dried as a flavoring in many foods.

Other names include True sage, Meadow sage, Common sage, Garden sage, Golden sage, Kitchen sage, Culinary sage, Dalmatian sage, Broadleaf sage, Salvia officinalis, Adaçayı, Maramia and Valmiki.

One of the longest histories of use of any cooking or medicinal herb, ancient Egyptians used it as a fertility drug. The ancient Greeks used it as part of a decoction to stop bleeding of wounds and clean sores and ulcers. Today, it is used for hoarseness and coughs. Externally, herbalists use it to treat swelling, bleeding ulcers, sprains, insect bites, skin, throat, mouth and gum infections and vaginal discharge. Internally, a tea made from sage leaves has been used to treat indigestion and sore throats.

Containing an anti–spasmodic agent, it reduces tension in smooth muscle and it can be used in a steam inhalation for asthma attacks. It is a proven remedy for helping to remove mucous congestion in the airways. It is used to improve the nervous system, memory and sharpening the senses. It has been used for excessive menstrual bleeding, rheumatism and to dry up a mother's milk when nursing ends.

The acids in Sage have been shown to be effective against bacteria like Staphylococcus aureus, Salmonella species and against fungi and yeasts such as Candida albicans. Sage has been used in the treatment of diarrhea in infants. It has been taken to reduce griping and other symptoms of indigestion. It is well documented that Sage leaf helps to reduce menopausal sweats. It has been use as a general tonic, for fatigue, immune system depletion, anxiety, depression, poor memory, concentration and nervous exhaustion at any age.

Sage essential oil, extract and tincture are all used in prepared medicines for stomach, mouth and throat remedies. The essential oil should not be used at high dosage or for long periods, as toxicity can occur. It is potentially toxic to nerve tissue, brain or spinal cord and should be avoided internally. People suffering from epilepsy, nervous disorders and high blood pressure should not use this oil since large doses may cause seizures. It should also not be used by lactating or pregnant women since it may cause contractions of the uterus.

"Salvia Officinalis"
http://bit.ly/1K3S3kw
"Common Name: Sage Scientific Name: Saliva officinalis"
http://bit.ly/1GA4GBL
"Sage" http://bit.ly/1ezIZso
"Sage (Garden sage) Saliva officinalis"

http://bit.ly/1LeA9MQ

Sumac: A member of the cashew family, which includes mango, poison oak, ivy and sumac, imparts a tangy lemony taste to dishes. Sumacs grow in temperate and subtropical regions such as North Africa, Iran, South Europe, Afghanistan and the Mediterranean countries. It is native to the Mediterranean and Middle East.

Other names include Rhus Coriaria, Sumach, Elm–leafed Sumac, Gewürzsumach, Kankrasing, Shumac, Sicilian Sumac, Somagh, Sommacco, Soumaki, Sumac, Somak, Sumaq, Summaq Zumaque, Summak and Tanner's Sumach.

There are different types of sumac plants. Edible sumac plants are different from poison sumac. Edible sumac has reddish, purplish or brownish berries. The berries of poison sumac are white. Sumac powder is made from the ground berries of the sumac bush. This bush grows wild in the Mediterranean region, especially parts of the Middle East and southern Italy.

Sumac is a good source of Vitamin C and Omega 3 fatty acids, which help prevent cardiovascular disease and strokes. It helps get rid of free radicals in the body, mainly in the gastrointestinal tract. The spice's antimicrobial activity may combat Salmonella bacteria. Water mixed with sumac extract has been used to wash fruits and vegetables to get rid of bacteria on them.

Research has shown that seeds of the plant are effective against Aspergillus fungus which causes lung infection and infection to other organs. Its antioxidant and antimicrobial activity could be helpful in blood sugar control.

"Health benefits of Sumac" http://bit.ly/1BDXTrX

"All About Sumac" http://bit.ly/1dYSGjl

"Sumac" http://bit.ly/1TH7qUy

Thyme: A member of the mint family, it is related to basil, rosemary, sage, savory, marjoram, oregano and lavender. It originated in the southern Mediterranean. Grown throughout North America, it is native to Europe, Asia and North Africa. About 350 thyme species exist. Today, the top producers of thyme are France, Portugal and Spain.

There are many different colors and shapes of thyme. These plants have different scents, which can give aromas such as eucalyptus, lemon, tangerine, celery, orange, pine and caraway. The subtle differences in the essential oil within the plant cause the different aromas and flavors.

There are different names for the various thyme types, which include Lemon Curd, Golden King, Goldstream, Archer's Gold, Silver Posie, Silver Queen, and Rainbow Falls. Other names include Thymus vulgaris, Thymus herba–barona, Thymus serpillum, Thymus citriodorus, Creeping Thyme, Timo, French Thyme, Garden Thyme, Common Thyme, English thyme, Mother–of–thyme and Mountain Thyme.

The types typically used in cooking are lemon thyme, common thyme, caraway thyme and wild thyme. All have mild, sweet pungent flavors. The dried or fresh sprigs, leaves and flowers can be used in dishes or for medicinal purposes. Ancient Romans used it to treat melancholy (a gloomy state of mind) and added it to cheese and alcoholic beverages. Ancient Greeks would use it in incense. During medieval times, the herb was used to give courage and vigor.

The essential oils contain large amounts of thymol, which gives the herb its flavor, its strong antiseptic, antioxidant and antibacterial properties. Today, this essential oil is widely used as an antiseptic and disinfectant. The oil has been used in mouthwashes to treat mouth inflammations and throat infections. It is also used often in cough drops.

It is used in the treatment of bronchitis, whooping cough and upper respiratory tract inflammation. It has been used to repel beetles and cabbage pests. Thyme, like all members of the family of mint, contains terpenoids that are well known for combating cancer. It also contains Curcumin, a substance in turmeric, which may help to reduce inflammation and inhibit the growth of cancer cells.

No known side effects, it is completely safe to use. However, thyme's essential oil could cause mucous membrane irritation, skin and allergic reactions. It is also recommended that thyme should not be used medicinally during pregnancy since it may cause contractions of the uterus.

"Thyme" http://bit.ly/1IYMQt2

"Varieties of Culinary Thyme" http://bit.ly/1Ghdxpol

"Thyme Leaf" http://bit.ly/1LuOnaB

"Thyme (Thymus)" http://bit.ly/1H86iWJ

"Lamiaceae" http://bit.ly/1GBKm2U

Turmeric: A member of the ginger family, which includes cardamom, it is native to and grows wild in the forest of South and Southeast Asia. It is grown in Vietnam. It has been used as a dye, medicine, and flavoring since 600 BC. Today, India is the world's largest producer of Turmeric.

A root, it is boiled, then ground into a powder. Turmeric is mildly aromatic with a pungent, slightly bitter flavor. It is deep yellowish orange in color and widely used as a food coloring for mustard, butter and cheese. It is used to make dye for clothing and textiles. It is also used to make curry and other South Asian dishes.

Other names include Turmeric Root, Indian Saffron, Yu Jin, Curcumin, Curcumine, Curcuma, Curcuma aromatica, Yu jin, Curcuma domestica, Curcumae longa, Curcuma longa, Curcuma kunyit, Jiang huang, Pian Jiang Huang, Taamerikku, Haldi, Khamin, Safran Bourbon, Safran de Batallita, Safran des Indes, Rajani, Rhizoma, Curcumae Longae Rhizoma, Curcuminoid, Curcuminoids, Halada, Haldi, Haridra, Nisha, Racine de Curcuma, Radix Curcumae, and Cucurmae Longae.

Medicinally, turmeric has been used throughout Asia to treat liver and stomach ailments. It was used externally, as a cosmetic and to heal sores. Studies have shown that turmeric can help in preventing breast cancer from spreading to the lungs. It has shown itself to be helpful in reducing inflammation and fighting infection. Turmeric contains high amounts of antioxidants, which are thought to reduce the body's risk of cancer.

Taken internally, turmeric is used to treat diarrhea, headaches, colds, fevers, bronchitis, colic, flatulence, leprosy, edema, and kidney inflammation. It has been proven to help in the relief of digestive complications and inflammation. Due to its anti–inflammatory and detoxification qualities, turmeric is used as a dietary supplement for stomach disorders and relief from irritable bowel syndrome. It has been taken to reduce gas and bloating.

Research has shown that it helps clear LDL (bad cholesterol) from the liver and improves liver function. Turmeric prevents and slows the progression of Alzheimer disease by removing protein pieces that clump together (amyloid plaque) in the brain, which otherwise would gather in the brain to form plaque and lead to brain complications. Turmeric has been used as an anti–depressant.

Antioxidants contained in turmeric help remove free radicals from the body. Free radicals damage cell membranes and cause cell death. They can also damage DNA. Curcumin, the active ingredient in turmeric, has demonstrated anti–inflammatory and disinfecting properties. It is often applied to abrasions and cuts. Turmeric also tends to deter ants.

“Turmeric (Curcuma Longa)” http://bit.ly/1SBZSRC

“Turmeric”http://bit.ly/1ItsAgf

“Turmeric” http://bit.ly/1MZArFO

“Introduction to Turmeric” http://bit.ly/1LoMxuY

“Basil” http://bit.ly/1K65gLr

“12 Amazing Benefits Of Basil Oil For Skin And Hair” http://bit.ly/1GunW08

CHAPTER 19
Healthy Grains

EATING GRAINS, ESPECIALLY WHOLE grains, provides many important health benefits. Eating whole grains as part of a healthy diet may reduce the risk of heart disease, and some chronic diseases. Consuming whole grains containing dietary fiber may help with constipation, type 2 diabetes and obesity. Many nutrients are provided by grains that are vital for the health and maintenance of our bodies including minerals (magnesium, iron and selenium) and several B vitamins (niacin, thiamin, riboflavin, and folate).

Listed below are some of the healthiest grains:

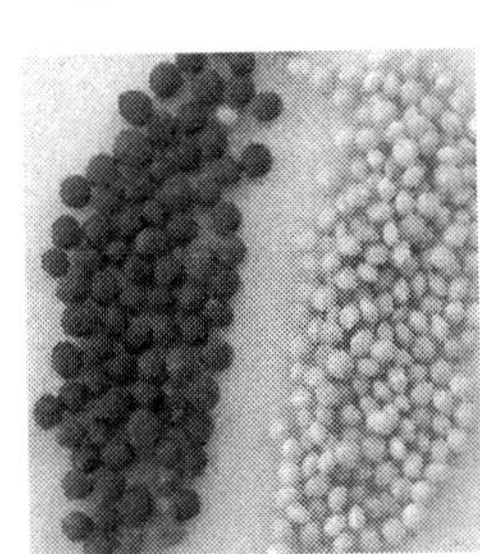

Amaranth – This tiny seed has a slight peppery flavor. It originated in South America. In the U.S., amaranth shows up in breads, cereals, and muffins. It is a delicious addition to pancakes. The oils and phytosterols in amaranth help lower cholesterol levels, including LDL (bad cholesterol) and triglycerides. The anti-inflammatory properties in the oils and peptides in amaranth can reduce inflammation and ease pain. Amaranth is a very rich source of protein, which is more digestible than other grains and has been compared to the digestibility of milk protein. Amaranth also comes in the form of flour, which can replace the white flour in recipes.

Barley – Barley has a chewy texture and a slightly sweet taste. Commonly used in soups, it's a good substitute for potatoes in stews. It is loaded with nutrients and fiber. The eight essential amino acids contained in barley represents a complete protein in our diet. The particular fiber in barley is especially helpful in lowering cholesterol and regulating blood sugar to a great extent. Barley's fiber also helps to reduce the risks of constipation.

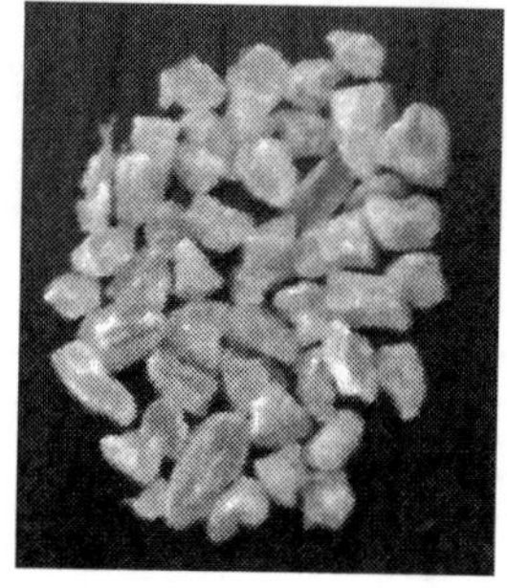

Bulgur – Bulgur is a staple of Middle Eastern cuisines. Also called cracked wheat, it has a sweet, nutty flavor. Bulgur has more fiber than quinoa, oats, millet, buckwheat, or corn. A cup of bulgur has less fat, fewer calories, and more than twice the fiber of brown rice. It is packed with a wealth of fiber and B vitamins and is a low glycemic index food, which is good for your insulin levels and blood glucose. Low glycemic index foods are better for you because they produce only small fluctuations in insulin levels and blood glucose compared with high glycemic index foods like rice.

Corn – Corn is high in antioxidants that help prevent free radicals and damaging LDL cholesterol, thus reducing the risk of cardiovascular disease. The high fiber content in corn helps prevent digestive ailments like constipation and hemorrhoids. The folic acid in corn is an important factor in preventing heart disease and lowering hypertension. If possible, choose organic corn. This is the only way to ensure that you are not eating genetically modified corn, which has long–term health risks.

Millet – Millet is tiny in size and round in shape. It can be gray, white, red or yellow. Millet can have the texture of light fluffy rice or mashed potatoes. It is a staple food in many Indian and African countries. It is high in protein. The magnesium in millet helps to reduce the severity of asthma and the frequency of migraine attacks. Magnesium also helps lower high blood pressure and reduce the risk of heart attack. The phosphorus provided by millet plays a role in the development and repair of body tissue.

Oats – Part of their distinctive flavor comes from the roasting process they undergo after being harvested and cleaned. Like barley, the fiber in oats protects against harmful LDL cholesterol in the blood. Oat's unique antioxidants reduce the risk of cardiovascular disease.

Quinoa – Pronounced keen–wah, is a small round seed. There is white, red and black quinoa. It is considered the "mother" of all grains. Considered a complete protein, it is packed with about eight grams of protein per cup. It is naturally gluten–free, high in iron and vitamin E. Incorporating quinoa into your diet could reduce the risk of cardiovascular disease, high blood pressure, type 2 diabetes, obesity and colon cancer.

Brown rice – High in selenium, brown rice is especially protective against heart disease, arthritis and colon cancer. The natural oil in brown rice also helps lower cholesterol. It is high in manganese. One cup provides 80% of our daily requirements. Manganese helps the body synthesize fats and also benefits our nervous and reproductive systems.

Black rice – Grown primarily in Asia, due to its dark color, black rice bran contains the same antioxidants found in blueberries or blackberries. Black rice is high in antioxidants, selenium, and rich in fiber. This helps reduce high blood pressure, heart disease, and inflammation.

Red rice – Red rice is grown in the agricultural parts of India, Southeast Asia and Europe. It is rich in fiber, high in selenium and antioxidants, low–calorie and low in fat. It is packed with nutrients such as B–vitamins, iron, calcium and zinc. Red rice reduces symptoms of inflammation, gives allergy relief, offers cancer prevention and assists in weight loss management.

General Cooking Directions for Plain Grains

Cooking most grains is similar to cooking rice. Put the dry grain in a pan or pot with broth or water. Bring it to a boil. Let it simmer until the liquid is absorbed. Pasta is generally cooked in a larger amount of water. Drain the excess water away after cooking.

Cooking Time Varies

Grains can vary in cooking time. This depends on the age of the grain, the variety, and the pans or pots used to cook it. When they're tender and tasty, they're done. If the grain is not as tender as you like when the "time is up," simply add more water and continue cooking. Or, if everything looks fine before all the liquid is absorbed, simply drain the excess.

Shortcuts

To cook grains more quickly, let them soak in the allotted amount of water for a few hours before cooking. Just before cooking, add extra water if necessary, then cook. The cooking time is much shorter with a little pre–soaking.

Another shortcut would be to cook the whole grains in big batches. That is, cook a large amount at one time. Grains can keep 3–4 days in your refrigerator. They take just minutes to warm up with a little added broth or water. You can use the leftovers for cold grain salads. Just toss grains in with chopped veggies and dressing.

"Cooking Whole Grains" http://bit.ly/1FvYk2a

"Great Grains and Seeds You're Not Eating"
http://wb.md/1MZAJfW
"11 Health Benefits of Amaranth" http://bit.ly/1GunXBn

"The Benefits of Bulgur" http://nyti.ms/1LeB0NO

"Health Benefits of Barley" http://bit.ly/1FvYnLq

"Health Benefits of Corn | Organic Facts" http://bit.ly/1daOnR8

"What Are The Health Benefits Of Quinoa?" http://bit.ly/1I85osf

"Top 10 Health Benefits of Brown Rice" http://bit.ly/1Gu6jgW/

"Which Is Better: Red Rice Or Brown Rice" http://bit.ly/1LsUH24

"Black Rice Beats Brown When It Comes To Its Health Benefits" http://bit.ly/1SBofvH

PART 3

CHAPTER 20

Diseases And Bad Nutrition

Candida

CANDIDA HAS BEEN CALLED the "American Parasite." This is an overgrowth of fungus acting as a parasite that uses you body as its personal feeding ground. First, it takes over your stomach and then your entire gastrointestinal (GI) tract. It forces you to crave the foods it wants, like bread, refined sugar, and alcohol, while slowly destroying your body from the inside out. You may not realize the weight gain, fatigue or lack of sleep is the result of this bug until it takes over your body forcing you to seek medical attention.

At least 70% of Americans (mostly women) are infected with the Candida fungus. Candida is a form of yeast. A very small amount of it is in your mouth and intestines. Its job is to aid with nutrient absorption and digestion. But when overproduced, it can break down the walls of the intestine and penetrate the bloodstream. This releases toxic byproducts into your body and can cause a leaky gut.

This can lead to many different health problems. They can range from skin and nail fungal infections, autoimmune disorders and chronic fatigue to skin issues. There can be difficulty in concentrating, vaginal and urinary tract infections, rectal or vaginal itching. There can also be severe seasonal allergies, itchy ears, digestive issues and depression. Doctors are now saying it could be the widest–spread health hazard to since polio, HIV, cigarettes or Hepatitis to hit North America.

What causes Candida overgrowth?

The healthy bacteria in your gut typically will keep your Candida levels in balance. The normal balance is about 80% (good bacteria) to 20% (bad bacteria). However, several factors can cause Candida overgrowth. The major factor is eating a diet high in refined carbohydrates and sugar that feeds the yeast. Consuming a lot of alcohol (which the body turns into sugar) will result in overgrowth of this fungus. Steroids and some cancer medications can weaken the immune system and allow yeast overgrowth.

There are other factors that can play a part in the overgrowth of Candida. Taking oral contraceptives, eating a diet high in beneficial fermented foods like pickles, olives and sauerkraut can contribute to the overgrowth of Candida. Taking antibiotics that kills too many of those friendly bacteria can contribute to fungus overgrowth. Stress has been pointed out as a factor. Hot weather and tight clothing are also risk factors because they create the ideal environment for the Candida fungus.

In women, Candida can be present in the vagina where damp warm conditions enable it to thrive. This overgrowth of Candida that causes a fungal infection in the genital area called candidiasis or yeast infection. At least three out of four women experience a yeast infection in their lifetime.

On contact with the penis it can spread to the male. Likewise, a male may have an overgrowth of Candida on his penis. Candida is most likely to be found underneath the foreskin where conditions enable it to grow and thrive. Men can carry the fungus without any symptoms and not know they have infected their partner. To prevent the possibility of a yeast infection coming back women and their partners should both undergo the protocol for getting the Candida back in balance.

Generally, the protocol for getting Candida under control is to remove all sugar from the diet for at least six months. "No sugar" doesn't just mean to avoid cookies, cakes, or candies. It also means not to have starchy carbohydrates like yams and potatoes and fruit. No bread or yeast. This includes peanuts, which contain fungus. Avoid fermented foods such as vinegar, sauerkraut, olives, and Kombucha. Essentially, the only things you can eat are green vegetables, certain meats and some nuts.

Because leaky gut is often involved with Candida, it is also recommended to take a probiotic, like alphadophilus to help raise the level of "good" bacteria found in the gut and help repair it. Omega-3 fatty acids will help reduce inflammation in the gut and in the body. Take grapefruit seed extract. This is a naturally occurring, antifungal agent. Drink 8–10 glasses of purified water (no chlorine or fluorine) each day. Reduce your stress by including regular exercise and/or meditation.

How To Cure Candida http://bit.ly/1QM7vay

10 Signs You Have Candida Overgrowth: What to Do About It http://bit.ly/1GCxvxm

Cure 4 Candida

http://bit.ly/1BwYOoK

Candidiasis
http://bit.ly/1Je89K7

Gout

Several of my uncles suffered from gout. Gout is one form of arthritis. It is an extremely painful inflammation of joints caused by a build-up of needle sharp uric acid crystals. This occurs when the body breaks down the chemical substances called purines producing uric acid in the blood.

Normally, uric acid dissolves in the blood, passes through the kidneys, and is excreted out of the body through the urine. When the level of uric acid in the blood becomes excessive the kidneys are not able to get rid of enough uric acid. This can also occur when the body increases the amount of uric acid it makes, or the person eats too many foods high in purines. Foods high in purines, include beer, seafood, meat, meat organs (liver), and HFCS drinks. Obesity, high blood pressure, lead poisoning, heavy alcohol consumption, fast weight loss, cyclosporine (medicine used by transplant patients), regular use of aspirin, niacin, and diuretic medicine have also been known to bring about a gout attack and may be some of the contributing causes of gout.

Obesity, Diabetes, Liver Damage, Tooth Decay and Leaky Gut

High doses of free fructose have punched holes in the intestinal lining. That is because free fructose requires more energy to be absorbed by the gut. This depletes the energy fuel source required to maintain the integrity of the intestinal wall or lining. When this lining is compromised because of the depletion of the body's energy source, food and bacteria "leak" across the intestinal membrane. An immune reaction and body wide inflammation are triggered when toxic gut bacteria and partially digested food proteins enter your bloodstream. This inflammation is the root of obesity, heart disease, diabetes, accelerated aging, dementia and cancer because of the affect on the immune system.

High fructose corn syrup (HFCS) and foods rich in sugars and sweeteners like HFCS, rot the teeth by decaying the enamel coating. Like other refined sugars, HFCS contain no vitamins or nutrients. The vitamins and nutrients needed to digest the carbohydrates must be drawn from your body's bone and tissues. This depletes your body of its valuable nutrients.

Even though foods that contain high levels of HFCS provide lots of calories, those calories have no nutritional value. Foods containing high amounts of HFCS are a source of body fatigue because they cause your body to release great amounts of hormone and endorphins. Too much of this refined sugar will cause your body to crave more. This results in mood swings when trying to cut back because the desires and craving only increases.

This is the major cause of liver damage in this country. This condition is called nonalcoholic "fatty liver" disease (NAFLD). It affects about 70 million people today. NAFLD in turn leads to hepatic insulin resistance, type II diabetes, and a host of other obesity–related conditions

When glucose is rapidly absorbed into the bloodstream, this triggers spikes in insulin. Insulin is a hormone produced by the pancreas to regulate carbohydrates and fat metabolism in the body. The continued spikes in insulin lead to leptin being inhibited. Leptin is a protein hormone that acts on receptors in the hypothalamus of the brain where it controls appetite. When leptin is limited, appetite control is hindered since this interferes with the body's hormones signaling the brain that one is full (satiated). This leads to increased food intake, weight gain, diabetes, heart disease, cancer, dementia, and more.

Obesity and irregular fluctuations of insulin lead to diabetes in many people. This is because of the continual damage to the pancreas caused by these irregular spikes of insulin production. This overworking of the pancreas causes the pancreas to stop producing insulin or insufficient amounts of insulin produced to regulate carbohydrates and fat metabolism.

Attention Deficit Hyperactivity Disorder (ADHD)

In 1968, Dr. Leon Eisenburg was considered by some to be the "scientific father of ADHD". He was the first person to actually coin the term ADHD. In his last interview before his death, in the Spiegal Magazine in Germany on February 2nd 2012, he said he made up the name of the disease and it does not exist.

The primary treatment and protocol of children diagnosed with ADHD is Ritalin (methylphenidate) or Adderall (amphetamine and dextroamphetamine). These two drugs contain a mixture of amphetamine salts. Both drugs are schedule 2 narcotics. They are in the same category with cocaine, opium, morphine, and demerol.

These drugs are incredibly strong and addictive. About 4 to 6 million children take Ritalin daily.

A major factor contributing to this is the huge increase in the number of prescriptions written for Ritalin and other stimulants. In the U.S., the number of stimulant prescriptions rose from around 5 million in 1991 to nearly 35 million in 2007. The rise of ADHD diagnoses and prescriptions for stimulants over the years was accompanied by a moneymaking campaign by pharmaceutical companies to publicize ADHD and promote the pills to doctors, educators and parents.

Dr. Umar Johnson, a noted clinical and school psychologist, points out that these drugs don't solve hypertension, anger or aggression. They only suppress the symptoms. They kill brain cells, interfere with heart function, cause instant death, liver damage, kidney failure, epilepsy, diabetics, schizophrenia, psychosis, interference with sleep–wake cycle, effect diet (eating too much or not enough) and erodes ability to produce healthy semen.

The U.S. uses 85% of the world's supply of Ritalin. Dr. Jean Haslet, former head of Diversion for the FDA stated "Ritalin is like cocaine. If a cocaine addict is given Ritalin, he can not tell the difference between cocaine and Ritalin." In the U.S. armed forces, if you are on either Ritalin or Adderall on a regular basis, they will not allow you to enlist in the armed forces.

As a classroom teacher for 30 years, I have observed many of my students diagnosed as ADHD. While on medication they could not concentrate. Many would simple fall asleep. Some could not keep still. A few would have a far off stare. At times, there were classroom disruptions. Many expressed their frustration because they could not concentrate.

Dr. Ted Broer, M.D., author of "Breakthrough Health", believes the huge problem that we are now having with Meth and Amphetamines is because of the Ritalin we have given these children since the time they were five years old until they are 18. Children get addictive and grow up to be addictive adults. That may explain why Meth labs are all over the place cooking this stuff.

As parents and guardians, we have the responsibility to protect our children from unsafe food and drugs. We should not allow our children to ingest food with artificial colors, sugar and HFCS and when they react to this junk by becoming hyperactive and unable to concentrate have them drugged with very powerful and potent drugs. Especially, when this drugging of our children appears motivated by the financial gain.

Inventor Of ADHDs Deathbed Confession ADHD Is A Fictitious Disease http://bit.ly/1TIoKWd

Living In Color The Potential Dangers Of Artificial Dyes http://onforb.es/1TIoO8D

Dr. Umar Johnson "The Planned Drugging Of The Black Community" YouTube Video Published September 13, 2013

The Selling Of Attention Deficit Disorder http://nyti.ms/1GCy5Lr

Is Ritalin chemically Similar to Cocaine http://slate.me/1K723Lv

Poor Man's Cocaine http://onforb.es/1TIoO8D

Breakthrough Health Book by Dr. Ted Broer Publisher: Dr. Ted Broer (1999);

CELIAC DISEASE

About 1 out of 200 of all Americans, experts estimate, have celiac disease. This condition causes an abnormal immune response to gluten that damages the lining of the small intestine. That, in turn, can prevent important nutrients from being absorbed by the body. This causes both gastrointestinal distress and nutritional deficiencies. If untreated, this can then lead to intestinal cancers as well as complications such as infertility and osteoporosis. More than 55 diseases have been linked to gluten, the protein found in barley, wheat, and rye. There is a wide range of disorders in which gluten has an adverse effect on the body. This includes minor rashes, high blood sugar, unattractive stomach bulges, to celiac disease. It is also estimated that 99% of the people who have either celiac disease or gluten intolerance are never diagnosed.

HIGH BLOOD PRESSURE AND KIDNEY DISEASE

The vast majority of sodium in the typical American diet comes from foods that are processed and prepared. These processed foods include fast foods, most canned foods, some frozen vegetables, soups, pizza, bacon, cheese, prepared dinners, smoked and cured meat, sauces, salad dressings, and egg dishes. Many commercially prepared condiments and seasonings are also high in sodium.

If you ingest too much salt you raise the amount of sodium in your bloodstream. This reduces the ability of your kidneys to reduce the water. The extra water stored in your body raises your blood pressure. High blood pressure can cause a strain on your kidneys, heart, arteries, and brain. This can lead to strokes, kidney disease, heart attacks, and dementia.

The adequate intake of sodium for African–Americans, those with hypertension, diabetes, or over the age of 50 is 1,500 milligrams daily. The maximum is up to 2,300 for all other males and females ages 9–50. The value is less than one teaspoon of table salt per day.

CHAPTER 21
Uterine Fibroids

UTERINE FIBROIDS ARE MUSCULAR tumors that grow from the smooth tissue in the wall of the uterus. These fibroids are almost always noncancerous. They often appear during childbearing years. This firm rubbery mass distinct from the nearby tissue is created when a single cell repeatedly divides. Fibroids may be single or multiple tumors. The size and growth patterns of the fibroids vary. The fibroids may grow slowly, rapidly, or remain the same size.

Fibroids can be as small as an apple or as large as a grapefruit. Some fibroids may shrink on their own. Many fibroids that have been present during pregnancy shrink or disappear after pregnancy. This occurs as the uterus goes back to normal size.

As many as three out of four women have uterine fibroids at some time during their lives, but most are unaware of them because they often cause no symptoms. Women who do have symptoms can find fibroids very challenging. Some have pain and heavy menstrual bleeding. Fibroids can put pressure on the bladder or rectum. This can cause frequent urination or rectal pressure. Some women look pregnant when fibroids get very large causing the abdomen to enlarge.

Fibroids become more common in women during 30s and 40s through menopause. After menopause, fibroids usually shrink. Overweight women are at a three to four times greater risk than the average for developing fibroids. Having family members with fibroids increases your risk. This is especially true, if the family members share the same unhealthy diet.

Warm baths, reasonable exercise, proper diet, and positive attitude are the best defense against uterine fibroids. According to Dr. Jewel Pookrum, the prostate of a man and a woman's uterus are made out of the same tissue. It is the same organ. It is in the same place in the body. The biggest difference is that the uterus has estrogen and the prostrate does not. This estrogen creates the different functions between the two. Everything that damages the prostate gland also damages the uterus.

As with the location of the prostate and rectum of men, the uterus and rectum is separated only by a thin wall of tissue. As long as feces flows through and out of the rectum there is no problem. The problem develops when there are no regular bowel movements. This results in stool setting in the rectum two or three days and not being evacuated. For many women, like many men, having a bowel movement once every two to three days is far too common.

If the brain gives a signal that it is time to have a bowel movement, we should act upon it. Some women may not follow their brain's urging to eliminate the body's waste. Perhaps, they may want to wait until they get a break from the activity they are currently engaged in, or wait for a more convenient place. An example would be to wait until they get home, or another place that makes them feel more comfortable. Delaying the bowel movement until we get home or another place of comfort does not always guarantee that we will still have the urge to release our waste.

The brain will stop sending normal signals to defecate if we continue to not heed the brain's urging. By not acting upon the brain's urging to eliminate, the urge may go away. Often, the urge to eliminate the waste may not return again until there is a large build–up of waste in the colon. The pressure from that build–up becomes so great it forces the signal to discharge on the anus.

By the time the signal to discharge waste is forced upon the anus, the waste build–up in the colon is usually compacted (pushed tightly together). Constipation often results. This compaction can extend to our lower intestine and start our bellies to extend. Being full of waste, we can become bloated and uncomfortable. Waste lines will often disappear.

The waste setting in the rectum must go somewhere. If the waste setting in the rectum does not exit out of the rectum, it will begin to migrate to the surrounding areas. Since there is but a thin membrane separating the uterus and rectum, the stool can seep onto the uterus causing it to be infected.

This type of infection can be avoided. It is more common in the man's prostate gland than in the woman's uterus. That is because women usually take regular baths in very warm water. Most men have been socialized not to take regular baths. Many men believe that taking a bath is a "woman's thing". Some men believe that men should only take a shower.

Both men and women should submerge in very warm water to keep their prostate gland and uterus healthy. We both were formed in very warm water in our mother's womb. It makes sense that being in warm water would assist in our cleaning, healing, and regeneration. The warmer (closer to hot), the better. Formed in our mother's womb we were subjected to 98 degrees Fahrenheit (37° Celsius). It seems to make sense that soaking in very warm water would result in health benefits.

The uterus has a tendency to get congested. This is because it is cushioned in the pelvic area with many other body structures. The bladder, ovaries, sigmoid colon, cervix, rectum, vagina, and fallopian tubes are lodged in the same closely packed area. A warm bath is one of the most effective treatments where there is congestion, inflammation, and irritability of the uterus.

Bathing in warm water assists the body in bringing the waste matter back into the rectum. Submerging in warm water stimulates the blood vessels. This allows the build–up of toxins and waste particles to be reabsorbed into the bloodstream. The toxins and waste particles are then transported from the bloodstream to the kidneys, or liver, and back into the colon. The waste matter is then pushed from the colon to exit from the rectum.

Very warm water can also help soften the stool. This allows an easier elimination of the stool and less stress on the body. Stress is often relieved when bathing in warm water. Warm water baths can provide the benefits of relaxation along with assisting the body with its elimination.

Black women

According to the statistics given, Black/African American women are more likely to develop uterine fibroids than white women. Statistics vary, showing the rate in African American women 2 to 3 times the rate seen in white women. There are many reasons for this. The maturation rate, physiology, and neurology of the Black and white women are very different.

Blacks reach 90 percent of their maturity about the age of 14. Whites reach 90 percent of their maturity about the age of 21. This points to the fact that Black's window of opportunity for proper nutrition is smaller than that of the whites. Blacks have from infancy to about 14 to actualize their best physical and neurological development. Whites have about 7 more years to reach their physical and neurological maturity.

The hemoglobin count of black women is lower than that of white women. Generally, it is 1 gram to a gram and 1/2 less than the norm for whites. The white cell count of black women is generally 1000 to 2000 lower than whites. The T–cell count is normally lower than that of white women and the bone mass of black women is ten times that of white women. It should be no surprise that African American women require much more calcium than white women.

White women have more ammonium salt, and sulphur in their bodies than Black women. Black women have more water in their bodies than white women. The ammonium and sulphur gives the smell on white women's hair when it is wet. The ammonium in their body makes white women feel warm in conditions that would feel cold to most Black women.

One example of this would be members of a polar bear club. The ammonium in their bodies allows them to feel warm enough to jump in cold water in the winter. Another example would be white women feeling warm in a cold office room. The temperature in the room would be fine for whites. But for most Black women, the temperature would be uncomfortably cool.

This blood chemistry difference creates other problems for Black women that white women do not have. When a white woman goes to her physician for consulting, treatment, or dispensing of drugs, a white woman's standard is used. When Black women go to the physician, the same white women's standards of measurement is used to diagnose, consult, or dispense drugs, even though the chemistry of the two is vastly different.

An example given by Dr. Jewel Pookrum is as follows: If an African woman is measured by the same standard as a white woman for calcium, by the time (the Black woman's) level falls to that of a low level for a white woman, she (the Black woman) has already suffered irreparable damage.

This results in many misdiagnoses. Black women are often given the wrong medical treatment. Misinformation given is not uncommon. Drugs have been dispensed based on a standard that should not apply to Black women. One can only imagine the fatalities that may have resulted because of the lack of a correct standard used for Black woman's body.

"Rise Of The Immortals" Dr Jewel Pookrum And Dr. Delbert Blair http://bit.ly/1dZo9Sl

Dr. Llaila Africa "Understanding Melanin" Published on Jan 22, 2014 http://bit.ly/1BwYkUH

Handbook Of Hair In Health And Disease – page 38 Victor R. Preedy – 2012 – Wageningen Academic Publishers

Drug Testing In Hair – p. 73 Edited by Pascal Kintz Published by Robert B. Stern. 1996

Textbook Of Aging Skin – p.509 Editors: Miranda A. Farage, PhD, Kenneth W. Farage, PhD, Howard I. Maibach, M.D. Publisher: Springer–Verlag Berlin Heidelberg 2010 p.509

"Racial Differences In Bone Strength"

http://1.usa.gov/1TI15bu/

Stress

Dr. Jewel Pookrum points out in "The Psychology of Uterine Fibroids", that African women living in the presence of a European cultural value system have fibroids. An Eurocentric cultural value system (ECVS) is a system of society or government in which Europeans (especially men) hold the power and people of color are largely excluded. This is in contrast to African women who live under their own cultural belief system. This disease does not plague these African women even though they may have 14–15 children.

The ECVS is in contrast to the matriarchal system, where the woman rules a family, clan, or tribe. Africans have lived under the matriarchal system for eons. Women have not been honored in the modern ECVS. In Africa, South America and other countries that have been colonized and accepted Eurocentric values, women suffer from the same disease.

Blacks nursed on the ECVS try to adapt and live through it. This creates a conflict with their genetic memory of how they are to live. This conflict manifests throughout their physical bodies and demonstrates that the life style that they have selected is not conducive to the way their tissues would like to function.

One example would be diet. Blacks' diet is created on their ancestry. They do not require large concentrations of fats and proteins. They require different types of nutrients in different concentrations. Eating a European diet instead of our forefather's alkaline diet (fruits, vegetables, grains, legumes), which originates from a different climate, does not support Blacks' body type and has been considered alien to our race.

Because Black's have so many more blood vessels than Europeans, if they eat foods high in quantities that close up or obstruct the blood vessel passages the nervous system is compromised. There is less blood to go to the brain. This can cause them to use only the lower stem of the brain, which can cause them to be more irritable, irrational, and even violent.

Wigs, Weaves

Many Black women wear wigs or hair weaves. Many to make Europeans feel less fearful wear this "straight hair" look. Europeans' fear is the foundation of their racism, which poses may problems for Blacks. Many Blacks take on this look to help them maintain their present jobs with Europeans and assist them in obtaining new ones. Some have even bought into the propaganda and conditioning, believing it is best to look and be like Europeans.

Years ago, I applied for a job wearing my hair in a "natural" style. I was turned down. The next day I came to the same white woman who had turned me down the day before with attached weaved on straight hair. She immediately hired me to go to work that day.

This quest to calm European's fear has come with a price. Many wear the lace front wig. This is usually applied to the front hairline area and attached with the assistance of glues and tapes. Once applied the wig will usually stay bonded for up to a week. Some lace wigs are treated with chemicals that may react with your skin. Many have experienced headaches, hair loss, dandruff, and damaged hair. Some may have a bad reaction to the glue used to apply the wig. Experts say that the high toxic levels of hair glue can cause allergic reactions, which can cause death.

Inspired by the high cost of hair, some procurers of hair have obtained hair to be sold, not just from living people. Some "human hair" used for weaves have come from the heads of dead people. This subjects the women to organisms that can get into the scalps and cause problems.

The weave is considered to be a graduation from the wig. It is a form of hair extensions often used by black women, and celebrities. Hair extensions are woven, or glued, into the hair from the track. Most start at $1,000.00. There is also the cost of the hair and the washing and conditioning every two to three weeks. This can cost from $18,000 to $150,000 each year. Most women would consider this a financial stress.

Hair Relaxers – Perm

Chemicals that straighten or relax hair can destroy hair and decrease the vitality of your system. Chemicals kill nutrients in the hair and the electromagnetic information that your body receives. Your hair is an antenna that communicates directly to the brain. When you decrease its ability to pick up electromagnetic information, you decrease the value of your system.

In 2011, at Beebe Memorial Cathedral in Oakland, California, I heard the Honorable Dick Gregory say in his speech "There were no fibroid tumors before the perm". This statement has been supported by research at Boston University. The research links chemical hair relaxers with uterine fibroids. The study's research reveals that Black women who had used chemical relaxers over a long period of time were at a greater risk for fibroids.

Relaxers contain chemicals like sodium hydroxide (lye). This chemical can eat through the skin and cause bald spots. If it is inhaled it can cause permanent lung damage. The study theorizes that chemicals like phthalates (industrial chemicals used to make plastics more flexible) get into the scalp through chemical burns and lesions. Once inside the body these phthalates can mimic estrogen.

This causes excess estrogen, resulting in hormone imbalance, which can lead to uterine fibroids.

In addition to phthalates, parabens have been associated with fibroid development. Parabens are chemicals used as a preservative in cosmetics and food. Like phthalates, parabens mimics estrogen and can result in hormone imbalance and the growth of fibroids. Both chemicals are unlike plant estrogen, which are water soluble and can be easily eliminated by the body. Phthalates and parabens dissolve in body fat and remain in the body for a very long time. This can lead to various cancers.

The Federal Drug Administration (FDA) does not regulate the hair care and cosmetic industry. Manufacturers do not have to state what chemicals are contained in hair care products and cosmetics commonly used by African–American women. Most relaxers contain fragrance. Manufacturers can legally have phthalates and parabens contained in the products without individually listing them by name. They can be put in the product as part of the "fragrance" along with the other listed ingredients.

The Black hair care is a multibillion dollar industry. The FDA doesn't regulate the hair care industry. So, there's no way to tell what black women are putting in their hair and how harmful these products may be. We have no way of knowing the many harmful additives that can be legally added to hair care products. Especially, since producers do not have to list ingredients they deem as part of the fragrance.

Families

Many Black women feel they have to make a choice between having a career and family in this present ECVS. In our African culture, this would not be the case. The family would always come first and children would be considered a blessing. Many that do have children, are the head of single families. Either choice can be a source of stress for a Black or Brown woman living under an ECVS.

Recommendations

Melanin–dominate people should use coconut oil and Shea butter on their hair rather than chemicals that straighten the hair. Coconut oil and Shea butter are natural and originate from the areas where people of color originate. It is also best to follow the rule of not putting anything on your skin or hair that you can not safely eat.

Blacks should open more of their own businesses. This would eliminate the stress of working for someone with a different cultural perpective. Since the FDA doesn't regulate the hair care industry, this creates a wonderful opportunity for the establishment of a new industry of safe and healthy cosmetics and hair care products for Black women.

Dr. Jewel Pookrum *The Psychology of Uterine Fibroids*

Dr. Jewel Pookrum, *Vitamins and Minerals from A to Z* 1993, 1999 A & B Publishers Group Brooklyn, New York

Dick Gregory: 2011, at Beebe Memorial Cathedral in Oakland, California

Good Hair Sit Back And Relax Chris Rock Lion Gate Films Inc. Ó2009 Home Box Office, Inc.

"Are Hair Relaxers To Blame For Uterine Fibroids"

http://bit.ly/1LfZt59

Hair Relaxer Use And Risk Of Uterine Leiomyomata In African–American Women" http://wb.md/1IueDyG

"Study: Hair Relaxers Linked To Fibroids"

http://bit.ly/1FwFoQN

"Rise Of The Immortals" Dr Jewel Pookrum & Dr Delbert Blair Part 1 YouTube

http://bit.ly/1NoZcBC

"Hair Weaves From Corpses Are Filled With Flesh–eating Worms"

http://bit.ly/1Gvg52x

"Why I'll Never Wear Hair Extensions Again, By Pop Star Jamelia" http://dailym.ai/1IueGKR

"Countress Vaughn On The Medical Dangers Of Wearing Lace Front Wigs" http://bit.ly/1BwYwTI

"Wigs Cause Health Problems"

http://bit.ly/1Gimwqp

"Lace Wigs" http://en.wikipedia.org/wiki/Lace_wig

Proper Diet

Proper diet and reasonable exercise will assist in deterring uterine fibroid challenges. Eating fruits, grains, and vegetables provide the nutrients to help our bodies grow and repair themselves. Roughage from the proper foods helps to clean out the colon and move the waste out of the body. Reasonable exercise helps to strengthen the body and aid body functions. All of this aids the body in proper elimination of its waste.

I would also recommend a body detoxification where there is excessive waste build–up. This will rid the body of unneeded waste, inflammation, parasites, and their parasitic eggs. More, importantly, it will help the body in its regulation of regular bowel movements.

Proper diet is profoundly important in protecting women from developing fibroids. Eating plenty of green leafy vegetables (vitamin A source) seems to safeguard women from developing fibroids. Eating a lot of red meat (e.g. beef) and ham is associated with the presence of uterine fibroids.

The synthetic growth hormones and antibiotics in poultry and beef has been linked to uterine fibroids. Animals raised on growth hormones and antibiotics grow at an unnaturally fast rate in order to meet demand. The hormones produce heavier flesh. The heavier animals are sold for a bigger profit. The animals are slaughtered with these unhealthy additives still in their systems.

Eating the beef and poultry means ingesting the same growth hormones and antibodies. Too much of this can cause higher estrogen activity in women. This seems to be a major contributing factor in developing uterine fibroids. This can lead to hormone imbalance, weight gain, reproductive health issues, and cancers. The excess estrogen produced also feeds the fibroids, thus encouraging these fibroids to grow even bigger.

Unfermented soy contains compounds that mimic and sometimes block the hormone estrogen. Unfermented soy includes tofu, soy milk, soy meat, soy protein, soybean oil, soy yogurt, edamane, soy infant formula, soy cheese, soy burgers, and soy ice cream. When the compounds mimic estrogen, excess estrogen is produced. This can cause uterine fibroids or feed existing fibroids to become larger. These compounds are known to disrupt endocrine function. This may cause infertility and breast cancer in women.

Fermented soy, includes natto, soy sauce, tempeh, and miso. Fermentation reduces the adverse effects of the compounds in soy. This allows the beneficial properties to become available to your digestive system. Fermented soy is what Japanese people eat to live longer and have lower rates of cancer than Americans.

There are reasons to leave all soy grown in the U.S. alone. Over 80 percent of soy grown in the U.S. and more than 90 percent of American soy crops are GM (genetically modified). Soy causes red blood cells to clump together, limiting proper absorption and distribution of oxygen to your tissues. Soy contains substances that interfere with iodine metabolism and thyroid function. Soybeans are processed by acid washing in aluminum tanks. This creates toxic levels of aluminum and manganese.

It is important to be committed and dedicated to the proper diet. This will reduce the fibroids and prevent other fibroids from developing. Even in women who have had fibroids removed, when these women abandon their healthy diets, the fibroids return. If you must eat animal products, choose organically fed and grown animal products without hormones.

A high–fiber diet of vegetable–based foods is one of the most important things to combat fibroids. Apples, whole grains like cereals, oats, millet, oatmeal, nuts, and seeds are all good sources of fiber. This keeps constipation away. Constipation can increase fibroid symptoms worsening the pain and the pressure.

Green leafy vegetables like lettuce, spinach, orka, celery, cabbage, and fruits like cucumber, kiwi, avocado, and plum are rich sources of vitamin K. This encourages blood clotting and helps to reduce excess menstrual flow. Plant foods that contain high amounts of plant estrogen, like nuts, seeds, and ground flax seed, help to properly regulate the body's estrogen production.

Dandelion, Milk Thistle, and Yellow Burdock help to metabolize estrogen in the body. Goldenseal also helps stimulate the liver to metabolized excess estrogen. Avoid foods that contain non–plant source estrogen. Increasing your intake of fresh fruits and vegetables keeps estrogen levels low. A plant–based diet creates a more alkaline body.

"Estrogen Dominance"
http://bit.ly/1GimChH

"The Meat You Eat: Steroid Use in Livestock" http://bit.ly/1GvgmT7

"Steroid Hormone Implants Used For Growth In Food–Producing Animals" http://1.usa.gov/1QM8mrR

"Rise Of The Immortals" Dr Jewel Pookrum And Dr. Delbert Blair
http://bit.ly/1dZo9Sl

"Four Foods Women With Fibroids Should Avoid"
http://bit.ly/1Lw8GnT

"Soy Can Damage You Health"
http://bit.ly/1BGYs4c

"The Top Ten Worst Foods For A Uterine Fibroid"
http://bit.ly/1NoZXuz

"Kidney Stones In–Depth Report"
http://nyti.ms/1H914Kn

"Racial Differences in Bone Strength"
http://1.usa.gov/1LgoESc

Alkaline Body

The human blood can be measured on an acidic/alkaline scale (ph). The scale ranges from 0–14. 0 is the most acidic, and 14, the most alkaline. The blood ph is considered neutral at 7.0. Human blood should be slightly alkaline (7.35 – 7.45). A blood ph below 7.0 is acidic. This generally means symptoms of disease.

An acidic ph in the blood causes the body many problems. It decreases the body's ability to absorb minerals, oxygen, and other nutrients. This impairs the body's ability to repair damaged cells and detoxify heavy metals. There is a decrease in energy production in the cells, and tumor cells thrive. Alkalinity thwarts fibroid growth. When the body is acidic, fibroid growth is enhanced.

To maintain health, the body's diet should consist of about 60 per cent alkaline forming foods and about 40 per cent acid forming foods. To restore health, increase your intake of alkaline foods. The restoration diet should be increased to about 80 per cent alkaline forming foods and decrease acid forming foods to about 20 per cent.

Generally, alkaline forming foods include most fruits, seeds and nuts, green vegetables, beans, peas, lentils, millet, blackstrap molasses, herbs, spices, and seasoning.

Generally, acid forming foods include animal products such as red meat, dairy, and eggs. Steer clear of acid producing processed foods like refined carbohydrates such as white sugar, pastries, and white flour. Avoid drinking acid producing beverages like coffee (caffeine) and soft drinks. Alcohol, artificial chemical sweeteners, and saturated fats form acid.

"A Detailed List of Acid/Alkaline Forming Foods"
http://bit.ly/1Io5JeO

REDUCING FIBROIDS

If you presently have fibroids, your intake of detoxifying foods will help to reduce or shrink the fibroids. Below are examples of detoxifying foods. Fruits are important in detoxifying the body. Garlic may be one of the best detox foods there is. Garlic helps stimulate the liver into producing detoxifying enzymes. These enzymes help to filter residues from the digestive system. Garlic may be eaten cooked or raw. We would recommend eating a raw bulb of garlic with slices of oranges.

Fruits like pears, rich in phytonutrients, prevent disease and keep the body working properly. Fruits that are high liquid content help the body wash out toxins. These fruits are easy to digest. They are high in antioxidants, nutrients, fiber, and vitamins.

Green foods like barley, wheatgrass, kale, spinach, spirulina, alfalfa, chard, arugula and other organic green leafy vegetables gives chlorophyll to boost your digestive tract. Chlorophyll helps aid the liver in detoxification. It also rids the body of harmful environmental toxins.

Citrus fruit like oranges, lemons, and limes aid the body in flushing out toxins and providing enzymes to aid the digestive tract. Lemon juice supports the cleansing process of the liver. Start each morning with a warm glass of lemon juice to increase detoxification.

Broccoli sprouts are extremely high in antioxidants. The ability of the broccoli sprout to stimulate the detoxification enzymes of the digestive tract is amazing. The sprouts are more effective in detoxification than the fully-grown broccoli.

Green Tea is packed with antioxidants. Its high liquid content washes toxins out of the body. Green tea contains a special type of antioxidant called catechins. This antioxidant is known to aid in the increase of liver function.

Mung Beans are used in the body's detoxification. Ayurvedic doctors have used Mung Beans for thousands of years. Mung Beans are easy to digest. The beans absorb toxic residue from the intestinal walls.

Raw Vegetables are great for detoxification. They are best juiced or eaten raw. Examples are onions, artichokes, carrots, broccoli, cauliflower, kale, Brussel spouts, cabbage, asparagus, garlic, oregano, beet, and turmeric. The combination of these foods will help aid your liver in purging toxins during the cleansing process. These vegetables are high in sulphur and glutathione. The liver uses sulphur to help it detoxify harmful chemicals.

Hemp, sunflower, sesame, pumpkin, and chia seeds are good sources in developing healthy bodies and aiding detoxification. Organic seeds in their raw state are best. Avoid irradiated or roasted seeds. Seeds and nuts are high in fiber, vitamin E, and monounsaturated fats that help the body keep disease free. Healthy seeds are a great source of protein, minerals, zinc and other nutrients. Seeds and nuts can prevent weight gain, the development of heart disease, and LDL (bad) cholesterol.

Omega–3 oils like hemp, avocado, or flax seed oil help lubricate the intestinal wall. This allows the toxins absorbed by the oil to be eliminated by the body.

The uterus, like the prostate gland, is harmed by fried foods and alcohol. Vinegar will dehydrate (dry) the uterus. Salt and sugar also pulls moisture out of the uterus. Coffee (both caffeinated and decaffeinated), soda, chocolate, and tea containing caffeine allows the development of uterine fibroids by decreasing the blood flow to the uterus. This causes waste to accumulate. This waste is called fibroids. Fibroids are waste material isolated in a bump form called a tumor.

Herbs that aid uterine fibroids

Herbs can assist in the healing process of uterine fibroids. Witch Hazel (the herb), Shepard's Purse, White Oak Bark, Thuja, and Burdock Root, help to shrink uterine fibroids naturally. Red Cover, Dandelion Root, Chaparral, Echinacea and Goldenseal help to cleanse the blood and eliminate waste. Camp Bark, Boswella, and White Willow help to relieve pain.

Red Raspberry, Chaste (also called Vitex), Black Cohosh, Squaw Vine, Damiana, and Blessed Thistle cleanses the blood and strengthens the uterus. Feverfew and Saint John's Wort helps to relieve tension and stress. Saw Palmetto and Pygeum (African) reduces estrogen levels which reduces fibroids. Wild Yam helps to balance hormones and Alum Root (also known as Crane's Bill or Wood Geranium), causes the blood to clot.

Other herbs like False Unicorn, a uterine and ovarian tonic, helps to regulate menstration. Dong Quai aids in balancing estrogen levels naturally. Pau d'Arco is a powerful anti–tumor herb that is helpful in fibroid reduction. Evening Primrose Oil offers hormone balancing Essential Fatty Acids. Ginger is important to help the lymph and blood system eliminate fibroid tissue from the body as it breaks down. Dandelion and Goldenseal also help stimulate the liver to metabolized excess estrogen.

Herbs that aid in healing the prostate gland are also useful in maintaining the health of the uterus and reducing fibroids. Gotu Kola, Ginkgo Biloba, Glucosamine, Maca, and Mira Puama help both the prostate gland and uterine fibroids.

Dr. Llaila O. Afrika: *Holistic Health*. Revised edition June 17, 2004

"Foods That Detox The Body"

http://bit.ly/1RpKdCp

"How Can I Eat To Shrink My Fibroid"

http://bit.ly/1BwYStE

"Uterine, Fibroids, and Endometriosis"

http://bit.ly/1ftm95M

CHAPTER 22
Prostate

THE PROSTATE OF A man and a woman's uterus are made out of the same tissue. It is the same organ. It is in the same place in the body. The two have different functions. The biggest difference is that the uterus has estrogen and the prostrate does not.

The prostate is said to be a walnut–sized gland located between the bladder and the penis. It is located just in front of the rectum. The uretha is a tube that runs through the center of the prostrate, from the bladder to the penis. The uretha lets urine flow out of the body through the penis.

The prostate secretes fluid that protects and nourishes sperm. During ejaculation, the prostate squeezes this fluid into the uretha. The fluid is expelled with the sperm as semen. The prostate is said to grow larger with age. If it gets too large it can cause problems. An enlarged prostate will make urination difficult. This may result in frequent visits to the restroom to urinate. This is very common for men after age fifty.

According to Dr. Jewel Pookrum, the prostate gland and the rectum are separated only by a thin wall of tissue. As long as feces flows through and out of the rectum there is no problem. The problem develops when there are no regular bowel movements. This results in stool setting in the rectum two or three days and not being evacuated. For many, having a bowel movement once every two to three days is far too common.

If the brain tells us it is time to have a bowel movement, we should act upon it. Some of us do not follow the urging of our brain to eliminate the body's waste. Perhaps, we might want to wait for a more convenient time or place. An example would be to wait until we get home or another place that makes us feel more comfortable. Often, waiting until we get home or another place of comfort does not guarantee we still have the urge to release our waste.

The brain will stop signaling us when it is time to have a bowel movement if we continue not heeding the brain's signal. By ignoring the urge to act upon the brain's signal to defecate, the urge may go away. The urge may not return again until there is such an exceedingly large build–up of waste in the colon that the pressure is so great it forces the signal to eliminate on the anus.

By that time, the waste build–up in the colon may be impacted. That is because there may be so much waste in the colon as a result of the build–up, the stool is pushed together or compacted. Constipation often results. This compaction can extend to our lower intestines and can start our bellies to extend. Being full of waste, we can become bloated and uncomfortable.

The waste setting in the rectum must go somewhere. If the waste setting in the rectum does not exit out of the rectum, it will begin to migrate to the surrounding areas. Since there is but a thin membrane separating the prostate and rectum, the stool can seep onto the prostate. This can cause the prostate to be infected.

Taking baths in warm water is one of the ways to avoid this infection. Most men have been socialized not to take baths. Many men believe that taking a bath is a "woman's thing". Some men believe that men should only take a shower.

Men, like women, were formed in warm water in their mother's womb. Being formed in warm water, it makes sense that it would assist in our cleaning, healing, and regeneration. I would say, the warmer (closer to hot), the better. Formed in our mother's womb, we were subjected to 98° Fahrenheit (37° Celsius). It seems to make sense that soaking in warm water would result in health benefits.

Men should bathe in warm water to keep their prostate gland healthy. The prostate gland has a tendency to get congested. This is because it is cushioned in the pelvic area with many other body structures. The bladder, seminal vesicles, rectum, vas deferens and penis are lodged in the same closely packed area. The prostate is located in the lower part of the body where there is a great tendency for heavy waste particles to accumulate. A warm bath is one of the most effective treatments where there is congestion, inflammation and irritability of the prostate.

Bathing in warm water assists the body in bringing the waste matter back into the rectum. Submerging in warm water stimulates the blood vessels. This allows the build–up of toxins and waste particles to be reabsorbed into the bloodstream. The toxins and waste particles are then transported from the bloodstream to the kidneys, or liver, and back into the colon. The waste matter is then pushed from the colon to exit from the rectum.

Men should imitate women in their practice of regular bathing to help keep their prostate healthy. Bathing in warm water often relieves stress. This allows the body to relax and and can assist the body to release some of the waste. The warm water can also soften the stool, allowing an easier exit of the feces.

The prostate is harmed by fried foods and alcohol. Vinegar will dehydrate (dry out) the tissue in the prostate. Salt and sugar pulls moisture out of the prostate. Coffee (both caffeinated and decaffeinated), chocolate, soda and tea containing caffeine dehydrates the prostate. Bleached or polished white flour also dehydrates the prostate gland.

Herbs can assist in the healing process of the prostate gland. Gotu kola, Ginkgo Biloba, Glucosamine, Saw Palmetto and Pygeum (African), Maca, Mira Puama are some of the herbs that help to heal the prostate gland. Saw Palmetto reduces night–time urination and helps to reduce the prostate. If the prostate is enlarged, Shepard's

Purse, Witch Hazel (the herb), Crane's bill (also known as Wild Alum Root, or Wood Geranium), are some of the herbs that will help shrink it.

Try to urinate when you first feel the urge to go. Waiting too long may overstretch the bladder muscle and may cause damage. Never pass up a chance to use the bathroom, even if your bladder does not feel full.

Proper diet and reasonable exercise will assist in deterring prostrate challenges. Eating fruits, grains, and vegetables provide the nutrients to help our bodies grow and repair themselves. Roughage from the proper foods helps to clean out the colon and move the waste out of the body. Reasonable exercise helps to strengthen the body and aid body functions. All of this aids the body in proper elimination of its waste.

We would recommend a body detoxification. This will rid the body of unneeded waste, inflammation, parasites, and their parasitic eggs. More, importantly, it will help the body in its regulation of regular bowel movements.

Since the bodies of men and women are anatomically similar, see pp. 224-227.

"Prostrate" http://en.wikipedia.org/wiki/Prostate

"Rise Of The Immortals: Dr Jewel Pookrum And Dr. Delbert Blair" http://bit.ly/1dZo9Sl

"The Troublesome Prostate Gland"
http://bit.ly/1K73wS4

"Incontinence& Overactive Bladder Health Center"
http://wb.md/1H6VuWO

"Give That Thing A Rest"
http://bit.ly/1BwYZ8C

CHAPTER 23
Melanin and What Melanin Does

MELANIN IS MOST FAMILIAR to us for its role in giving the skin pigmentation. But did you know it is also present in all parts of our body including the heart, liver, muscles, nerves, brain and intestines? Melanin is produced by the pineal gland, a flat, pine coned shaped gland of the endocrine system deep at the center of the midbrain. The endocrine system is a collection of glands that produce hormones that regulate your body's growth, metabolism, sexual development and function.

The pineal gland is also known as the "third eye" because it has rods and cones just like the eye. When you meditate and your visualizations are strong enough, you can actually see the image visualized. The pineal gland is often associated with the sixth chakra in yoga. It is believed to be the dormant organ which when awakened can unlock our hidden powers and telepathic abilities.

Melanin is part of your nervous system and brain. Most of the brain is heavily melaninated. The purest form of melanin is black. All individuals have this black brain–melanin, regardless of race. Melanin is concentrated in the area of the brain responsible for sensory, motor, emotional, and motivational activities. Melanin is present in both the sperm and the egg of the female, and is essential in the development of the child. The absence of melanin in the embryonic development of a child can cause defects and miscarriage.

Melanin is the original "superconductor ", meaning it has the ability to capture light to reproduce and duplicate itself. Melanin in the skin has the potential to transform electricity, electro–magnetic energy, solar energy, thermal waves, microwaves, music/sound waves, radar waves, radio waves, TV waves, cosmic rays, X–rays, and ultra violet light into kinetic energy. Kinetic energy is energy we derive from food for things like growth and bodily repairs.

To put it plainly, Melanin absorbs nearly all forms of energy while reflecting very little. Melanin captures and stores various forms of energy it comes in contact with, then absorbs that energy, stores it, and passes it to other cells of the body so that they can charge and regenerate themselves. Melanin permits people to charge up, or acquire energy without the need to eat or drink. This energy absorption is done simply by being out in the sun, or in the presence of the right type of music and other forms of energy. Since melanin converts sunlight to energy, sunlight is a form of nutrition for the melanin dominant (those with lots of melanin). It is important for the melanin dominant to get regular direct sunlight. This 'free energy' will boost their mental and emotional states, as well as strengthen their immune systems.

Melanin gives us the ability to delay the aging process and gives protections from the development of skin cancer. Melanin behaves like a sun umbrella for our cells, protecting the protein inside the chromosomes from excessive ultra violet (UV) radiation from the sun. It also allows sufficient UV radiation to enter the body to strengthen the bones. Without this protection, the skin wrinkles and burns. UV radiation is a main factor in the introduction of skin cancer.

Melanocyte cells located in the bottom layer of the skin produce melanin. Caucasians who are melanin recessive produce very little melanin in the melanocyte. Africans (those of African descent) who are generally melanin dominant with melanocytes produce the darker and purer form of melanin. Those individuals whose bodies can produce sufficient quantities of melanin will have dark skin, black hair and brown eyes. Individuals with bodies that are not able to produce significant amounts of melanin will have pale skin, blond or red hair, and light colored eyes (blue, green, hazel etc).

Melanin is heat absorbent. Melanin can be subjected to 1,000 degrees Fahrenheit (537°Celsius) and still maintain it's function. It can maintain 50 per cent of its integrity at 120,370 degrees Fahrenheit (66854° Celsius). That is why synthetic melanin is used to cover the spaceships and wiring on all space flights. Otherwise, their ships could not make it through Earth's stratosphere.

Serotonin and Melatonin

Serotonin is Melanin produced by the pineal gland during the day. Melatonin is Melanin produced at night. Both melatonin and serotonin are hormones and also neurotransmitters. Neurotransmitters are chemical substances that transmit nerve impulses across the spaces in between nerve cells. Nerve cells are also known as neurons. This allows faster communication across nerve cells.

Melatonin affects the wake/sleep cycle, sexual development and regulates all of the rhythms of the body, such as when organs should be fed, hair grows, and puberty begins. Melatonin helps to regulate potassium and sodium levels in the body, and control mental stability. The pineal gland releases melatonin only during times when the level of light is low, usually at night. It contains a mild sedative effect. This assists in keeping us calm and collected under pressure and maintaining a humorous disposition. It slows the heart rate and lowers blood pressure.

Melatonin has been described as a humanizing and civilizing hormone because it allows one to feel, have compassion, and reach higher consciousness. Melatonin also prevents senile dementia and cancer.

Serotonin is a natural stimulant. It works by enhancing the mood, reducing pain, appetite, sexual behavior and providing energy. Eighty percent of serotonin is found in the digestive tract, where it regulates intestinal movements. The remaining twenty percent is found in the central nervous system, blood platelets, and the pineal gland. Researchers at Princeton University say serotonin is also known as a happiness hormone because it contributes to feelings of well–being.

According to researchers at Macalester College, greater aggressive behavior has been associated with the absence of serotonin. They have observed that low serotonin levels have been correlated with higher levels of irritability, impulsivity, aggression, disordered eating, and sleeping problems. It has also been shown that the brain has a larger production of serotonin during full moons.

"Dr. Llaila Afrika Understanding Melanin"

http://bit.ly/1K73Wbh

Dr. Jewel Pookrum, MD, Ph.D. *Vitamins & Minerals from A to Z* © 1999 eeworldinc@yahoo.com

"What is Serotonin and What Does It Do?"

http://bit.ly/1dZpcSg

"Serotonin"

http://bit.ly/1FwGwE1

Types Of Melanin

There are two types of melanin. The type of melanin is based on the light frequency it absorbs and reflects. Pheo–melanin is yellow to reddish in color. Fair skinned people generally have a higher percentage of Pheo–melanin. It is found in red hair and blonds. It is concentrated in the redder areas of the skin such as the lips, nipples, glands of the penis, and vagina. It is prevalent in Scandinavian countries like Sweden, Denmark, Native Americans, and the Asian Mongolian race.

Pheo–melanin absorbs the ultra violet radiation and attempts to break the energy down. But it tends to break down with too much ultra violet exposure. The Pheo–melanin types with red hair are less able to make the dark Eu–melanin pigment. Their skin is generally quite pale and burns easily with sun exposure.

Eu–melanin is brown to black. Darker skinned people have a higher percentage of Eu–melanin. It is found in Africa, Australia, and India. The difference in the melanin types affects the color you get from being out in the sun. Those with more Pheo–melanin would have more of a red tan. Those with more Eu–melanin would have a brownish or blackish tan. It predominates in black and brunette hair. Eu–melanin is more protective against ultra violet radiation exposure. It absorbs the ultra violet radiation and then disperses the energy.

Whether Pheo–melanin or Eu–melanin, no one thing is superior to the other. Like the relationship of a bee to a flower, you simply acknowledge the differences when interacting with it.

Albino

A person lacking normal pigmentation is called an Albino. This is a congenital disorder characterized by the complete or partial absence of pigment in the hair, skin, and eyes. This is due to the absence or defect of a rare limiting enzyme (Tyrosinase) involved in the control of the production of melanin. Albinos either don't secrete any melanin, don't have much, or they are not making it in abundance. This lack of pigmentation results in the skin being abnormally white or milky. The eyes have a pink or blue iris and a deep–red pupil.

Individuals with little melanin are more likely to develop genetic disorders than individuals with substantial amounts of melanin. It is important for melanin recessive people who have very little melanin to use topical chemicals such as sunscreen to protect their skin from direct sun. They should also stay out of the sun for prolonged periods of time. The opposite is true for melanin dominant individuals. They should have 30 minutes to an hour of direct sunlight to keep their melanin activated each day.

Active Melanin

Brown and Black peoples, whose melanin is active, can withstand much hotter temperatures than whites. Melanin is considered active when it is fully functioning. Like a computer that is "on–line". A well functioning melanin system elevates the efficiency of our entire body.

An active or functioning melanin is determined by whether you have an alkaline or acidic diet, enlightened or unconscious thought, toxic and cold or adequate sunlight and non–toxic environment. Diet keeps melanin from becoming toxic and non–functional. The sun keeps the melanin molecule charged. Positive, loving thoughts heal. Fearful and angered thoughts harm the body.

Physiological Differences

The melanin dominants have more melanin sites than whites. They have 12 melanin sites in their brain. This is opposed to the 4 sites Europeans have. Europeans have sulphur in the middle of their melanin cells. The melanin dominants have selenium in the middle of their melanin cells. The Melanin dominant body contains the highest quantity of vitamins and minerals. The European person's body contains the least amount of vitamins and minerals. The chemical difference between Black and white people is largely due to the amount of melanin produced in the pineal gland.

Europeans have more ammonium salt and sulphur in their bodies than most Brown or Black people. Melanin dominant people have more water in their bodies than Europeans. The ammonium and sulphur gives the smell on European's hair when it is wet. The ammonium in their body makes Europeans feel warm in conditions that would feel cold to most Brown or Black people.

An example would be members of a polar bear club. The ammonium in their bodies allows them to feel warm enough to jump in cold water in a lake or ocean in the winter. Another example would be Europeans feeling warm in a cold office room. The temperature in the room would be fine for Europeans. But for most African/Blacks, the temperature would be uncomfortably cool.

The natural habitat for the melanin dominant has always been a warm and sunny environment. The cold western environment causes depression in the melanin dominant. The reason is that our melanin inside us is manifesting its disapproval of the cold whether. In contrast, even if they like summertime to tan themselves, Europeans, consider the sun as being their worst natural enemy.

The nervous system of the melanin dominant is more extensive then that of Europeans. That is because Brown and Black people have highly developed deep and superficial circulation systems. The deep system consists of the body's organs. Blood is contained deep in the organs, which includes the brain. The superficial circulation is carried by the blood vessels lying directly beneath the surface of the skin.

Europeans (melanin recessives) have a highly developed deep circulatory system and a partially developed superficial circulatory system. That means that most of their blood is in their organs. It also means that they do not have as many highly developed nerve fibers going to muscle fibers as the melanin dominants.

The superficial veins of the melanin dominants are arranged as a network of thousands of vessels. The vessels are spread throughout the area from the outside of their muscles to the surface of their skin. Melanin in our skin is connected to the nerves and muscles. It refines the nervous system in such a way that messages from the brain reaches the other areas of the body more rapidly. This network allows the fastest nerve and muscle response. It also results in the ability to have the movement, speed, and awareness that Pheo–melanin types do not possess. An example would be the flexibility and dexterity of Eu–melanin women like Dominique Dawes (Olympic gold in gymnastics) or Shelly–Ann Fraser–Pryce (the world's fastest woman). The more melanin present in the person, the faster the nerve transmissions.

Melanin in the ears of melanin dominants allows them to hear better than Europeans. It gives them the ability to absorb a full range of sound. They can hear sound within sound. Melanin also makes the melanin–dominant people more sensitive to their environment and music than whites. Melanin in the iris of the eye causes melanin dominant people to see better. They can see more color in the color they see. The field of vision is wider. Melanin allows them to see more light.

Melanin gives the melanin dominants more taste in their taste buds. It allows them to taste the full flavor in foods. Melanin also stimulates enzymes that help break down food to digest it with less energy expended.

Melanin dominant people vibrate more electromagnetic energy than whites and are able to perceive huge portions of the electro–magnetic spectrum. Portions of this spectrum that are within the reality of the melanin dominant person are completely imperceptible to other races.

Melanin Makes One More Human

Melanin is what makes people human. It has been called the key to life because it is considered to be a harmonizing chemical. The more melanin, the more physic, spiritual, and intelligent one can become. It helps keep us more in tune with others. The ability to feel produces within us a compassion for others and ourselves. Melanin sharpens our psychological awareness. This gives us a deeper understanding of life. It also allows us to reach higher levels of consciousness.

Melanin–dominant children are often considered "hyperactive" or "acting out" in a classroom and they are unable to pay attention in class. Often this behavior is the result of fluorescent lighting in the classroom. The florescent lights concentration of particular frequencies is too much stimulation to their nerve endings. The melanin–dominant children are not able to focus well because their nerves have to process this extra stimulation.

In my classrooms with my students, I made a practice of turning off the lights or replacing them with healthy non–florescent lights. The difference in their behavior was amazing. Instantly, the children were able to pay attention and focus better. When their nerve endings were not taxed with processing these particular concentrated frequencies, more learning took place.

Intelligence

Melanin gives us more intelligence because we are able to use a larger percentage of our brain. Most people do not use the full capacity of their brains. Their thinking is typically concentrated in the left hemisphere of the brain. Melanin gives the ability to make use of both sides of our hemisphere at once. Melanin in the brain helps to store more information and gives better memory recall. This has been called ancestry memory.

Melanin cells have intelligence. They can analyze and initiate physiological functions without the need to report to the brain. These cells have the ability to free the brain from its responsibility of bodily coordination. This brings about a quickening of our bodily responses and reflects against detectable changes in the internal or external environment.

An example would be LaBron James (basketball champion) dribbling the basketball down the court before making a shot. All of his body movements, nerve and muscle coordinations need not be reported to the brain. If the melanin is fully functioning, the entire body is like an eye, completely aware of its surroundings.

Melanin gives an ability to reach higher levels of performance. There is also an increase of the brain's ability to concentrate further on emotional, intellectual, and spiritual matters. Melanin dominant people possess the highest brain activity and are the most psychic, spiritual and civilized.

Drug Testing

According to James Woodford, a toxicologist associated with Emory University labs, who testifies frequently in court cases concerning drug abuse, melanin breaks down into fragments in the urine that are chemically similar to the active ingredient in marijuana, THC (tetrahydrocannabinol). Melanin, in addition to being chemically similar to THC, also "acts like a sponge" soaking up chemical compounds similar to THC that can also mimic marijuana in the urine. In very sensitive urine drug tests, melanin can produce false positive results in people who have not used marijuana. Dark–skinned (melanin–dominant) people are therefore more likely than others to be wrongly accused of marijuana use.

I have known two dark skinned men who claim that they have never taken any drugs. Yet they have taken and failed drug tests for marijuana. We can only imaging the scope of the harm that has possibly been caused to individuals, families and communities as a result of such tests. Consider the financial profits to jails, prisons, courts, child protective services, and the criminal justice administration system.

Dr. Carol Barnes, Senior Chemist and author of Melanin: The Chemical Key to Black Greatness, has charged that white scientists deliberately created drugs, such as cocaine, structured to bind chemically with melanin. Barnes asserts that cocaine and melanin have a natural attraction (high affinity) for each other because both have ring structures and alkaloids. Alkaloids are a group of naturally occurring chemical compounds containing mostly basic nitrogen atoms.

Dr. Barnes also points out that Black people get addicted faster, stay addicted longer, can test positive for cocaine up to a year after its most recent use, and suffer more from these drugs because cocaine co–polymerizes into melanin. That means, since the two chemicals have similar structures, they will dissolve into, or chemically react to, each other. Any significant event including stress, dietary change, climate flux, environmental shifts can trigger unknown amounts of cocaine into the blood stream. This in turn can cause spontaneous highs, delayed "trips", seizures, and even death.

It has been argued that when hair samples are used for drug testing, those with darker hair may be more likely to test positive for cocaine use. This may be because the binding with melanin ensures that traces persist for a longer period. This would apply to any race of people with dark hair. Dark skinned people usually have dark hair.

Furthermore, researchers in the journal Pharmacology, Biochemistry and Behavior concluded that, while the mechanism for nicotine addiction is not fully understood, melanin has a "biochemical affinity for nicotine," and that the "greater the amount of melanin people have, the harder it could be for them to quit smoking."

Other evidence has shown that even though African Americans smoke fewer cigarettes than some other groups, they have a higher intake of nicotine from each cigarette. Health advocacy and civil right organizations have criticized the tobacco industry for "aggressive" advertising and promotional campaigns targeting African–Americans. Research is required to produce drug tests that are scientific and accurate, not drug tests that might be used as tools in discrimination, victimization and domination of people of color.

Calcification

African/Blacks were the first inhabitants of this planet. Most races of people mutated from Blacks to their present form. When most whites mutated into their present condition, they grew a bony substance, calcium, on their pineal gland. This calcium can restrict their production of melatonin to a minimum amount. In some, melatonin is no longer produced. This makes their pineal gland inactive or non–functional. This is called calcification.

Most Europeans are unable to produce much melatonin because their pineal glands are often calcified and non–functioning. As you age the pineal gland can become calcified, causing calcium phosphate to develop over the gland. Calcification rates vary widely by country. Calcification occurs in an estimated 40% of Americans by their 17th year.

Generally, pineal calcification rates with Africans/Blacks are 5–15%, Asians 15–25%, and Europeans 60–80%. All races have some calcification. African/Blacks have less calcification, while whites have more. This results in African/Blacks having more melatonin and Europeans having less. The lack of melatonin is said to be the chemical basis for the cultural differences between Blacks, Asians, and Europeans.

Melanin in Brown and Blacks can be non functional if they develop bad sleeping and eating habits. We shouldn't eat too late. If we have to eat something late at night, it should be something light. This is because the pineal gland normally produces the hormone melatonin on a daily basis. During the night, melatonin levels rise in the body. The levels reach a peak from about 10 in the evening until about 3 in the morning. It drops dramatically when the new day dawns.

Heavy eating and not sleeping during this time interferes with melatonin production. Not sleeping during this time reduces the amount of melatonin that can alleviate mental stress, improves sleep and strengthens the immune system. When the eyes perceive light, melatonin production is reduced. The reduction of melatonin lowers the body's resistance germs and viruses.

That is why night workers and those who sleep with the light on have a higher propensity to develop cancers than others. For women night workers, bright light at night reduces the production of melatonin. It also induces estrogen secretion. This in turn increases the risk of breast cancer.

Jewel Pookrum, 'Vitamins and Minerals from A to Z 1993, 1999 A & B Publishers Group Brooklyn, New York

'Suzar, 'Blacked Out Through Whitewash

'C. Barnes, 'The Chemical Key to Great Blackness

Do More Good Deeds: the biggest Secret

http://bit.ly/1H92a8K

Eating Low On The Food Chain http://www.rawfoodexplained.com/why-we-should-not-eat-meat/eating-low-on-the-food-chain.html

What Calcifies the Pineal Gland

An acidity diet does not support the melanin system. An alkaline diet does. Browns and Blacks do not require large concentrations of proteins and fats. They have so many blood vessels, if they eat foods in high quantities that block the flow of blood, the nervous system is compromised. When blockages occur there is less blood to the brain. This causes them to only use the lower stem of the brain. This results in very irrational, violent behavior, creating havoc to themselves and others.

Choose an alkaline as opposed to acidity diet. There are two types of foods, acid-forming or alkaline forming. The worse acid forming foods include alcohol, caffeine, dairy products, artificial sweeteners (aspartame), cakes/pastries, white flour, sugar filled juices, refined starches (pasta), refined grains, table salt, soda, sugar and meat.

Meat should be avoided in the diet. Research has shown that pesticide residue levels are the highest in meat eaters. That is because the animals they eat have already concentrated the pollutants in its body. The meat eater may eat in a just few moments the pesticides that an animal has accumulated over a lifetime. This is a large reason why it is considered acid forming to the body.

Whenever you eat something that is acidic or incomplete (not wholesome), your body has to pull the nutrients out of your body's minerals to try to neutralize the acidity. Once you began to consume more alkaline foods you will start to increase your intuition, "psychic" powers, calmness and peace of mind. There will also be an increase in dreams, happiness, creativity, and overall energy!

Chemicals that straighten or relax hair can destroy hair and decrease the vitality of your system. Chemicals that kill nutrients in the hair kill the electromagnetic information that your body receives. Your hair is an antenna that communicates directly to the brain. When you decrease its ability to pick up electromagnetic information, you decrease the value of your system.

Environmental factors such as halides (fluoride, chlorine, bromide) and pollution should be avoided. Both are contributing factors in the calcification of the pineal gland and should be remove from your diet. Fluoride (sodium fluoride) is a toxic aluminum industrial waste product that is poison to your body. There are no nutrients or benefits to the body. The fluoride added to water supplies may be contaminated with lead, arsenic, aluminum and other industrial contaminates.

Fluoride chemicals are likely to decalcify the pineal gland by accumulating in the pineal gland. This "build–up" comes from fluoride substances in the high volume of blood flow it is exposed to in the brain. The fluoride accumulation in the pineal gland reduces the production of melatonin. It lowers the levels of melatonin in the body. The lower levels produced impair the sleep–wake cycle, shortens the time to puberty, and decreases the efficiency of other body functions.

Fluoride chemicals are found in public water systems and toothpaste, mouth rinses, hormones and additives put into processed foods. They are in sugars and artificial sweeteners in soft drinks, sport drinks, showers (without fluoride filters), red meat (organs) and mechanically deboned meat. This includes chicken nuggets. They are also found in inorganic grape juice and wine, many fluoride pharmaceuticals and reconstituted juices.

Chemical substances such as Bromide and Chlorine seem to have similar effects on the pineal gland. These substances will reduce pineal gland activation and prevent the awakening of your third eye. Chlorine is deadly in gas form. It gets into your body primarily through the water you drink and bathe in.

Fluoride is a cumulative toxin. That is, over time serious health concerns will emerge. It has been proven to cause damage in bones, brain, nervous system and glands that produce hormones that regulate your body's growth, metabolism, sexual development, and neurological system.

Instead of using fluoride toothpaste, switch to fluoride free toothpaste, baking powder, or miswak sticks to clean your teeth. These fluoride alternatives whiten teeth, remove bad odors, fight bacteria and germs. Miswak sticks are known to improve the sense of taste, strengthen and stops bleeding gums.

Drink spring or filtered water. Generally, spring or filtered water does not contain fluoride, chloride, and bromide. Distilled water can be harmful in the long run. That is because distilled water does contain vitamins and nutrients found in spring or filtered water. Unless vitamins and nutrients are added along with the distilled water, your body will pull the vitamins and nutrients from your body's tissues that the distilled water is lacking. Nevertheless, distilled water is better than tap water.

Sodium Chloride (table salt) interferes with the transfer of water in the cell to water outside the cell. This creates bloating and interferes with the function of your thyroid and can cause weight gain. Use sea salt or mineral salt to replace table salt. There are many minerals and nutrients in sea and mineral salt. Not so with table salt.

Bromide is an endocrine disrupter that depletes your body's iodine. It can be found in seafood, pesticides (Methyl Bromide), and soft drinks (Brominated Vegetable Oil (BVO). It is in fire retardants, medications, hot tub and swimming pool treatments and plastic (computers). Bromide can also be found in dough conditioner (Potassium Brominate), toothpaste and mouth rinse. Read the labels. Avoid products containing BVO and Potassium Brominate.

Mercury is toxic to the pineal gland and should be avoided. It is very difficult to get mercury out of the brain once it is there. Tooth fillings with mercury should be removed. Medical vaccines that contain mercury (Thimersal, a vaccine preservative) should be avoided. Fish and bottom feeders (crabs, lobsters, prawns, shrimp) should not be eaten. Tuna and dolphin meat be avoided because the meat contains high concentrations of mercury.

Eco light bulbs should be used with care because they contain mercury. If an eco light bulb is accidentally broken, harmful mercury vapor is released and can be inhaled. Mercury can be removed from the brain with a daily use of wheatgrass, chlorella, cilantro, and spirulina. It just takes time.

Stop taking Calcium supplements. This is one of the biggest contributors to calcification. In most cases, the supplements do not work for your body. Some do more harm than good. That is because many of the calcium supplements contain synthetic ingredients. Look on the back of a Calcium supplement bottle (or any other supplement). If you can read precise measurements of ingredients, ask yourself this question. How could the measurements be measured to such precision unless the ingredients added were synthetic? Natural plant based ingredients could not be measured with such precision. The natural ingredients are listed by name. Only synthetic or unnatural ingredients could be measured with such accuracy.

Antiperspirants, deodorants, and tobacco should be avoided. Cell phones are also being pinpointed as being harmful to the pineal gland due to high concentrations of radiation. Some pesticides are pineal toxic. Food grown with these chemical pesticides should be avoided. Fresh organic food that has not used these pesticides would be recommended. A lifestyle free of these things will help to flush out the system. It will also bring a greater mind/body balance.

Rapid Detoxification of the Third Eye Pineal Gland
http://bit.ly/1dbwf9I

Fluoride Denialism http://bit.ly/1GvhExh
Pineal Gland http://bit.ly/1N11NeR
Detoxification Of The Third Eye http://bit.ly/1IufU91
Ten Ways To Reduce Fluoride Exposure pineal–gland
http://bit.ly/1Jeah4k
Avoid This If You Want To Keep Your Thyroid Healthy
http://bit.ly/1Lg2N0g

Effects of Calcification

An active or functional pineal gland produces melatonin that enhances feelings and moral capacity. A calcified pineal gland would limit feelings and moral capacity. This often results in what is called the "European approach". That is, the rigid, logical, analytical, objective, erect, methodical, and anti–feeling posture. This also represents what is called a left– brain orientation.

According to the right–brain or left–brain dominance theory, each side of the brain was said to control a different type of thinking. People are said to have either one personality preference or the other. The right–brain orientation prefers a type of thinking that is creative, artistic, intuitive, thoughtful, subjective, and pro–feeling posture. An active pineal gland allows elevated levels of melatonin in the body that permit access to both sides of the brain (right and left) and to get into one's feelings.

Most Europeans have a calcified pineal gland. The lower the levels of melatonin produced, the less moral and harmonious one becomes. Dr. Cress–Welsing writes "the fact that the albinos (whites) lack melanin may also help to explain...why, in the view of many non–whites, they (whites) lack 'spirituality' and the capacity to tune in to, and thereby establish harmony and justice..."

Carol Barnes writes: "Melanin is responsible for the existence of civilization, philosophy, religion, truth, justice, and righteousness. Individuals (white) containing low levels of Melanin will behave in a barbaric manner." A closed third eye in Hindu tradition brings with it confusion, jealousy, cynicism, pessimism, uncertainty, envy and one sidedness. Most whites have a calcified pineal gland, which prevent melatonin production. As a result of a non–functioning pineal gland or the low levels of melanin produced, the moral capacity and harmony of the European is limited.

Carol Barnes "The Chemical Key To Greatness", Published by C. Barnes 1988 Box 3009189, Houston, Texas, 77230

Albinism http://en.wikipedia.org/wiki/Albinism

How Toxic is Black Hair Care http://bit.ly/1IZUh3a

Study: Hair Relaxers Linked to Fibroids http://bit.ly/1FwFoQN

Hair Relaxer Use And Risk Of Uterine Leiomyomata In African – American Women http://bit.ly/1SD7PGd

Left Brain Right Brain http://abt.cm/1eDRoel

Pineal Gland http://en.wikipedia.org/wiki/Pineal_gland

Pineal Gland Calcification http://bit.ly/1dZpKrs

Detoxing Calcification (Decalcifying)

To detox the calcified pineal gland is like trying to open a glued shut closet door. The secret to opening the door is dedication and commitment. Just as you would push at the closet door, you must be willing to be committed and dedicated to the proper diet and herbs. Crystals and magnets have also been known to help in detoxing calcification of the pineal gland.

Be patient with yourself. It took time to calcify the pineal gland. The calcification did not happen overnight. It will also take time to detox. But through continuous application of the right tools – diet, herbs, crystals, and magnets – just like the closet door will open, so will your health be opened to vast improvements in your life.

The first step is to stop the activity that is causing the calcification. This may be lifestyle choices or environmental factors. The second step would be to reduce and remove the existing calcification. The third step would be to help further develop the pineal gland.

There are a several ways to decalcify the pineal gland. Mercury can be eliminated from the brain with a daily use of chlorella, cilantro, spirulina and wheatgrass, it just takes time. Other pineal decalcifiers include MSM, raw chocolate, raw lemon juice, garlic, raw apple cider vinegar, oregano oil, neem extract, baron (present in beets), Vitamin K1 (found in green leafy vegetables), iodine, tamarind (pulp, bark, and leaves for tree), and distilled water.

Garlic (especially black) is good for decalcification because it not only is able to dissolve calcium, but also acts as an antibiotic. Added benefits are that it gives your immune system a boost. Consume about half a bulb to two bulbs daily (or more if you like). To keep your breath from scaring anyone off, you can crush the garlic and soak in fresh lemon juice or raw apple cider vinegar to deodorize it.

Certain foods such as raw cacao, goji berries, cilantro, watermelon, bananas, honey, coconut oil, hemp seeds, seaweed, lemons, raw apple cider vinegar and noni juice help to detox the pineal gland. Pineal gland stimulants include Hydrilla Verticillata, blue–green algae, iodine, Zeolite, ginseng, borax, D3, Bentonite clay, chlorophyll, and blue skate liver oil. They help to activate your third eye.

Essentials oils can be used to help stimulate the pineal gland and facilitate states of meditation, spiritual awareness and astral projection, Good essential oils for the pineal gland include sandalwood, lavender, parsley, frankincense, davana, pine, pink lotus, and mugwort. Excess use of mugwort has a neurotoxin effect if inhaled directly, so be careful. Essential oils can be burned in a diffuser or nebulizer, inhaled directly, and added to bath water.

Crystals that benefit the pineal gland include amethyst (wand), moonstone, laser quartz (wand), purple violet tourmaline, pietersite, purple sapphire, rhodonite, rose aura, and sodalite. Indigo, violet, or dark purple gemstone or crystal can be used to stimulate the pineal gland. A good exercise for pineal gland stimulation and health is to take an amethyst wand with the point of the wand touching your skin over your 3rd eye or an amethyst obelisk crystal pointing it at the 3rd eye. The 3rd eye is located between your two physical eyes but slightly higher or slightly above the eyes.Look up directly at the sun with your eyes closed. Do this everyday for about 5–10 minutes or whenever you feel like it. The Sun's rays will penetrate through the end part of an amethyst wand or the base part of the obelisk and stimulate the pineal gland by beaming directly into it. The Laser Quartz (wand) can also be used as well. Quartz crystals can benefit every single chakra.

Attaching a magnet that sticks by adhesive to the part of your skin above your 3rd eye for a few hours throughout the day will stimulate the pineal gland and help to decalcify it. Magnets cause the body to become alkaline. This is especially true for the part of the body where the magnet has been attached. You can use any strength (gauss) magnet. Only use magnets on the head area during waking hours. The sun's energy will magnify the strength of the magnet's effect on the pineal gland.

Regular meditation and chanting causes the tetrahedron bone in the nose to resonate and this resonance causes the pineal gland to be stimulated. When it is stimulated it secretes more beneficial hormones. These beneficial hormones help to keep your appearance youthful. Gazing at the sun (sun gazing) during the first 15 minutes of sunrise and last 15 minutes of sunset will also do wonders for your pineal gland.

Natural entheogens ("generating the divine within") are chemical substance used in a religious, shamanic, or spiritual context that may be synthesized or obtained from natural species. The chemical induces altered states of consciousness, psychological or physiological. These chemical substances are not for everyone. Entheogens help to stimulate the pineal gland. Enthogens include ayahuasca, psilocybin mushooms, peyote, changa, cannabis, salvia, DMT and more.

Benefits of Detoxifying and Activating Your Pineal Gland

Detoxification and activation of the third eye can bring vast improvements into our life. An open third eye brings intuition, clarity, concentration, bliss, decisiveness and insight. It can also bring lucid and vivid dreams, better sleep and enhanced imagination. It is easier to astral project, see energy, see beings, and see with eyes closed. Aura viewing, astral projection, as well as the ability to feel energy, are brought about with the detoxification and activation of the 3rd eye.

Alkaline Foods to Help Decalcify the Pineal Gland
http://bit.ly/1Iugfse

How to Decalcify The Pineal Gland http://bit.ly/1Cor9xA

Detoxification of The Third Eye
http://bit.ly/1dbwf9I

Pineal Gland Detox And Activation
http://bit.ly/1TI3wLm

Radid Detoxification of The Pineal Gland
http://bit.ly/1dbwf9I

The Mysterious Pineal Gland
http://bit.ly/1ftoopV

Umar Johnson Amerika's Attack on Black Youth Part 1 & 2 posted June 2013

Melanin http://en.wikipedia.org/wiki/Melanin

Melanin and the Pineal Gland
http://bit.ly/1LpvBo4
http://bit.ly/1I9Od9N

Fibroids
http://mayocl.in/1TI3JhA

Uterine Fibroids
http://1.usa.gov/1RpOdD8

CHAPTER 24
Vitamins

NATURAL, SYNTHETIC OR PLANT BASED

TODAY, MILLIONS OF PEOPLE are taking vitamin supplements as a means to prevent nutritional deficiencies. Many believe they actually compensate for bad diets and poor eating habits. Some believe soil depletion, storage conditions, industrial food processing, and often the low accessibility to fresh nutrient–dense food make it necessary to supplement our diet with vitamins.

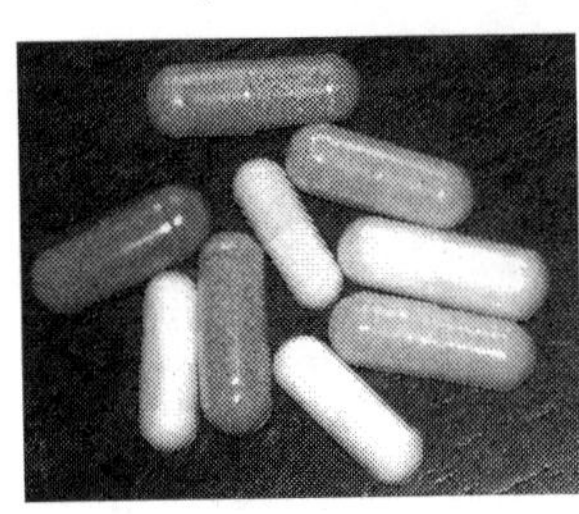

Synthetic

Most vitamins are made from non–plant or non–animal sources. These vitamins are considered synthetic. Organic vitamins that are certified organic are free of man–made fertilizers and pesticides. Synthetic vitamins are made from man–made ingredients. Chemical sources for synthetic vitamin supplements include petrochemicals, chemically manipulated sugar, wood pulp, inorganic minerals and coal tar. Coal tar is a known carcinogen found in cigarette smoke.

Manufacturers of vitamin and mineral supplements typically add synthetics to their vitamin products to increase the potency. Almost all multivitamins and fortified foods are from synthetics. Synthetic vitamins are cheaper to produce and have a longer "shelf life" and are considered more stable. This means they can last on shelves for months or years. They can be added to foods and beverages in high doses. They can also create small dense tablets packed with various types of synthetic vitamins.

Toxicity

Research shows that vitamin supplements can become toxic to the body if they're synthetically produced and if taken in overly high unnatural dosage. In nature, vitamins always appear in a group, balanced with other nutritional cofactors and in the right biological concentrations. These cofactors are the co–enzymes, phytonutrients and enzymes. They work together to help your body absorb and utilize vitamins and increase their potency. The body can't absorb synthetic vitamins properly because they lack the accompanying natural chemicals found in a variety of plant foods.

The National Institutes of Health (NIH) warns that excess amounts of synthetic vitamin D can lead to an accumulation of calcium in the blood. This can lead to kidney failure, bone loss and other complications. The body can only utilize vitamins as they naturally occur in food. It makes no difference whether these vitamins are fat or water–soluble.

Moreover, fat–soluble vitamins such as A, E, K and D are dissolved in fat instead of water. If you take more of these fat–soluble vitamins than your body can metabolize, they will be stored up within your fat cells. Over time they can accumulate in the body, resulting in an array of toxic reactions including the risk of birth defects and cancer.

100 Percent Natural

Check the product label for the words "100 percent natural". This could be "100 percent plant–based" or "100 percent animal–based" as recommended by the Organic Consumers Organization. If the product states, "100 percent natural", the vitamin supplement does not contain synthetics.

Manufacturers can state "natural" on their nutritional products if at least 10 percent of the product comes from natural food sources. Some vitamins are called "natural" even when they are actually synthetic because scientists say the synthetics are virtually identical to the ones found in food.

Natural Food Source

Look for the food source list on the product's label. This is the source of food from which the vitamin or mineral supplements came. Organic vitamins state the source for the vitamin. Synthetic vitamins contain a chemical name. Examples of food sources for organic vitamins include citrus, vegetable, fish, brewers yeast, lemon grass, or the organ of the animal used to obtain the vitamin. If the product's label contains no list of natural food sources, then the product is probably synthetic.

Identify Whole Foods

Look for whole foods in the product's ingredients label that contains certain vitamins. An example would be "acerola cherry powder", which contains vitamins C. Dr. Ben Kim, a chiropractor and acupuncturist with his own radio show, says if you can identify "vitamin C" in the ingredient list listed as the vitamin itself, you can almost guarantee that the vitamin is synthetic.

Key Words

Key words on the products label will indicate if the supplement is synthetic. Words ending in "ide" or "ate" indicate that the product contains salt forms. These salt forms are synthetics. So if the label lists such ingredients as acetate, chloride, hydrochloride, or nitrate, the manufacturer used synthetics for the product.

When a word also contains the letters "dl" in the prefix, it is an indication that the vitamin is synthetic. Examples would be "dl–alpha tocopherol acetate" and "dl–alpha tocopherol". Both are synthetic forms of vitamin E.

Below is a list of common synthetic vitamins to avoid:

Vitamin A: Palmitate, Acetate

Vitamin B1 (Thiamine): Thiamine Hydrochloride and Thiamine Mononitrate

Vitamin B2 (Riboflavin): Riboflavin

Pantothenic Acid: Calcium D–Pantothenate

Vitamin B6 (Pyridoxine): Pyridoxine Hydrochloride

Vitamin B12: Cobalamin

Vitamin C (Ascorbic Acid): Ascorbic Acid

Vitamin D: Calciferol, Irradiated Ergosteral

Vitamin E: dl–alpha tocopherol, dl–alpha tocopherol acetate or succinate

Biotin: d–Biotin

Choline: Choline Bitartrate, Choline Chloride

Folic Acid: Pteroylglutamic Acid

PABA (Para–aminobenzoic Acid): Aminobenzoic Acid

Recommendations

Talk to the vitamin or supplement worker in the Health Food store or pharmacist in the drug store before purchasing any vitamin or mineral supplement. A pharmacist can identify a synthetic or natural vitamin supplement. They can also help you learn to identify them yourself. Let them know if you are allergic to any medications or foods. If you use vitamins or mineral supplements, 100 percent food or plant based are best.

"Synthetic Versus Natural Vitamins" http://bit.ly/1dZqaho

"Natural Versus Synthetic" http://bit.ly/1JeaZyI

"What Are the Dangers of Synthetic Vitamins?" http://bit.ly/1dbwX6S

"Organic Vs. Synthetic Vitamins" http://bit.ly/1dZqgph

"Vitamin Poisoning: Are We Destroying Our Health With Hi–Potency Synthetic Vitamins?" http://bit.ly/1IugKme

CHAPTER 25
Antiperspirant and Deodorant

WE SPEND $18 BILLION a year trying to avoid wetness and odor in the armpit area. Even though we sweat to cool off our bodies and release toxins, many people wear antiperspirant and deodorant to avoid odor and wetness.

Sweat doesn't always stink. It is nearly odorless. The odor comes from bacteria breaking down the sweat on the skin. Deodorant contains antibacterial agents to stop the smell before it starts. Antiperspirants deal with sweat directly by temporarily blocking sweat ducts, reducing the amount of perspiration produced. This means less sweat in the underarm area.

Our lymph system has nodes in the armpit area and all over the body. The nodes act as tiny septic tanks, filtering, neutralizing, and destroying antigens and toxins. Most deodorants and antiperspirants have known toxins in them. We inhibit nodes from doing their job by rubbing or spraying these toxic ingredients on them. When these toxins are not purged, when trapped, find their way into the lymph nodes, where they concentrate and contribute to the cellular changes that can lead to cancer.

Ingredients To Avoid

Aluminum is one of the sweat–blocking ingredients found in many antiperspirants. A known toxin, it acts as a solvent and creates a temporary plug in the sweat glands. Sweat is then unable to reach the skin's surface. This leaves your underarm area dry. Linked to Alzheimer's, breast and prostate cancer, people are warned not to use antiperspirants if their kidneys are not fully functioning.

Phthalates are a group of chemicals, often called "plasticizers", used to make plastics harder to break and more flexible. They are often used to maintain fragrance and color in products and known as "endocrine disruptors" because they mimic the body's hormones and have been proven in laboratory tests to cause neurological and reproductive damage. They can increase your skin's absorption of parabens.

Phthalate Loophole

Phthalates and many other chemicals can be combined to create a "fragrance," and manufacturers are not required to list them in the ingredients. The International Fragrance Association (IFA) published a list of all of the ingredients a manufacture could potentially put into a product for "fragrance". Of the 3,163 ingredients on that list, 1 in every 20 was found to be highly hazardous by the Environmental Working Group (EWG).

Parabens are chemicals with estrogen–like properties. They are added to antiperspirants and deodorants to prevent bacterial growth and have also been shown to mimic the activity of estrogen. They enter your bloodstream and attach themselves to the nearest estrogen receptor and mimic the activity of estrogen. Too much estrogen in your system can be responsible for male reproductive disorder, breast and skin cancer. While many manufacturers in the U.S. have stopped using parabens in their products, they are still found in some as a type of preservative.

Triclosan is a chemical compound that acts as an antibacterial and is currently listed by the Environmental Protection Agency (EPA) as a pesticide. Studies have shown that it can alter hormone regulation. While the FDA has found no evidence that it is even an effective antibacterial agent in antiperspirant and deodorant, there is concern that it can be contributing to bacterial resistance. Triclosan is extremely toxic to aquatic wildlife and has been detected in many U.S. waterways.

Propylene Glycol is a synthetic liquid used to absorb water (sweat) and maintain moisture and a common ingredient used in antiperspirant and deodorant. It is a petroleum–based material used to soften cosmetic products. It can be an irritant to the skin and can cause immune system toxicity or allergies. Consumer safety advocates have questioned the argument that it is safe in small amounts. In large quantities, studies have shown that it can cause damage to the heart, liver and central nervous system.

Recommendations

Alternatives for deodorant and antiperspirants can be found at most health food stores. But use caution and read the labels. Just because a product is sold in a health food store does not necessarily mean it's healthy. For example, some of the crystal deodorants sold on the market are toxic.

- ·Ask for "paraben–free" deodorants and antiperspirants at health food stores.
- Use Patchouli oil (flash back from the hippy days).
- Baking soda can be mixed with paraben–free body lotion, your own deodorant cream, coconut oil and/or shea butter.
- Rub cut lemons under your arms.
- Apple cider vinegar. Dabbing it under your arms after your shower or bath may inhibit odor–causing bacteria from growing on your skin. Apply lightly with a cotton ball and wait a few minutes for the smell to dissipate.
- Shave. Body odor is caused by a combination of bacteria and perspiration. Body hair creates a lot of heat, which leads to more perspiration. Keeping your armpits groomed can help cut down on body odor and make you less dependent on deodorants in general.
- Remember anything you put on your skin is also absorbed into the bloodstream. So, if you can't safely eat it, don't put it on your skin.

"Deodorant Dangers And Your Health Options"
http://bit.ly/1GCB7zf
"Top Five Ingredients To Avoid In Deodorant"
http://bit.ly/1SD9oEo
"8 Things You Probably Didn't Know About Deodorant"
http://huff.to/1GvkfYo
"Is Antiperspirant Toxic?"
http://bit.ly/1TI5qLY
"Factsheet: Phthalates"
http://1.usa.gov/1QMasbd
"Why You Need to Switch Deodorants"
http://www.rodalenews.com/natural–deodorants

CHAPTER 26
Water

WATER IS THE MOST important nutrient for our bodies. A man's body is composed of 60% water and a woman's body about 50%. We can go for weeks without food but only 5–7 days without water. Our brain is about 75% water. If your brain does not get enough water, you will get dehydrated and your brain will actually shrink. This can greatly increase the risk of senile dementia.

You become thirsty when water in your body is reduced by just 1%. If water in the body is reduced by 5%, endurance and muscle strength decline considerably and you become hot and tired. At a 10% reduction, delirium and blurred vision may occur. A 20% reduction of water in the body can result in death.

Water is very important for transporting substances that are dissolved in water. Blood is about 83% water. It transports oxygen, nutrients, carbon dioxide (CO2), waste products and more from cell to cell. Urine, which is mostly water, removes waste products from the body. If we do not have enough water to produce urine, toxic levels of wastes build up in the body. We can become very sick or even die.

We use water to maintain our body's pH level of 7.4. The pH is a measurement of how acidic or alkaline a substance is. In this case, the substance is our blood. The pH scale ranges from 0 to 14. A pH of 7 is neutral. A pH less than 7 is acidic. A pH greater than 7 is alkaline. pH values are life threatening if less than 6.9 and greater than 7.6. Water is essential for keeping the pH within normal range.

Water regulates our body temperature through sweat. Sweat is a way the body can cool itself down. When sweat evaporates on our skin, it draws heat away from the body and cools us down. Water is essential in transporting oxygen to muscles and helps the body perform physical activity more efficiently and many other important functions.

Blood is primarily water and when you don't get enough water in your system the blood gets too thick. Thick blood is much harder for the heart to pump. This can lead to strokes, heart attacks and other problems. To keep blood thin like water you should drink ½ your body weight in ounces of water per day. For most, that is about 8–10 glasses per day. The more you weigh, the more water you should drink.

Don't Drink The Fluoride or The Chlorine.

Fluoride

Avoid drinking water containing fluorine or chlorine. Fluoride damages enzymes which causes premature aging. This affects the immune, digestive and respiratory system, blood circulation, liver, kidneys, thyroid and brain function. Fluoride can also cause hyperactivity. A recently–published Harvard University study has concluded that children who live in areas with highly fluoridated water have "significantly lower" IQ scores than those who live in low fluoride areas.

According to Dr. Ted Broer, a noted nutrition expert, there is not a single reputable scientific or laboratory study which proves that fluoridation reduces tooth decay in humans. There are, however, many published scientific papers which show that water fluoridation is dangerous to human, animal, aquatic and plant life. This should come as no surprise since fluoride is more toxic than lead and only marginally less so than arsenic. (Clinical Toxicology of Commercial Products, 5th ed., Gosselin, et al, 1984.).

Flouride was given in Nazi concentration camps to make the inmates infertile and suppress the will and vigor of the prisoners. This made them docile and easier to control. It also calcifies the pineal gland. The pineal gland is called the 3rd eye. Our third eye helps us to have insight and reasoning skills. Fluoride destroys this ability. **Fluoride** is also one of the active ingredients in **Prozac and Zoloft.** Do not use toothpaste or mouthwash with fluoride. Never let a dentist do a fluoride treatment on you.

What is put in tap water that most of us drink isn't pharmaceutical grade nor is it natural "calcium fluoride". It's a by–product of the fertilizer industry. What is added to tap water is nothing more than toxic waste or pollution. Robert Carton, PhD formerly President of the Union of Government Scientists working at the US Environmental Protection Agency said: "Water fluoridation is the greatest case of scientific fraud of this century, if not of all time."

Chlorine

Chlorine is perhaps one of the most dangerous poisons in our drinking water supply. Many municipal water treatment facilities use chlorine as a powerful disinfectant to kill or inactivate biological water contaminants. But chlorine is also poisonous to our bodies. It interacts with some of the other toxic chemicals to create even more toxic compounds. Chlorine in drinking water is currently a leading cause of rectal and bladder cancer and asthma. Health officials are now linking breast cancer to chlorine ingestion as well.

Chlorine acts as a corrosive agent on the hair and skin. When combined with other things chlorine basically attaches to the thyroid gland. The thyroid gland is a vitally important hormonal gland. It plays an essential role in metabolism, growth and maturation of the human body. This gland helps to regulate many body functions and affects every tissue in your body.

Chlorine competes for the same receptors that are used to capture Iodine on the thyroid gland. If you don't have sufficient quantities of

Iodine in your system to attach to the thyroid gland, fluorine will attach itself. If exposed to enough chlorine, your body will not hold on to the iodine that it needs. This slows the healing process and contributes to premature aging.

Lead

Lead often gets into tap water in a home's plumbing system through the corrosion of the water pipes. This contamination occurs after the municipal water treatment. Municipal facilities can't provide control for it. Lead in drinking water is especially harmful for pregnant mothers and young children. Ingestion of lead can result in severe learning disorders and /or developmental delays in children.

Exposure to lead may also cause development of autoimmunity, in which a person's immune system attacks its own cells. This can lead to joint diseases such as rheumatoid arthritis and diseases of the kidneys and circulatory and nervous systems.

Consumer Product Chemicals and Pharmaceuticals

Pharmaceuticals and other consumer product chemicals are called "emerging contaminants". These are chemicals like BPA (used in some plastics, paper receipts and canned–food linings) and PFOA (used to make pans non–stick and to make clothing). They end up in tap water in low levels. Few, if any, municipalities test for them.

Cryptosporidium and Giardia

Cryptosporidium and Giardia are resistant to chlorine. If released into the municipal water system, these protozoa can lead to severe and widespread outbreaks of gastrointestinal disease. They often get into tap water through sanitation breakdowns. Most municipal water treatment facilities have no way to control them.

Mercury

Mercury is a liquid metal found in natural deposits such as ores that contain other elements. 50 percent of the mercury used is for electrical products such as fluorescent light bulbs, switches, dry–cell batteries and other control equipment. Most sources of mercury contamination come from discharges from refineries and factories, runoffs from landfills and croplands.

If you suffer from a high exposure to mercury, you could have tremors, psychotic reactions and suicidal tendencies. Exposure to mercury may also cause development of autoimmunity, in which a person's immune system attacks its own cells. This can lead to rheumatoid arthritis and diseases of the kidney, circulatory and nervous systems. Mercury is something to take very seriously. If you consume too much, it could become fatal.

Other Heavy Metals

Water is stored in metal tanks. It travels through pipes. Corrosion of water tanks or pipes can result in metals in our water. Heavy metals such as Copper, Arsenic and Cadmium may find they way into the water. Toxic metals can be present in industrial, municipal and urban runoff.

Increased industrialization and urbanization are to blame for an increased level of trace metals, especially heavy metals, in our waterways. This can be harmful to both humans and aquatic life. Heavy metals can be very harmful to your health if found in your drinking water. Heavy metals, including copper, zinc and chromium, are actually required by the body in small amounts, but can be toxic in larger doses.

Energy Medicine Technologies: Ozone Healing, Microcrystals and the Future of Health Edited & Copyrighted by Finley Eversole, PH.D 2013 Inner Traditions One Park Street Rochester, Vermont 05767

www.InnerTraditions.com

"4 Things You Must Know about Your Water | Rodale News" http://bit.ly/1GvkmTJ

"How Dangerous is Your Tap Water?" http://bit.ly/1SDa9No

"Health Risks Of Heavy Metals" http://bit.ly/1H71oZC

"VOCs (Volatile Organic Compounds)" http://1.usa.gov/1IZWN9u

Alternatives to Tap Water

Boiling Water:

In an emergency, boiling is the best way to disinfect water that is unsafe because of the presence of viruses, bacteria or parasites. Water that is cloudy should be filtered before boiling. Coffee filters, towels (cotton or paper), cheesecloth, a cotton plug in a funnel or filters designed for use when camping are effective ways to filter cloudy water.

Using a clean container, bring water to a full boil for at least 3 minutes. Cover the container to help reduce evaporation. If you are more than 5,000 feet above sea level increase the boiling time to at least 5 minutes. Add one minute to boiling time for every additional 1,000 feet over 5,000 feet. Cover the boiled water while it is cooling.

The advantages of boiling water include killing pathogens in your water if the water is boiled long enough. It will also drive out some of the Volatile Organic Compounds (VOCs) that might also be in the water. "Volatile Organic Compound" or VOC is the name given to a substance that contains carbon and evaporates or "off–gases" at room temperature. Some examples of VOCs include methylene chloride, hexane, benzene, styrene and heptane.

VOCs are widely used in commercial and household products. Some disinfectants, glues, cleansers, cosmetics, waxes, dry cleaning products, varnishes, paints and preservatives include VOCs. VOCs are also found in new carpeting, cigarette smoke, pesticides, gasoline, kerosene and other fuels.

Although boiling works well and will make water that is contaminated with living organisms safe to drink, because of the inconvenience, boiling is not routinely used to treat drinking water except in emergencies.

Bottled Water

In the last two decades, consumers have begun to shy away from tap water, due to such public health scares as the 1993 Milwaukee cryptosporidium outbreak that infected more than 400,000 city residents. Promising to be purer and healthier than tap water, bottled water companies have expanded greatly in order to supply the public demand for quality drinking water.

But how can you be sure the water you purchased in the bottle is any safer or cleaner than your tap water? Like other water treatment solutions, you will find reputable companies that provide a safe, quality product. You can also find that 40% of bottled water comes from companies that fill their bottles using local, municipal tap water with minimal treatment. This includes ones labeled "Spring Water".

The U.S. Environmental Protection Agency (EPA) is in charge of tap water. Under The Safe Drinking Water Act, the EPA has the power to require water testing by certified laboratories and that violations be reported within a specified time frame. Tap water is tested more frequently. Water utilities are required by law to release reports to all of their customers. The reports must point out the source of the water, the treatment techniques used and the levels of contaminants found.

The Food and Drug Administration (FDA) lacks the regulatory authority of the EPA. It can only regulate bottled water as a food and cannot require certified lab testing or violation reporting. The FDA does not require bottled water companies to disclose to consumers where the water came from, which contaminants they test for, what contaminants it contains and which filtration technologies they use to remove them. So there's no way to know what exactly is in the bottled water.

According to the latest data available from the Beverage Marketing Corp. (BMC), Americans spent $11.8 billion dollars on 9.7 billion gallons of bottled water in 2012. This is an average cost of $1.22 per gallon nationwide, 300 times the cost of tap water. If we consider the fact that almost 64% of all bottled water sales are the single 16.9oz (500 ml) bottles, this cost is much higher. According to the American Water Works Association, that would be about $7.50 per gallon, almost 2,000 times the cost of a gallon of tap water.

Water is often bottled in plastic with recycle codes #1 PET or PETE bottles (polyethylene terephthalate). These bottles may leach DEHA, a known carcinogen into the water. #1 plastic bottles, experts agree, should not be reused. Plastics numbered 3, 6 and 7 are considered worst. They contain Bisphenol A (BPA), which is suspected of causing behavioral and neurological problems in fetuses and children. BPA mimics the female hormone estrogen. This may have detrimental effects on the immune system in adults and the female reproductive system, and may cause cancer of the breast, brain and prostate. Bottled water can be an emergency source of water. Since it does not contain chlorine, it may contain a mixture of minerals to enhance the flavor. It may taste even better than tap water. It may be inconvenient because it requires moving and storing jugs or bottles of water. At about eight pounds per gallon, or about 40 pounds per five gallon bottle, water can be heavy.

Reused bottles may contain bacteria. You will have to be diligent in maintaining the cleanliness of your bottles or you may increase your exposure to bacteria. Bacteria grow best in moist, warm areas like the threaded cap of an unrefrigerated bottle of water. This is a perfect place for bacteria to grow. These bacteria can cause gastrointestinal problems and other health risks, if ingested.

Producing bottles uses nonrenewable resources. Unless the bottles are recycled or reused, they cause a waste disposal problem. The inability of plastic to biodegrade causes environmental concerns. It takes about 1,000 years for plastic water bottles in a landfill to biodegrade. Plastic waste often ends up in waterways and landfills, where it has formed a floating patch of garbage like the one in the Pacific Ocean roughly the size of Texas. This has a devastating effect on sea life.

"Fewer Regulations For Bottled Water Than Tap, GAO Says"

http://nyti.ms/1Nfw8qC

"Bottles Water Costs More Than 2000 Times More Than Tap Water"

http://read.bi/1IZWXOj

"U.S. CONSUMPTION OF BOTTLED WATER SHOWS CONTINUED GROWTH, INCREASING 6.2 PERCENT IN 2012; SALES UP 6.7 PERCENT"

http://bit.ly/1Nfw8qOt

"The Dangers of Plastic Water"

http://bit.ly/1K6yw2W

Reverse Osmosis

With Reverse Osmosis (RO) water pressure is used to force water molecules through a membrane that has extremely tiny pores. This leaves the larger contaminants behind. Purified water is collected from the "clean" side of the membrane. The water containing the concentrated contaminants is flushed down the drain from the "contaminated" side. The average RO system unit consists of the reverse–osmosis membrane, a sediment/chlorine pre filter, an activated–carbon post filter and a water storage tank. They can cost from about $150 to over $1,500 for point of use systems.

Reverse Osmosis has many advantages. These systems do not use electricity. Although slower than a sediment or carbon filter, RO systems can typically purify more water per day than distillers and are less expensive to maintain and operate. Most point of Use RO units make 12 – 24 gallons of treated water per day for drinking or cooking. This is ok for most homes since the treated water is stored in a tank for use.

Microscopic parasites (including viruses) are usually removed with RO. It significantly reduces salt, most other inorganic material present in the water and some organic compounds. When using a quality carbon filter to remove any organic materials that get through the filter, the purity of the treated water is close to that produced by distillation.

There are a few disadvantages of the RO systems. They require relatively high water pressure to operate. RO systems can waste water. It takes two to four gallons of "waste" water flushed down the drain for each gallon of filtered water produced. Some solvents, chlorine, pesticides and other volatile organic chemicals (VOCs) are not completely removed by RO. A good activated carbon post filter is required to reduce these contaminants.

The RO membrane's efficiency in reducing the amount of contaminants in the water can be affected by many conditions. These would include chemical properties and contaminate concentration, the membrane condition, type and operating conditions (like water temperature, water pressure and pH). Any defect in the membrane would allow these organisms to flow undetected into the "filtered" water. For that reason, RO systems are not recommended for use on biologically unsafe water.

RO systems require maintenance. The reverse osmosis membranes and the pre and post filters must be changed according to the manufacturer's recommendation. The storage tank must be cleaned periodically. It is not easy to detect if membranes are damaged, so it is hard to tell if the system is functioning normally and safely.

Water Filtration

There are many types of filtration strategies and combinations of strategies used. But the basic concept behind most filters is fairly simple. The contaminants are prevented from moving through the filter. This is done by screening them out with very small pores and/or by chemical absorption with carbon filters. The carbon filters trap contaminates within the filter matrix by attracting them to the surface of carbon particles. Sediment and Activated Carbon are the two main types of filters. Sometimes they are combined in a single unit.

Sediment Filters

With Sediment filters solid particles are strained out. There are two types of Sediment filters, Fiber and Ceramic. The Fiber filter typically contains rayon, cellulose or some other material spun into a mess with small pores. These filters come in a variety of sizes and meshes from fine to coarse. The finer the filter, the more particles will be trapped and the more often the filter must be changed.

Fiber filters will not remove contaminates that are dissolved in water. This includes chlorine, mercury, lead, trihalomethanes (a byproduct of the water treatment process) and other inorganic or organic compounds.

Ceramic filters are much like Fiber filters. They use a process where water is forced through the pores of a ceramic filtration media. This type of filter can reduce cysts, asbestos fibers, some bacteria and other particulate matter if the pores are small enough. Like Fiber filters, Ceramic filters will not remove contaminants that are dissolved in the water, like chlorine, lead, mercury, trihalomethanes and other organic or inorganic compounds, nor will they remove viruses. These filters may provide a more thorough removal of contaminants when used as a back–end to an activated carbon filter.

Activated Carbon Filters

Activated carbon (AC) is charcoal that has been treated with oxygen to open up millions of tiny pores between the carbon atoms. This increases the surface area and the ability to adsorb a wide range of contaminants. The carbon source is a variety of materials, such as coal, peanut shells, or coconut husks. AC is particularly good at absorbing organic compounds. These are molecules that contain carbon and hydrogen atoms, like bacteria and alcohols.

AC filters reduce contaminates by two processes, blocking contaminates that are too large to get through the pores and attracting dissolved contaminates to and holding them on the surface of the carbon particles. The large surface area of activated charcoal gives it countless bonding sites. When certain chemicals go by the carbon surface, they attach to the surface and are trapped.

Activated charcoal is good at trapping chlorine and other carbon–based compounds ("organic" chemicals) like carbon dioxide, methane and citric acid. Many other chemicals, like sodium, nitrates are not attracted to carbon. They pass right through. Once all of the bonding sites on the carbon are filled, an activated charcoal filter stops working. At that point the filter must be replaced. Since there is often no noticeable indication that contaminates are no longer being removed by the carbon filter, it is important to replace the cartridge according to the manufacturer's instructions.

There are basically two types of carbon filters, **Granular Activated (GAC)** and **Solid Block Activated Carbon (SBAC).**

Granular Activated Carbon (GAC)

In a GAC filter, water flows through a bed of loose activated carbon granules. This traps some particulate matter and removes some, organic contaminants, chlorine and undesirable odors and tastes. GAC filters are effective and valuable water treatment devices. They require simple, economical maintenance. Typically, an inexpensive filter cartridge needs to be changed every few months to a year, depending on water use and the manufacturer's recommendation. They do not require electricity, nor do they waste water.

But they do have their limitations. GAC filter carbon granules are fairly large and can't significantly reduce bacterial contamination by themselves. Contaminated pockets of water can form in a loose bed of carbon granules. Changes in water pressure and flow rates could cause these pockets to collapse, "dumping" the contaminated water through the filter into the "filtered" flow.

Water might channel around the carbon granules avoiding filtering. A uniform flow rate which does not exceed the manufacture's specifications must be maintained for optimal performance. The filter cartridge must be changed after treating the number of gallons the filter is designed for. These filters might become breeding grounds for the bacteria they trap. Warnings on the filters suggest running water through them for a few minutes each morning to flush out bacteria.

Unless you notice an odor or the filter plugs up, it may be difficult to know when the filter has become saturated with contaminants. This would make the filter ineffective. That is why it is best to change filter cartridges according to the manufacturer's recommendation.

An activated charcoal filter will remove certain impurities while not removing others. GAC filters do not naturally reduce dissolved minerals or salts (including nitrates), fluoride and some other potentially harmful minerals like cadmium and arsenic unless the filter is specially designed and certified to do so. If these contaminants are in your water, reverse osmosis would typically be the most economical alternative followed by distillation.

It is important to note, when using a counter–top and faucet–mount carbon filtration systems, hot water should NEVER be run through a carbon filter. There is a possibility of damage to the filter from hot water. More importantly, hot water will tend to release trapped contaminants into the water flow. This could potentially make the water coming out of the filter more contaminated than the water going in.

Solid Block Activated Carbon (SBAC):

Activated carbon is the primary raw material in solid carbon block filters; but instead of carbon granules comprising the filtration medium, the carbon has been specially treated, compressed bonded to form a uniform matrix.

The absorption or trapping process of SBAC filters depends on several factors. This includes the physical properties of the AC, the surface area and pore size distribution, the chemical nature of the carbon source, or the amount of oxygen and hydrogen associated with it. We also must consider the concentration and chemical composition of the contaminants, the pH and temperature of the water, the water flow rate or time of exposure of water to AC.

SBAC provide a larger surface area for absorption to take place than Granular Activated Carbon (GAC) filters for better contaminant reduction. They provide a small pore size to physically trap particulates. If the pore size is small enough, bacteria that become trapped in the pores do not have enough room to multiply. This eliminates a problem common to GAC filters. SBAC provides a longer contact time with the activated carbon for more complete contaminant reduction.

Depending on the manufacturer, the filters can be designed to better reduce specific contaminants like arsenic, MTBE and others. SBAC completely eliminates the channeling and dumping problems associated with GAC filters and does not waste water like reverse osmosis. SBAC is the least expensive process and easiest to maintain.

All home sediment and activated carbon filtration systems do not require electricity to filter the water. Normal water pressure can be used to force the water though the filter. In emergencies, water can even be siphoned through them to provide some water treatment.

There are some disadvantages to SBAC filters. The effective pore size can be very small. SBAC, like all filter cartridges, eventually become saturated or plugged by contaminants. As SBAC filters are no longer able to adsorb the contaminants, they gradually lose effectiveness.

There is no easy way to determine when a filter is nearing the end of its effective life unless the 'filtered' water eventually begins to taste and smell like the unfiltered water. That is why the manufacturer's guidelines for changing filter cartridges should always be followed. As with Fiber filters, hot water should NEVER be run through a carbon filter.

SBAC filters, like all activated carbon filters, do not naturally reduce the levels of dissolved compounds. This includes nitrates, fluoride and some other potentially harmful minerals like arsenic and cadmium (unless specially certified and designed to do so). When these contaminants are in your water, the most economical alternative would be reverse osmosis followed by distillation. Check NSF International (The Public Health and Safety Organization) or Water Quaility Association (WQA) if there is a SBAC filtration system you are interested in obtaining. NSF and WQA gives information to help you determine if the marketing claims are accurate and the filtration system is certified to significantly reduce the contaminants you are concerned about.

Inexpensive GAC Pitchers

The effectiveness of these pitchers for your purification needs depends on your water treatment goals and the amount of water you plan to filter. They do reduce some contaminates. But they are limited in the type and number of contaminates they remove. Usually chlorine and perhaps copper, lead and/or cysts are reduced.

The most popular brands of filters will sometimes contain granules of an ion exchange medium you can hear and see rattling around. The small amount of GAC granules can not be considered effective treatments for most harmful biological or chemical contaminates. Some pitcher filters contain a microfilter that may be certified to reduce cysts.

All of these filters are mostly designed to improve the taste, odor and reduce a limited number of harmful contaminates. These filters may have possible bacteria growth channeling and all the other problems of larger GAC filters. The filter cartridge, capable of treating about 50 – 100 gallons, will cost about $0.14 – $0.25 per gallon.

Solid Carbon Block Faucet Mount Filters

Solid carbon block faucet mount filters are more effective than GAC filters in reducing harmful contaminates. But these filters are quite small. The larger solid carbon block filters have over 7 times more filter media. Since, the effectiveness of a filter is dependent on contact time of the water with the filter media, a larger high quality solid carbon block filter would be more effective in reducing contaminates at the same flow rate of the water.

Like pitcher filters, the replacement cartridges for faucet mount filters will be about $0.14 – $0.25 per gallon. It is relatively expensive compared to a high–quality solid block activated carbon replacement filter which will filter water for about $0.08 per gallon.

Looking at the long term costs and comparing it with other solutions, it seems that owning even a high–end water filter can be very inexpensive as long as the cost of the replacement filter elements is reasonable.

Distillation

The process of distillation has been used for centuries. It has primarily been a way of producing alcoholic beverages like vodka and whisky. Distillation provides mineral–free water that is required for use in science laboratories or for printing purposes. This process also works as a water purification technique. Distillation separates pure water molecules from contaminants in the water with a higher boiling point.

To remove contaminates from water, the water is usually boiled in a chamber. This causes the water to vaporize. The temperature is maintained at a constant to ensure continued water evaporation. The constant boiling temperature prohibits drinking water contaminants like salts, metals, sediment, most minerals, most bacteria, viruses or anything that will not boil or evaporates with a higher boiling point.

Steam is guided to a different part of the chamber where it is cooled until it condenses back into liquid water in a storage container.

Contaminants having a higher boiling point than the vaporized water remain in the original chamber and must be removed.

However, some contaminates evaporate along with the water boiled in the chamber. Good examples of contaminants that will evaporate and condense with the water vapor are chlorine, chlorine byproducts or Volatile Organic Compounds (VOCs). VOCs are commonly used in commercial and household products. Some examples of VOCs include chloride, methylene, benzene, hexane and toluene.

A carbon filter, vapor trap, or other device should be used along with the distillation unit to ensure a more complete removal of contaminants.

Advantages of the Distillation process includes:

A good distillation unit kills pathogens (anything that can produce disease). It can remove heavy metals, nitrates and other salts that carbon filtration can not remove. A distillation unit that is kept clean and in good working condition is the most effective water treatment method by providing a consistent quality of treated water regardless of the incoming water.

There is no filter cartridge to replace, unless a carbon filter is combined with the unit to remove volatile organic compounds (VOCs). It is often preferred in developing nations or area where the risk of air–borne disease is high to remove viruses and bacteria in the drinking water.

Some of the disadvantages include:

Distillation does not remove chlorine, chlorine byproducts, or VOCs. These are major contaminates in municipally treated water. It takes time. It takes 2–5 hours to make 1 gallon of treated water. The Distillation unit requires periodic cleaning of the boiler, condensation compartment and storage tank. Distillation wastes water. 80% of the water used is discarded with contaminates.

Since distillation, like reverse osmosis, provides mineral–free water, there have been concerns that the distilled water, due to it acidity, might be harmful to our body's system when ingested.

Distillers cost from $200 to $1500 for home use models. It requires electricity. In case of an emergency where there is no electricity the unit will not work. The initial cost of the unit and electrical use make distillation one of the most expensive water treatment methods. It cost about $0.25–$0.35 of electricity per gallon.

I would suggest checking NSF International (The Public Health and Safety Organization) or Water Quality Association (WQA) if there is a distillation unit you are interested in obtaining. NSF and WQA gives information to help you determine if the marketing claims are accurate and the distillation unit is certified to significantly reduce the contaminants you are concerned about.

Make your own distilled water

You can make your own distilled water. The basis principle is the same. Boil water. Water creates steam. Steam hits a cool surface. Steam turns into water again. We call it condensation. The condensation is collected into a clean drip tray or another container.

There are many variations to this principal of making distillation water. But here is one. You will need a heat source. This can be a campfire, stove, or other heat source. A clean large pot with a lid, glass bowl and ice cubes, ice packs or cold water.

Get the large pot with the lid. Add water to pot to about ¼ full. Sit the glass bowl on top of water in the pot. Make sure the bowl floats on the water. Place lid of pot up–side–down on top of pot. If the lid has a tiny hole in it, fill it with part of a toothpick or place tape over the tiny hole. To produce condensation, fill the up–side–downed lid with ice packs, cold water or ice cubes. Bring the water inside the pot to a boil, then lower the heat.

The steam will rise and hit the lid. Condensation will collect on the up–side–downed lid and drip into the bowl inside the pot. Use a potholder to carefully lift lid, not spilling the water inside the up–side–down lid. Pour the melted water out. Check on the level of distilled water inside the glass bowl. Place more ice cubes, cold water or ice packs on top of the up–side–down lip. Place the lid back on top of the pot. Repeat this process until the desired amount of distilled water is collected in the glass bowl. Store distilled water in glass instead of plastic so you don't pick up residue.

Purchasing Distilled Water

Many prefer not to purchase a distillation unit and electe to purchase distilled water at the store. There may be concerns about plastic residue and the lack of minerals leading to mineral deficiencies. Dr. Delbert Blair addresses these concerns:

"One aspect in the use of water is distilled water. It is rejected by many because distilled water can not grow fish and can not grow plants. I personally love distilled water and unfortunately I can't find it in a glass bottle in many cases. When I don't find a glass bottle I buy the distilled water in a plastic bottle. I take the plastic bottle and I pour it into a glass container that has a top to it so I can screw it tight. I then add as much liquid oxygen as I think I want for that time. I then add Q–5 (liquid mineral supplement) to it, a 96 mineral type of an essence is there.

Then, I put it onto a diode plaque. I leave it on the diode plaque for at least one hour. You can do it a shorter time. But I would suggest at least one hour. Then I put it on a magnet. I use the north pole side of the magnet only. Once that is done I've got a water I find that helps to draw out impurities, gives me my minimum oxygen and flushes out the colon, the liver, the bladder and the body itself.

That's my methodology. It works for me. I hope it works for some."

"Drinking Water Treatment Methods"

http://bit.ly/1FwJFDP

"The Phosphate Fertilizer Industry: An Environmental Overview"

http://bit.ly/1dZrLDL

"Did Hitler Really Put Fluoride In The Water At Concentration Camps? If So Why Do We Put It In Our Water?" http://yhoo.it/1dZrMrj

"Importance Of Water In The Diet" http://bit.ly/1GvkVN2

"Harvard Study Confirms Fluoride Reduces Children's IQ" http://huff.to/1IZXBey

"Dr. Ted Broer – 10 Foods to Never Eat – YouTube" http://bit.ly/1GZDVrN

"Why Choose Filtered Water?" http://www.allaboutwater.org/filtered–water.html

"Search for NSF Certified Drinking Water Treatment Units, Water Filters" http://bit.ly/1Ho9CfU

"Water Quality Association" http://bit.ly/1GCCZYT

Dr. Delbert Blair, www.themetacenter2.com

"What is a Diode?" http://bit.ly/1K6yR5T

"How To Make Distilled Water" https://www.youtube.com/watch?v=NpkDJ6yIN8I

Alkaline Water Systems

Water ionization was first developed in Japan in the early 50's as part of an effort to help their people injured by the atomic bombs. Alkaline water is made by using electronic devices to split filtered tap water into alkaline and acidic streams, feeding each into separate chambers. One chamber contains the alkaline water. The second chamber contains the acidic water.

In 1958, the first units were large and could only be afforded by hospitals. In 1966, the Health and Rehabilitation Ministry of the Japanese Government acknowledged the alkaline ionic water ionizer as a legitimate medical device for improving human health. Today, these machines are still part of medical treatment programs in Japan.

Both alkaline and acidic water have benefits, especially, acidic water. Nursery farmers that supply cut flowers for flower shops use it to keep flowers longer before delivery. It is used on golf courses in place of chemicals on the greens and fairways. In hospitals, it is used as an astringent for killing bacteria and germs. In the 1990s, more people worldwide began to recognize the benefits of alkaline ionized water and the market for these machines grew.

Some of the advantages claimed by proponents of Alkaline water include: Better hydration. The minerals contained in alkalized water increase absorption that supply the cells throughout the body. Many alternative medicine practitioners believe this hydrating effect can prevent or cure many diseases.

Alkaline water is said to contain antioxidants, molecules that inhibit the oxidation of other molecules that may prevent or delay some types of cell damage. The negatively charged molecules are said to capture positively charged free radicals in your body that cause oxidation. Oxidation damages the DNA of a cell causing it to age drastically.

Proponents say that it can boost your metabolism and help your body absorb nutrients more affectively. Drinking alkaline water may also counter the acidity of the food we eat and drink. Since most of the food we eat and drink is acidic, including coffee, meat, tomatoes and orange juice, alkaline water may restore a more balanced pH.

Alkaline water may aid in the treatment of disease for patients suffering from a variety of medical conditions such as diabetes (reported drops in blood sugar), liver disease, asthma, allergies, osteoporosis (brittle bones) high or low blood pressure and gastroduodenal ulcers. Some believe alkaline water may prevent or treat cancer because cancer cells cannot grow in an alkaline environment.

One of the primary claimed benefits of alkaline water is more "available" oxygen in the system. Cancer is related to an acid environment (lack of oxygen). The higher the pH, the more oxygen will be present in the cells of the body. This makes it harder for cancer to thrive.

Alkaline water systems produce acidic water for cleaning. Acidic water is a good cleansing agent. It is like cleaning windows with a water–and–vinegar mixture.

The disadvantages include claims that it does not balance pH. Because the human body expels excess acid in many ways, such as urine, sweat and exhalation (CO_2 expelled during respiration is an acid), alkaline water is likely to have no effect on the body's pH.

Alkaline water does not change the pH in your stomach because everything that passes through the stomach is highly acid. Alkaline water does not change the pH of the intestines. Strong alkaline enzymes in the intestines further break down food to advance digestion after the acidification in the stomach.

Proponents of alkalinity suggest that alkaline water balances the pH throughout the body. If this is implying the entire body has the same pH, it is not true. The pH varies widely throughout the body.

Most alkaline water ionizers are being marketed by multi–level marketing (MLM) companies with less than "heavenly ethics" and through which you pay inflated prices. Alkaline water ionizers are expensive ranging from $1,000.00 to over $4,000.00. The Ionizers require maintenance and have filters you need to buy and replace periodically.

"Pros–Cons: Alkaline Water" http://bit.ly/1ftsiyS

"Alkaline Water" http://bit.ly/1Bx1LdZ

"The History of Alkaline Water"
http://bit.ly/1FwK2hV

"The History Of Alkaline Water"
http://bit.ly/1dZs9Cs

"Healthy Living: Nutrition And Healthy Eating: Expert Answers"
http://mayocl.in/1I9Rbep

Make Your Own Alkaline Water

You can make your own alkaline water with baking soda, lemons or limes.

Add 1/8 tbsp (600 mg) baking soda to an 8 oz. (2 liters) glass of water. Baking soda has a high alkaline content. When the baking soda mixes with the water, it increases the alkaline properties of the water. Shake well (if you are using a water bottle) or stir (if using a glass) the mixture vigorously to make sure the baking soda mixes in thoroughly with the water. If you are on a low sodium diet, do not add baking soda to your water. Baking soda is high in sodium.

Use lemons or limes. Lemons are anionic, so when you drink lemon water, your body reacts with the anionic properties of the lemon making the water alkaline as your body digests it. Fill one pitcher (64 oz.) with clean water. Filtered water is the best way to go, but if you don't have a filter, tap water is okay to use.

Cut up one lemon into eighths. Add the lemons to the water but do not squeeze them. Simply place them in the water. Cover the water and let it sit overnight for 8 to 12 hours at room temperature.

"Make Alkaline Water"

http://www.wikihow.com/ Make–Alkaline–Water

Recommendations

We would recommend reverse osmosis, distillation and then alkaline water. For each method I would suggest adding additional filters and changing the filters as often as possible.

CHAPTER 27
Microwave Ovens

AN ELECTRON TUBE, CALLED a magnetron, produces microwaves inside the oven. The microwave energy is absorbed into the food as they reflect within the metal interior of the oven. Microwaves cause water molecules in food to vibrate at very high frequencies. This vibration produces heat that cooks the food. Foods high in water content, like fresh vegetables, can be cooked more quickly than other foods because they contain more water molecules.

The Food and Drug Administration (FDA) have regulated the manufacturing of microwave ovens since 1971. The agency states that on the basis of current knowledge about microwave radiation, ovens that meet the FDA standard and are used according to the manufacturer's instructions are safe for use. It states that microwave cooking does not reduce the nutritional value of foods any more than conventional cooking and that foods cooked in a microwave oven may keep more of their vitamins and minerals, because microwave ovens can cook more quickly and without adding water.

However, there seems to be views to the contrary. One view is that while microwaves heat food by causing water molecules in it to resonate at very high frequencies and eventually turn to steam, which rapidly heats your food, it also causes a change in your food's chemical structure. Microwaving deforms and distorts the molecules of whatever food or other substance you "microwave". One simple test is to take two potted plants. Water one with tap water and the other with water that was heated in the microwave oven and cooled before giving it to the plant. Within a few weeks the plant watered with "microwaved" water will be dead.

The few studies done generally agree that microwaving food damages its nutritional value. Nutrients, minerals, and vitamins of all microwaved food is altered or reduced. This renders food of little or no benefit to the body. The body also absorbs altered compounds that cannot be broken down without pulling nutrients from your bones and tissue to do so. One study in the November 2003 issue of The Journal of the Science of Food and Agriculture found that broccoli "cooked" in the microwave with a little water lost up to 97 percent of its beneficial antioxidants. By comparison, steamed broccoli lost only 11 percent or fewer of its antioxidants.

When microwaving creates deformed and altered compounds, the human body cannot metabolize (break down) the unknown by–products created in microwaved food. This creates tremendous stress on the pancreas to produce insulin to help break down the "dead" food without the benefit of nutritional exchange. Prolonged production of insulin with little or no nutritional exchange can lead to diabetes.

There are many other problems reported with "microwaved" food. Eating microwaved food can cause loss of concentration, memory, emotional instability, and a decrease of intelligence. The minerals in vegetables may be altered into cancerous free radicals. Hormone production is shut down and/or altered by continually eating microwaved foods. Continually eating food "microwaved" can cause long term – permanent – brain damage by "shorting out" electrical impulses in the brain and immune system deficiencies through lymph gland and blood serum alterations.

"Hot spots" in microwaved food can cause burns or build up to a "steam explosion". Boiling water on a conventional stove allows steam to escape as the water begins to boil through bubbling action. By contrast, in a microwave oven there may be no bubbles on the walls of the container. The water will super–heat and may suddenly boil. The introduction of a foreign element such as a spoon or a single bubble in the liquid may trigger this sudden boiling. This super–heated water has caused severe burns. This is a good reason not to use the microwave to heat up baby bottles containing liquid, since babies have been burned by super–heated formula that went undetected.

Certain items with non–porous surfaces such as hotdogs or items composed of materials that heat at different rates such as the yolk and white of eggs, heat unevenly and may explode. This can happen if chestnuts and eggs are cooked in their shells. These ovens may produce uneven cooking because microwave energy does not penetrate well in thicker pieces of food. If parts of the food are not heated sufficiently to kill potentially dangerous micro–organisms this can lead to a health risk. To compensate for the potential for uneven distribution of cooking, food heated in a microwave oven should rest for several minutes after the cooking is completed. This allows the heat to distribute throughout the food.

Carcinogenic toxins can leach out of your paper and plastic containers, and into your food. Only use dishes and containers specifically designed for microwave cooking. One of the worst contaminants is BPA (Bisphenol A), an estrogen–like compound used widely in plastic products. Dishes made specifically for the microwave often contain BPA. It is not too hard to see why their use was outlawed in the Soviet Union and the Soviets issued an international warning on the health hazards, both biological and environmental, of microwave ovens and similar frequency electronic devices.

Recommendations

Stay clear of an operated microwave oven. Even if there is nothing wrong with your microwave, just standing a foot away from it while it is on can expose you to upwards of 400 milliGauss (units of measurement of a magnetic field). A mere 4 milliGauss has been firmly linked to leukemia.

Our eyes are known to be particularly susceptible to microwave radiation. High microwave exposures are known to cause cataracts.

Do not let your children stand near the microwave when it is running. Avoid it yourself as much as possible, especially if you are pregnant.

Follow the instructions that come with each microwave oven. They should indicate the kinds of containers to use. They also should cover how to test containers to determine whether or not they can be used in microwave ovens.

Alternatives

A toaster oven is great for heating up leftovers! Keep it at a low temperature — like 200–250 degrees F — and gently warm a plate of food in about 20–30 minutes.

The convection oven is another great alternative. They can be built in or purchased at a relatively inexpensive price and this is another quick safe way to heat foods.

Prepare your meals in advance. This way you always have meals available on those days when you're too busy or too tired to cook.

Eat more organic raw foods. This is probably the best way to improve your health over the long run.

"Electromagnetic Fields & Public Health: Microwave Ovens" http://bit.ly/1BH4BgP

"Why Did The Russians Ban An Appliance Found In 90% of American Homes?" http://bit.ly/1SDcRmc

"Radiation–Emitting Products" http://1.usa.gov/1JedOjk

"The Dangers of Microwave Ovens" http://bit.ly/1K6zrR8

CHAPTER 28
Food for Thought

Why is processed food so cheap?

The food industry has great power and influence. Powerful food industry lobbyists have influenced the government to pass laws that give subsidies (money from our taxpayer dollars) to the food industry. Campaign contributions of large sums of money are given to Congressional members running for re–election by the food industry. These contributions go to the politicians who will favor the food industry's position. The United States Department of Agriculture (USDA) gives subsides to the food industry to make the cost of production cheaper.

These subsidies allow them to make food at a lower cost and increase their chances of making a profit. Since we pay them to produce or not to produce, many consider this "corporate welfare". In addition, the food industry has put pressure on Congress to maintain subsidies (corporate welfare) and promote other laws that favor the food industry. This results in the production of cheaper food. That is why it costs less to purchase the supersized Pepsi, fries and chili burger or a Big Mac with fries and a coke than fresh organic fruits, vegetable, legumes, and whole grains.

Why is Junk Food addictive?

The food industry has also invested time, money, and resources researching our body's reaction to certain foods. Their geneticists, bio–engineers, microbiologists and other scientists have found that the combination of salt, sugar, and fat has a <u>predictable addictive chemical effect</u> on our bodies. The food industry's research has lead to increased profits. It has also lead to the lower cost of food containing sugar, salt and fat. The increased consumption of food containing this unholy trinity of sugar, salt and fat has lead to many health challenges.

Obesity rates have tripled among children between 12 and 19 years old in the U.S. in the past 30 years. A third of the children are officially overweight or obese. These over–weight or obese children are more likely to suffer from diseases such as high blood pressure, high cholesterol, and Type II diabetes. These diseases were once limited to adults, but are common today among children.

In "The End of Overeating" David Kessler, M.D. says processed food is loaded with sugar, salt, and fat. This addictive food combination stimulates the release of dopamine. This is a feel good brain chemical that can lead to over eating. Once the food is eaten, the brain releases opiates, which bring emotional relief. In time, the brain gets programed, or "wired" so that a pathway is created and every time one is reminded of a particular food, they will want to eat it.

What is the effect of advertisements?

Each year food corporations spend hundreds of millions of dollars on food advertisement in the U.S. The vast majority of the ads are designed to convince children to eat unhealthy food such as fast and processed foods, treats and snacks. Many adults are also influenced by this advertisement. Many adults have been influenced by advertising since they were children. Very few of advertisements are for healthy foods such as fresh organic fruits, vegetables, whole grains, and legumes.

Dopamine is a chemical that helps control the brain's reward and pleasure centers. At the mere suggestion of a food, the brain releases dopamine. To make sure there are plenty of reminders of a particular food, the food industry has ads. Radio, T.V., billboards, internet and poster ads are designed to remind us of particular foods. This chemical (dopamine) released from the brain gives a strong urge to eat the suggested food. Opiads then bring an emotional relief after eating the food.

This cycle is repeated over and over by many unsuspecting eaters having no knowledge or awareness of this addictive combination. Often, this results in over eating. This can lead to obesity and the many health challenges this brings. This seems to point to an addictive chemical trap laid by the food industry. Most likely, this was done in an effort to make a profit. Perhaps that is why salt, fat, and sugar are in almost all processed food produced by the food industry.

How helpful are the USDA Guidelines?

The USDA's nutritional guidance is misleading. The Dietary Guidelines for Americans are jointly issued and updated every 5 years by the Department of Agriculture (USDA) and the Department of Health and Human Services (HHS). It is supposed to provide science–based nutrition guidance for Americans ages 2 and older to promote healthy lifestyles and dietary habits. In practice, this does not always seem to be true.

The USDA nutritional guidelines appear to be based on the increasing profits of the food industry. The guidelines do not tell you what foods may cause a health risk if too much is consumed. For example, the consumption of soy beans, tofu, shellfish, meat, and dairy are recommended, notwithstanding the known related health risks for obesity, mercury poisoning, or chronic diseases that can lead to suffering or death.

The End of Overeating David Kessler, M.D. Publisher: Simon & Schuster 2009

"Choose My Plate" http://1.usa.gov/1K791jF

Protein Myth

As vegans, my wife and I have been asked many times "how do you get enough protein?" We usually answer, "If one eats a healthy vegan diet, there is an abundance of protein". This question assumes that, meat and dairy products are the only source of dietary protein worth eating. We are told, without plentiful amounts of animal protein, it's impossible to be healthy, let alone perform as an athlete at your peak.

Powerful and well–funded meat and dairy lobbies have spent their marketing dollars on a campaign of disinformation to convince society that we absolutely need these products to live. This notion is at best misleading, if not altogether false. The animal protein push is killing us by luring us to feast on factory farmed, pesticide and hormone induced foods. These foods are generally high in saturated fats, which clog the arteries; contribute to heart disease and many other congenital problems.

First, let's make it clear. Protein should not be considered a food group. Protein is considered one of the six essential nutrients along with water, carbohydrates, minerals, vitamins and fats. These nutrients are necessary for the body to properly function. Protein is about twenty percent of the body and next to water, the most plentiful substance in the body. It is the major structural part of cells and is critical in building and repairing muscle tissue and many important bodily functions.

MyPlate is the current nutrition guide published by the United States Department of Agriculture (USDA). It consists of a diagram of a plate and glass divided into five food groups, fruits, vegetables, grains, protein and dairy. It replaced the USDA's MyPyramid diagram on June 2, 2011. The guide is displayed on food packaging and used in nutritional education in the United States. This guide is also very misleading.

Protein is not a food group. There is protein in fruit, vegetables, whole grains and dairy. Why the confusion? Disinformation and confusion has been an important marketing tool for some companies. When the public is confused as to what protein is and how our bodies use it, it is easier to give them misleading or false information that can lead to them purchasing or consuming animal or protein products.

Proteins consist of twenty different amino acids. Your body can make eleven of the amino acids. The remaining nine we call essential amino acids because it is essential that they be eaten from an outside food source.

Plants can make all twenty amino acids. They are also found in meat and dairy products only because the animals eat the plants. Protein foods (plant or animal) are broken down into amino acids during digestion. So, technically, our bodies only require certain amino acids, not protein per se. Protein can be considered the "middleman". You don't need proteins. You need amino acids.

It is healthier to get protein from plant foods than from animal source foods. Since meat is not the original source of amino acids, when we eat meat, the amino acids we consume are considered second–hand. When we eat meat we not only get the secondhand amino acids, but all of the toxins the animal has consumed its entire life. So, contrary to the popular disinformation given, you do not need to eat animal protein to get all the protein you need in your diet. Also, it should be clear that protein does not equal meat nor does meat equal protein.

All plant–based proteins are not "complete", containing all nine essential amino acids. Examples of this are beans, nuts, peas, seeds, grain products like bread and vegetables. But a well–rounded whole food plant–based diet that includes a colorful rotation of these foods will satisfy the demanding protein needs of even the hardest training athlete. These plant–based proteins do not contain the saturated fat in meat that gives us heart disease, the casein in cow's milk that has been linked to a variety of congenital diseases, or the whey, a low–grade discard of cheese production.

The body does not require a large daily intake of proteins. The current Recommended Dietary Allowance (RDA) for protein is 50 grams a day for adult women and 63 grams daily for adult men. Considering the high amounts of protein contained in plant foods, most people meet this daily requirement easily and usually exceed it. As an Example: A breakfast consisting of one–cup oatmeal, a sliced medium banana, ¼ medium avocado and ¼ cup almonds is over 16 grams of protein.

A lunch consisting of one–cup cooked lentils, one–cup of brown rice, and one slice of spouted grain bread is over twenty–five grams.

A dinner of one–half cup quinoa, one–cup cooked spinach and a small salad is about 30 grams of protein.

This totals more than seventy grams of protein. This is more than the recommended RDA for protein for a male.

Most plant legumes, vegetables and whole grains supply between 10–15 percent of their calories from protein or about 50–70 grams a day, which matches the RDA recommendations. Pregnant, lactating women, or the very physically active need more protein than the average person. Their needs can be easily met by increasing the total amount of protein–rich grains and legumes they eat each day.

According to surveys, Americans eat almost twice as much protein as their bodies need. This may be because of a preference for meat and other animal sources of protein created by the meat and dairy industry and the ample supplies of protein. The average protein intake is approximately 100 grams per day.

Long term, excessive animal protein intake can be harmful. There is evidence that it is often stored in fat cells. This contributes to the onset of a variety of congenital diseases such impaired kidney and liver function, heart disease and cancer. The protein from animals is too acidic for our bodies. So, in order for our bodies to neutralize the acidity, it takes calcium phosphate from the bones. We pee out the calcium. That is why so many meat eaters end up with osteoporosis (brittle bones).

If you are still not convinced consider this: Some of the strongest, largest and fiercest animals in the world such as the elephant, rhino, hippo and gorilla are plant powered. Along with the giraffes, horses, and buffaloes, they all share one thing in common. They all get all of their protein from plants. So, rather than consuming steak, eggs, milk, and whey supplements, opt instead for healthy plant–based protein sources such as kidney, black and pinto beans, lentils, almonds, hemp seeds, spirulina, spinach, broccoli and quinoa.

Protein In The Vegan Diet by Reed Mangels, PhD, RD From "Simply Vegan 5th Edition"

http://www.vrg.org/nutrition/protein.php

"Protein In Diet"

http://1.usa.gov/1dbArX9

"What Is Protein? By Georgia C. Laurizen"

http://bit.ly/1Nfxamv

"Plant Protein"

http://bit.ly/1CovKjn

CHAPTER 29

Cookware – from the worst to the best

THE POTS, PANS AND other cookware we use are made from a variety of materials. These materials can get into the food we cook in them. Most of the time, this material is harmless. However, caution should be taken with some materials. As a general rule, most cookware should be replaced if it is worn or pitted. Not knowing what to replace your old cookware with can be a problem. For that reason we have listed the cookware from what is reported to be the worst to the best.

Teflon and nonstick

Avoid Teflon and non–stick pots, pans, bakeware and utensils! These surfaces can release toxic fumes into the air when overheated. According to the Environmental Working Group, nonstick coatings can "reach 700 degrees Fahrenheit in as little as 3–5 minutes, releasing 15 toxic gases and chemicals, including two carcinogens. Perfluorooctanoic acid (PFOA), also known as C8 is a man made chemical that is used in the process of making Teflon and similar chemicals.

PFOA is considered a likely carcinogen. It is associated with birth defects and raised levels of cholesterol. The chemical is present in the blood for up to 4 years and can show up in breast milk. Workers exposed to PFOA have increased risk for bladder, kidney, pancreas and testicular cancer. Additionally, overheated chemical nonstick finishes release fumes that are known to kill birds. If those toxic Perfluorooctanoic Acid (PFOA) fumes can kill birds in a few minutes, what can they do to you?

If you must use non–stick cookware keep this in mind:

Do not use metal utensils on nonstick cookware. Wash the cookware by hand using nonabrasive cleaners and sponges. Do not use steel wool. This cookware scratches easily.

If you're not careful flecks of non–stick material can mix in unnoticed with your food.

You should not use non–stick cookware if the coating is coming off.

Never leave nonstick pans unattended while cooking.

Avoid heating the cookware above 450° Fahrenheit (232° Celsius). At this temperature toxic gases are released.

Your food is exposed to the metal underneath–most likely aluminum when this cookware is damaged or worn.

Use an exhaust fan over the stove.

Do not leave your birds in the kitchen when cooking with non–stick cookware.

"Teflon and Perfluorooctanoic Acid (PFOA)" http://bit.ly/1LwfPVl

"Which Is The Safest Cookware" http://bit.ly/1H97dGt

"Dangers Of Cookware: Safest Alternatives" http://bit.ly/1eDYsro

"Hidden Dangers in Cookware" http://bit.ly/1I9S4DK

"Cookware: What Is Safe and What Is Toxic" http://bit.ly/1Lgajbk

Copper

Copper leaches into food when it is heated. Large amounts of copper from unlined cookware can cause diarrhea, nausea, and vomiting. This prompted the FDA to warn against using unlined copper for general use. According to the National Institute of Health, some copper and brass pans are coated with another metal to prevent food from coming in contact with copper and allowed to dissolve in food. Older copper cookware may have tin or nickel coatings and should not be used for cooking.

Aluminum

This is a soft, highly toxic and reactive metal. Aluminum is often used in cookware because it conducts heat quickly. The problem is the metal can leach into your food. This is especially true when aluminum is used for cooking or storing salty or highly acidic foods such as tomatoes. These foods may cause more aluminum than usual to enter the food. The metal–food reaction can form aluminum salts that are associated with Alzheimer's disease and impaired visual motor coordination. Also, the more pitted and worn the cookware, the greater the amount of aluminum that can be released into food.

According to Dr. A. McGuigan's Report on Findings for the Federal Trade Commission, "All Vegetables cooked in Aluminum produce hydroxide poison which neutralizes digestive juices, producing stomach and gastrointestinal trouble, such as stomach ulcers and colitis." It should also be noted that the sale of aluminum cookware is prohibited in Germany, France, Belgium, Great Britain Switzerland, Hungary and Brazil.

"Safe Cookware: The Safest Cookware and the Most Toxic Cookware by Elizabeth Walling"

http://bit.ly/1Lgajbk

Anodized Aluminum

Most cookware today is made of anodized aluminum. This has become a popular alternative to aluminum. Anodized aluminum is cookware that has an aluminum core surrounded in a safer cooking material. As long as the cookware is in good shape, this may be considered a safe option. But anodization can break down over time causing the surface of the cookware to become worn or damaged. This risk is increased, especially with the frequent cooking of highly acidic foods such as pasta sauce, well–water use or the caustic soaps used in the dishwasher. The more worn the cookware becomes, the greater the amount of aluminum that can come in contact with the food. You do not want your food touching aluminum, especially if it's heated

"Be Cautious With Cookware"

http://bit.ly/1ftucQ8

Stainless Steel

This cookware is quite durable. Stainless steel can be used for any type of cooking. It can be used for quickly heating food up. It is particularly useful for quick dishes, sautéing quickly, or for recipes that require gauging the color of a broth or a sauce. Stainless steel is one of the few metal cookwares that are relatively nonreactive. This means the metal does not interact with the food or affect the final flavor of the dish.

There are many grades of stainless steel. From regular stainless steel cookware made from different alloys including scrap metal to high–grade surgical stainless steel. Stainless steel is a mixture of different metals, including nickel, chromium and molybdenum and often cobalt, as well. If your cookware is worn or damaged these metals can migrate into food. However, unless the cookware is damaged or worn, the amount of metals likely to leach into your food is reportedly small.

Stainless steel cookware is known to release more metals into the food when cooking with liquids and acidic ingredients like tomatoes, apricots or rhubarb. Most high–grade stainless steels are unstable when cooking in tomato acids and salt, or salt and citrus. To avoid the leaching of metals, we would caution against storing highly acidic foods in stainless steel containers or using this cookware for slow cooking acidic dishes. If theses dishes need to be slow–cooked for a long period of time, we would suggest adding salt after cooking or to use a lead free crock pot.

Stainless steel is easier to clean and maintain than cast iron and is far less expensive than ceramic. As with other non–stick surfaces, it is suggested to avoid abrasives for cleaning stainless steel cookware. Frequent use of abrasive materials can scratch the surface and lead to the release of small amounts of chromium and nickel.

People with nickel allergies (an itchy rash commonly associated with earrings and other jewelry, particularly jewelry associated with body piercings) should use a stainless steel cookware with less nickel or avoid cooking with stainless steel cookware.

"Mad As A Hatter by Kaayla T. Daniel, PhD and Galen D. Knight, PhD" http://bit.ly/1JefoTO

Cast Iron

Cast iron is a popular and traditional style of cookware that has been used for hundreds of years. It is durable, provides even heat distribution and good heat retention. It is very versatile and can be used for a variety of recipes. Cast iron cookware is great for cooking dishes that need to go from the stovetop to oven. It can also be used on a campfire.

Cast iron cookware does require some extra effort in its maintenance. Cast iron cookware needs to be "seasoned" with oil before it is used because it will rust. Seasoning is the term used for treating cast iron with oil and baking it. This makes it pretty non–stick if seasoned properly. This fills in the small holes that allow leaching to pass through the surface of the cookware.

Never use soap or an abrasive cleaning pad on a seasoned cast iron cookware. Wipe it out with a nonabrasive washcloth, sponge or nylon dish–brush. Salt can be used as an abrasive if extra cleaning is needed. Dry immediately. Rub with a light coat of coconut oil after every wash. Rub in enough to restore the sheen, without being "sticky". This will keep the iron "seasoned" and protected from moisture.

I would suggest seasoning cast iron by coating with coconut oil. Put it in a 300° Fahrenheit (148° Celsius) oven for three hours. While it is heating, remove it at least three times to wipe it clean and re–grease it. Seasoning your cast iron cookware will prevent rusting and help give it a good natural nonstick coating.

Cast iron pans that have not yet built up a finish of seasoning can leach small amounts of iron, particularly when cooking with liquids and acidic ingredients like tomato or citrus. However, the amount of iron that is leached into the food is generally safe for those who do not have any issues with excess iron.

For some people, excess iron can be a problem. If you suffer with an iron overload like haemochromatosis or similar conditions you should probably not use iron cookware.

Enameled Cast Iron

Enameled cast iron is a versatile cookware material that can be used for many types of dishes. The heat retention of cast iron and the benefits of porcelain combine to perform many cooking techniques. It can easily go from the stovetop to the oven use, so these pots and pans are great for sautéing, frying, braising, stewing, roasting, broiling and baking. The cookware is easy to use and clean up after cooking. It is dishwasher safe.

This is one of the safest types of cookware that comes close to a non–stick surface. The cooking surface is also nonreactive, so there are no dangerous chemicals or metals leaching into food. Porcelain enamel is resistant to alkaline and acidic foods and can be used to marinate and refrigerate. Although it can take a little time to heat up, the heat is distributed evenly and is easily maintained.

You don't have to season enameled cast iron cookware. The porcelain finish is hard, but can be chipped if dropped or banged. Use interior protection to prevent chipping if the cookware is stacked. Enamel cookware also tends to be very expensive. But if you have the cash to spend, high quality enamel pots and pans can be a worthwhile investment, as they will last for many years and are extremely durable.

Glass

Glass bakeware comprises 27% of the total bakeware market today. A good reason is because glass is the most inert of all the cookware. That means it doesn't leach metals or other ingredients into the food. It is one of the best surfaces to cook on. Because it has a smooth, nonporous surface, food particles and odors do not stick to the surface. It can be heated to fairly high temperatures. Glass cookware allows one to see how the food is cooking without needing to lift the lid. It is sturdy, resistant to wear and corrosion and is easy to clean.

Glass cookware can be used for stovetop cooking and baking. It can go from oven to table, with leftover storage in the same container in the refrigerator or freezer. Glass cookware absorbs more heat and bakes faster than metal pans. The cooking temperature is 25 degrees less than a metal pan. This causes the food within to cook faster and brown more. This makes glass cookware a good choice for casseroles, cobblers, breads or pies, but metal cookware is better for cakes, cookies or roasting.

When glass cookware is manufactured, small amounts of lead and cadmium or lead–traced pigment may be used in the process. These materials are harmful if they enter the body. Glassware is considered safe for cooking by the Food and Drug Administration when it contains trace levels of lead or is considered lead free. Use caution when purchasing glass cookware abroad. Not all countries have standards on allowable levels of lead that are as strict as the standards in the United States.

Glass cookware can break when dropped. **If it is designed specifically for baking it should not be used on stovetops.** It can crack or shatter violently when exposed to quick temperature changes resulting in dangerous broken glass pieces. There are reports that the present glass cookware is subject to more shattering because it is not made of the same strong material since 1980. While this is debated, it is still best to use caution when baking or cooking with glass cookware. Here are a few guidelines:

Never heat your glass cookware under a broiler or directly on a stove burner.

Always preheat your oven before putting your glass cookware in it.

Be sure to cover the bottom of your pan with liquid before cooking meat or vegetables.

When you remove the glass cookware from the oven, do not place it directly on the counter top, the stovetop or in a sink. Place it on a dry cloth, pot holder or towel.

Do not immerse the hot cookware in water until it has reached room temperature.

Clean with mild, nonabrasive cleanser. When scrubbing is required, use plastic or nylon scouring pads, not metal.

Ceramic

This cookware is one of the safer options. It is the most inert. This means it does not easily take part in chemical reactions with other metals to leach anything into foods. Ceramics cook better than cast iron or stainless. It has a non–stick cooking surface, holds in flavors in foods and heats evenly.

Ceramics are technically dishwasher, oven, microwave and stove safe. It is easier to clean than cast iron or stainless steel. It can be scrubbed with steel wool or scrubbing pads without scraping or damaging the surface.

Ceramics can chip easily. You have to be careful when stacking or storing them. They can break if you drop them. Their longevity is limited by breakage. Avoid ceramic dishware that is cracked or chipping because the glazes or decorations used in ceramic dishware often contain lead. Cracked or chipping glazes may be more likely to release lead into liquids and foods.

Look out for lead or cadmium in certain ceramics. If it is produced by individuals or made in a foreign country it could very well contain unacceptable levels of lead or cadmium. Both of these highly toxic substances have been phased out in the U.S. or at least limited in cookware manufacturing. So, larger, domestic producers of ceramics in foreign countries would probably be a safer bet.

"The Best (and Worst) Cookware Materials by CHRIS KRESSER"

http://chriskresser.com/the-best-and-worst-cookware-materials

"Be Cautious With Cookware"

http://healthychild.org/easy-steps/cautious-with-cookware/

"What's the Safest Cookware"

http://bit.ly/1GvmISu

"What Are The Safest Cookware Options?" http://bit.ly/1Nfxemo

"Dangers Of Cookware: Safe Alternatives"

http://bit.ly/1Bx3EXV

"Hidden Dangers in Cookware"

http://bit.ly/1fFaQr1

"What is Safe Cookware and Healthy Cookware July 21, 2013 By Mark Jala" http://bit.ly/1ftuNBr

"Kitchen calamity: Reports of shattering cookware on the rise"

http://on.today.com/1TI82cP

"Glass bakeware that shatters"

http://bit.ly/1Jo16BG

"Safety Alert: Your Bakeware Can Potentially Explode Don't Put Yourself, Your Family or Your Kitchen at Risk"

http://bit.ly/1OAkczK

"Glass Cookware Dangers" http://bit.ly/1eDZiEx

"Glass Cookware Dangers" http://bit.ly/1K6AikC

Woks

I have used a wok for 36 years feeding my family that began as 3, then it grew to 5. It was my first kitchen appliance. The wok has inspired me to creatively cook our plant-based foods. It is a strong recommendation to have one.

A Wok is a bowl-shaped frying pan used typically in Chinese cooking. It is often used for stir frying, steaming, deep frying, braising, stewing, or making soup. Woks come in many sizes. A wok can range from about a foot (30 cm) to 6.5 feet (2 m) or more in diameter. For a family of 3 or 4, a Wok of about a foot (30 cm) to 3 feet (91 cm) would be appropriate.

Woks can be as small as 8 inches (20 cm) to nearly 6.5 feet (2 m). Woks that are several feet across are mainly used by restaurants or community kitchens for cooking rice, soup, or boiling water. The smaller woks are typically used for quick cooking at high heat such as stir frying.

Non Stick

We would not recommend these. But some people like them because they do not require seasoning and they're easy to clean. However, we would suggest avoiding non–stick woks coated with Teflon and Polylactic acid (PLA). Teflon emits toxic fumes when overheated. PLA, a corn–based plastic, is typically made from genetically modified corn, at least in the United States. The world's largest producer of PLA is NatureWorks, a subsidiary of Cargill, which is the world's largest provider of genetically modified corn seed.

Non–stick woks seem to scratch easily (like the one I had), and the coating can flake off into your food. They're not good for some types of recipes. For example, some ingredients such as tamarind (often used in pad Thai recipes) go sour/bitter when they mix with the non–stick coating. These woks cannot be used with metal utensils, and foods cooked in non–stick woks tend to hold on to juices instead of browning in the pan.

Stainless Steel (Clad): Woks are also now being introduced with clad or five–layer construction, which sandwich a thick layer of copper or aluminum between two sheets of stainless steel. These woks can cost five to ten times the price of a traditional carbon steel or cast–iron wok, yet cook no better. This is the reason they are not used in most professional restaurant kitchens. They are also slower to heat than traditional woks and not nearly as efficient for stir–frying. There is also the possibility of leaching of copper or aluminum in foods with worn or dented woks.

Cast Iron: This is a traditional, heavier wok that must be seasoned before using. There are two types of cast–iron woks, Chinese and Western–style. Chinese–made cast–iron woks are very thin sized (3mm), weighing only a little more than a similar sized carbon steel wok, while Western–style cast–iron woks typically produced in the West tend to be very heavy and much thicker. Western–style cast–iron woks take much longer to heat up to cooking because of the thickness of the cast–iron. Its weight also makes stir–frying difficult.

Cast–iron woks form a more stable carbonized layer of seasoning which makes it less likely to have food sticking on the pan. While cast–iron woks are superior to carbon steel woks in retaining heat and even heat distribution, they respond slowly to heat adjustments and are slow to cool once taken off the fire. Because of this, food cooked in a cast–iron wok must be quickly removed from the wok as soon as it is done to prevent overcooking. Chinese–style cast–iron woks are relatively light. This makes them fragile and prone to shattering if mishandled or dropped.

Carbon Steel: This is your best bet. It is reasonably durable and inexpensive. It is a good, sturdy wok that's a little lighter than the cast iron and easier to lift. It is heavier than non–stick. Although, a carbon steel wok tends to be more difficult to season, when properly cared for, it will end up with a practically nonstick surface that heats quickly and evenly. Look for carbon steel woks that are about 2 mm (0.1inch) thick (at least 14–gauge). It should not bend when you press on the sides. This wok varies widely in price, quality and style based on how the wok is assembled.

Aluminum

An aluminum wok is a lighter and thinner choice. It is very soft and not as durable as carbon steel. Although it is an excellent heat conductor, it does not retain heat as well as cast iron or carbon steel. Aluminum does not stand up as well to the high temperatures needed to cook with a wok and tend to scorch the food, as it is too thin. It can rust or corrode when frequently used to cook acidic foods like tomatoes. The more damaged the wok, the greater the amount of aluminum that can be released into food. Although anodized aluminum alloys can stand up to constant use, plain aluminum woks are too soft and easily damaged. If you are looking for something light, a better choice is carbon steel, which is thin and durable and can endure high temperatures.

"How To Buy A Wok" http://bit.ly/1gkDD52

The best quality woks are almost always hand–made. Flat–bottomed and electric woks are also available for those cooking over electric burners or wanting a stand–alone heat source.

The best way to clean your wok once it is seasoned is to use only hot water right after you finish using it. Wipe it dry immediately or put it under a low heat to dry. Rub some coconut oil inside the wok if you are not going to use it for a while to prevent rusting. You can also repeat the seasoning any time you think is necessary.

"Wok cooking: A guide to buying and cooking with a wok"
http://hubpages.com/hub/Wok–cooking
"Wok" http://en.wikipedia.org/wiki/Wok

Crock Pots (Slow Cookers)

Crock–Pot is a trademark name that may sometimes be used generically when referring to a slow cooker. This is an electrical cooking appliance used for simmering food at a relatively low temperature for 8 to 12 hours. Most are ceramic pots which drop inside a metal 'base' that has various heat settings.

Glazed Ceramic

Ceramic crock–pot inserts (what you put your food into) are most commonly made of glazed ceramics. The glaze in ceramics is the smooth, often brightly colored coating on the inside of the slow cooker. The problem is the potential for lead to leach out of these glazes into your food. Most of the lead leaching is believed to come from the glaze. Lead compounds, such as lead oxide, have historically been used in glazes. Lead can be absorbed from glazes by acidic food or drinks.

The FDA limits the amount of lead that is allowed to leach from cookware. Anything below 2.0 parts per million is considered acceptable by the FDA. But there is no safe amount of lead to have in your body. Crock–pots that leach potentially harmful amounts of lead, may not kill you in one meal, but over the years, could lead to lead poisoning. These pots can be legally sold. Companies can even declare the pots "lead–free".

Plastic

It has been suggested to use plastic (often nylon) liners in your crock–pot so lead doesn't leach into your food. We would not recommend doing that because plastics heated to high temperatures leach other kinds of toxins into the food. Although, one company claims their slow cooker liners are made from a high resin nylon which is suitable for high temperature cooking, we are still concerned about heating plastic.

Aluminum

The aluminum crock–pots that have non–stick interiors can also leach toxins that you don't want accumulating in your body. Many improvements have been made in aluminum pots and pans with the advent of anodized aluminum (in which a thicker aluminum oxide layer is created on the surface). Yet, we would still recommend avoidance of aluminum cookware due to the potential toxicity of aluminum itself. Additionally, many of them have non–stick coatings (Teflon or some variation thereof).

Stainless Steel

With stainless steel comes the risk of nickel leaching. Because the combination of metals used in stainless steel cookware is more stable than most other cookware materials, the amount of any metal, including nickel, likely to get into your food is reportedly small. An exception would be when highly acidic foods such as tomato sauce and salt remain in stainless steel for long periods.

Since the purpose of the crock–pot is to cook food for 8 to 12 hours, such leaching may occur when cooking highly acidic foods. Leaching may also occur when the cookware has been worn or damaged by harsh scouring with an abrasive material like steel wool.

We would suggest checking with the manufacturer before purchasing a crock–pot. Ask if the cookware is truly lead–free. Beware if the manufacturer states that the cookware meets the FDA requirements. Although this allows the manufacturer to declare that is legally "lead–free", no amount of lead that can leach into your food is considered safe.

There are a few lead–free alternatives to slow cookers. The cast iron Dutch ovens or unglazed clay cookers for example, can achieve the same effect with food, but require a little more monitoring during cooking and maintenance afterwards.

As of this writing we would recommend Miriam's Earthen Cookware for crock–pots. It is pure–clay cookware that is tested to ensure the raw material is indeed pure. It has no lead or any other heavy metals that react and leach into your food. The cookware is made in the USA. The pots are 100% Non–toxic, healthy and Green. The cookware is multi–functional and can be used in your slow cooker, on your stovetop and in the oven.

"Are Crockpots Worth The Risks"
http://bit.ly/1OAk2Zb

"Is There Lead In Slow Cookers And Is It Getting Into Your Food"
http://bit.ly/1GCFWbT

"Miriam's Earthen Cookware"
http://bit.ly/1ONw6an

"The Skinny On Lead In Crock Pots, It May Surprise You"

http://bit.ly/1GvmTNH

"Housekeeping Home Garden: Lead Poisoning And Crock Pots"

http://bit.ly/1GvmY3O

Protein Myth

Protein In The Vegan Diet by Reed Mangels, PhD, RD From "Simply Vegan 5th Edition"

http://www.vrg.org/nutrition/protein.php

"Protein In Diet"

http://1.usa.gov/1dbArX9

"What Is Protein? By Georgia C. Laurizen"

http://bit.ly/1Nfxamv

"Plant Protein"

http://bit.ly/1CovKjn

CHAPTER 30
Polystyrene (Commonly known as Styrofoam) Containers

MANY RESTAURANTS AND EATERIES give you polystyrene food containers and cups to take your food home. In offices all over the country, workers take breaks and drink coffee or tea out of polystyrene cups. We recently attended a party where the guests drank alcohol and other beverages out of polystyrene cups. These containers and cups are inexpensive to manufacture, but the quality of your food can be affected by these containers and cups. They pose certain health risks. To be safe, we recommend avoiding polystyrene for cups, plates and carry out containers for any food or drink. Avoid all plastic containers for hot food. Bring your own coffee or teacup to work to use at breaks.

Styrofoam is actually a Dow Chemical company trade name for a certain type of polystyrene foam and is often misused as a generic term for polystyrene. Polystyrene is the disposable foam that makes products such as coffee cups, coolers and packaging materials. Its primary ingredient, styrene is the danger. Another toxic substance contained in polystyrene is Benzene. Both are suspected carcinogens and neurotoxins that are hazardous to humans.

In the 12th Edition of its Reports on Carcinogens, the National Toxicology Program (NIP) stated that styrene is "reasonably anticipated to be a carcinogen," and the International Agency for Research on Cancer classified styrene as a possible human carcinogen." According to the Agency for Toxic Substances and Disease Registry food products placed in polystyrene containers may become contaminated with styrene. Eating and drinking such contaminated products can lead to anything from gastrointestinal difficulties to liver and kidney damage.

Polystyrene is very light in weight because 95% of its bulk is air filling. It is a petroleum–based plastic that can release potentially toxic breakdown products (including styrene), particularly when heated. The migration of styrene from polystyrene containers into your food has been shown to be dependent on a few other factors. That is, oils, acidity, alcohol and the presence of vitamin A.

Entrees, soups, or beverages that are high in fat (like fried chicken, noodles, and coffee with milk) will suck styrene out of polystyrene containers. Acids (like tea with lemons) produce the most marked change in the weight of the foam cup. The polystyrene cup will weigh less after the beverage has been consumed because the styrene that is ingested reduces the overall weight of the cup.

Styrene tends to migrate from polystyrene containers more quickly into drinks or foods when they are hot. Examples would be hot tea, coffee or foods heated in the microwave that are in polystyrene cups and containers. The presence of ethanol, commonly found in alcohol will dissolve styrene. An example would be red wine. It will instantly dissolve styrene. This means one will ingest styrene when drinking alcohol, beer, wine or mixed drinks in polystyrene cups.

In packaged foods with the addition of heat (such as microwave temperatures), vitamin A (betacarotene) will decompose and produce solvents that will dissolve polystyrene. An example would be heating "Instant Soup Cup" in a polystyrene cup containing carrots in the microwave. You can usually recognize styrene foam cups at a glance. To find out whether a container is made out of polystyrene, look for the number 6 inside the recycling symbol.

In your quest for better health, watch not only what you eat, but what you eat out of. The containers you use can affect your health.

"Styrofoam, The Silent Killer"

http://bit.ly/1LgdAYi
"Is Styrofoam Safe?"
http://bit.ly/1NfxlOE
"Skip Styrofoam Cups...for Your Health"
http://bit.ly/1H774RK
"Are Polystyrene or Styrofoam food containers harmful?"
http://exm.nr/1GCGPkL
"The Health Hazards of Styrofoam: What is Styrofoam"
http://yhoo.it/1BH6Ali

CHAPTER 31

Plastics and Recycle Codes

Another product in our daily lives that is widely used and misused is plastic. We believe you need to be informed of the dangers of plastics because they come into contact with nearly everything we touch and/or consume. Although plastics have some benefits, be aware of their interactions with your food and the fact they have to be handled in environmentally safe and efficient ways to sustain a healthy lifestyle. This lifestyle includes recycling.

In 1988, the Society of the Plastics Industry (SPI) developed an international set of symbols placed on plastic to help consumers and manufacturers efficiently sort plastics for recycling. The symbols identify the polymer types with a resin code. The codes allow efficient separation of the different polymer types for recycling. Separation must be efficient because even one item of the wrong type of resin can ruin a mix.

Look at the numbers inside the triangles on plastics you recycle. The numbers inside the triangle are numbered 1–7, and 9.

Most recycling companies do not accept certain numbers for recycling. The plastics to avoid are the numbers 3, 6, and 7. Get rid of all 3 and 7 plastic containers and never purchase products packaged in them.

Number 1 is polyethylene terephthalate (PET or PETE).

This is high impact plastic. This is commonly used for beverage bottles, food jars, and frozen food trays. It is cheap, light, and easily recycled. It has the lowest risk of chemical leaching into food. It is intended for one use. Repeated use increases the risk of leaching and bacterial growth.

It has been shown that high temperatures can cause the release of the heavy metal antimony by PETE or PET. Antimony is toxic. Although the toxicity level is far lower than arsenic, the effects of antimony poisoning are similar to arsenic poisonings. Recycled, PET or PETE becomes bottles and containers again as well as fleece jackets, carpet fiber, stuffing for pillows, life jackets, and comforter filling.

Products made of PET or PETE should be recycled but not reused.

Number 2 is high density polyethylene (HDPE).

This is the stiff plastic used in butter and yogurt cartons, shopping bags, box liners, toys, water jugs, and bottles for milk, juice, bleach, liquid detergent, and cosmetics. It is durable and weather resistant. It is easily recycled and is a low risk for chemical leaching. Recycled HDPE becomes waste bins, park benches, picnic tables, garden edgings, flowerpots, buckets, plastic lumber, and bottles for non-food items.

Products made of HDPE are reusable and recyclable.

Number 3 is polyvinylchloride (PVC) or vinyl (V).

This is a soft, flexible plastic called the “poison plastic”. This is because it contains numerous toxins. These toxins can leach into food or the environment throughout their entire life. They have been found to contain BPA and phthalates that can be released into food and drinks. The highest risk is when the containers are heated, micro waved, put through the dishwasher, or start to wear out. Number 3 plastic is used to make clear plastic food wrappings (clamshell or blister packs), cooking oil bottles, teething rings, toys, and medical items. Because V or PVC is durable and relatively resistant to sunlight and weather, its used to make construction pipes, tubing, window frames, garden hoses, and trellises. Recycled, it lives on in fencing, decking, carpet backing, gutters, traffic cones and paneling.

PVC contains chlorine. As it is manufactured, it releases highly toxic dioxins into the environment. Dioxins are a group of chemically related compounds that are environmental pollutants. Examples where dioxins can result are the production of PVC or the bleaching of paper. In nature, they are produced in volcanoes and forest fires. They are highly toxic and can cause reproductive and developmental problems, damage to the immune system, interference with hormones and also cause cancer.

Products using PVC or V plastics are not recyclable.

Number 4 is low density polyethylene (LDPE).

This is a flexible plastic considered less toxic than other plastics, and relatively safe for use. It is found in squeeze bottles, shrink wrap, dry cleaner garment bags, container lids, trash bags, frozen food, various molded laboratory equipment, and shopping bags. It is the type of plastic used to package bread and to make the plastic grocery bags used in most stores today.

Not all recycling centers accept LDPE, but many stores have plastic shopping bag recycle boxes. Much of LDPE tends to litter the earth and use up energy resources. Recycled, it becomes plastic lumber and bins, garbage bag liners, and floor tiles.

Products using LDPE plastics are reusable, but not always recyclable. Check with your local collection service to see if they are accepting LDPE plastic items for recycling.

Number 5 is Polypropylene (PP).

This plastic is tough and lightweight. It has excellent heat–resistant qualities and is used for containers for hot liquids. PP is the thin plastic liner in a cereal box. It is commonly used for disposable diapers, syrup and catsup bottles, auto parts, frozen food containers, margarine and yogurt containers, potato chip bags, packing tape, rope, plastic bottle caps, drinking straws, medicine bottles, dishware and take–out containers.

PP is considered safe for reuse. It is gradually becoming more accepted by recyclers. Recycled, it is used to make brooms, bins, trays, landscaping border stripping, and battery cases.

Number 6 is polystyrene (PS).

This is an inexpensive, lightweight and easily–formed plastic. PS is commonly used to make disposable Styrofoam drinking cups, disposable plastic picnic utensils, aspirin bottles, take–out food containers (clam shell), foam packaging, meat trays and egg cartons. PS is used to make the foam chips (packing peanuts) to protect contents in shipping boxes. It is used in home construction as foam insulation and underlining sheeting for laminate flooring.

PS breaks up easily and leaches toxins including styrene, a possible human carcinogen into food products (especially when heated). It should not be used for coffee cups or other hot beverages. **It is not accepted widely by recyclers** and tends to litter the earth. Beaches all over the world have bits of PS on the shores. Untold numbers of marine life have ingested PS with dire consequences. Chemicals present in PS have been linked to human health and reproductive system dysfunction. PS should be avoided where possible.

Number 7 is designed as a miscellaneous category for a variety of plastic resins that do not fit in the other categories.

Some plastic resins are safe. A few are made from plants (polyactide) can be used as compost. A new generation of compostable plastics made from bio–based polymers like corn–starch are being developed. These are also included in the number 7 category. These have the initials "PLA" or say "Compostable" on the bottle of the container near the recycling symbol.

A scary member of this group is polycarbonate (PC). This is hard plastic. Polycarbonate plastics are often used in containers that store food and beverages. Typically, PC is used in rigid plastic baby bottles, five–gallon water bottles, car parts, "bullet proof" plastic materials, and certain food containers. Of primary concern with PC plastic is the potential for leaching of BPA into food and drink products packaged in PC containers.

Some PC water bottles are marketed as "non–leaching" for minimizing plastic odor and taste. However, there is still a possibility that BPA will leach from these containers, particularly if it is used to heat liquids. An example would be heating up milk in a PC plastic baby bottle.

When possible it is best to avoid number 7 plastics, especially for children's food or drink. Numbers 1, 2, 4 and 5 are less damaging plastics. Exchange all number 7 baby bottles for shatter–resistant glass, number 1 or 5 plastic or corn–based plastics. These plastics are still not as safe as glass, ceramics, or stainless steel. But if you must use plastic containers, avoid numbers 3, 6, and 7.

Recommended websites for safe food storage containers are the MightyNest website (http://bit.ly/1fFbo1w), Life Without Plastic (lifewithoutplastic.com), and the Mercola Healthy Cookware

http://bit.ly/1dbCt9H

"What do the Recycle Triangles on the Bottom of the Plastic Mean?"

http://bit.ly/1GvnUFv

"Plastic By the Numbers"

http://bit.ly/1JekH43

"What does the Recycle Number Mean on a Plastic Container?"

http://bit.ly/1eE1rjA

"Best Food Storage Containers"

http://exm.nr/1LpAQUK

"Dioxin"

http://bit.ly/1JSwhNd

CHAPTER 32

Basic Kitchen Safety Tips

Cooking is life sustaining, creative and fun, but disasters can occur in the kitchen. There are knives that cut fingers, bacteria that cause disease, fires that burn people and houses, glass that breaks and cuts, electrical shocks, water that scalds, and slips and falls from spills. To avert unpleasant cooking experiences, these tips are good to remember.

Wash your hands in hot, soapy water before cooking. We recommend healthy, environmentally friendly hand soaps.

Pay attention or focus on what you're doing in the kitchen.

Immediately clean up any spill. Wet floors are dangerously slippery.

Never leave children unsupervised in the kitchen. All knives, ovens, hot liquids, hot pots of food and electrical appliances present a potential danger.

Do not wear loose sleeves or sweaters while cooking. They can catch on to handles of pots on the range or stove. Wearing an apron also will protect your clothes.

Do not leave food unattended while cooking on top of the stove or range. Cut off each burner on the stove or range as you finish cooking each dish. If you have food in the oven and you must go into another area, set and take your timer with you.

Always turn pot and skillet handles away from the front of the stove, toward the back of the range or stove so they cannot be reached by children or accidentally pulled off the stove as you walk by.

Use one or more timers in the kitchen. This alerts you when food is cooked and helps avoid overcooking and starting fires.

When handling knives:

(a) Always cut away from your body.

(b) Always use a chopping or cutting board.

(c) Keep knives sharpened. A dull knife is more dangerous than a sharp one. The pressure you use to cut with a dull knife can cause it to slip, resulting in injury. Also, a cut with a dull knife is not a straight one.

(d) Do not place knives in a sink of soapy water. They may not be seen and injury can occur.

(e) When washing and drying knives, always keep the sharp edge away from your hands.

(f) Do not place knives in drawers with other utensils. This can result in injury.

(g) Store knives in a wooden block or in a separate section of a drawer.

(h) Keep knives out of the reach of children.

(i) Do not attempt to catch a knife if it falls. It is better for it to hit the floor than cut your hand.

10. Scalding can occur from hot steam. Be careful when opening hot ovens or lifting lids from hot food. Move your head away from hot steam before viewing the food.

11. If you are cooking in two or more pots on top of the stove or range at the same time, when the dish next to those still cooking is done, take it off the stove or range. The heat coming from those dishes still cooking can overcook the done dish, resulting in less nutrition and diminished flavors.

12. Keep paper towels, potholders, oven mitts and dishtowels nearby. Use them, but be careful to keep them away from an open flame or heated electrical range.

13. Keep salt, flour or baking soda close in case of a grease fire. Douse it with one of these if you do not have a fire extinguisher. Never pour water on a grease fire; it will only spread.

14. Be sure all appliances such as mixers, blenders, and can openers are unplugged before touching their sharp edges. Also, check carefully to be sure no utensil is left in an electrical device before it is turned on. Never stick a fork or knife into a toaster when it is plugged in.

15. Do not add water to a pan containing hot oil. It could make the oil spatter and cause injury.

16. Turn the oven off and unplug all cooking devices before you leave the kitchen.

"Basic Rules of Kitchen Safety"
http://bit.ly/1Bx4zbo
"Safety Tips in the Kitchen"
http://bit.ly/1dZv5ij
"28 Basic Kitchen Safety Tips"
http://bit.ly/1GiyNva
"Basic Rules of Kitchen Safety"
http://bit.ly/1Bx4zbo

PART 4

CHAPTER 33

Recipes

ALL RECIPES ARE VEGAN, GLUTEN–FREE & NON–SOY!

Spicy Tasty Recipe Categories:

Baked Items

•Banana Fruit Cookies – 345
•Banana Fruit Loaf – 347
•Cornbread – 362
•Baked French Fries – 340
•Lasagna with Basil Cashew Cheese – 364
•Pizza – 376
•Baked Sweet Potatoes/Yams – 394
•Roasted Eggplant Vegetable Casserole – 390
•Baked Butternut Squash – 339
•Portobello Mushrooms – 382

Grains

•Quinoa, Black and Red Rice Mix – 375
•Polenta – 385
•Millet – 372
•NaaCereal – 373
•NaaCereal Non–Infant Formula – 374
•Quinoa Tabouli – 399
•Steel Cut Oats – 397
•Wild Rice – 350
•Fruit Grain Cereal – 359

Vegetable

•African Stew – 335
•Pulp Burger/Juice – 389
•Plant Protein Filling - 382
•Collard Green Veggie Wraps – 349

•Daikon Kale Stir–Fry – 357
•Simple Kale Stir–Fry – 367
•Potato Salad – 387
•Roasted Eggplant Vegetable Casserole – 394
•Mixed Spiced Tossed Salad – 400
•Raw Salad – 391

Fun Foods

•Cocoa Mousse – 352
•FuFu – 360
•Shallot Popcorn – 361
•Guacamole – 362
•Kale Chips – 366
•Real Waffles – 392
•Real Banana Pancakes – 377
•Almond Coconut Date Roll – 336
•Raw Ice Cream – 390
•Variety Fruit Salad – 401
•Spicy Plantain – 384

Drinks/ Beverages

•Pineapple Rind Drink – 379
•Spicy Citrus Drink – 351
•Blueberry Almond Butter Smoothie – 349
•Almond Banana Smoothie – 341
•Almond Milk – 342
•Hemp Milk – 365
•Earthy Root Detox Tea – 358

Dressings/Pesto

•Almond Arugula Pesto – 339
•Hemp Basil Salad Dressing – 364
•Salad Dressing – 396

Other

•Egg Substitute – 358
•Natural Hair Conditioner – 363

Spicy African Stew

THIS AMOUNT OF STEW is designed to last for 5 days. The stew is the foundation for the salad, pizza, Sloppy Joes, eggplant casserole, lasagna and other recipes. The vegetables are soaked, rinsed, and cut up. The salad is put together in a large bowl from the cut up vegetables. The salad is then covered and refrigerated before the cooking of the stew. Most of the vegetables left after making the salad are put in the stew.

Keep in mind the vegetables listed are based on the season. All the vegetables listed may not be available. Other vegetables that are in season or available may be substituted. If there are any vegetables left that are not used in the salad or stew, cover and store them in the refrigerator for use in other recipes. Add more spices to the stew each day before reheating the portion of the stew to be eaten that day. This adds more flavor and taste.

Cook time about 1 hour Serves 8–12

Large Pot (8 Quarts)

To make the paste or rue, heat the pot on low.

Add: 2–3 tablespoons Oil (Coconut or Olive)

Increase heat to medium low, then sauté these seeds in the oil for 6–8 minutes:

1 ½ tablespoons Fennel Seeds

2 tablespoons Cumin Seeds

1½ tablespoons Coriander Seeds. Increase heat to medium.

Add: 1 cup scallions (chopped) Sauté scallions with seeds until brown.

Add:

2 Tomatoes (medium sized). Lower heat to medium low

1 can Tomato Paste (6 oz)

2 Vegetable Bouillon Cubes

Add: 1 cup chopped Leeks

½ cup Shallots

½ cup Ginger

2 Bay Leaves (medium sized)

2 tablespoons Oil (Coconut or Olive)

Add: 2 cups of vegetable stems from collards, broccoli, kale, beet, and cauliflower. Stir occasionally to avoid sticking to bottom of pot for 4–6 minutes. Add:

1 quart Vegetable Broth

1 Cinnamon Stick

1 teaspoon Thyme

1 teaspoon Rosemary

2 tablespoons Ground Cumin

2 tablespoons Ground Coriander

2 tablespoons Turmeric

Optional Dry Spices:

1 teaspoon Paprika

1 teaspoon Sage

½ teaspoon Marjoram

½ teaspoon Fenugreek

1 can Coconut Milk (13.5 oz)

1 tablespoon Almond Butter

½ cup Beans (Soak beans overnight or at least: 1 hour for Lentils, 2–4 hours, for Mung, Adzuki, Red, Kidney or Black Beans)
1 cup Water
1 cup Yellow Squash/Zucchini
Place lid on pot. Boil 10–15 minutes on medium high heat. Stir occasionally.
Add: 1 Glass jar – Organic Salsa (12oz)
Cover pot with lid. Turn heat low for 10 minutes.
2 tablespoons Oregano
1 tablespoon Chipotle
1 teaspoon Ground Basil

Optional
1 tablespoon Dried Seaweed
½ teaspoon Sumac
½ teaspoon Jalapeño Peppers

½ teaspoon Mineral Salt
¼ teaspoon Cayenne Pepper
1½ tablespoons Bragg Liquid Aminos
2 tablespoons Chickpea Miso Non–Soy, Non–GMO
1 tablespoon Maple Syrup
1 cup chopped Beets
Continue to stir for 4–6 minutes on medium heat. Then
Add: 1 Vegetable Bouillon Cube
1 cup thinly sliced Potatoes (Purple, Red, Yukon)
Place lid on pot. Stir occasionally 5–8 minutes: Add chopped:
1 cup Fresh Basil
1 cup Bok Choy (seasonal)
1 cups Daikon
1 cup Celery
1 cup Green or Red Bell Pepper
1 cup Cauliflower
1 cup Beets Greens

1 cup chopped Fennel

Optional Vegetables:

½ cup Dill Weed

1 cup Dandelion

1 cup Carrots

½ cup Spearmint

1 cup Water if needed (if you desirer a thicker stew, use less water)

Place lid on the pot for 10–15 minutes. Stir occasionally. **Add:**

2 cups Cabbage

2 cups Collard Greens

1 cup Parsley

3 cups Kale (Curly or Dinosaur)

1 cup Broccoli

Optional Vegetables:

2 cups Green Beans

1 cup chopped Asparagus

½ cup Cilantro

Cover pot with lid. Turn heat low for 10 minutes.

Almond Arugula Pesto

Prep Time: 15 minutes **Makes 1½ –2 Cups**

Ingredients:

¾ teaspoon Mineral or Sea Salt
1 tablespoon chopped Shallots
3 bunches Arugula or Basil Leaves (no stems)
¾ cup Coconut or Olive oil
1 teaspoon Turmeric
1 teaspoon Omega or Flax Oil
1½ tablespoon Lemon Juice
2 tablespoons Whole Almonds
½ cup Hemp Seeds
3 tablespoons Nutritional Yeast
¼ teaspoon Cayenne

Optional:

1 tablespoon Pine Nuts

Directions:

Place all ingredients except for hemp seeds and almonds in a food processor fitted with the "S" blade. Pulse and scrape down the sides of the bowl until smooth. While processor is running add the almonds and hemp seeds. Pulse until desired smoothness. Eat immediately or store in airtight container in the refrigerator.

Almond Coconut Date Rolls

Prep Time: 15 minutes
Blend Time: 2–3 minutes **Makes 10–12 Rolls**

Ingredients:

1 cup pitted Dates
1 cup raw Ground Almonds
1 pinch of Mineral or Sea Salt
¼ cup shredded unsweetened dried Coconut
½ teaspoon Cinnamon
½ teaspoon Cardamom
1 tablespoon Coconut Oil

Blending Instructions:

Blend cardamom, cinnamon, almonds, oil, salt, dates and coconut in a blender or food processor 2–3 minutes until it becomes a paste. Roll tablespoonfuls of the paste into 1–2 inch balls.

Eat, refrigerate, or freeze until later. Enjoy!

Optional: Sprinkle coconut on top of rolls.

Almond Banana Smoothie

Prep Time:15 minutes **Makes 4–6 Cups**

Ingredients:

Nuts: ¼ cup Almonds: Soak almonds overnight or 8 hours or longer. If there is a time crunch, soak almonds for at least 2 hours. Rinse and drain almonds and place them in the blender.

Dry Ingredients:

1 tablespoon Flax seed
1 tablespoon Chia Seed
1 tablespoons Maca
½ teaspoon Chlorella
2 pitted Medjool Dates
1 teaspoon Cinnamon

Optional:

½ teaspoon Spirulina
½ teaspoon Iris Moss
½ teaspoon Psyllium Husk
1 teaspoon Hemp Seeds
2 Prunes
¼ cup Walnuts, Sunflower, Pumpkin Seeds

Liquids:

1/2 cup Hemp Milk
½ cup Water
1 cup Ice
½ cup Coconut Water
1 teaspoon Omega Twin

Optional:

1 teaspoon Aloe Vera Gel
½ cup Apple Juice

Fruit:

2 Banana
¼ cup chopped Pineapples
½ Apple
¼ cup Blueberries

Optional

¼ cup Strawberries
1/4 cup Kale

Directions:

Pour all ingredients into Blender for 2–3 minutes.

Serve immediately or refrigerate. Enjoy!

Almond Milk

Prep Time: 10 minutes
Makes 3 ½ Cups
Ingredients:
Nut milk bag or Cheesecloth
1 cup Raw Almonds
3½ cups Water
3–4 pitted Medjool Dates
½ teaspoon powdered Vanilla
½ teaspoon Cardamom
½ teaspoon Cinnamon
1/8 teaspoon of Mineral or Sea Salt
Optional:
1 tablespoon Raw Cacao
½ teaspoon Allspice
½ teaspoon Nutmeg
½ teaspoon Iris Moss

Directions: Soak almonds overnight or 8 hours or longer. If there is a time crunch, soak almonds for at least 2 hours. Rinse and drain almonds and place them in the blender. Add water, dates and vanilla. Blend on high speed for 2 minutes or until smooth. Place a nut milk bag or cheesecloth over a large bowl. Pour the milk mixture into the bag or strain through cheesecloth.

Gently, squeeze the bottom of the milk bag or squeeze milk from cheesecloth. This may take 3–4 minutes. Rinse out the blender and pour the milk back into the blender. Add cinnamon, cardamom and salt. Blend on low for 30 seconds. Serve immediately or refrigerate in an airtight glass jar container for up to 3–5 days.

Baked Butternut Squash

Prep Time: 10 min.
Cooking Time: 1hour
9x13 Baking dish
Serves 6–8
Ingredients:

2 Butternut Squash
½ cup Water
1½ Vegetable Bouillon cube
1 tablespoon chopped Ginger
1 teaspoon Maple syrup
1 tablespoon chopped Shallots
2 tablespoons Oil (Coconut or Olive)
1 cup chopped Scallions
¼ cup Parsley
Mineral or Sea Salt to taste
1 tablespoon Bragg Liquid Aminos
1 tablespoon ground Basil
1 tablespoon ground Thyme
1 teaspoon Chipotle

Optional:

1 teaspoon Rosemary
1 teaspoon Fennel
1 teaspoon Coriander
1 teaspoon Turmeric

Directions: Preheat oven to 400 Fahrenheit (204 Celsius). Rinse off each squash. Cut each squash into halves. Place each half in a large baking dish flesh side up. Put ½ tablespoon Oil in the middle of each squash. Sprinkle herbs and seasoning on the halves to taste. Cover pan and bake 45–60 minutes or until skin is tender and easily pierced with a fork. Eat. Enjoy!

Baked French Fries

Prep Time: 15 minutes

Cook Time 25–30 minutes

Serves 2–4

Ingredients:

6 Yukon potatoes
3 Sweet potatoes
½ cup Coconut or Olive Oil
1 tablespoon chopped Shallots
1 teaspoon Allspice
1 teaspoon Sumac
1 teaspoon Turmeric
1 teaspoon Cayenne Pepper
1 teaspoon Paprika
1 teaspoon Mineral Salt
1 teaspoon Italian Seasoning

Directions:

Preheat oven to 400 Fahrenheit (204 Celsius).

Wash potatoes. Leave as much skin on the potatoes as possible. Cut potatoes into French fry slices. Place potatoes in oiled pan. Sprinkle spices evenly on potatoes. Massage potatoes with oil and spices. Place the pan of potatoes into the oven at 400 degrees Fahrenheit (204 Celsius) for 25–35 minutes.

Remove cooked potatoes from oven and place on plate. Eat. Enjoy!

Banana Fruit Cookies

Makes 36–40 Cookies

Cook Time: 10–15 Minutes

Dry Ingredients:

½ cup Barley Flour
½ cup Quinoa Flour
½ cup Buckwheat Flour
½ cup Rolled Oats
2 tablespoons Baking Powder
½ teaspoon Anise Powder
½ teaspoon Baking Soda
1½ teaspoon Vanilla Powder
1 teaspoon Mace powder
1 teaspoon Clove Powder
1 teaspoon Nutmeg Powder
1 tablespoon Cinnamon Powder
1 teaspoon Allspice
1 teaspoon Mineral or Sea Salt
2 tablespoons Flax Seeds
2 teaspoons Dry Yeast (1 packet)
¼ cup Raisins

Optional

¼ cup pitted dried Dates
¼ cup chopped Walnuts
1 teaspoon Ginger Powder
¼ cup Pineapple
¼ cup Strawberries
¼ cup Coconut chips

Wet Ingredients:

4 Bananas (ripe)
1 cup Water
¼ cup Orange Peel
½ cup grated Carrots
¼ cup Blueberries

Optional

¼ cup chopped Prunes
¼ cup Oil (Coconut or Olive)
¼ cup chopped Apples
1 cup Coconut Milk
1 cup water

Instructions:

In a small bowl warm the 1 cup of water
Add a drop of maple syrup in the water and stir

Mix in the active yeast

Keep in warm place for the yeast to froth for 10 minutes

Combine flour, oatmeal, baking soda and powder, vanilla, mace, cloves, nutmeg, cinnamon, allspice, mineral or sea salt, flax seeds into a large bowl. Grade carrots and orange peel and add chopped apples, bananas, raisins, blueberries, prunes, oil, maple syrup, into another large bowl. Spoon flour into bowl with the fruits and add water and coconut milk stirring or blending everything together.

Preheat oven to 325 Fahrenheit (162 Celsius). Grease baking sheet really well and sprinkle a little flour on it to prevent cookies from sticking to baking sheet. Drop in 2 tablespoon sized mounds on baking sheet. Allow cookies to bake 10–15 minutes or until edges are barely golden brown.

Temperatures may vary. The gas oven may need to bake 5 minutes longer than an electric oven. Cookies may bake up to 20 minutes and it does not matter if they are a little dark. Remove cookies from oven. Allow them to cool for 10–12 minutes. Use spatula to remove cookies from baking sheet

Banana Fruit Loaf

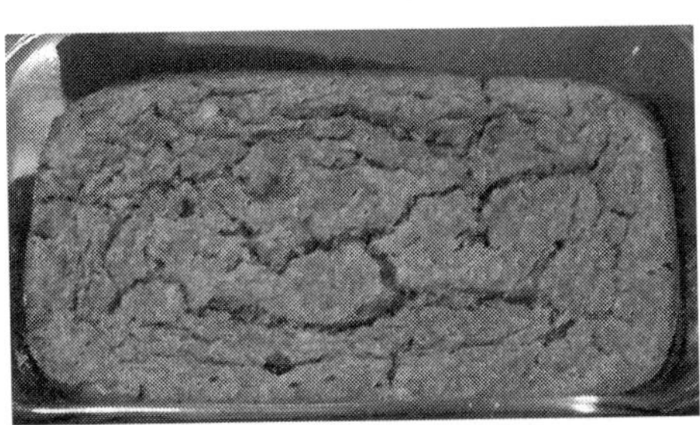

Makes 2–3 loaves
Cook Time: 2 Hours 10 Minutes

Dry Ingredients:

½ cup Barley Flour
½ cup Quinoa Flour
½ cup Buckwheat Flour
½ cup Rolled Oats
2 tablespoons Baking Powder
½ teaspoon Baking Soda
1½ teaspoon Vanilla Powder
1 teaspoon Mace Powder
1 teaspoon Clove Powder
1 teaspoon Nutmeg Powder
1 tablespoon Cinnamon Powder
1 teaspoon Allspice
1 teaspoon Mineral or Sea Salt
2 tablespoons Flax Seeds
2 teaspoons Dry Yeast (1 packet)
¼ cup chopped Prunes
¼ cup Raisins

Wet Ingredients:

4 bananas (ripe)
¼ cup Orange Peel
¼ cup chopped Apples
½ cup grated Carrots
¼ cup Blueberries

Optional:

¼ cup pitted dried Dates
¼ cup chopped Walnuts
½ teaspoon Anise Powder
1 teaspoon Ginger Powder
¼ cup Pineapple
¼ cup Strawberries
¼ cup Coconut chips

Preheat oven to 325 Fahrenheit (162 Celsius).

Instructions:

In a small bowl

Warm the 1 cup of water

Add a drop of maple syrup in the water and stir

Mix in the active yeast

Keep in warm place for the yeast to froth for 10 minutes

Combine flour, oatmeal, baking soda and powder, vanilla, mace, cloves, nutmeg, cinnamon, allspice, mineral or sea salt, flax seeds into a large bowl. Grade carrots and orange peel and add chopped apples, raisins, blueberries, prunes, oil, maple syrup, into another large bowl. Add a couple of spoons of flour into bowl with the fruits and add water and coconut milk stirring everything together.

Grease 2 to 3 bread pans really well and sprinkle a little flour on greased pans to prevent fruit bread from sticking to pans. Allow bread to bake 2 hours and 10 minutes. Check loaf with toothpick by inserting it in the middle and remove. If done there should be a few moist crumbs attached, but not batter.

Temperatures may vary. The gas oven may bake 20 minutes longer than an electric oven. The bread may bake over 2 hours and 30 minutes, and it does not matter if it is a little dark. Remove bread from oven. Allow loaves to cool 1 hour. Use spatula to remove fruit bread from pan.

Blueberry Almond Butter Smoothie

Prep time: 5 minutes

Makes 1 large Smoothie

Ingredients:

1 cup frozen Blueberries

1 cup frozen Banana

½ cup Almond Milk

1 heaping tablespoon Almond Butter

½ teaspoon Vanilla Powder

1 teaspoon Maple Syrup or to taste

1 cup Water

Directions:

Combine all ingredients into a blender. Blend until smooth. Drink! Enjoy!

Optional:

½ cup Strawberries

½ teaspoon Cinnamon

Wild Rice

Serves 6–8

Cooking Time: 45 minutes

Wild rice is not really rice, but a delicious member of the grass family. It is a native of North America and is traditionally grown (wild) in river beds and isolated lake locations. It holds its long shape with cooking and retains a nutty texture.

Wild rice contains twice as much protein as brown rice. It is rich in antioxidants, containing up to 30 times more than white rice. Wild rice is a good source of essential minerals and vitamins A, C and E. It can be eaten by diabetics, since it is lower in carbohydrates and calories and higher in fiber than rice.

Ingredients:

1 cup Wild Rice
2 cups Water
¼ teaspoon Mineral or Sea Salt
¼ teaspoon ground Cumin
1 teaspoon Turmeric
½ teaspoon Paprika
¼ teaspoon Coriander
¼ teaspoon Basil

Optional:
¼ teaspoon Saffron
3 Cardamom Seeds
¼ teaspoon Cloves

Directions:

Boil 2 cups of water adding salt, Cumin, Turmeric, Paprika, Coriander and Basil for 3–5 minutes. Pour in Rice and stir. Turn heat to low, cover and let rice simmer 25–30 minutes, stirring occasionally to avoid burning the bottom of the pot or pan. Remove from heat. Stir, leave uncovered 15–20 minutes to let the grains separate. Eat, enjoy!

Citrus Drink

Makes ¾ –1 Gallon

Ingredients:

1 quart Water
2 quarts Apple Juice
or Apple Cider
2 Oranges
1 Apple
2 Lemons
2 Limes
1 Grapefruit
1 tablespoon sliced Ginger
1 tablespoon chopped Shallots
¼ teaspoon Cayenne pepper
1 Cinnamon Stick
1 teaspoon Cinnamon Powder
2 whole Nutmeg
4–6 whole Allspice
4–6 whole Cloves
1 teaspoon Turmeric Powder
½ teaspoon Burdock Root

Optional:

¼ cup Scallions
1 teaspoon Dandelion Root

Directions:

Wash fruit
Slice fruit
Place sliced fruit in pot
Pour water and apple juice or apple cider in pot
Add ginger, shallots, cayenne pepper, cinnamon and turmeric powder.

Place cinnamon stick, whole nutmeg, whole allspice, whole coves, dandelion and burdock root in a muslin bag or cheesecloth mesh.

Place Muslin bag in the pot. Simmer on medium heat 1 hour with lid slightly jarred. The longer it simmers, the thicker the drink.

When drink is gone, you can refill pot with water, apple juice or cider and simmer for 25 minutes. Enjoy!

Cocoa Mousse

Total Time: Prep: 15 min. + 1 hour Chilling

Makes: 6 Servings

Ingredients:

1 ripe Avocado

1¼ cups Hemp or Almond Milk

1/3 cup Coconut Nectar or Maple Syrup

¼ cup Cocoa Powder

1 teaspoon Vanilla extract

Directions:

In a blender, combine milk, coconut nectar or Maple syrup, avocado, cocoa and vanilla. Puree until smooth and well combined.

Spoon mixture into glasses or serving bowls. Cover and chill in the refrigerator for at least 1 hour.

Eat, enjoy!

Collard Green Wraps

There are 4 parts:
Spread Wraps,
African Stew or
Wrap Sauce,
Plant Protein Filling
Added ingredients.
Makes 10–12 wraps
Prep Time: 40 minutes
Plant Protein Filling
Ingredients:
2 cups Raw Sunflower Seeds
5 oz Olives (Black, Green or Kalamata)
1 cup chopped Shallots
¼ cup Lemon or Lime Juice
½ teaspoon Mineral or Sea Salt
1 teaspoon Turmeric
½ teaspoon ground Basil
1 tablespoon Sesame Seeds
½ cup chopped Scallions
1 tablespoon Cumin
2 tablespoons Cilantro
½ cup Beets
¼ teaspoon Cayenne Pepper
½ cup Bell Pepper
2 tablespoons Oil (Coconut or Olive)

Optional:
¼ teaspoon chopped Ginger Root
¼ cup chopped Celery
¼ teaspoon Chipole
2 tablespoons Tomato
2 tablespoons Parsley
½ cup Carrots
1 teaspoon Oregano

Add and place in four (4) separate bowls:
1 chopped Mango or Persimmon
1 sliced Avocado

1 chopped Cucumber (medium sized)

1 cubed or chopped Baked Yam or Sweet Potato (medium sized)

Directions:

In a food processor combine oil, salt, seeds, olives, vegetables and spices. Add lemon or lime juice and pulse until smooth but still slightly crumbly.

Spread Wraps

To rinse collards: place in a large bowl with water and teaspoon sea salt. This will rid the collards of critters that want to hold on to the succulent collards. Rinse again without the sea salt.

Blot dry with paper towel. With a sharp knife slice the thickest part of the vein or stem thinly. Slice from the larger part of the vein or stem toward the narrow end of the vein or stem of the collards.

Boil one gallon of water. Generously salt with mineral or sea salt.

Drop 4–5 leaves in the pot of boiled water about 2–5 seconds. Remove and place in a bowl of ice cold water. Spread out collards on paper towels and blot dry.

African Stew (2–3 cups) or Wrap Sauce

Add 2–3 cups of blended Africn Vegetable Stew or Wrap Sauce.

Wrap Sauce:

1 tablespoon Coconut or Olive Oil
¼ teaspoon Mineral or Sea Salt
¼ cup chopped Shallots
¼ cup chopped Scallions
½ teaspoon Oregano
1 teaspoon Turmeric
½ teaspoons dried Basil
2 cups Salsa (medium or mild)
½ teaspoon Thyme
1 teaspoon Maple Syrup
1 Vegetable Bouillon cube

Sauté the shallots and scallions in oil for 1–2 minutes in a saucepan on medium heat. Add the other ingredients and stir. Reduce the heat to low and let it simmer, stirring occasionally for 5 –10 minutes. Remove from heat.

To Make Wrap:

Spread 1–2 teaspoons of blended "stew" or Wrap Sauce across collard leaf. Place 1–2 teaspoons of Plant Protein Filling on top. Feel free to add sliced avocado, yam or sweet potatoe, persimmon, mango and cucumber.

Roll the collards like you would a burrito. Cut in half and serve.

Optional sauce: Mix lemon juice, Shoyu, Tamari or Liquid Braggs Aminos, to taste. Drizzle over wraps or use for dipping.

Vegan Real Cornbread

10 –12 servings
PrepTime: 10 minutes
Cook Tme: 35 minutes
Ingredients:
Dry:

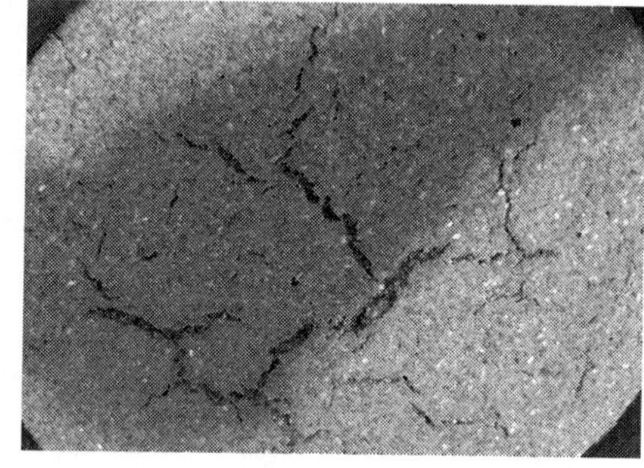

1 tsp Baking Soda
¼ cup Polenta
1½ cups Cornmeal (blue or yellow)
1 cup flour (Quinoa, Buckwheat, Spelt, Rye, Amaranth, or Coconut)
½ teaspoon Mineral Salt or Sea Salt
2½ tablespoons Sesame Seeds
1½ tablespoon Flax Seeds
1½ tablespoon Baking powder (aluminum free)

Wet:

¼ – 1/3 cup Maple Syrup (to taste)
1/3 cup Olive Oil or Coconut Oil
1 cup Unsweetened Hemp or Almond Milk
1 cup water

Directions:

Preheat oven at 350°

Oil bottom of a large pan, large skillet, or Pyrex dish (9x13 inch). Sprinkle Sesame Seeds evenly on the oiled bottom. Mix dry and wet ingredients together in a large bowl. Pour mixed ingredients into pan, place in oven for 35 minutes. Remove from oven and allow to sit about 20 minutes. Be sure oven is off. (if cornbread is placed on top of the stove, it will continue to cook) Enjoy!

Daikon Kale Stir–Fry

Total Time: 23 min

Prep: 15 min

Cook: 8 min

Ingredients:

3 tablespoons Coconut or Olive Oil

¼ cup chopped Ginger

¼ cup chopped Shallots

3⁄4 cup chopped Scallions

1 cup thinly sliced Bell Peppers

½ cup shredded Daikon

¼ cup chopped Pineapple

1 teaspoon Turmeric

¼ teaspoon Mineral or Sea Salt

1 teaspoon Cumin

1 teaspoon Oregano

1 teaspoon Basil

1 tablespoon Chipotle

2 bunches kale with leaves torn, stalks discarded, coarsely chopped.

Preparation Instructions:

Thoroughly soak kale in a large bowl with cold water with a dash of Sea Salt to remove grit and discourage little critters. Rinse off kale in cold water. Tear the leaves from the stalks, coarsely chop kale leaves.

Heat oil in a large skillet or wok over medium heat with bell pepper, daikon, scallions, shallots, ginger, salt, cumin, oregano, basil and chipotle. Stir it around 2–3 minutes so it won't burn.

Add kale and pineapple and stir around 3–5 minutes.

Remove cooked dish to a plate and serve!

Earthy Root Detox Tea

We suggest drinking one glass of water with a squeeze of lemon upon rising each day to aid your body moving out waste. To help in cleansing the body there seems to be nothing better than the roots of nature.

Ingredients:

1 Gallon Water
Chaparral
Patchouli
Shepherds Purse
Wild Yam
Oregon Grape
Yellow dock
Gota Kola
Dandelion
Red Clover
Cohosh
Bilberry
Licorice

Optional:

Lavender

Directions:

Place 1 teaspoon of each root in a Muslin bag or cheesecloth mesh in a large pot. Pour in 1 gallon of water over roots. Boil 40–45 minutes on medium high heat. Turn off heat and let steep for 1 hour. Drink immediately, reheat or refrigerate.

Be Healthy!

Egg Substitute

2 tablespoons corn starch = 1 egg
2 tablespoons arrowroot flour = 1 egg
1 tablespoons flax seeds + 1 cup water = 1 egg
1 banana or
¼ cup applesauce = 1 egg in baked goods such as pancakes, muffins or yeast–free quick breads, such as banana and pumpkin.

Fruit Grain Cereal

6–8 Servings –
Cooking Time:
25–30 minutes
Ingredients:

4 cups Water
¼ teaspoon Mineral or Sea Salt
½ teaspoon Mace
½ teaspoon Cloves
¼ cup Rolled Oats
1 teaspoon Turmeric
½ teaspoon Cardamom
½ teaspoon Cinnamon
½ teaspoon Nutmeg
1 tablespoon Coconut or Olive Oil
¼ cup Black Rice
¼ cup Red Rice
½ cup Quinoa
½ cup Steel Cut Oats
¼ cup Millet

Directions: Pour water into pan or pot. Add oil and spices and bring to boil 8–10 minutes. Adding Cinnamon Stick is optional. Pour in Grains. Reduce heat to low, cover and cook 15–20 minutes. Add Rolled Oats and stir. Cover for 3–5 minutes at low heat. Turn off heat and remove from burner. Remove lid. Stir and leave uncovered for 25–30 minutes to let the grains separate.

Place in large bowl:

¼ cup Blueberries
¼ cup Strawberry
¼ cup Banana
¼ Peach
¼ cup Apples
¼ cup Orange
¼ cup Mango
¼ cup Pineapple

Fruit is seasonal. If certain fruits are not available simply substitute other fruits. Mix fruit with desired amount of grains. Add Almond, Hemp Milk or Smoothie to taste.

Select from desired Power Boosters below and sprinkle to taste: raisins, dates, almonds, mulberries, goji berries, pates, hunza berries, hemp seeds, chia seeds, maca, spirulina, psyllium husk, moringa powder, Irish moss powder.

Refrigerate all fruit and grains that are not used for another day or other recipes.

Simple African Fufu

Prep Time: 10 minutes
Cook Time: 5 minutes
Serves: 2–4
Ingredients:

2 cups water
¼ teaspoon Mineral or Sea Salt
¾ or 1 cup Cassava Flour

Directions:

1. Boil two cups of water in a small pot or pan.
2. Remove boiling water from the burner.
3. Pour Cassava flour clockwise in the water.
4. Stir it slowly until it is thick enough to roll into a ball.
5. Dip or serve Fufu with soup or stew.

Enjoy!

Shallot Popcorn

Prep Time – 5 minutes –

Cook Time 2–3 minutes

Serves 2–4

Ingredients:

2 tablespoons Coconut or Olive oil

½ cup Popcorn

¼ teaspoon chopped Shallots

Directions:

Put the oil (Coconut or Olive) and chopped shallots in a large, deep pot or pan with a lid. Turn to medium–high heat. Add 2 kernels of popcorn, and cover.

Once the kernels pop, remove the cover and pour in the remaining popcorn. Cover and move pot or pan on top of heat in a circular motion, holding the cover on, until the popcorn is no longer popping. Remove popcorn from heat.

Optional:

Pour popcorn in a large bag. Sprinkle Mineral or Sea Salt, Cayenne pepper, Paprika, Cumin, Turmeric and/or Nutritional Yeast into the bag with the popcorn. Close the top of the bag. Shake bag of popcorn with the ingredients for about 5 –10 seconds. Eat popcorn. Enjoy!

Tasty Guacamole

Prep Time: 20
Makes 1 Batch
Ingredients:
3 ripe Avocados
1 cup Tomato
½ teaspoon Cumin
½ teaspoon Mineral or Sea Salt
½ Jalapeno Pepper (medium) minced
½ cup chopped Cilantro
½ teaspoon Cayenne
¼ cup chopped Shallots
1 tablespoon Lemon Juice

Optional:
¼ cup Bell Pepper

Directions:

Cut avocados in half and remove the seed. Scoop out flesh and place it in the blender. If you do not have a blender, place all ingredients in a large bowl and mix well. If you do have a blender, place all other ingredients into the blender. Select low speed. Turn machine on and quickly increase speed to medium. Run for 15–20 seconds or until the ingredients are well mixed. Stop machine and use a spatula to remove the mixture. **Enjoy!**

Natural Hair Conditioner

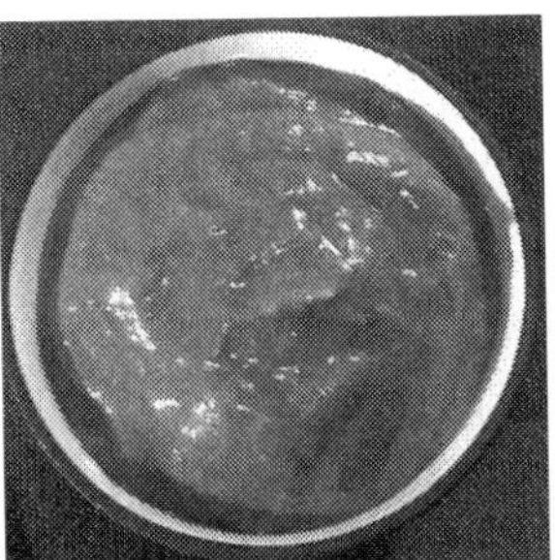

Makes 14 ounces

Total time: 25 minutes

Ingredients:

1 Mashed Ripe Avocado *(medium sized)*

1 cup Parsley

1 cup Banana

1 tablespoon Coconut or Olive Oil

1 teaspoon Jojoba, Grape Seed, or Almond Oil

½ teaspoon Molasses

1 tablespoon Dairy–Free Yogurt or Soy–Free Veganaise

1 teaspoon Lemon Juice

½ teaspoon Cayenne

4 – 6 Drops Essential Oils. Select three (3) from the four (4) listed below:

Lavender, Rosemary, Tea Tree or Peppermint Oil.

2 tablespoons Bulk Herbal Teas: Select 1 teaspoon each from four (4) out of seven (7) herbal teas listed below:

Chamomile, Calendula, Nettle, Marshmallow, Rosemary, Burdock Root or Dandelion

Directions:

Put tea in two cups of water. Bring to boil. Let tea steep for 20 minutes. While tea is steeping, place all other ingredients into blender. Strain tea. Add 1 cup of strained herbal tea to the other ingredients in the blender. Blend all ingredients until smooth.

Pour conditioner in a jar with a lid or top or in a clear condiment squeeze bottle. Squeeze and massage it throughout your hair and scalp. After you are done, cover your hair with a plastic cap. Leave conditioner on hair for 30–60 minutes or overnight. It works well on gray hair too.

Hemp/Basil Dressing

Prep time: 20 minutes

Makes 3½ Cups

Ingredients:

½ cup soaked Sunflower Seeds
(presoaked for at least 2 hours)
1 cup Coconut or Olive oil
1 cup Water
½ cup Lemon Juice
½ cup chopped Parsley
½ cup chopped Basil
½ cup Cilantro
1 teaspoon chopped Shallots
1 tablespoon chopped Jalpeno Pepper
1 tablespoon Bragg Liquid Aminos or Shoyu
1 cup Hemp Seeds
¾ teaspoon salt
1 teaspoon Dill Weed
1 teaspoon Oregano
½ teaspoon Chipotle
½ teaspoon Cayenne

Directions:

Place all ingredients into blender. Start at low speed and gradually increase until smooth. If there is no blender, mix well. Serve immediately or refrigerate.

Enjoy!

Hemp Milk

Prep Time: 10 minutes

Makes 2 Cups

Ingredients:

½ cup Hemp Seeds
2 cups Water
2 Medjool Dates
½ teaspoon Vanilla
½ teaspoon Cardamom
½ teaspoon Cinnamon

Optional:

1 tablespoon Raw Cacao
½ teaspoon Allspice
½ teaspoon Nutmeg
½ teaspoon Iris Moss

Directions:

Place all ingredients in blender on high speed for 20 seconds. Optionally, you can strain the mixture through messbag or cheesecloth to remove the seed particles. The seed particles can be refrigerated for use in other recipes or put in cereal, pancakes, waffles, smoothies, soup or stew. Serve immediately or refrigerate in an airtight glass container for up to 3–5 days.

Kale Chips

Prep 10 minutes

Cook 7–8 minutes

Ingredients:

2 tablespoons Olive Oil

Liquid Braggs Amino

Chipotle	Paprika
Cumin	Shallots
Turmeric	1 bunch Curly Kale (Dinosaur optional)
Italian Seasoning	2 large cookie sheets or pans
Cayenne Pepper	Mineral or Sea Salt

Directions: Preheat an oven to 450 degrees F (232 degrees C). Thoroughly soak Kale in a large bowl with cold water with a dash of Sea Salt to remove grit and discourage little critters. Rinse off Kale in cold water.

Carefully remove the leaves from the stems of the Kale. Thoroughly dry kale with a paper towel or a salad spinner and cut into bite size pieces.

Massage and rub each kale piece with the Olive Oil on the cookie sheets or pans.

Sprinkle with seasoning to taste. Rub and massage spices on the Kale.

Place Kale in the oven. If more than one oven rack is used for the two pans or cookie sheets (one above the other), after 3 minutes, switch the Kale on the top with the Kale on the bottom. Keep in oven for the remaining time. Check it after 5 minutes.

Bake until the edges are brown, but not burnt, 5 to 7 minutes.

Simple Kale Stir–Fry

Total Time: 18 min

Prep: 10 min

Cook: 8 min

Ingredients:

3 tablespoons Coconut or Olive Oil

¼ cup chopped Shallots

¾ cup chopped Scallions

1 bunch Kale with leaves torn, stalks discarded, coarsely chopped.

1 tablespoon Turmeric

¼ teaspoon Mineral or Sea Salt

1 teaspoon Cumin

¼ teaspoon Cayenne

Instructions: Thoroughly soak kale in a large bowl with cold water with a dash of Sea Salt to remove grit and discourage little critters. Rinse off kale in cold water. Tear the leaves from the stalks, coarsely chop kale leaves.

Heat oil in a large skillet or wok over medium heat with Scallions, Shallots, Salt, Turmeric, Cayenne and Cumin. Stir it around 2–3 minutes so it won't burn. Add Kale and stir around 3–5 minutes. Remove cooked dish to a plate and serve!

Optional: Serve with Quinoa, Pasta, Black, Red, or Brown rice.

Lasagna with Basil Cashew Cheese

Prep Time 1 Hour

6–8 Servings

Cooking Time 35– 45

Makes 1 9x13 Pan

Basil Cashew Cheese Topping:

¼ cup Raw Cashews (soak in 1 cup of water for 30 minutes)

Pour the 1 cup of Water containing the Soaked Cashews into the blender or food processor.

2 ½ tablespoons Tapioca Starch

1 cup – fresh Basil

¼ teaspoon Mineral or Sea Salt

1 tablespoon Oil (Olive or Coconut)

½ cup Nutritional Yeast

1 teaspoon fresh Lemon Juice

¼ cup chopped Shallots

Add all ingredients into a high–powered blender or food processor and blend until smooth. Pour topping into a small saucepan and cook. Continue to stir over medium high heat. After a few minutes the mixture will start to look like its curdling or separating. Reduce heat to medium and continue stirring so you don't burn the bottom of the saucepan.

Keep cooking and stirring until the mixture gets real thick and becomes like melted dairy cheese. In about 2–3 more minutes, remove from heat and let it cool. As soon as it has cooled enough pour the topping into a container. Cover the container and place it in the refrigerator for later use.

The Sauce or African Stew (page 335

Lasagna Sauce Ingredients:

1 tablespoon Coconut or Olive Oil
¼ teaspoon Mineral or Sea Salt
¼ cup chopped Scallions
¼ cup chopped Shallots
½ teaspoon Oregano
½ teaspoon Thyme
1 Vegetable Bouillon cube
1 teaspoon Turmeric
½ teaspoons dried Basil
2 cups Salsa (medium or mild)
1 teaspoon Maple Syrup

Sauté the shallots and scallions in oil for 1–2 minutes in a saucepan on medium heat. Add the other ingredients. Reduce the heat to low and let it simmer, stirring occasionally for 5 –10 minutes. Remove from heat.

Plant Protein Filling:

2 cups Raw Sunflower Seeds
5 oz Kalamata or Black Olives
½ cup chopped Shallots
¼ cup Lemon or Lime Juice
½ teaspoon Mineral or Sea Salt
1 teaspoon Turmeric
½ teaspoon Basil
1 tablespoon Sesame Seeds
¼ cup chopped Scallions
1 tablespoon Cumin
2 tablespoons Parsley
½ cup Beets
¼ teaspoon Cayenne Pepper
½ cup Bell Pepper
2 tablespoons Tomato
2 tablespoons Oil (Coconut or Olive)

Optional:

½ cup Carrots
1 teaspoon Italian Seasoning
¼ teaspoon Ginger Root
¼ cup chopped Celery
¼ teaspoon Chipotle
2 tablespoons Cilantro

Put Sunflower seeds into food processor. Pulse seeds until semi–smooth and set them aside in a bowl. Put salt, shallots and olives in processor using the S–blade until smooth. Combine Sunflower seeds and add all other ingredients with the oil and blend until semi–smooth.

Lasagna

Vegetable Stir–fry

Ingredients:

2 tablespoon Oil (coconut or Olive)

1 cup chopped Scallions

2 tablespoons chopped Shallots

1 cup Zucchini (chopped)

½ cup sliced Mushrooms

1 cup Spinach

1 cup Kale

1 box of Brown Rice Pasta or Lasagna Noodles

Optional:

¼ teaspoon Cayenne

½ cup Red Pepper

¼ cup chopped Ginger

¼ cup chopped Shallots

1 teaspoon Soy Free Chick–pea Miso

½ teaspoon Mineral or Sea Salt

STEP 1– Preheat oven to 375°Fahreheit (190 Celsius).

Optional to Sauté seeds: Caraway, Fennel, Cumin and Coriander in large skillet, wok or pan before sautéing onion, bouillon cubes and shallots in oil over low–medium heat for 3–5 minutes.

Otherwise, sauté onion, bouillon cubes and shallots in oil over low–medium heat for 2–3 minutes. Add Zucchini and Mushrooms, sauté for 2–3 more minutes. Add Kale and Spinach and sauté for additional 2–3 more minutes.

Optional to add: Cabbage, Asparagus, Carrots, Parsley, Cilantro, Basil or Tomato

Optional to Sprinkle: Ground Turmeric, Cumin, Tarragon, Thyme, Oregano, Rosemary, Fenugreek, Sage, Marjoram

STEP 2 – Cook 1 box of brown rice pasta or lasagna noodles. Check the box directions for boiling pasta or noodles. Generally, add 3–4 quarts water. Bring water to rapid boil. Add ½ teaspoon mineral or sea salt to reduce sticking. Lower heat to low and add noodles 2–3 pieces at a time and stir. Return to rapid boil. Cook uncovered while stirring for 3–4 minutes with brown rice pasta or 8–10 minutes with lasagna noodles, stirring occasionally. Watch lasagna or pasta to prevent over cooking. Drain pasta or noodles well in strainer or colander. Pour cold water over noodles or pasta to cool and prevent sticking. Separate cooked lasagna or pasta and lay on wax paper.

STEP 3 – Layer the Lasagna: Pour about a cup of sauce or African stew into a 9×13 inch pan and spread it evenly. Add a layer of sautéed vegetables. Then add another layer of pasta or noodles. Then, spread sauce on top of noodles or pasta along with the plant protein filling. Add another layer of pasta or noodles.

STEP 4 – Repeat layers of sauce and plant protein filling. Then, add a layer of sautéed vegetables. Add basil cashew cheese topping. Optional to sprinkle herbs and spices: ground turmeric, cumin, tarragon, thyme, oregano, rosemary, fenugreek, sage, marjoram or cayenne

STEP 5 – Bake for 35–45 minutes, watching closely so as not to burn the edges.

Tasty Millet

Makes 6–8

Cooking Time:

25–30 minutes

Millet is gluten free and a good source of fiber. The main grain in China before rice, it has a sweet nutty flavor. Considered to be one of the most digestible and non–allergenic grains available, it is high in protein and antioxidant activity. Importantly, millet hydrates the colon to keep you from being constipated. It is one of the few grains that are alkalizing to the body. It contains magnesium that can help reduce the effects of migraines and heart attacks. The serotonin in millet is calming to moods.

Ingredients:

1 cup Millet

2 cups Water

¼ teaspoon Mineral or Sea Salt

¼ teaspoon ground Cinnamon

1 teaspoon Turmeric

Optional:

¼ teaspoon Allspice

¼ teaspoon ground Ginger

Directions:

Boil 2 cups of water adding salt, cinnamon and turmeric for 3–5 minutes. Pour in millet and stir. Turn heat to low, cover and let millets simmer 25–30 minutes, stirring occasionally to avoid burning the bottom of the pot or pan. Remove from heat, Stir, uncovered 15–20 minutes to let the grains separate. Eat, enjoy!

NaaCereal

Makes 6–8 Servings

Cooking Time: 30–35 Minutes

For Infants or Adults

Ingredients:

2 cups water

1 cup grains: Select four of the five grains below.

Add ¼ cup of each:

Steel Cut Oats, Millets, Quinoa (Black, Red, Beige or Tri–color),

Black Forbidden Rice or Red Rice

1 teaspoon Olive or Coconut oil

1/8 teaspoon Mineral or Sea Salt

Select four (4) out of the seven (7) spices:

1/8 teaspoon ground Cinnamon

1/8 teaspoon Mace

1/8 teaspoon Turmeric

1/8 teaspoon Nutmeg

1/8 teaspoon Cardamom

1/8 teaspoon Sage

1/8 teaspoon Cloves

Fruits: Select desired fruit from those listed below equaling one cup. Seasonal fruit is best.

Oranges	Strawberries	Pears
Pineapple	Blueberries	Persimmons
Bananas	Apples	Kiwi

Super–foods

¼ teaspoon Chia seeds	¼ teaspoon Nutritional Yeast
¼ teaspoon Ground flax seeds	1 large Date

¼ teaspoon Pea Protein

1 tablespoon Raisins

Wet Ingredients:

½ cup to taste: Water, Almond or Hemp milk

Cooking Directions:

Boil 2 cups of water adding oil, salt and spices for 3–5 minutes.

Pour in grains and stir. Turn heat to low, cover and let grains simmer 25–30 minutes, stirring occasionally to avoid burning the bottom of the pot or pan. Remove from heat. Stir the grains and leave uncovered 10–15 minutes to let the grains separate.

Place in blender, Vita–mix, Nutra bullet or Baby Ninja

1 cup grains

1 cup Fruit

½ cup or to taste: Water, Almond or Hemp Milk

Super–foods

Blend course or puree, depending on the ability of child or adult to chew.

• See Almond and Hemp milk recipes

NaaCereal Non–Infant Formula

Optional: Non Infant Formula:

After cooking grains and allowing them to separate, place grains in bowl with fruit, water, almond or hemp milk and super–foods. Stir and eat.

Quinoa, Black and Red Rice Mix

Serves 6–8

Cooking Time: 45 minutes

Quinoa is gluten free. It has been called "The Mother" of all the grains. One of the most protein–rich foods we can eat, it is a complete protein containing all nine essential amino acids. It contains almost twice as much fiber as most other grains. Fiber helps to relieve constipation and prevent heart disease by reducing high blood pressure and diabetes. Fiber lowers blood sugar levels and cholesterol and may help you to lose weight.

It has a good amount of iron, which helps keep our red blood cells healthy and increases brain function. It contains lysine, which is essential for tissue repair and growth. It is rich in magnesium, which helps to relax blood vessels and thereby alleviate migraines. It also contains Manganese, which is an antioxidant, which helps to protect red blood cells and other cells from injury by free radicals.

Ingredients:

2 cups Water
¼ teaspoon Mineral or Sea Salt
¼ teaspoon ground Cinnamon
¼ teaspoon Cumin
¼ teaspoon Thyme
¼ teaspoon Cayenne powder
½ cup Quinoa
1 teaspoon Turmeric
¼ cup Red Rice
¼ cup Black Rice
1 vegetable bouillon cube

Optional:

¼ teaspoon Shallots
¼ teaspoon ground Parsley
3 Cardamom Seeds
¼ teaspoon Saffron

Directions:

Boil 2 cups of water adding salt, cinnamon, turmeric, cumin, thyme and cayenne for 3–5 minutes. Pour in quinoa, black and red rice, stir. Turn heat to low, cover and let grains simmer 25–30 minutes, stirring occasionally to avoid burning the bottom of the pot or pan. Remove from heat. Stir, leave uncovered 15–25 minutes to let the grains separate. Eat, enjoy!

Real Banana Pancakes

8 –10 Pancakes
Prep time 15 minutes
Cook time 40 minutes
Ingredients:
¾ cups Buckwheat Flour
¾ cups Quinoa Flour
(optional) Spelt, Amaranth, Rye, Coconut
1 teaspoon Nutritional Yeast
½ teaspoon Baking soda
1 tablespoon Flax Seeds (ground)
1½ teaspoons Baking Powder (aluminum free)
½ teaspoon Cinnamon
½ teaspoon Mineral or Sea Salt
1 tablespoon Maple Syrup or Coconut Nectar
1 cup Almond or Hemp milk
1½ Bananas (medium sized)—mash into mix
¼ cup Coconut (Olive) Oil
(optional) Top with strawberries, mango, blueberries or other fruit

Directions:

Mix flour, baking powder, baking soda, cinnamon, salt and flax seed, into a medium–large bowl.

Whisk the bananas, milk and oil together in a medium–large bowl.

Make a well in the center of the dry ingredients, and pour in the wet. Stir or use blender until mixture is smooth

Wipe the surface of the griddle, skillet, or pan with the oiled napkin or paper towel.

Heat the lightly oiled griddle, large non–stick skillet, or frying pan over low medium heat.

Drop 1/4 cup of batter onto a hot oiled griddle, or well–greased frying pan or skillet over medium high heat.

When bubbles appear on the surface of the pancake, approximately 3 minutes, flip, and cook until browned on the other side for another 2 minutes.

Drop another 1/4 cup of batter onto the hot oiled griddle, well greased frying pan, or skillet

Repeat with remaining mixture until the batter is gone. Enjoy!

Pineapple Rind Drink

Prep Time: 10 minutes

Serves 4–6

Cook Time: 35–40 minutes

Ingredients:

1 Medium Pineapple

4 cups Water

Directions:

Rinse pineapple
and remove rind and core

Cut rind and core into
strips or pieces

Place water and pineapple
rinds into pot

Bring water to medium high and boil covered for 35–40 minutes

Remove pot from heat

Keep lid on pot

Let pineapple drink steep for 30–60 minutes

Remove pineapple rind and strain

Serve immediately or refrigerate.

Can store refrigerated for 2 weeks. Enjoy!

Pizza

Prep Time: 1 hour
Cook Time:10–15 minutes
Makes 12 –16 Slices
The pizza is made in 5 parts:
The basil cheese topping, crust, African Stew or sauce, plant protein filling and raw salad.
First, you'll need to make the
Basil Cashew Cheese Topping:
¼ cup Raw Cashews (soak in 1 cup of water for 30 minutes)
Pour the 1 cup of Water containing the Soaked Cashews into the blender, or food processer.

2 ½ tablespoons Tapioca starch
¼ teaspoon Mineral or Sea Salt
½ cup Nutritional Yeast
¼ cup chopped Shallots
1 cup fresh Basil
1 tablespoon Oil (Olive or Coconut)
1 teaspoon fresh Lemon Juice

Add all ingredients into a high–powered blender or food processer and blend until smooth. Pour topping into a small saucepan and cook. Continue to stir over medium high heat. After a few minutes the mixture will start to look like its curdling or separating. Reduce heat to medium and continue stirring so you don't burn the bottom of the saucepan.

Keep cooking and stirring until the mixture gets real thick and becomes like melted dairy cheese in about 2–3 more minutes. Remove from heat and let it cool. As soon as it has cooled enough pour the topping into a container. Cover the container and place it in the refrigerator for later use.

The Crust:

2 cups Quinoa or Barley Flour

1 teaspoon Mineral or Sea Salt

Buckwheat or Spelt Flour

1 teaspoon Maple Syrup

2 tablespoons Dry Yeast (1 packet)

1 tablespoon Coconut or Olive Oil

½ cup Flax Seed

1 cup warm Water

Combine all ingredients in a large bowl and stir to create dough. Add additional flour to dough as needed to keep dough from sticking to bowl or to hands. Place dough on slightly floured flat surface and knead for 10 minutes. This means, to press, massage or squeeze the dough with your hands blending the mixture together. If the underside or bottom of dough is sticking to the surface, pull up dough and add additional flour and re–knead. Repeat process until the underside or bottom of dough no longer sticks. Knead dough into a half rounded ball or dome shape. Place dough in a large bowl and cover to let it rise in a warm place for 60 minutes while you complete the other parts of the pizza.

The Sauce: Use 2–3 Cups of African Stew or Pizza Sauce:

1 tablespoon Coconut or Olive Oil

¼ teaspoon Mineral or Sea salt

¼ cup chopped Scallions

1– teaspoon – Turmeric

¼ cup chopped Shallots

½ teaspoons dried Basil

½ teaspoon – Oregano

2 cups Salsa (medium or mild)

½ teaspoon Thyme

1 teaspoon Maple Syrup

1 Vegetable Bouillon Bube

Sauté the shallots and scallions in oil for 1–2 minutes in a saucepan on medium heat. Add the other ingredients. Reduce the heat to low and let it simmer, stirring occasionally for 5 –10 minutes. Remove from heat.

Plant Protein Filling

Makes about 2 Cups

2 cups – Raw Sunflower Seeds
5 oz Kalamata or Black Olives
½ cup chopped Shallots
¼ cup Lemon or Lime Juice
½ teaspoon Mineral or Sea Salt
1 teaspoon Turmeric
½ teaspoon Basil
1 tablespoon Sesame Seeds
½ cup chopped Scallion
1 tablespoon Cumin
2 tablespoons Cilantro
2 tablespoons Parsley

Put Sunflower seeds into food processor. Pulse seeds until semi–smooth and set them aside in a bowl. Put salt, shallots and olives in processor using the S–blade until smooth. Combine Sunflower seeds and all other ingredients with the oil and blend until semi–smooth.

Raw Vegetables: Sprinkle vegetables on top of Pizza.

¼ cup Cilantro
¼ cup Tomatoes
¼ cup thinly sliced Cauliflower
¼ cup fresh Basil
¼ cup thinly sliced Broccoli

Optional:

¼ cup chopped Celery
¼ cup chopped or thinly sliced Scallions
2 tablespoons thinly sliced Daikon
¼ cup shredded Cabbage

¼ cup Bell Pepper	2 tablespoons Olives
¼ cup Parsley	¼ cup Kale
¼ cup chopped Pineapple	2 tablespoons Carrot (grated)

Putting The Parts Together: Preheat the oven to 500 Fahrenheit (260 Celsius).

When dough is ready after 60 minutes, roll out dough on a floured surface as thick or thin as you desire. Spread pizza with the Pizza Sauce or African Stew. Then spread the Plant Protein Filling on top of the Sauce or African Stew. Sprinkle the Raw Vegetables on top of the Filling. Add drops of the Basil Cashew Cheese Topping on top of the pizza.

Bake pizza on a slightly oiled baking sheet for 10–15 minutes or until the crust is nicely browned. If desired, sprinkle pizza with additional fresh chopped Basil, ground Oregano, Cayenne or Paprika after is comes out of the oven. Eat! Enjoy!

Spicy Vegan Plantain

Prep Time: 10 minutes
Serves 4–6
Cook Time: 20–25 minutes
Ingredients:
4–6 very ripe Plantains
½ cup Raisins
1 teaspoons Cinnamon
½ teaspoon Cloves
1 teaspoon Nutmeg
¼ cup chopped Pineapple
4 tablespoons Oil (Coconut or Olive)
1 teaspoon Allspice
½ teaspoon Mace
½ tablespoon chopped Ginger
Optional:
½ cup dried unsweetened Cranberries
½ cup Blueberries

Directions:

Peel plantain and cut into thin slices. Heat oil in large skillet or wok. Place over medium low heat and sauté the plantain in a single layer. When golden on the bottom, turn plantain over with spatula. Add nutmeg, cloves, cinnamon, allspice, mace, pineapple and ginger. Stir continuously until plantain begins to caramelize.

Serve immediately and enjoy!

Tasty Polenta

Serves 6–8

Cooking Time: 15 minutes

Polenta is made from corn, grains and legumes. It is gluten-free. A good source of fiber, it originated as a peasant food in Northern Italy. Freshly made polenta from whole-grain corn can supply long-lasting energy and has the consistency of grits. It is considered easy to digest. It contains good amounts of magnesium, iron, thiamine, phosphorus and zinc. The zinc contributes to a healthy immune system.

The complex carbohydrates in corn help slow the rate of glucose absorption, thereby controlling blood sugar levels. It is a good source of Vitamins A and C, which benefit cancer and heart disease prevention. It can also be made into cakes for frying or grilling. Since, today's corn is almost entirely genetically modified, use only organic polenta.

Ingredients:

2 cups Water
¼ teaspoon Mineral or Sea Salt
¼ teaspoon ground Paprika
1 teaspoon Turmeric
1 teaspoon ground Cardamom
1 teaspoon Thyme
½ teaspoon Basil

Optional:

¼ teaspoon Saffron
½ Vegetable Bouillon cube
¼ teaspoon Parsley

Directions: Boil 2 cups of water adding salt, paprika, cardamom, basil, thyme and turmeric for 3–5 minutes. Pour in polenta and stir. Turn heat to low, cover and let polenta simmer 15–20 minutes, stirring occasionally to avoid burning the bottom of the pot or pan. Remove from heat. Stir, leave uncovered 15–20 minutes to let the grains separate. Eat, enjoy!

Portobello Mushrooms

Prep Time: 10 minutes

Cook Time: 20 minutes

Serves 4

Ingredients:

4 Portobello mushroom caps
¼ cup Bell Pepper
2 tablespoons freshly chopped Mint
¼ cup Coconut or Olive Oil
1 cup chopped Tomatoes
3 tablespoons chopped Scallions
3 tablespoons chopped Shallots
1 teaspoon finely chopped Rosemary
2 teaspoons Bragg Liquid Aminos
½ teaspoon Mineral or Sea Salt
½ teaspoon Cayenne
2 tablespoons fresh Lemon or Lime Juice

Optional:
1 tablespoon Balsamic

Directions:

Preheat oven to 400 Fahrenheit (204 Celsius)

Clean mushrooms and remove stems, reserve stems for other recipes. Place the mushroom caps on a plate with the gills up. Use a spoon to remove gills. In a small bowl, combine the rosemary, cayenne, scallions, tomatoes and shallots. In another bowl combine oil, juice, salt and Bragg.

Bush over both sides of mushroom caps with the oil, juice, salt and Bragg mixture. Spoon the mixture of rosemary, cayenne, scallions, shallots and tomatoes evenly into each mushroom cap. Place mushrooms on baking sheet or dish. Place the baking dish on middle rack in the oven. Bake for 20 minutes. Serve immediately.

Tasty Potato Salad

Serves 6–8
Cooking Time: 25 minutes
Ingredients:
3 lbs Potatoes
(Yukon, Red or Purple)
(About 8 medium sized)
Finely chopped:
3 tablespoons Parsley
¼ cup fresh Dill Weed
¼ cup Dinosaur Kale
¼ cup Bell Peppers
¼ cup Beets
½ cup Broccoli
¼ cup Cilantro
3⁄4 cup chopped Scallions
¼ cup Cucumber
1 teaspoon Chipotle
1 tablespoon Oregano
1 tablespoon Water
1 tablespoon Pea Protein
2 tablespoons Olive Oil
2 tablespoons Maple Syrup or Coconut Nectar
2 tablespoon Mustard
2 teaspoons Lemon or Lime Juice
1 teaspoon ground or fresh Basil
1 tablespoon Mineral or Sea Salt
1 tablespoon Turmeric
¼ cup Olive oil
2 tablespoons Bragg Liquid Aminos
Optional:
¼ cup Red Cabbage

¼ cup Cauliflower
¼ cup Celery
1 Tomato sliced on top
¼ cup fresh Fennel
½ teaspoon Paprika
1 teaspoon Marjoram
½ teaspoon Cayenne
½ cup Olives

Directions:

Wash potatoes with skin on. Cut potatoes into quarter or eights. Place in large pot. Fill pot with water over the level of the potatoes. Boil potatoes with skin on medium heat for 20 minutes or until tender. Squeeze juice from lemon or lime in a small bowl.

After boiling, place potatoes in a large bowl. Add: All vegetables, herbs, seasoning, mustard, lemon or lime juice, Bragg, maple syrup and olives into large bowl with the potatoes. Stir well. Sprinkle ½ teaspoon lemon juice on top. Eat. Enjoy!

Pulp Burger/Juice

Makes 10–12 Open faced Sandwiches & about 2 quarts Juice

Juice Ingredients:

4 Apples
3 Oranges
1 Pear
½ cup Dandelion
1 Daikon
½ cup Parsley
¼ cup chopped Ginger
2 Carrots
½ cup Cabbage

½ bunch Kale
4 Celery Stalks
1 cup Pineapple
2 Beets (medium sized)
3 Cucumbers (medium sized)

Burger Ingredients:

Catsup, mustard, sliced cucumber (pickles), grain bread, 4–6 beds of lettuce, 1 sliced tomato,1 thin sliced shallot, 1 avocado

Directions:

1. Rinse all items.
2. Remove stems and cut seeds out of apples, oranges and pears.
3. Juice all items.
4. Collect pulp from juiced items.
5. Toast bread.
6. Spread catsup, shallot, avocado and mustard on toasted bread.
7. Spread pulp evenly on top of catsup, mustard and avocado.
8. Place thinly sliced cucumber (pickles), shallot and sliced tomato on top of pulp.

Raw Ice Cream

Prep Time: 5 min.
Serves 4–5
Ingredients:
1 cup frozen Blueberries
1 cup frozen Strawberries
3 frozen ripe Bananas
2 cups Almond or Hemp Milk
¼ cup Maple Syrup or Coconut Nectar or to taste

Optional:
1 teaspoon Vanilla Powder

Directions:
1. Blend the frozen strawberries with milk until semi–smooth.
2. Add the frozen bananas, blueberries and blend until creamy.
3. Serve immediately or store in the freezer.

Raw Salad

Prep Time: 40 minutes

Serves 8–12

Ingredients:

1 cup Carrots
¼ cup Cilantro
½ cup chopped Cauliflower
1 cup sliced Collar Greens
¼ cup Parsley
½ cup Celery
¼ cup chopped Zucchini
1 cup Swiss Chard
1 cup Spinach
1 cup chopped Beets
¼ cup Basil
1 cup Napa Cabbage
¼ cup Mint
1 cup chopped Broccoli
¼ cup Fennel
¼ cup Dill Weed
1 cup Dinosaur Kale
1 cup Purple Kale
1 cup Beet Greens

Optional:
¼ cup chopped Asparagus
¼ cup Green Beans (seasonal)
¼ cup dried Seaweed
1 cup chopped Cucumber
½ cup Boc Choy
½ cup Leeks
¼ cup Brussels Sprouts
¼ cup Daikon

Directions: Pour the following vegetables into a large bowl and toss.

Vegan Real Waffles

12 –14 Waffles

Prep time 15 minutes Cook time 30 minutes

Ingredients:

¾ cups Buckwheat Flour

¾ cups Quinoa flour (optional) Spelt, Amaranth, Rye, Coconut

1 teaspoon Nutritional Yeast

½ teaspoon Baking soda

1 tablespoon Flax Seeds (ground)

1½ teaspoons Baking powder (aluminum free)

½ teaspoon Cinnamon

½ teaspoon Mineral or Sea Salt

1 tablespoon Maple Syrup

1 cup Almond or Hemp milk

1½ Bananas (medium sized)—mash into mix

¼ cup Coconut or Olive oil

Optional:

Top with strawberry, mango, blueberries or other fruit.

Mix flour, Nutritional Yeast, baking powder, baking soda, cinnamon, salt and flax seed, into a large bowl.

Whisk or mix the bananas, milk and oil together in a medium-large bowl.

Make a well in the center of the dry ingredients, and pour in the wet. Stir or use blender until mixture is smooth

Preheat the waffle iron per the machine's instructions.

Brush the waffle iron with oil (Coconut or Olive). Use a paper towel or pastry brush to oil both the bottom and top plates of the waffle iron. Repeat this process of oiling the plates before you make each waffle, or it is most likely that the waffles will stick to the plates.

Spoon in, depending on the waffle iron, about ¼ – ½ cup of batter evenly into the bottom plate of the waffle iron and close to cook.

The first waffle will be the tester. So, if you have poured in too much batter, not enough or more oil is needed to avoid sticking, you can make the adjustments for the next waffle.

Close the lid and wait until the waffle iron's indicator light shows that cooking is complete, or until no more steam comes out. This may be 3–5 minutes, depending on the waffle iron. The cooked waffle should be crispy and golden brown.

Remove the waffle with a spatula or butter knife to help you lift it without burning your fingers or breaking the waffle. Place the cooked waffle on a plate or place the cooked waffle in a 200 degree Fahrenheit (93 Celsius) oven until serving. Oil the plates and pour more batter into the waffle iron to make another waffle. Repeat until all the batter is gone.

Roasted Eggplant Vegetable Casserole

Cooking time: 50 Minutes
Serves 2–4 For 3–4 Days
Ingredients:

2 (medium sized) Eggplants
2 tablespoons Sesame Seeds
¼ cup finely chopped Shallots
¼ cup chopped Ginger Root
1 teaspoon Parsley
1 teaspoon Chipotle
2 large Tomatoes
1 cup Bell Peppers
¼ cup Broccoli
½ teaspoon Mineral or Sea Salt
1½ cup Kale
½ cup fresh Mint
¾ cup Coconut or Olive oil
2 tablespoons Bragg Liquid Aminos
2 tablespoons Lemon or Lime Juice
2 teaspoons Oregano
1 teaspoon Thyme
1 teaspoon Rosemary
1 teaspoon Cumin
1 cup fresh Basil
1 teaspoon Turmeric
¼ cup chopped Beets
1 cup chopped scallions
½ teaspoon Cayenne
1 Glass Jar Salsa (12 oz) or 1½ cup African stew

Directions:

Preheat oven 450 Fahrenheit (232 Celsius). Grease bottom of large Pyrex or Baking pan (13x9 pan) with oil. Cut 2 Eggplants (medium) in half the long way. Slice each half into ½ inch cuts. Place Eggplant in bottom of pan.

Pour ½ cup Oil on Eggplant. Massage Oil on both sides of Eggplant. Sprinkle Bell Peppers and Shallots on top of Eggplant. Slice 2 large Tomatoes and one cup chopped Scallions on top of Eggplant.

Sprinkle Turmeric, Cumin, Mineral or Sea Salt, Chipotle, Rosemary, Cayenne, Thyme, Parsley, Oregano, Mint, Ginger, Basil,

Sesame Seeds, Broccoli, Kale, Lemon or Lime Juice and Beets on top of Eggplant. Pour ¼ cup of Oil and Bragg on Casserole. Add either African Stew or Salsa on top.

Place in oven for 25 minutes at 450 Fahrenheit (232 Celsius). Remove from oven. Turn Eggplant over in Pyrex or pan. Place Eggplant back into oven for another 25 minutes. Check to see if skin of eggplant is soft. If eggplant skin is not soft, bake up to an additional 20 minutes in the oven. Take Eggplant out of oven. Eat, enjoy!

Salad Dressing

Ingredients:

3 tablespoons Water
1 teaspoon Turmeric
1 tablespoon Pea Protein
1 tablespoon Hemp Seeds
1 tablespoon Organic Shoyu
¼ cup Bragg Liquid Aminos
1 tablespoon finely chopped Shallots
½ teaspoon Mineral or
Sea Salt or to taste
1 teaspoon Organic Braggberry
¼ teaspoon Cayenne
2 tablespoons Olive Oil
¼ cup Lemon or Lime Juice
1 teaspoon Sesame Seeds

Optional:

1 teaspoon Fig Balsamic Vinegar
¼ teaspoon Thyme
¼ teaspoon Paprika
¼ teaspoon Chipotle

Directions: In medium bowl

Add: All ingredients. Mix ingredients and pour in jar or bottle. Use immediately on salad or refrigerate.

Steel Cut Oats

Serves 6–8

Cooking Time: 45 minutes

Steel–cut oats are gluten free. They are the inner portion of the oat kernel which has been cut into two or three pieces. They differ from rolled oats, which have been flattened, steamed, rolled, re–steamed and toasted. Due to this additional processing, rolled oats lose some of their natural taste, nutritional value, texture and fiber.

Steel–cut oats are an excellent source of protein, fiber, rich in B–vitamins and calcium, while low in unsaturated fat and sodium. Steel–cut oats help eliminate fat and cholesterol from the body. This translates to lower cholesterol and a decrease in the risk of developing diabetes, cancer and heart disease.

Ingredients

1 cup Oats
2 cups Water
¼ teaspoon Mineral or Sea Salt
¼ teaspoon ground Cardamom
1 teaspoon Turmeric
¼ teaspoon ground Cinnamon
¼ teaspoon ground Cloves
½ teaspoon Allspice
1 teaspoon Coconut Oil

Optional:

¼ teaspoon ground Ginger
¼ teaspoon ground Nutmeg
¼ teaspoon ground Mace

Directions:

Boil 2 cups of water adding coconut oil, salt, cinnamon, cloves, allspice and turmeric for 3–5 minutes. Pour in oats and stir. Turn heat to low, cover and let oats simmer 25–30 minutes, stirring occasionally to avoid burning the bottom of the pot or pan. Remove from heat. Stir, leave uncovered 15–20 minutes to let the grains separate. Eat, enjoy!

Baked Sweet Potatoes/Yams

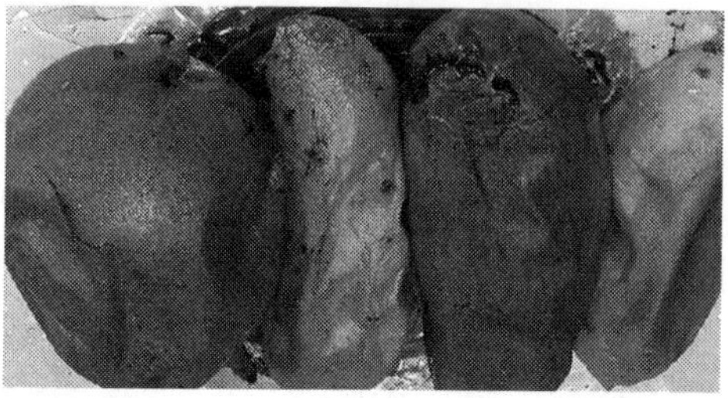

Prep Time:
10 minutes
Cook Time: 1 hour
Serves 4–6
Ingredients:

9x13 dish
4 large sweet potatoes or yams
Coconut or Olive oil

Directions:

1. Preheat oven to 400 Fahrenheit (204 Celsius).
2. Wash the sweet potatoes/yams and pat dry with a paper towel.
3. Lightly grease pan.
4. Lightly massage oil on the skins of the sweet potatoes/yams.
5. Use fork to pierce skin of potato in three (3) places.
6. Bake at 400 degrees for approximately an hour, or until tender.
7. Check potatoes/yams and rotate periodically to evenly cook.

Quinoa Tabouli

Serves 6–8

Cooking Time: 45 minutes

Ingredients:

1 cup Quinoa
2 cups Water
1 Vegetable Bouillon Cube
½ cup Shallots
1 teaspoon Turmeric
1 teaspoon Bragg Liquid Aminos
1 teaspoon Mineral or Sea Salt
½ teaspoon Cayenne Pepper
1 teaspoon Cumin
3 tablespoons Olive Oil
3 tablespoons Lemon Juice
1 cup chopped fresh Mint leaves
1 cup chopped Parsley Leaves
1 cup chopped Cilantro
½ cup chopped Green Onions
2 cups diced Cucumbers
Optional:
¼ cup Dandelion
¼ cup chopped Jicama
¼ cup chopped Cauliflower
2 cups diced Tomatoes or Cherry Tomatoes halved

Directions:

Boil 2 cups of water adding dash of salt, ground cumin, turmeric, cayenne pepper and 1 bouillon cube for 3–5 minutes. Pour in Quinoa and stir. Turn heat to low, cover and let quinoa simmer 25–30 minutes, stirring occasionally to avoid burning the bottom of the pot or pan. Remove from heat. Stir, leave uncovered 15–20 minutes to let the grains separate. Refrigerate 30–60 minutes.

In a large bowl, pour Quinoa, chopped herbs and vegetables, oil, Bragg, lemon juice and salt. Mix well. Chill, serve and enjoy.

Feel free to add additional spices...Mix well.

Mixed Spiced Tossed Salad

Prep Time: 15 minutes

Serves 8–10

Ingredients:

1 Head Romaine Lettuce (cut up or torn)

3 cups Spring Mix Salad

Dressing:

¾ cup Olive oil

¼ cup chopped Parsley

½ cup Water

½ cup Lemon Juice

1 cup chopped Shallots

1 teaspoon Cumin

¼ teaspoon Turmeric

2–4 un–pitted Medjool Dates

1 tablespoon Chick Pea Miso

1 teaspoon Oregano

1 teaspoon Bragg Liquid Aminos or Shoyu

Directions:

Blend dressing mixture in blender until creamy and smooth.

Make Topping:

1 teaspoon Chia Seeds

1½ cup Pine Nuts

2 tablespoon Flax seed or Omega Twin oil

1 teaspoon Mineral or Sea Salt

Pulse topping mixture in blender or food processor until coarsely chopped.

Toss spring mix and lettuce with dressing. Sprinkle topping mixture on top and serve.

Enjoy!

Variety Fruit Salad

Prep Time: 25 minutes

Serves 10–12

Choose 10 out of the 14 fruits below:

1 cup Apple
1 cup Blueberries
1 cup Banana
1 cup Oranges
1 cup Pineapple
1 cup Cherries
1 cup Strawberries
1 cup Mango
1 cup Raspberry
1 cup Grapes
1 cup Guava
1 cup Blackberries
1 cup Kiwi
1 cup Pear

Optional:

Persimmon, Peach, Apricot, Fig, Nectarine, Plum and Papaya. Add Almond, Hemp Milk to taste.

Directions:

Fruit is seasonal. If certain fruits are not available simply substitute other fruits. Mix fruit.

Sprinkle the below Power Boosters to taste:

Flax seed, Cacao, Raisins, Dates, Almonds, Mulberries, Goji Berries, Prunes, Hunza Berries, Hemp Seeds, Chia Seeds, Maca, Spirulina, Psyllium Husk, Moringa Powder or Iris Moss Powder.

Refrigerate all fruit salad that is not used for another day or other recipes.

General Index

Abscesses 182
Athlete's foot 182, 191
Acid reflux 125
Atherosclerosis 76, 85, 130, 148, 130, 156, 172
Acne 48, 103 -04, 158, 166, 181, 188, 193
Attention Deficit Disorder 62, 111, 129, 211
Adderall 211-12
Adrenal gland 124
ADHD 111, 211-13
Africans 50, 220, 238, 248, 238
Age spots 192
Aging 78, 86, 91, 99, 141, 169, 186, 238, 270
Alkaline 158, 220, 227-28, 242, 249, 256-57
Alkaline water 286–289
Allergic 144, 147, 198, 221, 262
All natural 136
African American 21, 214, 218, 223, 247
African Stew 44, 53, 335, 353, 383
Allergies 130, 132, 135, 144, 181, 207
Allspice 165
Almond 37, 131-32, 301, 339
Almond Arugula pesto 339
Almond Banana Smoothie 341
Almond Coconut Date Roll 340
Almond Milk 331
Aluminum 61, 226, 250, 263, 304-05, 313
Aluminum wok 313
Alzheimer's disease 61, 76, 174, 199, 305
Amaranth 201
Amino acid 108, 156, 189, 202, 299, 375
Ammonium 218-19, 242
Amphetamines 212
Ancestry memory 245
Anemic 19, 60
Antibacterial 85, 188, 192, 197, 199, 263
Antibiotic 50, 128, 137-39, 181, 225, 255
Antibiotic resistance 138
Anti–inflammatory 86, 119, 154, 165, 192, 199
Antiseptic 173, 167, 176, 185, 190, 197
Antiviral 85, 157, 167, 193, 185
Amenorrhea 179
Antifungal 85, 185, 191, 209
Antimicrobial 85, 166, 174, 196
Antioxidant 78, 86, 146, 155-58, 167, 203
Antiperspirant 252, 263-65,
Apple 145-46, 226, 255
Apple juice 145, 352
Aromatherapy 169, 185
Arteries 34, 76, 130, 156-157, 182, 187
Arthritis 104, 130, 148, 170, 192, 203, 209, 270
Artificial Colors 110, 213
Artificial growth hormones 128
Asparagus 155-56, 230
Aspartame 61, 106-08, 249,
Asthma 80, 176, 181, 269, 195, 202
Autoimmune 77, 192, 207
Avocado 227, 230, 300
B 6 105, 154, 159, 165, 192, 262
Bacillus thuringienesis 141, 144,
Bacteria 138, 141, 173, 181, 192, 263-65
Bad breath 169, 173, 169, 178, 188
Bad carbs 96
Baked French Fries 344
Banana 82, 148
Banana Fruit Bread 347
Banana Fruit Loaf 347
Barefootin' 119
Barley 114, 201-03, 229, 213
Basic Kitchen Safety 329
Basil 166
Bay Leaf 166-67, 184
Beans 78, , 114, 228, 299, 301
Beet 153, 230, 255
Beet greens 153
Beta–carotene 130, 146-47, 155-56, 168
Blackberries 203
Blackheads 175, 188
Black rice 42
Black women 218-24
Black Strap Molasses 43, 228
Bladder cancer 269
Bladder infection 139
Bleeding 104, 170, 194, 215, 251
Blood circulation 182-83, 185, 243, 268
Blueberry Almond Butter 349
Bipolar 108
Birth defects 60, 108, 147, 167, 260, 303
Bloating 125, 183, 188, 199, 251
Blood clots 104, 172
Blood Pressure 148, 156, 158-59, 165, 179, 187, 192, 203, 214, 239, 375
Blueberries 40, 42, 145, 162, 203
Bovine growth hormone 128, 135, 139
Boiled 48-49, 83, 174, 198, 272, 282
Boils 176, 182
Boost 84-87, 153, 156-57, 170, 179, 183, 229
Bottled water 272-74
Bowel Pain 158, 170
Bowel Movement 22, 216, 225, 233-34, 236
Bragg Liquid Aminos 42, 54, 62
Brain cancer 108
Brain tumors 108
Bran 96, 101-04, 203
Bread 96-97, 111, 189, 201, 207, 309
Breast 58
Breast Cancer 57, 60, 130, 147, 156, 179
Breast enlargement 61, 179, 180
Breast milk 85, 127, 177, 303

Breakfast 17, 22, 300
Broccoli, 132, 152, 156, 292, 301
Broccoli spouts 229
Bronchitis 180, 182-83, 198-99
Brown Rice 42, 114, 202-03, 350
Bulgur 202
Bulger 23, 48, 57, 226, 295,
Bunions 170
Burn 85, 87, 222, 239, 241, 293
B–vitamins 96, 189, 204, 397
C8 303
Cabbage 132, 152, 156, 198, 227, 230
Caffeine 123-27, 228, 230, 235, 249
Calcification 247-48, 250, 252-54
Calcium Info 61, 86, 129, 186, 247, 252, 300
Calcium Fruit Source 148
Calcium Grain Source 130, 204, 397
Calcium Herb/Spice Source 162-63, 165, 169-71, 174, 183
Calcium Vegetable Source 145–153, 156, 166, 178
Calcium Oil Source 82, 86, 169, 169,
Celiac disease 112, 213-14
Calories 84, 107, 139, 210, 145, 153, 156-157
Cancer 100, 104, 124, 219, 222, 234, 248
Cancer, Fruit 141-44, 150, 153, 188
Cancer, Grains 199-200, 381, 393, 397
Cancer, Herbs & Spices 167, 169, 172, 179, 192, 181, 180, 183, 192, 194, 198, 199,
Cancer, Vegetables 145-48, 151-158, 178, 179
Cancer, Oils 169, 181, 198
Candida 167, 171, 191, 194-95, 207
Cane 98, 104, 189
Canola oil 57, 65-66, 70-71
Candy 5, 97, 101
Cantaloupe 146-47, 163
Carbohydrates 86, 99-102, 113, 115, 211
Carcinogen 126, 176, 259, 303, 293, 319
Cardamom 168, 169, 182, 198
Cardiovascular 85, 138, 153, 187, 196, 202
Carnivore 19-20, 25
Carrots 156-157, 229, 320
Cashew 196
Cast iron 306, 307, 310, 313, 314, 316
Cataracts 146, 154, 294
Cayenne 169-170
Celery 157, 158, 178,197, 227
Cell 29, 74, 76, 113, 120, 267
Cellulite 104, 113
Ceramic 273, 306, 314, 327
Certified organic 133-34, 259
Ceylon 170-71
Chee (Qi) 121
Cheese substitute 189
Chemotherapy 24, 179
Chest 58, 153, 168,179
Chicken 47, 139, 50-51, 139, 250, 320
Chipotle 172
Chakra 237, 256
Chlorophyll 151, 229, 255
Chloride 186-87, 251, 261, 283
Chlorine 250-51, 268, 269, 277-78
Chocolate 72, 123, 230, 235, 255
Cholesterol 85, 131, 172, 201-03, 397
Chronic fatigue 207
Cilantro 173-75, 184, 252, 255
Cinnamon 39, 130, 165, 171,
Citrus Drink 18, 24, 351
Clean 130, 161, 163, 203, 272, 306
Cleanse 20,148, 150, 152, 184
Cleansing 55, 149, 229, 288, 358
Clotting 78, 103, 153, 181, 183, 277
Clove oil 173
Cloves 169
Cocaine 97, 211-13, 246-47
Coco butter 188, 224, 265
Coconut 65-68, 82, 83-85, 87, 224
Coconut nectar 43, 110, 130
Coconut oil 65-69, 73, 81-,85, 87, 224
Coconut sugar 109
Coffee 123-27, 230, 287, 319-20
Coffee alternatives 127
Cold 142, 168, 176, 182, 199, 219, 242
Colic 167, 179, 183, 199
Colitis 175, 305
Collard Green Wrap 14, 54, 353
Collards 152, 355
Colon 139, 203, 218, 234, 236, 372
Colon cancer 130, 139, 151, 153, 156, 157
Complex carbohydrates 101-02, 159, 385
Complexion 153, 183, 192
Congestion 146,151, 153, 168, 179, 195,
Conjugated linoleic acids 138
Constipation 148, 152, 168, 175, 185, 201-02, 227, 375
Conventional 45, 134, 136, 138, 161,
Convulsions 108, 190
Cooking Oil Alternatives 7, 65
Cookware 303–317
Cookies 75, 79, 101, 83, 208, 346
Copper 165, 167, 178, 187, 271, 304
Coriander 173-74, 175, 180, 184
Cortisol 125
Corn 101, 137, 202, 356, 385
Corn oil 57, 78
Cornbread 20, 44, 72, 356
Cosmetics 111, 223, 224, 272, 324
Cottonseed 78
Cough 152, 179, 182-83, 194,198,
Cow's milk 123, 127, 128, 129, 131, 299
Cramps 34, 170, 179, 183, 185, 186
Crockpot 316
Crystals 209, 254-56
Cucumber 40, 146, 162, 227

Cumin 39, 175, 176,
Daikon Kale Stir–Fry 357
Dairy 103, 128, 298, 135, 138-9 297
Dandruff 181, 221
Dandelion Greens 153
Decaffeinated 227, 230, 235
Decalcification 255
Demerol 211
Dementia 99, 210, 211, 214, 239 267
Deodorant 87, 90, 252, 263, 264, 265
Depression 125, 148, 169, 174, 179, 195, 207
Detox 148, 228-29, 254, 255, 257, 358
Diabetes 68, 86, 99, 110, 152, 172, 180, 210-11
Diabetic 86, 109, 171, 174, 177, 212,
Diarrhea 168, 174, 175, 186, 195, 304
Digestion 84, 114, 152, 165, 170, 171, 185
Dill 176
Dirty Dozen 161
Disinfectant 177,197, 269, 272
Distillation 276, 279, 281-84
Distilled water 284, 285, 251, 255
Dopamine 97, 107, 296-97
DNA 103, 141, 148, 151, 154, 159, 141
Dressing 72, 88, 97, 193, 214, 364
Drug resistance 138, 211
Dye 111, 198, 209, 213
Earache 168, 179
Ear infections 156, 138
Earthy Root Detox Tea 358
Earthing 119, 121-22
Eczema 180
Egg 137, 139, 214, 228, 237, 293
Eggplant 157, 163, 394
Egg Substitute 358
Eliminate 115, 181, 222, 216, 234, 255
Endocrine 60, 130, 226, 237, 251, 264
Energy 84-85, 99, 100, 121, 124-25, 210, 238, 257
Enriched 96, 132, 189, 350
Enzymes 105, 114, 145, 229, 244, 260
Enameled cast iron 308
Epilepsy 195, 212
Essential nutrients 61, 103, 174, 298
Essential fatty acids 78, 80, 231, 350
Essential oils 166, 182, 188, 197, 255
Estrogen 60-62, 129, 130, 27, 226, 264
Erectile dysfunction 61
Eugenol 177, 185
Eu–melanin 241, 243
European cultural value system 220
Exercise 137, 209, 215, 225, 236, 255
Extra light olive oil 90
Extra virgin olive oil 89
Eye 147, 192, 225, 241, 257, 294
Factory farms 138
Fake meat 111
Fatigue 104, 119, 125, 195, , 207, 210
Farmer's Market 37, 59, 136
Fat 65, 67, 73, 86, 98, 189, 220, 260
Fatty acids 66, 71, 78-80, 91, 103-104
Fast 33, 55
Fast food 5, 60, 65, 79, 214
FDA 106, 142-43, 223, 291, 315
Feet 49, 120-121
Fennel 39, 178-79, 184
Fenugreek 39, 179, 181-82
Ferment 59, 62, 110, 208-09,
Fertility 60, 100, 141, 170, 194
Fertilizer 129-30, 213, 255, 265
Fever 158, 180, 183, 176, 185, 199
Fiber 96, 102, 105, 145, 202, 243, 375
Fibroid 50, 215, 222, 223, 226, 230
Filling 13, 252, 320, 369
Fight–or–flight 124
Fish 47, 78, 102, 177, 252, 261
Flatulence 167, 183, 199
Flax 78, 227, 132, 230
Flavonoids 157
Flu 115, 146, 151, 183
Fino olive oil 90
Fleas 182
Flour 67, 97, 104, 228, 235, 331
Fluoride 250-51, 268, 269, 281
Folate 151-55, 157, 156, 167, 201
Folic acid 151, 154-57, 167
Food additives 107, 143, 186, 225, 250
Food For Thought 299
Food labels 96, 251, 265
Forgiveness 31
Formaldehyde 108
Fractures 153
Fragrance 90, 223, 264
Free fructose 99, 210
Free methanol 107-08
Free radicals 74, 77, 104, 120, 153, 199
Fried 49, 57, 72, 154, 230, 235,320
Fries 52, 295, 344
Frontal lobes 34
Fructose 96-99, 1101, 09, 110, 210
Fruit 38, 40, 45, 145, 209, 229
Fruit Grain Cereal 359
Fruit juice 97, 101, 145, 158
Fruitbread 17, 26, 347
Fully hydrogenated 71-73, 75
Fungi 85, 111, 171, 173, 188, 195
Fungal infection 85, 171, 191, 207
Fufu 54, 360
GAC 278-82
Gall bladder 84, 113, 186
Gallstones 123
Gamma rays 111
Gangrene 168
Gargle 179, 194
Garlic 169, 181-82, 229-30

Garlic popcorn 361
Gas 71, 125, 129, 170, 175, 251, 303
Gastrointestinal 141, 190, 196, 213, 305
Generally recognized as safe 142
Genetically engineered 60, 65, 70, 135
Genetically modified 70, 60-62, 134, 141, 159
Germ 96, 103, 185, 248, 251, 287
Ghee 65
Ginger 127, 168, 183-83, 198, 231
Ginger tea 127, 183
Ginseng 127, 255
Glands 114, 124, 149, 237, 247, 251
Glass 308-10, 327, 358
Glucose 98, 101, 103, 109, 202, 385
Glutamate 61, 113
Gluten 111, 112, 189, 214, 372, 385
Gluten intolerant 111
Glycemic index 109, 202
Goiters 60, 130
Good carbs 96,105
Gout 34, 113, 179-80, 209, 210
GMO 45, 58, 60, 62, 109, 141, 143,
Grains 201, 204, 372, 374, 375, 385
Granular Activated Carbon 278, 280
Grapefruit 146,163, 209
Grape 40, 148-50
GRAS 142
Green tea 126-27, 229
Growth hormones 128, 134, 138-39, 225
Ground 111, 119-122, 183, 191, 196
Grounded floor mats 122
Grounding 121
GSH 155
Guacamole 362
Gums 148-49, 251
Hair 192, 194, 221-224, 250, 363
Hallucinations 108
Hands 329-30
Hair conditioner 363
Hair products 111, 189, 194, 223, 224, 265
Hardening of the arteries 34, 110, 130, 154
Hay fever 181
HDL 74, 87, 91, 170
Headaches 108, 126, 174, 182, 185, 199
Head lice 171
Heal 19, 29, 199, 231, 235, 242
Health Food Store 45, 69, 110, 262, 265
Health hazards 143, 293
Heart 87, 98, 121, 131, 155 165, 268
Heart Attack, 48, 159, 100, 192, 194, 214
Heartbeat 100, 104, 147
Heart disease 65, 67, 99, 104, 157, 192, 202
Heart rate 65, 121, 165, 178, 239
Heartburn 125, 157, 178, 179, 183, 191
Heavy metals 174, 181, 187, 228, 283, 316
Hemp 7, 43, 78, 131, 230, 301
Hemp seeds 42, 78, 130, 230, 255, 301
Hemp Basil Dressing 364
Hemp Milk 7, 37, 130-31, 365
Hemoglobin 218
Hepatitis 5, 149, 175, 182, 207
Hepatitis B 5
Herbs 40, 165, 183-84, 191, 230-31, 235
Herbal teas 127, 358
Herbicide 70, 75, 141
Herbicide resistant 75, 141
Herbs de Provence 39, 183-84
Hernia 168
Herpes 85, 158, 170
High Blood Pressure, 34, 158, 203, 148, 210, 156
High– Fructose Corn Syrup 96-97, 99, 110, 109
High– Fructose Maize Syrup 97
Himalayan crystal salt 186–87
HIV 85, 207
Hoarseness 153, 179, 194
Honey 101, 188, 255
Hormonal mood swings 174
Hormonal balance 139, 231
Hormonal development 61, 129
Hormones 50, 78, 86, 138-39, 237, 256
Hormone production 99, 211, 292
Hot Dog 48, 57, 293
Humus 20
Hybrid 70, 111
Hydration 112, 287
Hydrates 372
Hydrochloric acid 114, 125
Hydrogenated oil 66, 68 71-75, 80
Hydrogenation 71-72
Hydrogen 71, 277, 280
Hyperactive 213, 244
Hypertension 175, 202, 212, 156, 214
Hypoallergenic 147
Hypoglycemic 174
Hypothalamus 99, 211
Hypothyroidism 60, 130
IBS 125
Ice cream 57, 226, 390
Illness 82, 84,96-97, 129, 138, 142
Indigestion 148, 168, 183, 195, 175, 191
Infants 62, 135-36, 145, 195
Infant mortality 62, 144
Infection 196, 199, 207-08, 217, 234
Injury 120, 122, 330-31, 375
Insomnia 108, 168, 178, 185, 189
Insulin 86, 99, 155, 171, 173, 202,
Insulin spike 99, 211, 86
Insulin resistance 99, 110, 211
Intestinal walls 116, 143, 229
Intestines 84, 148, 207, 234, 288
Intuitive 35, 253
Immune 131, 141, 176, 210, 268, 385
Immune response 112, 120, 144, 213

Immune booster 85, 167
Immune system 146, 153, 176, 195, 265, 270
Infant formula 59, 125, 226, 374
Infant mortality 62, 144
Infection 196, 199, 208, 217,
Infertility 60, 62, 130, 141, 213, 226
Infertile 62, 269
Inflammatory 79, 119, 144, 192
Inflammation 119, 149, 198-99, 201, 209
Insect bites 168, 179,194
Intestinal flora 182
Iodized salt 113, 186
Irradiation 111, 134
Irritate 112, 116, 180
Irritable 124-25, 145, 179, 221
Irritable bowel 125, 179, 183, 199
Irritability 125, 189, 217, 235, 240,
Iron 153, 165, 176, 192, 307, 310, 313
Italian seasoning 184
Jaundice 149, 175
Joints 157, 183, 188, 209
Joint pain 48, 168, 188, 209
Juice 97, 145, 158, 175, 229, 250, 255
Kale 78, 151, 153, 229, 230, 357, 366
Karma 30, 33
Kidney 126, 146, 179, 186, 212, 235, 300
Kidney 1 121
Kidney meridian 121
Kidney stones 113, 123 188
Kitchen Safety 329
Kiwi 146, 227
Kombucha 209
Labeling 91, 109, 143
Lactating 128, 195, 300
Larynx 156
Lasagna 55, 368
Lavender 184, 197, 255
Leaky gut 207, 209-10
Learning disabilities 61, 100
LDL 85, 87, 157-59, 172, 198-203
Legume 102, 114, 179-80, 300
Lemon 229, 255, 265, 288, 320
Lemon cakes 51
Lentils 101-02, 114, 228, 300
Leather 119
Leftovers 54, 112, 204, 294
Leptin 99, 110, 211
Leprosy 199
Lettuce 26, 227
Libido 61, 1186
Licorice 178
Liver 98, 144, 149, 199, 210, 221, 229
Liver cirrhosis 123
Longevity 26, 155, 310
Lotion 87, 194, 265
Low calorie sweetener 107, 109, 145
Low–density lipoprotein 120, 157-158
Low–level antibiotics 137-39
Lubricate 148, 230
Lung 146, 148, 151, 170, 179, 196
Lung infection 146, 151, 156, 196
Lye 115, 222
Maca 231, 235
Mace 188
Macular degeneration 146, 154-57
Malaria 158
Magnesium 61, 109, 130, 153, 167
Magnets 254, 256
Malnutrition 96
Manganese 131, 153, 167, 175, 178, 203
Manic depression 108
Manure 134
Margarine 65–66, 71–73, 325
Marjoram 184-85, 190, 371
Maple Syrup 110, 130
Mashed potatoes 47, 49, 51, 202
Marijuana 130, 246
Measles 85, 158
Meat 59, 83, 137, 210, 226, 250, 299
Medication 24, 208, 212, 251, 262
Medicinal 169, 173, 179, 185, 194, 197
Melanin 78, 192, 224, 237-57
Melanin dominant 238, 241–246
Melancholy 197
Melanocyte 78, 238
Melanin recessive 237, 241, 243
Melatonin 238, 247-48, 253-254
Membrane 79, 103, 157, 217, 234
Memory 130, 151, 188-189, 193, 195
Menopausal sweats 195
Menopause 57, 215, 180
Menstruation 179, 190
Menstrual bleeding 195, 215
Menstrual flow 174, 179, 185, 227
Menstrual cramps 34, 179, 183, 185
Meth 107-08, 212-13
Mercury 100, 197, 211, 255, 270-71
Meridian 121
Metabolic rate 84-85, 113
Metabolism 84, 99, 148, 170, 181
Metabolize 77, 145, 227, 231, 260
Methanol 107-08
Microbial infection 85, 174, 191, 196
Microwave 291-94, 238, 310, 320
Migraines 102, 372, 375
Milk 127-32, 138, 180, 299, 320
Millet 54, 202-203, 227-28, 372
Mineral salt 112, 230, 242, 251
Minerals 86, 145, 154, 186, 201
Mint 184, 193-94, 197-198
Miscarriage 237
Miso 43, 57, 59, 62, 226
Mixing Carbohydrates 48, 113
Molasses 43, 101, 189, 228

Mood 102-104, 125, 239
Mood swings 100, 108, 125, 174, 210
Monounsaturated 90–91, 230
Monsanto 62, 128, 142, 144
Mono–sodium–glutamate 113
Morning sickness 171
Most Men Are Slow 33
Motion sickness 183
Mouth infections 174, 194, 198, 207
Mouthwash 194, 197, 269
Mouth ulcer 174, 194
MSG 61, 113
Mucous congestion 195
Mutations 74, 111, 143, 194
Muscle 98, 116, 124, 237, 243, 245
Muscle pain 174, 180, 185, 193
Muscle spasms 175, 185
Mushroom 188, 386
Mustard Greens 153
NaaCereal 373
NaaCereal Non–Infant Formula 374
Naasira's Approach 37-45
Nails 131, 189
Narcotic 107, 211
Natto 59, 226
Natural 73, 109, 136, 252, 246, 260, 363
Natural Hair Conditioner 363
Natural flavor 107, 109
Nausea 168, 174, 183, 185, 304
Nearsightedness 156
Nerve 34, 103, 108, 130, 237, 244
Nerve cells 34, 103, 239, 245
Nervous disorder 190, 195
Nervous system 100, 121, 155, 167, 243
Neural tube defect 151, 154
Neurotoxin 61, 100, 108, 319
Neurotransmitter 97, 103, 239
Neutralize 78, 121, 128, 149, 155, 305
Neutral foods 114
Niacin 130, 152, 165, 201, 210
Nonalcoholic fatty liver 98, 211
Non–GMO 45, 62
Numbness 100
Nutmeg butter 188
Nutmeg 130, 165, 187-89
Nuts 37, 75, 103, 114, 227, 230
Nutrient deficiencies 97, 213, 259
Nutrient–dense 59, 259
Nutrients 61, 100, 105, 130, 145, 201
Nutrition 151, 86, 207, 218, 292, 298,
Nutritional 111, 174, 189, 259, 260, 291
Nutritional yeast 188-89
Nutritionally dead 96
Nutritionally dense 136
Nutritional value 111, 210, 292, 350, 397
Nutritious 41, 82, 104, 350
Oats 195, 202-203, 227, 401
Obesity 80, 145, 179, 203, 210, 297
Odors 76, 251, 278, 309
Oil 65-76, 82-87, 92-93, 166
Olive oil 88-93
Olives 91-92, 209
Omega–3 71, 78-80, 152, 209, 230
Omega–6 78-80
Opiads 297
Optimal 38, 55, 86, 279
Optimum 37, 55, 79, 95, 119
Onion 49, 169, 181, 229
Oral cavity cancer 167
Oral contraceptives 180, 209
Oral disorders 167
Orange 149
Oregano 190
Organic 45, 82, 134, 133-37
Organic food 136-37, 139, 252, 294
Organs 86, 141, 157, 210, 239
Osteoporosis 84, 126, 153, 183, 187
Ovarian cancer 152, 183
Oxygen 147, 191, 166, 287, 267-68
Oxidation 76–78, 81, 287
Oxidative stress 193
Oxidize 72, 74, 80-81, 88, 90
Palm oil 65–67, 73
Pain 34, 147, 170, 188, 192, 201
Papaya 147
Paprika 191
Pancakes 82, 201, 377
Pancreas 99, 114, 170, 292, 303
Pancreatic disorders 60
Panic attacks 108, 174
Parabens 223, 264
Paranoia 108
Parasites 116, 181, 187, 225, 236
Parkinson's 123, 194
Parsley 173, 175-76, 184, 255
Partially hydrogenated 66, 71, 73, 80
Pasta 96, 204, 249, 305
Pathogens 85, 111, 129, 187, 272, 283
Peanut butter 72
Pears 147, 229
Penicillin 181
Pepper 158, 162, 165-70, 172, 191
Peppercorn 167-68
Peppermint 127
Peppermint tea 127
Pepsin 114
Peroxides 76
Pesticide 70, 82, 123, 136, 141, 249, 264
Pesticide Data Program 136
Pesticide residue 136, 161, 249
PET 323–24
PETE 274, 323-24
Petroleum 270, 303-04
PFOA 270, 303-04

Pharmaceutical 212, 250, 269-70
Pheo–melanin 240, 241
Phenylalanine 107-08
Phosphorus 130, 152, 169, 192, 203, 385
Phytates 60
Phytoestrogens 60
Pig 49, 115-16, 139
Pigment 192, 237, 241, 309
Piles 176
Pimples 103, 175
Pineapple Rind Drink 379
Pineal gland 240, 247, 254-57, 269
Pituitary gland 124
Pizza 44, 190, 214 335, 380
Phlebotomist 5
Phthalates 222, 264, 324
Phytonutrients 152, 157, 166, 174, 229
Plague 220
Plantain 52, 384
Plant based 60, 130, 51, 259, 299
Plant based milks 37, 43
Plant killer 70
Plant oils 60, 78, 103, 197
Plastic 120, 270, 274, 315, 320, 324
Plasticizers 264
PMS 102, 180, 189
Pneumonia 138, 182
Popcorn 66, 101, 189, 361
Price–Look–Up–Code 134
Prostate 144, 153, 172, 231, 263, 233
Prostate cancer 57, 130, 153, 156, 172
Prostate gland 216-17, 231, 233, 235
Protein 113-14, 131, 141, 249, 299
Ptyalin 114
Poison 70, 100, 108, 115, 141, 250, 305
Poison oak 182, 196
Poison ivy 182, 196
Pollutants 120, 249, 325
Polystyrene 319–21, 326
Polyunsaturated oils 65-70, 72, 74, 76, 81
Poor memory 195
Popcorn topping 189
Pores 103, 275-77, 280
Pork 47, 49-50, 73, 115, 137
Portobello mushrooms 386
Potassium 109, 131, 146, 148, 156, 167, 174
Potato Salad 387
Poultice 180, 182
Poultry 100, 114, 134, 137,139, 225
PMS 102, 180, 189
Pre–diabetes 86
Premature aging 77, 121, 141, 268, 270
Processed 60, 76, 96, 102, 134, 186, 296
Produce 114, 134, 136, 161, 159, 237
Psoriasis 170
Puberty 34, 239, 250
Public health risk 137
Pulp sandwich 20, 27
Pulp Berger 372
Pumpkin seed 43, 78, 230
Pure olive oil 90
Purify 148-49, 192, 275
Pus 49, 115, 129
PVC 324–25
Psychosis 212
Qi 121
Quinoa 203, 301, 375, 399
Radiation 166, 179, 194, 238, 252, 294
rbGH 124, 135, 139
Rancid 66, 71-74, 81–82, 91-92
Rancidity 76, 91
Rapeseed 70
Raw 134, 152, 186, 229, 255
Raw coconut oil 7, 82
Raw ice cream 390
Raw salad 391
Real Waffles 392
Red blood cells 61, 104, 156, 192, 375
Recipes 333
Rectal cancer 269
Recycle codes 274, 323
Reducing Fibroids 228, 231
Red eye 148, 241
Red rice 203-204, 375
Red peppers 158, 191
Refined 70, 79, 89, 96, 99, 104, 210
Refinement process 90, 96, 102, 112
Regulate 99, 103, 112, 155, 187, 223
Regularity 126
Rejuvenate 55
Remedies 173-74, 195
Repair 86, 147, 203, 209, 225, 229
Reproductive issues 139, 226
Reproductive systems 62, 129, 203
Residue 136, 139, 161, 229, 249, 285
Respiratory 179, 181, 186, 190, 198, 268
Respiration 124, 288
Rest 49, 55
Resveratrol 148
Retinal damage 108
Ritalin 211-212
Reverse osmosis 275-76, 279-81, 284
Riboflavin 96, 130, 165, 201
Rice 114, 203, 204, 350, 375
Rheumatism 113, 147, 149, 170, 195
Roasted 55, 126, 180 230, 394, 398
Rosemary 41, 184, 193, 197
Root 119, 183, 198, 230-01, 236
Roasted Eggplant Casserole 398
Round–up 70
Roundworms 156
Safflower 70, 78
Sage 193-94, 197
Salad 53, 89, 177, 204, 387, 400

Salad dressings 79, 97, 214
Salivary glands 114
Salmonella 192, 195–96
Salt 97, 218, 235, 242, 249, 331
Salve 176
Satiated 99, 102-103, 211
Satisfied 103
Saturated 66, 68, 71, 73, 74, 82, 131
Sauce 107, 214, 226, 316, 355, 369
Saute´ 44, 54, 88, 90, 154, 306, 308
Scabies 173
Sea Salt 187, 251
Seafood 50, 114, 210, 251
Seasonal 207, 359, 401
Seasoning 37, 174, 177, 184, 185, 307
Seizures 87, 108, 175, 195, 247
Sediment filters 277
Seed 141, 159, 174, 188, 209
Seeds 60, 78, 130, 159, 174, 177, 180
Seizures 87, 108, 175, 195, 247
Selenium 165, 168, 201, 203, 242
Semiconductor 119
Senility 170
Sesame 43, 230
Sewer 115
Sex 179, 180, 185, 239, 251
Shakes 59
Shea butter 224, 265
Shelf life 73, 83, 91, 98, 102, 112, 259
Shingles 182, 185
Shortening 47, 71-72, 100
Shoyu 42, 59, 62
Sick 51, 115, 129, 171, 183
Side effect 77, 138, 143, 198
Silicon 147, 157
Simple carbohydrates 85, 101-02
Sinus headaches 178, 181
Skin 86, 238, 240, 241, 246, 247, 395
Skin cancer 74, 238, 264,
Sleep 119, 112, 145, 186, 240, 248, 257
Sleep–wake cycle 212, 250
Sloppy Joes 44, 54, 335
Sluggish 20, 121
Sluggish blood 121
Small pox 158, 174
Smell 71 87, 166, 171, 243, 263
Smoking point 90
Smoothies 44, 82, 131, 365
Snack 43, 59, 124, 148, 174, 296
Snake bite 115, 179, 181
Sniffle 24
Sodium chloride 186-87, 251
Soft drinks 97, 228, 250, 251
Solid Block Activated 278-79, 282
Sore throat 168, 176, 180, 182 188
Soul Food 47, 51-50,
Spaghetti 44, 54, 101
Spaghetti sauce 44
Spices 39, 52, 54, 95, 154, 165, 228
Spinach 78, 151, 153, 162, 229, 300
Spin–offs 44
Spinal cord 116, 195
Spleen 170, 179
Sprains 185, 194
Sperm count 61
Spoil 38, 71, 74, 76, 92, 102, 170
Spouts 230
Squash 141, 146, 158, 163, 343
Starch 96, 104, 114, 209
Strawberries 40, 143, 147, 162
Steam 153-54, 191, 195, 291, 330
Steel cut oats 42, 397
Sterile 62
Stew 9, 22, 44, 52, 54, 202,
Stevia 109
Stir–fry 54-55, 82, 313,357, 367
Stock Your Kitchen 38
Stomachache 18
Straight hair 221-22, 250,
Strep throat 138, 188
Stress 125, 139, 169, 193, 218, 231
Strokes 35, 51, 74, 157, 196, 214, 268
Styrofoam 319, 320, 326
Soda 51, 107, 110-11, 230, 235, 255
Sodium 44, 109, 170, 182-83, 210, 235
Sodium hydroxide 83, 222
Sore throat 168, 180, 182, 188, 195
Soul Food 9, 16, 47, 50-51
Soups 88-89,177, 201, 214, 312, 320
Soy 57, 65, 70, 78-79, 80, 130, 226
Soybean 43, 60-62, 66, 70, 78, 226
Soybean oil 60, 65-66, 70, 78-79, 226
Soy burgers 57, 226
Soy cheese 57, 226
Soy formula 59, 61-62, 129, 130, 226
Soy ice cream 57, 226
Soy milk 61, 58, 129, 132, 226
Soy protein 57, 226
Soy sausage 57
Soy sauce 57, 59, 62, 226
Soy wieners 57
Sperm 61, 178, 233, 237
Spices 39, 52, 54, 95, 154, 165, 228
Sports drink 100
Stabilize 77, 86, 132, 55
Stainless steel 306, 310, 312, 316, 327
Steroids 128, 180, 208
Stomach 148, 158, 167, 174, 195, 199
Stomach acidity 171, 178-79, 191-92
Stomach cramps 170, 179, 183
Stomach digestion 148, 152, 168, 195
Stomach ulcers 151, 158, 170, 194, 305
Stuffed Bell Peppers 47
Sucrose 98, 101

Subsidizes 98
Substitute 7, 65, 82, 131, 183, 189, 358
Sugar 98, 102, 105, 124, 145, 210
Sugar free 109, 189
Sugar levels 102, 104, 145, 174, 180
Suicide 35
Sulfur 113, 169, 182
Sumac 196
Sunburns 87
Sunflower oil 70, 78
Sunflower Seeds 78, 230
Superconductor 237
Superficial circulation 243
Supplemental dishes 54
Sunstroke 104
Sweat glands 115, 263
Sweeteners 107, 109, 228, 250
Sweet Potatoe 154-55, 163, 398
Swelling 146, 157, 182, 185, 194
Swine 50, 115-16, 137
Swiss Chard 42, 152
Synthetic 113, 252, 260, 265, 239
Synthetic chemicals 109, 111, 113, 260
Synthetic estrogen 180
Synthetic growth hormones 128, 225
Table salt 112, 186, 249, 251
Table sugar 96-97, 113, 109
Tabletop sweeteners 107
Tallow 65
Tacos 44
Talc 112
Tamari sauce 59, 62
Tangerine 149, 162, 197
Tempeh 57, 59, 62, 226
Taste buds 27, 244
Tea 124, 179, 190, 230, 359
Testicles 143
Teeth 61, 99, 103, 149, 251
Teflon 303, 312, 315
Tired 13, 20, 124, 267, 294
Teeccino 126-27
Tendonitis 183
Texture 34, 57, 111, 200-202
The Whole Soy Story 61, 129
Thiamine 96, 152, 261, 385
Third eye 237, 255, 257, 269
Throat infections 135, 194, 198
Thrush 171
Thyme 184, 193, 197-98
Thyroid cancer 60, 130
Thyroid gland 34, 270
Thyroid function 87, 113, 130, 226, 251
Tinctures 127, 193
Tissue 77, 105, 120, 210, 215, 226, 233
Toasted 48, 389, 397
Toe 100
Toothache 173, 179, 183, 185
Tooth decay 145, 168, 210, 268-69
Toothpaste 87, 188, 250, 269
Tomato 148
Tongue 114, 190
Tonic 149, 170, 195, 190, 231
Tonsillitis 181
Toxic 112, 195, 267-69, 303, 319, 320
Toxic chemicals 135, 250, 264, 269, 303
Trace elements 103, 112, 186-87
Traditional 59, 119, 190, 312-13
Trans fat 66, 72–75, 83
Trans fatty acids 66, 72, 74-76, 80
Transitioning to Healthy Foods 7
Trembling 189
Trichina 116
Triglyceride 110, 146, 172, 201
Tropical oil 65–67
Tuberculosis 182
Tofu 57, 59, 226, 297
Tumors 106, 172, 215, 222
Turnip greens 42, 153
Turkey 47, 51, 126
Turmeric 198-200, 175, 200, 230
Tuna 47-48, 78, 252
Twitching 22Type 1 Diabetes 23
Type 2 Diabetes 86, 156-57, 201, 203
Ultra violet 238, 240-41
Upset stomach 168, 171
Unhealthy 38, 48, 215, 225, 296
Unfermented 60-62, 226,
Ulcer 34, 148, 151, 170, 174, 194
Unrefined 81-83, 186-87,
Upset stomach 168, 171
Uric acid 110, 209
Urinary 146, 148, 158, 174, 169, 207
Urinary tract infections 146, 171, 174, 207
Uterine Fibroids 50, 60, 130, 222, 215-231
UV–A radiation 194, 238
UV radiation 194, 238
Vaginal discharge 194-95
Vaginal Itching 207
Variety Fruit Salad 401
Veggies 204
Vegan 5-6, 9, 19, 37, 95, 189, 356
Vegetables 45, 52, 151-160, 292
Vegetable stew 44, 53, 54, 335
Vegetable oil 65-67, 71-73, 78, 79
Vegetable based 226,
Vegetable protein 59, 114,
Vegetarian 26, 37, 95, 111, 131, 188
Vinegar 49, 209, 230, 235, 265, 288
Virgin olive oil 7, 43, 89-90
Viral infections 151
Viruses 85, 115, 157-58, 248, 272, 275, 283
Vitality 19, 222, 250
Vitamins 96, 102-103, 151-53, 155, 259-62
Vitamins grains 201, 204, 350, 385, 397

Vitamin vegetables 96, 151-160, 229
Vitamins fruits 145-149, 229
Vitamins herbs 165-167, 175-77, 189, 192
Waffles 82, 365, 392
Wake sleep cycle 212, 239, 250
Walnuts 43, 78
Waste 103, 216, 225, 230, 234 250, 358
Waist lines 51
Warts 158, 182
Water 158, 235, 242, 267-289, 291, 359
Watermelon 40, 146, 158-59, 163, 255
Water retention 179
Wax 45, 70, 272
Weave 221-22
Weight control 85, 99, 159, 172
Weight gain 99, 207, 211, 226, 230, 251
Weight loss 69, 84, 123 157, 172 210
Weight management 138, 152, 155-56, 204
Wellbeing 17, 190, 240
Wheat 96, 102, 111-12, 202, 213
Wheat grass 111, 229, 252, 255
Wheat protein 112
Wheat sensitivity 112
Whey 189, 299, 301
White blood cells 120
White bread 48-49, 96-97
White flour 47, 96, 97, 201, 228, 235
White rice 47-48, 96, 350,
White sugar 80, 97, 113, 228
White foods 96-97,
Whole 96, 127, 145, 177, 261
Whole fruit 145
Whole grain 96, 101-04, 114, 201, 300
Whole grain bread 96
Whole grain cereal 96
Whole Wheat kernel 96, 102
Whooping cough 152, 198
Wig 221-22, 225
Wild Rice 350
Woks 312-314
Worms 116, 152, 156, 170, 181
Wrinkles 86, 192, 238
X–ray 111, 238
Yams 53, 101, 159, 209, 398
Yeast 85, 171, 188-89, 191,194, 208
Yogurt 101, 107, 226, 324-25
Zeolite 255
Zinc 61, 103, 105, 167, 189, 230, 385
Zucchini 103, 141

Made in the USA
Middletown, DE
03 September 2024